Writing the Self

Essays on Autobiography and Autofiction

Edited by
Kerstin W Shands
Giulia Grillo Mikrut
Dipti R. Pattanaik
Karen Ferreira-Meyers

ENGLISH STUDIES 5

Södertörns högskola 2015

© 2015 Kerstin W. Shands and Södertörns högskola.
All rights reserved.
No portion of this book may be reproduced, by any process or technique, without the express written consent of the publisher.

Cover artwork: *Beyond the Face* by Mimo Listerfelt
Cover photo: Kerstin W. Shands
Cover design: Jonathan Robson
Layout: Kerstin W. Shands, Per Lindblom & Jonathan Robson

First published in 2015
Printed in Sweden by Elanders

English Studies 5
ISSN: 1651-4165

ISBN: 978-91-87843-21-1

Contents

Introduction
7

When I Think About Myself:
Identity Building Processes in Maya Angelou's Autobiographical Sequel
Alice Godfrey
29

The 'Absent Presence' and the Art of Autobiography:
Barack Obama's Dreams from My Father
Aparajita Nanda
39

Expressing Nonsuicidal Self-Injury:
Using Creative Writing and Autobiographical Fiction as Self-Care
Belinda Hilton
51

Memory, Trauma, and Resilience:
The Autobiographies of Winnie Madikizela Mandela
Ben Lebdai
61

Autobiography and the Scene of Speech
in Gertrude Stein's Everybody's Autobiography
Christine Savinel
71

When Worlds Collide: (Auto-)Biography, Truth, Identity,
and Normalcy in the Case of Elias Canetti
Claude Desmarais
81

'It's Our Shared Memories… The Stories We Tell…':
Politics and Identity in Two Memoirs by Hungarian-Canadians
Dagmara Drewniak
93

From Autobiography to Storytelling:
The Works of C.S. Lewis
Daniel Warzecha
103

Avoiding Self-Centered Fairytales:
Autobiographies by Female Singer-Songwriters
Daniela Chana
113

Four Moments of Self-Recovery:
Postcoloniality, Odia Identity and Autobiography
Dipti R. Pattanaik
123

Writing Me, Raising Me, Beating the Drums Louder:
Fictional Autobiography as a Feminist Tool for Expression
in African and Diaspora Women's Writing
Ebere Nnenna Agugbue Nweze
137

Maternity and Writing:
An Expedition into the Ojibwe Land of Letters with Louise Erdrich
Elisabeth Bouzonviller
147

"My Mother Composed Me as I Now Compose Her":
Catharsis and Cathexis in Alison Bechdel's Are You My Mother?
Eva-Sabine Zehelein
163

Like Father Like Daughter?
Autobiography as Defacement in Leslie Stephen's
Mausoleum Book and Virginia Woolf's Memoirs
Floriane Reviron-Piégay
173

What's Wrong with Me?
A Cautionary Tale of Using Contemporary 'Damage Narratives'

in Autobiographical Life Writing
Jo Woodiwiss
183

Trans-Autobiographies as Sites for Decolonization
John C. Hawley
193

Autobiography and Autofiction:
No Need to Fight for a Place in the Limelight,
There is Space Enough for Both of these Concepts
Karen Ferreira-Meyers
203

The Ordeal of the Soul:
Ordinary People's Autobiographies of Mental Illness in Finland 1870–1935
Kirsi Tuohela
219

Motions and Emotions in Jamaica Kincaid's
The Autobiography of My Mother
Lamia Mokrane
231

"No Shadows Under Us":
Fictional Freedoms and Real Violations in Louise Erdrich's Shadow Tag
Laura Castor
239

"My Own Face as Personal Vanishing Point":
Writing the Body in Lucy Grealy's Autobiography of a Face
Laure de Nervaux-Gavoty
257

Female Autobiography and Otherness in The Grand Piano:
An Experiment in Collective Autobiography
Manuel Brito
269

"Memoir as Well as Biography":
Generic Indeterminacy in Vikram Seth's Two Lives
Mélanie Heydari
279

The (Un)making of a Novelist's Self:
'Late Style' in Günter Grass' and J. M. Coetzee's Autobiographical Writing
Melissa Schuh
287

Eve Unchained:
Christina Stead's Recasting of the Christian Spiritual Autobiography
Michael Ackland
295

Retouching the Past:
Vladimir Nabokov's Speak, Memory as Fictive Autobiography
Mikołaj Wiśniewski
307

"Life Has Got Awfully Dramatic All of a Sudden, Hasn't It? Just Like a Fiction":
The Art of Writing Life in Donna Tartt's novels
Pamela J. Rader
315

Sexual Fingerprint:
Queer Diaries and Autobiography
Piotr Sobolczyk
329

"Glad Rags, Feather-Dusted Spiders and Horse-Drawn Harvesters":
Gender, Truth, and Imagination in Three Approaches to
Autobiography/Autoethnography at an Elder Care Home in Bristol
Seana Kozar
345

Rewriting Cure:
Autobiography as Therapy and Discursive Practice
Tanja Reiffenrath
359

Introduction

The present avalanche of autobiographical writing indicates that our time has a great interest in questions of self and identity. The culture pages in our national newspapers testify to a critical interest in autobiography. At our universities, new courses on autobiography and life-writing are being developed. Part of an expanding and complex genre, autobiographical texts increasingly attract critical attention, and work on autobiography from a number of perspectives has become a vital area of research, engaging in questions about what is private and public along with notions of truth and fiction, identity and authenticity, as well as in discussions of what constitutes experience and narration, and theories concerning the very boundaries and limits of the genre. New critical methods have been applied to areas such as the new media and reality television as performative genres, and the contemporary study of autobiography encompasses a broad variety of research perspectives.

Coming from the Greek αὐτός-autos self, βίος-bios life, and γράφειν-graphein write, the term autobiography may seem straightforward. But as James Olney asks in "Autobiography and the Cultural Moment: A Thematic, Historical, and Bibliographical Introduction": "What do we mean by the self, or himself (*autos*)? What do we mean by life (*bios*)? What significance do we impute to the act of writing (*graphe*)—what is the significance and the effect of transforming a life into a text?" (6). In Olney's view, "the subject of autobiography produces more questions than answers" (5). Not only do questions about the three aspects of the term arise but, more importantly, as Bruce Hindmarsh puts it, they intricately concern "the relationship between myself as author, myself as subject, and myself as portrayed in a literary text" (5).

Blurred and porous, the notion of genre raises many practical and theoretical controversies all the way to its perceived uselessness, according to Ernstpeter Ruhe, because it leads to "nullity, as it is neither this nor that" (qtd Garcia 151). According to Vincent Colonna, further, "virtually all good genre names are imprecise, ambiguous or polysemic, even malformed, yet effective and popular generic tools" (399). While gender as taxonomy enables professionals, critics, academic researchers to classify literary works, the purpose of the concept of genre, its theoretical relevance in a way, is essentially to provide a guide for the reader to decode a literary text, to "operate as a pattern of reception, a skill of the reader, confirmed and/or challenged by any new text in a dynamic process" (Compagnon 185).

Genre is a discursive convention brought back to the scene of literary studies, by several means, after a refusal on the part of formalist literary theory that dominated the twentieth century, from Russian formalism to structuralism, for which genre was irrelevant since only text and literariness counted. Today, the aesthetic of reception has shifted the emphasis of the theory of the text to its reading. Indeed, we need to return to the notion of reception, a key concept for understanding the rise of autofiction in the twentieth and twenty-first centuries. Suffice it to remember that genre becomes, through reception, a category of reading akin to what Hans Robert Jauss, in *Ästhetische Erfahrung und literarische Hermeneutik*, calls a horizon of expectations, a set of shared assumptions that can be attributed to a generation of readers. Annie Ernaux, responding to a question from the journalist of *Le Monde*, Raphaelle Rérole, stresses the importance of reception. Autofiction follows the autobiographical novel, but transposed to our times in different ways partly because readers' text reception changed.

In general, the reader makes an assumption about the type of text while reading. This hypothesis guides the reading; the reader will correct it if the text contradicts the assumption; in the reader's mind the thoughts that arise might be: no, this is not a non-fiction text, no, it is not an autobiography, etc. To classify a work, it must be read by making assumptions about its generic affiliation and revising these assumptions as it is read. These assumptions can only be verified and then accepted or rejected when the reader knows the intra-, extra-, or para-textual clues of a particular genre and is, as a detective or hunter, on the lookout for these indices. Reading can therefore be compared to puzzle-solving, in accordance with what Barthes called the hermeneutic code. The genre assists in interpreting the code, since it is an instance ensuring the comprehensibility of the text in terms of its composition and its content.

Thus, on a practical or pragmatic level, genre does not only produce and interpret the facts of language, it can also 'rate' or situate them within the field of discourse: genre is not only an isolated regularity, but a regularity that is part of a field of genres and specific 'tensions' that go through it in function of the position it occupies. In *Nouveau Dictionnaire Encyclopédique des Sciences du Langage*, Oswald Ducrot and Jean-Marie Schaeffer emphasize that "a literary work can always be understood on different levels, so its generic identity is always relative to the level(s) that one considers as relevant" (524). Hence the importance of taking into account the reception of a literary work by the reader. As a sub-conclusion, the importance of the concepts of reception, interpretation, and readers should be noted when talking about genre, which cannot be seen as a fixed essence, but rather, as Lejeune indicated in *Signes de vie: Le pacte autobiographique 2*, as a "precarious combination" (116).

Recent autobiographical theory has explored the troubled boundary between truth and falsehoods, how facts and beliefs are represented. A well-known example is the autobiography of Rigoberta Menchú, an activist from Guatemala who won the Nobel Peace Prize in 1992 and wrote an autobiography (*I, Rigoberta Menchú: An Indian Woman in Guatemala*) that was later shown to contain inaccuracies. An anthropologist, David Stoll, asserts that Rigoberta Menchú writes about experiences she never had herself. Discussing this in *The Limits of Autobiography*, Leigh Gilmore argues that "Menchú and her defenders have said that accusations about her truthfulness are political in that they mean to discredit her and thereby her efforts to raise international concern for the indigenous Guatemalan Indians of whom she is one and whom she represents" (4). In Gilmore's view, then, a "crucial limit in autobiography" is "not just the one understood as the boundary between truth and lies, but, rather, the limit of representativeness, with its compulsory inflation of the self to stand for others" (5). The question as to whether Stoll's findings are correct or if they constitute a form of "unsympathetic scrutiny" or an "adversarial account" as Gilmore suggests, (4), can be left open. "As a genre," Gilmore goes on to say, "autobiography is characterized less by a set of formal elements than by a rhetorical setting in which a person places herself or himself within testimonial contexts as seemingly diverse as the Christian confession, the scandalous memoirs of the rogue, and the coming-out story in order to achieve as proximate a relation as possible to what constitutes truth in that discourse" (3). As Gilmore argues in another book, *Autobiographics*, "autobiography draws its authority less from its resemblance to real life than from its proximity to discourses about truth and identity, less from reference and mimesis than from the cultural power of truth-telling (3, fn. 8). In Gilmore's view, then, the "demands made by autobiography" can lead to "silencing and shaming effects" (3). In particular, this may be the case with trauma stories, since "conventions about truth telling, salutary as they are, can be inimical to the ways in which some writers bring trauma stories into language" (3).

Notions of truth and truthfulness may of course also have a central function (for example, a political one). Contemporary critics sometimes defend or criticize the topics, views, and ideologies presented in autobiographical writings. One extraliterary and political purpose of Leigh Gilmore's *The Limits of Autobiography* is to help people recover from trauma while illuminating the history and recent theorization around its possibilities and purpose. Many essays in *Autobiography in Canada* (edited by Susanna Egan and Gabriele Helms) "are characterized by an authorial stance either as advocate or critic of the writer whose work is under discussion," one writer praising the coming out of a lesbian autobiographer and upbraiding another "for being less than frank about his sexual orientation," according to Rosamund Dalziell (215). While "the role of the scholar as advocate can be valid and useful," "the critic as advocate" also "raises major theoretical questions," according to Dalziell, who goes on to say: "When a scholar concerned about issues of agency in the life narrative of a marginalized writer implies that others associated with the writer are interfering, power seeking, and undermining individual agency, there is a danger that the apparently detached critic is positioning her/ himself inappropriately as having more developed and sensitive moral insight" (216). But whereas readers of autobiography have often approached autobiographical texts hoping to find authors displayed as they really are or were, a prevailing view in recent decades has been that autobiography, as Paul John Eakin argues in *Fictions in Autobiography: Studies in the Art of Self-Invention*, cannot "offer a faithful and unmediated reconstruction of a historically verifiable past" (5). Or, as an often quoted passage from Paul de Man puts it:

> Autobiography seems to depend on actual and potentially verifiable events in a less ambivalent way than fiction does. It seems to belong to a simpler mode of referentiality (…) But are we so certain that autobiography depends on reference, as a photograph depends on its subject? (…) We assume that life produces the autobiography as an act produces its consequences, but can we not suggest, with equal justice, that the autobiographical project may itself produce and determine the life and that whatever the writer does is in fact governed by the technical demands of self-portraiture and thus determined in all its aspects, by the resources of his medium?

Similarly, in Sidonie Smith and Julia Watson's view, "narrative performativity constitutes interiority. That is, the interiority or self that is said to be prior to the autobiographical expression or reflection is an effect of autobiographical storytelling" (109). *In Reading Autobiography*, Smith and Watson emphasize the intertextuality of autobiography whereby genres tend to merge. Like so many other contemporary critics, Smith and Watson underline that the autobiographical writer does not in any simple way convey the truth about his or her life. Proposing that the subject of the autobiographical narrative is complex, with four key aspects—the historical I who "lives or lived in the world, going about his or her business in everyday life" (59), the narrating I, the narrated I, and the ideological I—Smith and Watson argue that the subject dwells in conflicting positions inside the narratives of self. The supposedly unified subject of the narrative thereby becomes "both the observing subject and the object of investigation, remembrance, and contemplation" (1). Further, "[w]hile the historical I has a broad experiential history extending a lifetime back into the past, the narrating I calls forth only that part of the experimental history linked to the story he is telling" (60). If autobiography is self-invention, as Eakin proposes in his book *Fictions in Autobiography*, or if the self is "an effect of autobiographical storytelling" there is nothing wrong with writing about things one has not experienced personally.

In *Reading Room Only: Memoir of a Radical Bibliophile*, Phil Cohen ponders the reasons for writing a memoir. Is it about "a quest for roots"? he wonders. Is it "a search for, or a flight from" one's social or spiritual heritage? (12). If one's story, as in the case of Cohen, is "too disjointed" to fit into neat patterns, should it be formatted accordingly? "Should it then perhaps be an exercise in postmodernity, celebrating the fragmentary and contradictory aspects of [one's] life, while reflecting on the conditions of impossibility of the autobiographical enterprise itself?" (12). Looked at from the point of view of what function a memoir has, Cohen proposes that "[w]riting one's life can also be a way of learning from your mistakes, so that you can do better in future, a version of self improvement that again involves abandoning an idealized version of your past" (13). Cohen continues:

> Every life is an experiment, but unlike an experiment in chemistry or physics, not one that can be replicated, or has procedures that can control the outcome. It follows that the method of writing a life should

be equally open ended, alert to the contingency of events and the counterfactual. It is impossible to write any such account without pondering what might have been. It is tempting, then, to reach for the consolation of imagining life unfolding according to some ineluctable master plan, whether dictated by divine providence or DNA, or some imperious ambition. In default of that there is the equally dangerous lure of being so haunted by a sense of missed opportunities that life becomes a hard luck story, one long lamentation or angry tirade focused on injustices and misfortunes, real or imagined. (13)

Realizing that he is an "unreliable narrator," Cohen chooses to see his own autobiography, *Reading Room Only*, as "a narrative essay around [a] chosen theme," a narrative that does not have to be—that cannot be—inclusive, one that cannot "tell the whole story" (12).

Analogously, this anthology will not and cannot tell the whole story. It does hope, however, to give a sense of the broad range of perspectives one finds in autobiography studies today. Exploring autobiographical expression in many different forms, the thirty essays collected in this book were presented at an international conference held at Södertörn University, Stockholm, in October 2014. The essays will be arranged here in alphabetical order according to the first names of the contributors.

In the first chapter entitled "'When I think about myself'": Identity Building in Maya Angelou's Autobiographical Sequel," Alice Godfrey places Angelou's work within an Afro-American autobiographical tradition of the nineteenth and twentieth century and argues that the black feminist critique developed during the twentieth centuries helps shed light on processes of identity-building among Afro-American women and their relationship to Afro-American communities and culture. Godfrey points to Angelou's use of the first-person singular and her attempts to make it into the first-person plural; in highlighting her own story, Angelou shows how similar it is to the stories of many other Black American women. An important writer within Afro-American literature, Maya Angelou is well-known for her autobiographies. Travel constitutes an important motif, and Angelou's travels brought her into many different geographical and cultural territories, something that led to her reflections on American contexts. Importantly, too, while Angelou's travels took place in a physical realm, they were at the same time deeply spiritual.

In the second chapter, "The 'Absent Presence' and the Art of Autobiography: Barack Obama's *Dreams from My Father*," Aparajita Nanda looks at Obama's patriography through the lens of poststructuralist theory, especially Barthes' *Camera Lucida*. Nanda argues that the link she tries to establish between French theory and Obama's narrative is justifiable for several reasons. First of all, it was French poststructuralism that revitalized American literary criticism after the 1970s. Secondly, historically, France has been a land of various liberatory movements. In the past, it has sheltered the leaders of Black liberation movements. Moreover, there is a parallel between the way Barthes' autobiographical work communicates meaning through photographs, storytelling, dreams, and Obama's life-writing. The absent presence of his father is the main driving force behind Obama's life-writing which ultimately becomes a personal interior journey to connect the chasm between the ideal and the real, the abstract and the concrete, myth and history. In Obama's narrative, despite their personal failings, both father and son stand redeemed in a larger drama of human connectedness.

Until recently, there have been many misunderstandings about self-injury, something that can represent an added difficulty for those who engage in such behavior since it may deprive them of support and understanding which, in turn, may lead to silence around such behavior. In "Expressing Nonsuicidal Self-injury: Using Creative Writing and Autobiographical Fiction as Self-Care," Belinda Hilton points to therapeutic writing as a possible way forward, if not a complete cure. Careful not to overestimate the importance of therapeutic writing, Hilton nonetheless suggests that it can be seen as a tool for self-care, in being both an outlet for overwhelming negative emotions and a space in which to explore the reasons for such emotions. These emotions stem from one's own stories, stories that are often "full of fictions" that need to be uncovered and challenged. Relying upon Celia Hunt's ideas of fictional autobiography in "Therapeutic Effects of Writing Fictional Autobiography," Hilton proposes a process of 'repurposing' rather than recounting elements from one's life story, using fictional techniques to alleviate self-harming behaviors and render more apparent recurring themes and underlying reasons.

In his article entitled "Memory, Trauma, and Resilience: The Autobiographies of Winnie Madikizela Mandela," Ben Lebdai seeks to find the political, family-oriented, and individual woman behind the icon she has become. He does so by comparing and contrasting two autobiographical texts published by Madikizela Mandela, *Part of My Soul Went with Him* (1985) and *491 Days: Prisoner number 1323/69* (2013). In answer to a number of questions—What are the keys to Madikizela Mandela's discourse and her appealing storytelling? What are the sources behind her impressive resilience and resistance? Are they inspired by the culture taught by her father, by her social involvements, by politics or by love?—Lebdai explains Winnie Madikizela Mandela's capacity to speak her mind in the extremely hostile world of Apartheid South Africa.

In "The (Un)making of a Novelist's Self: 'Late Style' in Günter Grass' and J. M. Coetzee's Autobiographical Writing," Melissa Schuh specifically focuses on third-person autobiographies and on a deliberate shift from the first to the third person with all the literary and interpretative consequences this can carry. First outlining the use of lateness as a factor of style in autobiographical life-writing, drawing on Edward Said's theory of late style, Schuh then analyzes how narrative strategies are representative in conveying lateness and late style in the autobiographical context: first in Grass' *Beim Häuten der Zwiebel*, then in Coetzee's *Summertime*. Her conclusion evaluates Grass' and Coetzee's autobiographical portrayal of the novelist's writing life as a source of stylistic innovation.

In "Autobiography and the Scene of Speech in Gertrude Stein's *Everybody's Autobiography*," Christine Savinel focuses on how Stein addresses questions of singularity and generality of voice through discourse staging and reflexivity. Stein comes closer to a purely existential definition of the genre when she demands of her readers that they "listen" to her "being existing"—which means meditating and writing in a way that evokes Nietzsche's *Ecce Homo*. Savinel shows how Stein evolves a form of heterogeneous autobiographical discourse that is more associative and digressive than sequential, rechanneling events through analogy and difference. By multiplying the images of self, Stein creates a both general and singular instance of self. Savinel suggests Stein transforms autobiography into a scene of speech, where an ongoing conversation represents "Everybody's speech" in a singular way.

Autobiography and biography sail under different flags and answer differently to questions of shared and remembered truths. They move along similar routes, something that may lead to complementary or contradictory accounts of the same life story. In "When Words Collide: (Auto-)Biography, Truth, Identity and Normalcy in the Case of Elias Canetti," Claude Desmarais puts Canetti's three-volume autobiography side by side with the biography of Canetti by Sven Hanuschek published much later in order to problematize the issue of truth-claim in the genre of life-writing. Desmarais finds a number of rather startling differences between the two. In one sense, Hanuschek's biography gives a more complete picture in covering sixty years more of Canetti's life and in adding to the picture what are presumably historically correct descriptions of Canetti's relationships to family and acquaintances. Important details concerning his relationship to his father and his mother as well as to some friends are shown to be incomplete in their underplaying of interpersonal conflicts. The both dramatizing and idealizing narrative of the father's death, for example, is shown to be a "pure construct." The omission of a mention in his autobiography of his wife's disability may be seen as respectful but might also lead to a "questioning of the autobiographical portrait for leaving out such an important detail." The biography clearly suggests that the autobiography fails to tell the whole story. And yet, the biography could be questioned, too, for an approach that might "damage the literary text," and rob it of narrative agency. Using Paul Eakin's framework, Desmarais demonstrates how Canetti's autobiography and Hanuschek's biography of Canetti meet the expectations of truth, identity, and normalcy in different ways. While Canetti's unreliable memory, his inadvertent slips, and his deliberate omissions reveal his world-view, their documentary contextualization is revealing in more ways than one. In a sense, even when the words of the autobiography and the biography collide, they complement each other in the act of constructing Elias Canetti.

Dagmara Drewniak's chapter, "'It's Our Shared Memories. The Stories We Tell': Politics and Identity in Two Memoirs by Hungarian-Canadians," analyses works by two Hungarian-Canadian writers: *Shoshanna's Story: A Mother, a Daughter, and the Shadows of History* by Elaine Kalman Naves and *The Storyteller: Memory, Secrets, Magic and Lies* by Anna Porter. Both writers are interested in exploring the process of identity formation through a historical and political reconsideration of their homeland, Hungary. Drewniak describes how both individual experience and collective memory augment the process of self-formation. Through reconsideration of their homeland, Hungary, its history and politics, the above-mentioned authors attempt to analyze the formation of self. Collective memory as well as history are two fundamental components that are brought into Drewniak's analysis as well.

In his chapter, "From Autobiography to Storytelling: The Works of C.S. Lewis," Daniel Warzecha depicts the famous mid-twentieth century Anglo-Irish Christian apologist and novelist C.S. Lewis' journey and his description of the repercussion of death on the psychological and spiritual self, something he had himself experienced after his beloved's death. According to Warzecha, Lewis' childhood and youth are two of the factors that most deeply contributed to the author's development into a story-teller and apologist. Ultimately, Warzecha observes that Lewis's aesthetic autobiography is retrospectively fundamental as it sheds light on his state of mind as a fiction writer.

In "Avoiding Self-Centered Fairytales: Autobiographies by Female Singer-Songwriters," Daniela Chana writes about common points and differences between the autobiographies by singer-songwriter and pianist, Tori Amos and the rock star, Patti Smith. In Chana's perspective, Tori Amos writes a more experimental form of autobiography in which the artist does not write about the story of her life as an artist but provides an "accumulation" of fragments taken from interviews, as well as reflections by the artists and details from her songs. On the other hand, Patti Smith's autobiography intends instead to provide political, philosohical and sociocultural insights of the multilayered world of art and rock and roll as in the 1960s and 1970s.

In "Four Moments of Self-recovery: Postcolonality, Odia Identity, and Autobiography," Dipti R. Pattanaik demonstrates how the genre of autobiography in Odisha has been the site of a complex interaction between inherited tradition and acquired modernity. This literary genre, along with many other colonial forms of knowledge, was introduced into the rather self-effacing traditional Odia culture when the British occupied the territory in the nineteenth century. After the first indigenous autobiography in Odia was penned in the early part of the twentieth century, the Odia mind across the class divide has found the medium so conducive for self-expression that it has become the most dominant literary genre in Odia literature. The first Odia autobiographer, Fakirmohan, used the genre as an instrument of self-recovery, a mechanism to come to terms with the psychological loss his community felt under the rule of British colonial masters and their comprador Bengali subcolonialists. Fakirmohan's narrative strategically inhabits the crossroads where the personal and the communal, the private and the political meet. This model of autobiography as an instrument of identity politics continues to hold sway, as can be seen from the essay, even after the nature of political hegemony and actors of oppression have changed with the times.

Ebere Nnenna Agugbue Nweze focuses on autobiographical works by African and Diaspora (Anglophone Caribbean and American) women whose works are regarded as sources of inspiration for a female vocalism in society. In her chapter, "Writing me, Raising Me, Beating the Drums Louder: Fictional Autobiography as a Feminist Tool for Expression in African and Diaspora Women's Writing," Nweze maintains that autobiography as a genre can be deployed by female minority groups and feminists to obtain a more important role in literature and history. According to Nweze, when women writers use the form and especially when their protagonists are girls or women, they subvert the notion of the voicelessness of the second sex in black society and literature, and they become active subjects in the communities they live in.

Elisabeth Bouzonviller's chapter, "Maternity and Writing: An Expedition into the Ojibwe Land of Letters with Louise Erdrich," explores American novelist Louise Erdrich's autobiographies, *The Blue Jay's Dance: A Birth Year* and *Books and Islands in Ojibwe Country*. Pregnancy, birth, and early childhood are the subjects of Erdrich's first text, while the second deals with a family journey in the traditional Ojibwe land. In this chapter, Bouzonviller's intention is to argue that both texts tackle maternity and writing as the main subjects. In these books, literature and the act of writing become active components thanks to the re-telling of her life story. Bouzonviller explores the way Erdrich departs from the reality of her life, first by turning her various experiences into an experience that is unique, but most of all by questioning the essence of writing through the story of her family.

In "'My Mother Composed Me as I Now Compose Her': Catharsis and Cathexis in Alison Bechdel's Are You My Mother?" Eva-Sabine Zahelein narrativizes Bechdel's troubled quest for her self by analyzing her autobiography/memoir which combines both narrative and graphic art. Bechdel's graphic memoir of her mother ultimately doubles up as an autobiography of self-assertion by eliding the minor genre divide that usually sets a memoir and an autobiography apart. In the complex relationship she has with her mother, she has a mirror which shows her not only her mother's inability to perform as an expected cathectic object, but also her own troubled search for surrogate emotional succour. Her life-writing act helps her discover that her mother's failings are somehow also her own, and both mother and daughter are connected on a more subtle plane much after the umbilical cord is severed and their emotional bond has been traumatised. The book is a testament of mother–daughter bonding on a subtle plane, a recognition of their allegiance to the creative process which helps Alison empathise with her mother who, after all, introduced to her the healing powers of the creative process that enables her to better understand herself.

In "Like Father Like Daughter? Autobiography as Defacement in Leslie Stephen's *Mausoleum Book* and Virginia Woolf's *Memoirs*," Floriane Reviron-Piegay reads two life writing texts written by members of the same family in order to show how ideological differences result in creating two contrasting pictures of the same person. Leslie Stephen's portrait of his second wife is informed by a masculine and patriarchal Victorian voice which, while idealizing Julia Stephen, stifles and smothers her spirit. Virginia Woolf's feminist, modern attitude as revealed in her *Memoirs* conveys reservations about her father's attempt to portray the deceased mother's character and personality for the benefit of her children. Woolf describes how her father's protestations transform the living memory of their mother into an "unlovable phantom." Piegay argues that her father's auto/biography generates in Woolf a general mistrust of the genre of life-writing, a genre that her family across generations had contributed to so substantially. The comparative study of these two life-writing texts helps us to focus on the fictional dimension that underlies the genre.

In "What's Wrong with Me? A Cautionary Tale of Using Contemporary 'Damage Narratives' in Autobiographical Life," Jo Woodiwiss draws both on her own research on women's stories of childhood sexual abuse and stories of adoption as well as a wider engagement with self-help literature. Her intention is to argue for a need to examine limitations and constraints placed on contemporary stories aiming to question which stories can be told, and heard, and which cannot, and by whom, in a society where we are all engaged in a continuous process of re/telling our biographies and life stories. Proposing that we do not simply slot ourselves into readymade narratives but draw on stories or narrative frameworks currently in circulation, Woodiwiss looks at the role of contemporary storytelling whilst highlighting the limitations and dangers of currently available biographical framewords within which we make sense of our lives.

John C. Hawley writes about autobiographies by transsexuals and how their purpose is to carve a place for themselves in a society that does not fully comprehend who these authors really are. In his chapter, "Trans-Autobiographies as Sites for Decolonization," Hawley focuses on the reception of transsexuals' autobiographies in society, on the questions these autobiographies raise or attempt to address and, furthermore, on the mixed receptions these texts have had in gay and lesbian communities. Hawley teaches us that the necessity for such autography does not take special talents. There is a wish to carve out a place for the transsexual in a society that does not understand who the transsexual writer is.

In her chapter entitled "Autobiography and Autofiction: No Need to Fight for a Place in the Limelight, There is Space Enough for Both of these Concepts," Karen Ferreira-Meyers questions the possible links between autobiography and autofiction. The recent surge in published autofictions and the debate around concepts such as autobiography and autofiction make additional analyses of the literary concepts involved necessary. In his books, Philippe Forest tries to define autofiction and autobiography by exclaiming that autofiction is simply a form of autobiography that should be looked at with suspicion. For Forest, each narrative, even the most intimate, is necessarily fictional because each episode lived configures itself spontaneously according to the rules of literature. Thus, from his point of view, the Self exists only as fiction in the first-person novel. Jeannelle draws the following conclusion: "therefore, the only difference between the two competing models [autobiography and autofiction] is that, in the case of autofiction, the staging of the subject's identity is clearly fictional while it remains ambiguous in the case of the autobiographical novel" (26). In 2007, Serge Doubrovsky reaffirms that autofiction is the postmodern form of autobiography because life and how we regard it now has drastically changed. Autofiction allows for a distinction between a more classical and a modern/ postmodern sensibility.

In "The Ordeal of the Soul: Ordinary People's Autobiographies of Mental Illness in Finland 1870–1935," Kirsi Tuohela presents the autobiographies of three non-professional writers who had experienced a mental collapse: Karl Johan Lind, Maria Åkerblom, and Aino Manner, writing in the early twentieth century, in the 1920s and in the 1930s, respectively. In Finland as well as in other European countries both Christian thought and pagan rites were brought to bear on the treatment of the insane or mentally unbalanced with the aim of driving out evil spirits. Rewarding patients with food if they said the Lord's prayer was one method used in the eighteenth century. Although the autobiographies Tuohela discusses are from a later period, they, too, are informed by the thought that alienation from God and a deviation from a Christian path of righteousness could lead to madness. In the case of Karl Johan Lind, an ordained minister, that would seem not to have been the case, but in the course of caring for the souls of women in prison, he fell ill himself. For him, only a spiritual path of prayer could bring healing. Maria Åkerblom almost died from tuberculosis when, on her death bed, in a state of trance, she saw visions and started to preach. She herself rejected the idea that she was mentally ill and concluded that her state was God's will. Aino Manner, Tuohela's third example, had several stays in a mental institution after her breakdown. She compares herself to Dante in the *Divine Comedy* in touring hell. In Manner's view, nurses and patients had lost their souls, and salvation and a way out of madness consisted in following Jesus. What the three writers studied by Tuohela have in common is the ideal that mental illness is due to a disconnection from God, a sort of shipwreck of the soul on its spiritual journey.

Lamia Mokrane's chapter, "Motions and Emotions in Jamaica Kincaid's *The Autobiography of my Mother*," deals with Jamaica Kincaid's main character, Xuela, in *The Autobiography of my Mother* as compared to Donna Harraway's cyborg in *A Manifesto for Cyborgs*. Xuela has two sides: a human and a monstruous, unemotional one. The reader easily experiences sympathy for her as she is portrayed as a lost and abandoned orphan, but on the other hand she also seems arrogant and insensitive. Initially, Mokrane examines Xuela's motherlessness and her decision not to give or receive love. Building on Harraway's ideas of a cyborg, Mokrane argues further that Kincaid depicts Xuela as a possible cyborg who could be seen both as a creature made as a machine and as an organism.

In "'No Shadows Under Us': Fictional Freedoms and Real Violations in Louise Erdrich's *Shadow Tag*," Laura Castor analyses the multiple narrative perspectives adopted by Louise Erdrich in her autobiographical novel *Shadow Tag* in order to represent a self torn between complex and contradictory pulls of ethical restraint and commitment to truth. The author needs to record the factuality of her experience not just in order to gain a psychotherapeutic outlet from her traumatic marital experience, but also to indulge in an act of creative excellence. Both are necessary. But the more important concern for her is that this exercise could be a subversive testament of violating power structures of all kinds—colonisation, race, gender etc. At the same time Erdrich is very much aware that this is going to be only her side of the story because the possibility of a counternarrative which could have made it easier to discover the truth is forever lost with the suicide of her former husband, Michael Dorris. So now, how much she can reveal and how much truth-claim she makes for these revelations become ethical questions. Erdrich's choice of fiction as the genre to write her life is a deliberate attempt to not invoke what Lejeune calls the autobiographical pact. However, Castor argues that designating *Shadow Tag* as an autobiographical novel would be delimiting its possibilities. Using Leigh Gilmore's coinage, Castor shows how *Shadow Tag* is a 'limit-case autobiography' in which the autobiographical and narratorial 'I' has a shadow-like presence (from which the text draws its title) in the text very much like the trickster figure in Indian narratives. This 'tricksterial' quality of the author figure helps the novelist/autobiographer circumvent the ethical, moral, and generic questions and turns the text into a metanarrative of self-representation through narrative. Although this bestselling work has been seen as a *roman à clef*, the parallels between Erdrich's own life and her characters have so far not been sufficiently explored. Castor focuses on the politics of belonging. While pointing to a fleeting character in *Shadow Tag*, Louise, as a subtle indication of the author's presence as a 'shadow,' Castor does not so much search to determine the factuality of Erdrich's novel as to raise the question as to how Erdrich might "use memories and material from her experience as a way of getting readers to do their own cultural work of questioning violence in relationships between men and women," and she concludes that "Erdrich's personal process of healing the trauma in her marriage to Michael Dorris and of his suicide may be just as important as her cultural work on behalf of America's trauma as a nation from the time of contact between European immigrants and Native peoples."

In the chapter "'My Own Face as Personal Vanishing Point': Writing The Body in Lucy Grealy's *Autobiography of a Face*," Laure de Nervaux-Gavoty analyzes how illness complicates the task of providing the self access to itself through a coherent narrative—a task commonly incumbent upon an autobiographer. The illness in question is Ewing's sarcoma, a rare form of jaw cancer, and the autobiographer under consideration is Lucy Grealy who underwent major surgery that removed two thirds of her right jaw. The traumatic experience of the disease and the long process of healing is dealt with in *Autobiography of a Face*. Further, this pathography—the narrative of illness and loss—also deals with subsequent attempts to reconstruct a coherent self and identity in the face of a hostile environment. Nervaux-Gavoty's contentions in this regard are very apt: if an autobiographer's primary concern is to reconstruct a coherent self, how can Grealy achieve it when her self is mutilated to start with? Moreover, while conventional autobiographical texts assert the primacy of the mind at the expense of body, this text perforce has to assume the superior power of the body. The surgical restoration of the integrity of the body in Grealy's case doubles as the textual integrity even as the 'face' becomes the synecdoche of the whole self of the narrator. The 'hole' in the face created through surgery makes Grealy's encounters with the mirror difficult, reminding her time and again of her illusory quest for wholeness in life. Paradoxically, this lack of wholeness, the lack in the face becomes the source of her identity. She does not subscribe to any myths of panacea or catharsis that normal pathographies weave. Her attempts at self-recognition on the contrary undermines the fiction of a unified self, a task theoreticians like Gusdorf set for an ideal autobiography to achieve. In this and many other senses, Gavoty argues, Grealy's autobiography goes against the grain of most autobiographical texts. While most life writing texts concentrate on the effacement of the body, Grealy's account asserts the power of the body and the way it shapes identity and how the body itself turns into a text.

Manuel Brito analyzes how American women authors, Lyn Hejinian, Carla Harryman, and Rae Armantrout endorse a new literary genre in *The Grand Piano: An Experiment in Collective Autobiography*. This genre, considered by Brito as avant-garde and dynamic, went beyond the model of self determined by the cultural influences of the age. The three female authors were committed to the concepts of autobiography conceptualized by Sidonie Smith and Julia Watson while focusing on the continued action of writing, traversing both space and time as a modification of the author's self. An emphasis on community and otherness blurs the boundaries of literary genres and make self and language relevant components.

In "'Memoir as Well as Biography': Generic Indeterminacy in Vikram Seth's *Two Lives*," Mélanie Heydari proposes that the formal aspects of this work have received too little critical attention. On the border between biography and autobiography, *Two Lives*, an account of the relationship between Seth and his relatives, is "a book about borders, boundaries, the closing of borders, and the crossing into new ones" marked even by "porous geographical, linguistic, and even generic frontiers" whose metatextual commentary and troubling ending add to the generic indeterminacy and undermine the horizons of expectation. While some of Seth's work such as *An Equal Music* (1999) has received criticism for a perceived lack of 'Indianness' and a lack of the postcolonial perspectives expected from contemporary Indian authors, Heydari argues that Seth's place is indeed on the postcolonial scene, but that the place he occupies is an original one.

In "Eve Unchained: Christina Stead's Recasting of the Christian Spiritual Autobiography," Michael Ackland analyzes Christina Stead's abandoning of literary archetypes and genres that were closely identified with Christian teachings in favor of new, more transgressives ones. Ackland divides his chapter into three parts. The first part establishes Stead as a bone fide Marxist while concentrating on letters written in the aftermath of the Wall Street crash and on her portrayal of Roman Catholic faith in her first novel, *Seven Poor Men of Sydney*. The next section focuses on essays in which Stead, harnessing key biblical paradigms, depicts her childhood. In the last one Ackland turns to another two of Stead's works with the aim to show how their allegedly authobiographical content serves, in Ackland's words, as a "blind" or "screen" for a covert Marxist critique of key Western societies in the 1930s and in the Cold War period.

In his chapter entitled "Retouching the Past: Vladimir Nabokov's *Speak, Memory* as Fictive Autobiography," Mikołaj Wiśniewski writes about Vladimir Nabokov's *Strong Opinion* in which he describes the difference between "good" and "bad memoirists." Furthermore, Wiśniewski aims to show how Nabokov uses cinematographic effects to capture the past in order to embellish it and to even suppress its traumatic or otherwise disagreeable content. In particular, Wisniewski is attracted to the lines between memory and fiction (or even delusion), and between artistic genius and madness, which he argues can be very thin. Wiśniewski sees a contrast between the redemptive memory of *Speak, Memory* and the memory of what he calls 'mnemonic deviants,' those who remain in the past, unable to distinguish reality from the imaginings of their own paranoid minds.

In a chapter entitled "'Life Has Got Awfully Dramatic All of a Sudden, Hasn't it? Just Like a Fiction': The Art of Writing Life in Donna Tartt's Novels," Pamela J. Rader shows how representational strategies of life-writing are employed in the two novels of Donna Tartt, namely *The Secret History* and *The Goldfinch*, and how they complicate the traditional genre divide that exists between autobiography and fiction. The novels are supposedly the confessional accounts of the two protagonists, Richard Papen and Theo Decker, who invite readers to have a glimpse of their essential selves beneath the narratorial personae. At one level, the narration delineates their ideals of love and beauty, their aches of loss and loneliness, their secret crimes and lies to which others had not been privy, so far, but at another, it also raises questions about its own truth-claims. Readers are left wondering whether they are confronting a confession or just an artistic ruse or a contrivance, or if they should go for the message or the medium itself. What begins as an insider's view of truth about the characters' lives ends up as a literary artefact, an object of beauty. Their self-portraits, ultimately, a celebration of the life-sustaining power of art, align themselves with the great masters of art whose works have transcended the limitations of time to which ordinary human lives are subject. By borrowing representational strategies from master artists in order to tell their lives, the protagonists not only create an illusion of immortality for themselves—which probably is the human purpose behind artistic creation—they also succeed in lending beauty to the ugliness of ordinary life. Inevitably, the narration leads to a very fundamental question about autobiography writing in general: is autobiographic life writing a construction of an authentic self? Or is it the representational narrative that appropriates the self into a verbal artefact in which the self is totally lost? Rader argues that Tartt's novels primarily dramatize this paradox.

In his essay, "Sexual Fingerprint: Queer Diaries and Autobiography," Piotr Sobolczyk demonstrates how a particular culture influences the writing styles of sexuality in autobiographic literature. Citing the instances of "queer diaries" of a few Polish homosexual writers, he argues that the cultural ideology of sexuality relegated these autobiographic writings to a secretive private space. Although there was no specific law banning homosexual relationships in communist Poland, the prevalent culture forced the writers of these secret queer diaries to lead a double life. Some of them arranged to have their works confessing their deviant sexuality to be published posthumously, even as they published their official autobiographies during their lifetime, giving only broad hints about their queer orientation. The difference between these two autobiographic modes—the secret and the official—is, according to Sobolczyk, a response to the paranoid sexual politics and culture of Poland at that time. Reading the four secret diaries of Iwaszkiewicz, Andrzejewski, Bialoszewski and Gombrowicz closely, Sobolczyk shows how these writers alternate between what Melanie Klein calls paranoid, depressive, and reparative positions of writing sexuality. In the final analysis these autobiographic writings are as much individual confessions as they are a testimony to a corporate ideology of sexuality.

Seana Kozar's "'Glad Rags, Feather-Dusted Spiders and Horse-Drawn Harvesters': Gender, Truth and Imagination in Three Approaches to Autobiography/Autoethnography at an Elder Care Home in Bristol," is framed by an Irish folk tale, "The Wonders of the Three Donals," in which three men tell fantastic stories of journeys into remote and magic realms. Kozar's point is that even though autobiography as a genre clearly differs from folk tales, there are certain striking similarities in their narration of significant existential life events and stages. Thematically, both genres may relate maturation processes, life reviews, and ways of handling fears of death. Temporally, there may also be resemblances. Paying particular attention to autobiographical and autoethnographic styles, Kozar's chapter explores the oral and written reminiscences of three residents in an elder care home in Bristol. The three respondents mentioned in Kozar's essay were encouraged to remember and talk about their past while the researchers recorded their stories. Even though the respondents are not accomplished writers or story-tellers, their autoethnography, Kozar argues, in both style and content, has a striking resemblance to the manner of structuring folktales. Folktales and autobiographies, as literary genres, may be vastly different from each other, but they share certain key features. Using the framing narrative of an Irish folktale, "The Wonders of Three Donals," Kozar shows how the autobiographies of the three respondents are in fact narratives about coming of age concerned with a "reflexive past and future that serve the narrator's present understanding." This mode of autobiography certainly expands the limits of the genre and even has certain advantages over the traditional written autobiographies. Kozar is of the view that 'the intentional, systematic, contextualised self-consciousness of the method' gives these narratives a distinctive feature. Not adept at the traditional strategies of writing, these respondents might normally not have produced these narratives. Moreover, their cultural norms might have inhibited them from drawing too much attention to their own selves. With this interventionist attempt, not only a few more stories have been added to our corpus of life-stories, a whole new perspective for autobiographical studies has been inaugurated.

In her essay "Rewriting Cure: Autobiography as Therapy and Discursive Practice," Tanja Reiffenrath argues that certain illness autobiographies challenge established cultural constructions of disease and health, and destabilize the dichotomous relationship between the two. Citing the instances of Audre Lorde's *The Cancer Journals* and Siri Hustvedt's *The Shaking Woman*, Reiffenrath first justifies the need for a new theoretical framework to deal with the challenges these life-writing narratives pose to our collective scientific and cultural wisdom regarding the body, sexuality, disease, diagnosis, therapy, cures, identity, and health. These narratives call for a new nomenclature of illness autobiography with 'illness' being the focal point of the narrative rather than a rupture of 'normalcy' as in traditional autobiographies. These illness narratives give voice to experiences that are silenced in biomedical discourses. This assertion of the suffering self, hitherto not domesticated in scientific parlance and cultural discourses of health, is both cathartic and therapeutic. However, they are also different from the triumphant narratives which adopt a celebratory tone about overcoming the temporary phase of ill health. For illness narratives of the kind exemplified by Lorde and Hustvedt's stories do not see illness and health in linear terms or as dichotomies, but as contextual, dependent on a historical moment. They see illness and health as contingent experiences and the so-called healed patient as inhabiting an in-between space, or, to use Arthur Frank's terminology, as the members of a remission society. In the ultimate analysis, these illness autobiographies have succeeded in destigmatizing disease.

Recent discussions of autobiographical writing have led to a pléthora of new terms such as autographies, autre-biographies, nouvelle autobiography, autofiction, faction, égolittérature, circonfession. For some, autofiction is either a simple model of the autobiographical pact (Lejeune) with a marked psychoanalytic inflection (Doubrovsky), or the latest form of the autobiographical novel (Gasparini), for others, an intergeneric practice which is already ancient, and which can be taken as an arch-genre including the form of an autobiographical novel, but not limited in possibilities. Based on the work of Lucian, Vincent Colonna describes different autofictional categories such as fantastic autofiction that transfigures the existence and identity of the writer "in an unreal story, indifferent to likelihood" (75) and biographical autofiction, in which the author fantasizes about his existence from actual data, remaining closer to reality and crediting his text with a less subjective truth" (93);[1] mirror autofiction, in which the work reflects the presence of the writer as in a mirror, and intrusive authorial autofiction requiring a text in the third person with an author-narrator in the margins of the plot. Life is regarded as raw material which should provide a specific form: this work of the self, about the self is about inventing oneself through exercises in subjectivity.

Before the 1950s, autobiography criticism, far from being highly regarded, was seen as a nuisance or even a "moral perversion" (Olney 7). Even though the field of autobiography studies started to blossom after the 1950s, only a few decades ago Philippe Lejeune could still make the observation that "experts in autobiography [had] one thing in common," namely that "within their own disciplines, they [were] often challenged and marginalized." Within the field of literature, he said, "autobiography was long considered a secondary field" and being associated with subjective truth claims rather than objective science, it was not held to be serious. It was even "uncomfortable because it [referred] the researcher back to himself" (Lejeune "A Plea" 4).

Today, there is no doubt that there is a heightened interest in autobiography. Current approaches to autobiography and autofiction suggest that the literary field offers a renewal and sometimes even a revolution of life writing regarding views of recent world events (the Holocaust, the two World Wars, the postcolonial era, to mention but a few). Indeed, as the essays in this anthology suggest, we seem to be in the process of rethinking

---

[1] Examples of the first-mentioned category would be Lucian's *True History* and *The Aleph* by Jorge Luis Borges and of the second category, Christine Angot and Serge Doubrovsky.

our definitions of what constitutes autobiographical writing. It is our hope that this anthology, through the variety of papers included here, will offer an inspiring and thought-provoking overview of different approaches to autobiography and autofiction.

Kerstin W. Shands
Dipti Ranjan Pattanaik
Karen Ferreira-Meyers
Giulia Grillo Mikrut

Works Cited

Anderson, Linda. *Autobiography: New Critical Idiom*. London: Routledge, 2001. Print.

Cohen, Phil. *Reading Room Only: Memoir of a Radical Bibliophile*. Nottingham: Five Leaves, 2013. Print.

Colonna, Vincent. *Autofictions & Autres Mythomanies Littéraires*. Auch: Tristam, 2004. Print.

Compagnon, Antoine, *Le Démon de la Théorie. Littérature et Sens Commun*, Paris: Seuil, coll. Essais, 1998. Print.

Dalziell, Rosamund. "Speaking Volumes: About Auto/biography Studies in Canada." ESC 32.2–3 (2008): 211–27. Print.

de Man, Paul. "Autobiography as Defacement." *MLN* 94. 5 (1979): 919–30. http://seas3.elte.hu/coursematerial/PeterAgnes/AutobiographyAsDe_facement.pdf. Accessed 3 March, 2015.

Doubrovsky, Serge. *Fils*. Paris: Galilée, 1977. Print.

Ducrot, Oswald, and Jean-Marie Schaeffer. *Nouveau Dictionnaire Encyclopédique des Sciences du Language*. Paris: Seuil, 1995. Print.

Eakin, Paul John. *Fictions in Autobiography: Studies in the Art of Self-Invention*. 1985. Princeton, NJ: Princeton UP, 2014. Print.

Garcia, Mar. "L'étiquette Générique *Autofiction*: Us et Coutumes." *Cédille, Revista de Estudios franceses*, 5 (2009): 146–63. Print.

Gasparini, Philippe. *La Tentation Autobiographique de l'Antiquité à la Renaissance*. Paris: Seuil, coll. Poétique, 2014. Print.

Gilmore, Leigh. *The Limits of Autobiography: Trauma and Testimony*. Ithaca: Cornell UP, 2001. Print.

—. Autobiographics: *A Feminist Theory of Women's Self-representation*. Ithaca: Cornell UP, 1994. Print.

Hindmarsh, D. Bruce. *The Evangelical Conversion Narrative: Spiritual Autobiography in Early Modern England*. Oxford: Oxford UP, 2005. Print.

Jauss, Hans Robert. *Pour une Esthétique de la Réception*. French transl. Paris: Gallimard, 1975. Print.

Jeannelle, J. L., and C. Violet. *Genèse et Autofiction*. Louvain-la-Neuve: Academia Bruylant, 2007. Print.

Lejeune, Philippe. *On Autobiography*. Ed. P. J. Eakin. 1989. Print.

—. *Le Pacte Autobiographique*. 2, Signes de vie. Paris: Seuil, 2005. Print.

—. "A Plea for a Guide to Autobiographical Europe." A speech given at Life Writing Europe: Founding Conference IABA Europe. Amsterdam, 29 October 2009. http://www.autopacte.org/81amsterdamangl.pdf. Accessed 7 May, 2015.

Olney, James. *Autobiography: Essays Theoretical and Critical*. Princeton: Princeton UP, 1980. Print.

—. "Autobiography and the Cultural Moment: A Thematic, Historical, and Bibliographical Introduction." Olney 3–27

Smith, Sidonie, and Julia Watson. *Reading Autobiography: A Guide for Interpreting Life Narratives*. Minneapolis: U of Minnesota P, 2010. Print.

When I Think About Myself: Identity Building Processes in Maya Angelou's Autobiographical Sequel

Alice Godfrey

In attempting to find the roots of Black women's desire to set down their own stories during a long-lasting struggle for racial and gender equality in the United States, I address the question of how the autobiographical genre contributed to the identity process of Afro-American women specifically in Maya Angelou's works. Her autobiographical productions, written between 1969 and 2013, constitutes an important milestone in both Afro-American literature and the autobiographical genre. Understanding how her work can be viewed as an identity building process can be envisaged from different angles.

A preliminary phase involves examining the development of the Afro-American autobiographical tradition that Stephen Butterfield first started theorizing in 1974. His wide scope of analysis helps situate Angelou's works within this tradition in North American literature. To better understand their specific features, a second step involves studying them through a black feminist critique, which first appeared as early as the 1920s. That critique goes some way towards explaining how women autobiographers perceive the autobiographical act of writing and publishing their works as a part of personal identity building, and that of Black women in their communities. Another feature to be considered is the recurrence of a travel motif, particularly present in Afro-American autobiographies. In her article "Travel as Metaphor and Reality in Afro-American Women's Autobiography, 1850–1972," Mary G. Mason analyses the role of this motif in the works of May Church Terrel and Ida Wells. Studying this travel motif in African-American women's autobiographies, and specifically in Angelou's work, enables one to envisage it as a tool for comprehending the on-going identity building processes portrayed in several Afro-American autobiographies.

In *Black American Autobiography* (1974), Stephen Butterfield divides the development of autobiographies into three periods. He suggests that in the first period, "slave narratives at the time were essentially determined by the will and the determination to fight a social system" (qtd. in Weixlmann 382). The second period, defined as a 'Period of Search', is characterized by a "deep alienation and identity crisis in black writing" (Butterfield 93). Finally, the ensuing "Period of Rebirth" highlighted a "reawakened political commitment," a period during which "the black masses took the initiative, forcing the middle class to respond to their militancy one way or another" (183). Although criticized by certain scholars for not clearly distinguishing pre- and post-civil war productions,[1] Butterfield's classification still sheds light on some important tendencies within the works written by Afro-American autobiographers.

When asked about the influence of slave narratives on her writing, Angelou affirms that they certainly played a role in her works, as she re-read them before writing *Gather Together In My Name*.[2] For the slave narrative period, Butterfield chose to focus on several male autobiographers of the time, one of whom is Frederick Douglass. Although the narrative of Harriet Jacobs is often considered as the female counterpart of Douglass' work, there are significant differences. Initially published in 1861 under the pseudonym of Linda Brent, Jacobs' autobiography was frequently mistaken for a novel; it was not interpreted as the will of an individual to share her own experience in order to fight a political and social system. This thereby reduced its political and social impact at the time of its release. From a literary viewpoint, its use of the first-person was long misinterpreted as referring to a fictional character, whereas it referred to Jacobs herself. This seemingly insignificant difference is, in fact, crucial in analyzing Jacobs' work. Although publishing slave narratives formed part of the activism at work within the anti-slavery movement, most published slave narratives

---

[1] In his article "Black Autobiography in America by Stephen Butterfield: A Review," James M. COX suggests that Butterfield only views autobiographies through a Marxist prism. Dejin XU, in *Race and Form: Towards a Contextualized Narratology of African American Autobiography*, Peter Lang (2003), also challenges Butterfield's division of the development of the African-American autobiographical tradition.

[2] See Neubauer 288.

were written by men. The ulterior recognition of Jacobs' work as an autobiography, more than a century later, places Jacobs, *a posteriori*, as part of the anti-slavery movement, in two distinct ways. Firstly, as an individual, taking a clear stand against slavery; secondly and arguably more importantly, the publication of her work as an autobiography that situates her experience as a milestone in the abolitionist movement. On several occasions, Jacobs describes and denounces the system that keeps her enslaved: "Slaveholders have a method, peculiar to their institution, of getting rid of *old slaves*, whose lives have been worn out in their sense. I knew an old woman (...) She had become almost helpless, from hard labor and disease. [She] was left to be sold to any body who would give twenty dollars for her." (Jacobs 16). Jacobs' work thus sheds light on the position of women slaves within an institutionalized economic and social system.

Similarly, in her first autobiographical volumes, Angelou tackled the issues of racism and segregation, which affected the Black communities differently in the North and the South. She draws some parallels between her work and slave narratives. In an interview, she declared: "I love the idea of the slave narrative, using the first person singular, really meaning the third person plural" (qtd. in Neubauer 288). To some extent, the title of Angelou's second volume also embodies this idea of using the first person, meaning the third person plural, in which it appears that a group of people should assemble around a unifying figure, a direct allusion to a verse from the Bible "For where two or three are gathered together in my name, there am I in the midst of them" (King James Bible, Matthew 18:20).

However, in a later interview with George Plimpton, Angelou explained: "I'm using the first-person singular and trying to make that the first-person plural (...) It's a large, ambitious dream. But I love the form." (Plimpton 184). On the one hand, writing her autobiography tends to singularize her experience. Rather paradoxically, by setting down her own story, Angelou also stresses that it might, too, resemble that of many other Black American young women. Angelou's 'I' is used here as a collective force in both cases.

This motif is also present in her fifth volume, *All God's Children Need Traveling Shoes*, when she describes the complex relationship between herself and some Ghanaian women a few weeks after her arrival in Ghana. She recalls one occasion when she wished to submit a paper to *The Ghanaian Times*: "For a few days I examined whether in looking for a home I, and all the émigrés, were running from a bitter truth that rode lightly but forever at home on our shoulders" (*Traveling Shoes* 34). Her use of the first-person singular with that of the first person plural helps establish a form of association with the group of Black American women settled in Ghana.

As an heiress to the Afro-American autobiographical tradition, Angelou uses features found in each of Butterfield's periods. *Gather Together in My Name* (subsequently referred to as *Gather Together*) could be considered as being part of Butterfield's 'Second period.' Mary Jane Lupton reports that many scholars, including Selwyn Cudjoe, have found this volume particularly fragmented, and not as concise in structure as her first volume. Lupton addresses this issue by stressing that, "(these) so-called 'fragments' are reflections of the kind of chaos found in actual living" (Lupton 'SBM' 258). Another singularity of Angelou's autobiographical writings also concerns the sheer extent of her works: her sequel, if taken in chronological order, despite some overlapping, amounts to six volumes. As few African-American autobiographies seldom fill more than one volume, Angelou's choice of sequencing her autobiographical works renews and extends the possibilities of the genre.

At times, even, her narratives overlap, like at the end of *The Heart of a Woman* and *All God's Children Need Traveling Shoes*. Furthermore, the ending of Angelou's second volume recalls that of a novel sequel: "I had no idea what I was going to make of my life, but I had given a promise and found my innocence. I swore I'd never lose it again" (*Gather* 214). Although this last sentence of the autobiographical volume does seem to mark the end of a period, it also leads to several questions. The sense of an ending, marked explicitly by the verb "find," appears to symbolize the end of a quest. The ending is also ambivalent, however, as the end of one quest seems to open on to another. Angelou declares that she is not sure what her future projects will be, which seems to usher in the next step of her identity building process.

In the African-American autobiographical tradition, certain features are specific to Afro-American women's autobiographies. For Joanne Braxton, "black women autobiographers constitute a tradition within a tradition operating within the dominant, familiar, and essentially masculinist modes of autobiography" (128). Braxton further describes this as a "master's cardboard house," an expression that characterizes the shallowness of a patriarchal, white-dominated, society paradigm which needs to be challenged.

Butterfield's second and third periods also coincided with the development of African-American women's autobiographies. Black women's literature, particularly autobiographies, has often been subject to severe criticism, such accounts often being deemed too personal, or not political enough.

However, Braxton stresses how "black women autobiographers liberate themselves from stereotyped views of black womanhood and define their own experiences" (128). One example of the successful political autobiographies published at the time is that of Elaine Brown, a Black Civil Rights activist, and leader of the Black Panthers from 1974 to 1977. One of her autobiographical books, *A Taste of Power* (1992), details her activism within the Black Panther Party. As such, Brown's autobiography could correspond to the 'Period of Rebirth' depicted by Butterfield. However, her autobiographical accounts also portray how challenging it was for women to gain responsibilities within a political party at the time: "A woman in the Black Power movement was considered, at best, irrelevant. A woman asserting herself was a pariah (…) if a black woman assumed a role of leadership, she was said to be eroding black manhood, to be hindering the progress of the black race. She was an enemy of black people" (Brown 257). Similarly, Angelou declared the following to Claudia Tate: "A number of black men in the sixties fell for a terrible ploy. They felt that in order to be total and free and independent and powerful they had to be like white men to their women. So there was a terrible time when black men told their women that if you really love me, you must walk three steps behind me" (Tate 4). Hence, underlying sexism and gender discrimination showed the limits of this political reawakening, and fighting such gender prejudice is indubitably part of Angelou's work as an autobiographer and a poet.

Braxton goes on to highlight another theme: the importance of a working definition of 'black womanhood' within autobiographical productions. "Central to the early autobiographical writings by black women, as several scholars have argued, is a definition of black womanhood posed against conventional white notions of 'true womanhood' with their myriad pretentions" (Braxton 130). In an interview with Claudia Tate, Angelou briefly reflects on the writing process of her first autobiography: "I wasn't thinking so much about my own life or identity. (…) I used the central figure—myself—as a focus to show how one person can make it through those times" (Tate 6). Angelou, in close resonance with the slave narratives of Harriet Jacobs, aims at showing others how one overcame "those times," using her experience as a testimony of what the 1930s in Arkansas and California were like. Through her writing process, willingly or not, she portrays herself as emblematic of a young girl growing up in the South and the hurdles she had to face. The theme of overcoming is inherent in Angelou's writing, both in her autobiographies and in her poetry. An example of this can be found in the poem '*When I Think About Myself*':

"When I think about myself/ I almost laugh myself to death/ (...) Too proud to bend,/ Too poor to break,/ I laugh until my stomach ache,/ When I think about myself (...)" (*Collected Poems* 29).

The persona, via the repeated use of the personal pronoun 'I', the strong emphasis on the possessive 'my' and the reflexive pronoun 'myself', focuses the reader's attention on the poem. Not only is the persona at the center of the poem, so are the challenges it faces and its efforts to overcome them. The formal tension developed between the lexical fields of joy and death throughout the poem, recalls the struggle depicted in many Black women's autobiographies, between the hardships they are subject to and their determination to overcome them. Angelou's writing stresses the vital importance of overcoming these discriminations. Her work as an autobiographer focuses on creating what Eva Lennox calls a "positive black female self" (Lennox 11). Maya's character and its evolution throughout the sequel emphasize how she accomplishes herself as a Black woman living in both the United States and abroad.

In her article on the works of May Church Terrell and Ida Wells, Mason seeks to demonstrate "how travel, which was a reality in the escape of the slave narrative and a reality in the itinerant travels of the spiritual autobiography, becomes a metaphor for Afro-American women's life as journey" (337). One might wonder to what extent this statement could also apply to Angelou's own itinerary. In her first volumes, Angelou writes about how she often moved from Missouri to her paternal grandmother's house in Arkansas and later to her mother's home in California. In *Caged Bird*, Angelou writes that after her rape and the murder of her rapist Maya reduces herself to silence. These events lead her to travel back to Stamps, the place closest to a home for Maya. Her encounter with Bertha Flowers, her grandmother's neighbor, helps her regain the use of her voice:

> Now no one is going to make you talk—possibly no one can. But bear in mind, language is man's way of communicating with his fellow man and it is language alone which separates him from the lower animal." That was a totally new idea to me and I would need time to think about it.
>
> Your grandmother says you read a lot. Every chance you get. Words mean more than what is set down on paper. It takes the human voice to infuse them with the shades of deeper meaning. (*Collected Autobiographies* 78)

This memory from *Caged Bird* rooted in Angelou's childhood puts forward Angelou's early analysis of the use of words. While the journey forcing her to return to Stamps could be seen as a step back, it was also a journey home that helped her overcome this trauma and perhaps prepare her career as a writer.

Mason points out that May Church Terrell's journey motif in her autobiography is ambivalent. "The autobiography of Mary Church Terrell (1863–1954) (...) carries on the journey theme. Journey as commitment to action is a primary metaphor, but there is also a conflicting metaphor—journey as self-discovery" (345). Much the same could be said about the travel motif in Angelou's autobiography, especially in *Gather Together* and in *Traveling Shoes*. She traveled extensively during her life, first in the United States and later throughout the world, in Europe, but especially in Africa. She first traveled to Africa with her former husband, working as a journalist in Egypt. In *Traveling Shoes*, most of the action takes place in Ghana, where Angelou had to stay with her son, due to his severe car accident. Her extensive traveling allowed her to be confronted with various political, social and cultural contexts. In her autobiographies, she often reflects on her own position and identity as a black American woman within different contexts, as well as on the position of Black American women within diverse cultural frameworks. As such, it appears that the physical journeys Angelou undertook cannot be separated from the author's spiritual journey.

Yet, for William L. Andrews, the major theme of Afro-Americans' spiritual autobiographies is "the growth of authentic, individually authorized selfhood" (Mason 340). In the following volume, Angelou moved around on several occasions because of her work as a dancer and singer, travelling to San Francisco and to Hawaii. In the *Heart of a Woman*, which partly takes place in New York, Angelou was working as the Northern Coordinator of the Southern Christian Leadership Conference. In her autobiographical accounts one could argue that Maya's life progression is not only a physical journey, but also a journey towards gaining a better understanding of herself and asserting her financial and moral independence. Revisiting the journeys Maya undertook in *Gather Together* and *Traveling Shoes* could therefore provide a deeper insight into Angelou's ongoing identity building process. In an interview in the *Paris Review*, Angelou explains the choice of her title:

> I never agreed, even as a young person, with the Thomas Wolfe title, *You Can't Go Home Again*. Instinctively I didn't. But the truth is, you can never *leave* home. You take it with you; it's under your fingernails; it's in the hair follicles; it's in the way you smile; it's in the ride of your hips, in the passage of your breasts; it's all there, no matter where you go (…) So this book is about trying to go home. (Plimpton 190)

Whereas, at the beginning of *Traveling Shoes*, one can sense Angelou's strong desire to become part of the Ghanaian community, she comes to realize that she will always be considered as a foreigner. Nevertheless, her stay in Ghana helps her come to term with her African roots, a necessary step in fulfilling her identity quest before returning to her home in the United States.

Maya Angelou's works root her deeply into the Afro-American autobiographical tradition that developed during the nineteenth and twentieth centuries. Her works give us an insight into how writing one's autobiography can impact both the writer and the community. Her popularity as a writer, and her career as a teacher, also inspired her sequenced publications. In April 2013, at the age of eighty-four, her very last book was published, highlighting her on-going will to share her experiences as part of an identity building process. As she so forcibly puts it: "All my work, my life, everything I do is about survival, not just bare, awful, plodding survival, but survival with grace and faith. While one may encounter many defeats, one must not be defeated" (qtd. in McPherson 10).

Works Cited

Angelou, Maya. *I Know Why the Caged Bird Sings*. New York: Random House, 1969. Print.

—. *Gather Together in My Name*. New York: Random House, 1974. Print.

—. *The Heart of a Woman*. New York: Random House, 1981. Print.

—. *All God's Children Need Travelling Shoes*. 1986. London: Virago P, 1987. Print.

—. *The Complete Collected Poems,* New York: Random House, 1994. Print.

—. *The Collected Autobiographies of Maya Angelou,* New York: Random House, 2004. Print.

—. "Shades and Slashes of Light" in Evans, Mari, and Stephen E. Henderson, eds. *Black Women Writers (1950-1980): A Critical Evaluation*, Garden City, NY: Anchor-Doubleday, 1984. 4-8. Print.

Braxton, Joanne. Black Women Writing Autobiography: A Tradition Within a Tradition. Philadelphia: Temple UP, 1989. Print.

Brown, Elaine. *A Taste of Power: A Black Woman's Story*. 1992. New York: Anchor Books. 1993. Print.

Butterfield, Stephen. *Black Autobiography in America*. Amherst: University of Massachusetts P, 1974. Print.

—. "Autobiography and African Women's Literature" in *The Cambridge Companion to African American Women's Literature*, Cambridge: Cambridge UP, 2009. 128-149. Print.

Jacobs, Harriet. *Incidents in the Life of a Slave Girl*. 1861. New York: Modern Library, 2004. Print.

Lupton, Mary Jane. "Singing the Black Mother: Maya Angelou and Autobiographical Continuity." *Black American Literature Forum*, 24.2 (1990): 257-276, St. Louis U. Web. 8 June 2014.

—. 'Order Out of Chaos: The Autobiographical Works of Maya Angelou' by Dolly A. McPherson. A review by Mary Jane Lupton', *Black American Literature Forum*, 24. 4 (1990): 809-14. Web. April 15 2014.

—. "A Review by: Mary Jane Lupton." *Black American Literature Forum*, Vol. 24.4 (1990), St Louis U. 809-814. Web. April 15 2014.

Mason, Mary G. "Travel as Metaphor and Reality in Afro-American Women's Autobiography, 1850-1972." *Black American Literature Forum*, 24.2 (1990): 337-356. Web. 13 June 2014.

McPherson, Dolly Aimee. Order Out of Chaos: The Autobiographical. Works of Maya Angelou. New York: Peter Lang, 1990. Print.

Neubauer, Carol. "An Interview with Maya Angelou."*Massachusetts Review*, 28.2 (1987): 286-292. Web. April 28 2014.

Plimpton, George. Writers at Work: The Paris Review Interviews, Ninth Series. New York: Viking, 1992. Print.

Tate, Claudia. "Maya Angelou" in *Black Women Writers at Work*." New York: Continuum, 1984. Print.

Weixlmann, Joe. "African American Autobiography in the Twentieth Century: A Bibliographical Essay." *Black American Literature Forum*, 24.2 (1990): 375-415. Web. 7 June 2014.

The 'Absent Presence' and the Art of Autobiography: Barack Obama's *Dreams from My Father*

Aparajita Nanda

On the back cover of Barack Obama's *Dreams from My Father: A Story of Race and Inheritance*, Charlayne Hunter-Gault praises the autobiography as "One of the most powerful books of self-discovery I've ever read… It is also beautifully written, skillfully layered, and paced like a novel." Two words particularly caught my attention: "self-discovery" and "novel." The former virtually acknowledges the book to be a memoir whereas the latter compares it to a fictitious prose narrative. It is interesting to note that while an autobiography bases itself on facts (or truth), a novel easily embraces fiction (or lies). Even the title of the book seemed to straddle both zones: the dreams were *from* Obama's father, a father he almost never met, and according to the back cover, "a figure he knows more as a myth than as a man" while the subtitle promises a story grounded in the lived realities of race and inheritance. And yet a reading that attempts to segregate the concepts of myth and lived reality may be misdirected. One needs to keep in mind that the two are not exclusive; in fact, a blurring of fact and fiction leads to a fluidity of identity that, by Barack Obama's own admission, becomes a mainstay for the self-created narrative (vii).[1] The primary trigger of this self-creation is the haunting lack or void left by an absent father figure.

Filling this vacuum is a paternal presence that oscillates between the "real" father who had abandoned the son so early in life and a "mythical" father, resurrected through stories, whose dreams seem to act as milestones for the son's successful journey through life, an example as G. Thomas

---

[1] Given that father and son have the same name I have referred to the father as Obama senior. Wherever not specified the reference is to the son.

Couser argues of "patriography...life writing about fathers by their sons....inherently relational and inter-subjective" (259). In the first half of the narrative, the "absent" father figure haunts the life writing of the son as the latter struggles to measure up to the mythical personality of the former until, in the second half, the son understands the flawed human being his father was. Obama's initial reference to his father as "something unknown ... and vaguely threatening" (Obama 63) possibly creates a "metaphor for the way in which [the] son imagined Africa" (Smithers 494). In this second half, however, Michael Janis observes that "a political recognition of the significance of the African diaspora as a cultural entity and as a repository of intellectual history" is established (154). And Obama's father, I feel, given his intellectual brilliance, stands as a representational figure paving the way for the son to move from the postcolonial "periphery" to the twenty-first century "centre" (Baillie 317). Despite interesting critical appraisals of the father figure, no particular discussion, apart from Josephine Metcalf's, has taken its cue from the role structuralism plays in Obama's memoir. Whereas Metcalf makes just a passing comment on Stuart Hall's semiotic readings of texts, this paper argues that Obama's narrative can be read through a critical lens of cross-fertilization provided by Roland Barthes: from the absent father figure, a virtual semiotic signifier that communicates meaning within the text,[2] the narrative proceeds—with the help of photographs, storytelling, and dreams—to seek a sense of human connectedness in its final cathartic closure. The ending recalls Barthes' *Camera Lucida*, his emotional dependency on his mother, and at her death[3] the kindling of his desire to recover a lost relationship through nostalgia, sympathy, and filial devotion.

French scholars such as Barthes have been accredited for revitalizing the field of American literary criticism in the late 1970s and 80s. Jason Duell points out that French theory has been used as a form of "cultural capital" within the American academic literary field and "that... [French theories'] applicability to a wide variety of literary products has offered... way[s] of creating a degree of intellectual community across the divisions of periodization."[4] In his Presidential address at the 1992 MLA convention, Houston Baker brings to the fore the political angle achieved by the conflation of literary and cultural studies in America: how French theorists

---

[2] See Roland Barthes, *Elements of Semiology*, *S/Z* and *Image Music Text*.
[3] Obama's memoir starts with the death of his father.
[4] See Jason Duell, "Assessing The Literary: Intellectual Boundaries and Justification in French and American Literary Studies."

have virtually lifted the stranglehold of Enlightenment rationalism, thereby giving voice to minority (African American, Native American, Asian American) writings.[5]

France, the land of liberty,' was always associated with the idea of freedom. Abbé Grégoire's Société des Amis des Novis supported the first African American poet Phyllis Wheatley, who was a slave (Fabre 1). From the 19th century onwards, notable names like William Wells Brown, Paul Laurence Dunbar, W.E.B. Du Bois, Alain Locke, Countee Cullen, Langston Hughes, Richard Wright, James Baldwin and Claude McKay kept the French connection alive by visiting or living there in exile and finding, more often than not, a more conducive racial climate in France than in America.[6] In fact, W.E.B. Du Bois, at the Pan-African conference held at Paris in 1919, started to build bridges of understanding between anglophone and francophone African intellectuals (Janis 156). This cross-cultural influence often enriched African American writings, impacting their world views radically: Ralph Ellison relied on the techniques of French writers such as André Malraux and Paul Valéry; similar to French poets like Baudelaire and Rimbaud, the African American novelist Jean Toomer used changes in subject matter and style that parallel differences in lived realities, thus "reaffirming [the French poets] relevance in the Americas" (Hakutani XI, Ryder 802).

The relevance of the French in America, of Roland Barthes in particular, is quite apparent in how Barthes's essay "Photography and Electoral Appeal," included in *Mythologies* played a distinctive role in Barack Obama's 2008 presidential campaign. Michael Johnson and Sam Anderson point out that, though Barthes' essay was written about the French electoral process, his observations regarding the use of photographs in political campaigns is equally applicable to Obama's campaign poster in which he gazes up at the sky, while the colors of the American flag on display serve to give the image a purpose and intent paired with the single word HOPE. Photographs play a seminal role in Obama's autobiography, which he admits is a "personal, interior journey—a boy's search for his father" (xvi). The search is not an easy one given that Obama is dealing with a three-fold loss[7]: early abandonment,

---

[5] See Houston Baker, "Presidential Form on Multiculturalism: The Task of Literary Representation in the Twenty-First Century."

[6] See Michel Fabre, *From Harlem to Paris* for more details. Also see Virginia Whatley Smith's article in this context.

[7] Roland Barthes in his autobiography claims to suffer from "great Oedipal frustration" over the death of his father when Barthes was only two years old (*Roland Barthes* 45, qtd.

geographical distance, and the father's death. Naturally then, his reconstruction is based on arguments of familial memory (his mother's and his grandparents' on his mother's side) stitched together into "feasible stories" aided by some "old black-and-white studio" photographs retrieved from a "crumbling album" (Obama 8–9). The son's effort to reconstruct the father's image stems from his desire to recreate the past. This re-creation is again three-folded: via Barthesian *studium, punctum,* and the new *punctum.* Barthes defines *studium* as the appreciation of memorial artifacts (e.g., photographs) based on a sense of cultural participation in what they depict: "the figures, the faces, the gestures, the settings, the actions" (*Camera Lucida* 26). Whereas the interest that arises from *studium* is intentional and dispassionate, the *punctum* is feature of an artifact that literally punctures the *studium,* intensifying interest and stimulating an involuntary emotional or psychic investment ("that accident which pricks [one]") and the "new *punctum* ... which is no longer of form but of intensity, is Time, the lacerating emphasis of the *noeme* ("*that-has-been*"), its pure representation" (*Camera Lucida* 27, 96). As Obama looks at his father's photographs, the cultural connotations that these evoke combine with the quiet slide of the narrative to reconstruct the life story of the father—his birth, youth, arrival as a student in the United States, brief romance and marriage, abandonment of his wife and child (i.e., Obama and his mother) as he goes off to Harvard and, finally, his journey back to Africa to put his education to work (Obama 9–10). This story, if only temporarily, creates a sense of comfort (as Obama notes, "I would wander off content, swaddled in a tale that placed me in the center of a vast and orderly universe") in an otherwise uncomfortable "fatherless" world as he tries to "reach back into [his] memory for the words of [his] father ... irretrievably lost ... so that all [he] perceive[s] is the worn out shell" (10, 66). The Barthesian *punctum* here are itemized details: "the dark laughing face, the prominent forehead and thick glasses that made him appear older than his years" (9), the "prominent forehead and thick glasses" that possibly denote

---

in Kennedy 386). Kennedy is quick to point out that, despite the early loss of his father, there is no Freudian fantasy concerning his mother—only a deep sense of love and respect for the latter. On another note, David Dudley in his book *My Father's Shadow* attributes "a kind of Oedipal conflict" between Booker T. Washington and Frederick Douglass, James Baldwin and Richard Wright among others, where the younger writer needed to " overcome the older in order to clear imaginative space for himself" (1). I would like to suggest a unique combination of the two in Obama: his love and respect for his mother combined with a desire to go beyond the dreams of the "prisoner[s] of fate" (Obama 231)—his father and his racial forefathers, Washington and Douglass, Baldwin and Wright—to "clear imaginative space for himself" (Dudley 1) to fulfill the dreams from his father.

a scholar and a man of wisdom (who in reality was irresponsible and selfish,[8] though the narrative never directly so characterizes him). These revelations that "puncture" the *studium* of an otherwise sanitized, gentle portrait of Obama's father actually *do not* "sting, cut … [or] bruise" but further reinstate the propagated narrative (*Camera Lucinda* 27). Thus, though the stories draw sustenance from the past, the Barthesian *noeme*, they bring about a skewing of the reality in the fictionalized version of the father figure.

The past is one that is resurrected by the various stories told by Obama's mother and maternal grandfather. The nostalgic setting with "Gramps leaning back in his old stuffed chair after dinner, sipping whiskey and cleaning his teeth with cellophane from his cigarette pack" seems ideal for the stories to come: a story told by his grandfather of how Obama senior "almost threw a man off the Pali Lookout because of a pipe," a present from his father-in-law (Obama 6). Out on a sightseeing tour with his wife and friend, the latter had requested to take a puff or two from the pipe Obama senior was smoking. In a coughing spree, inadvertently, the friend had dropped the pipe way down the cliff. Obama senior "picked [the friend] clear off the ground and started dangling him over the railing" to teach him "a lesson about the proper care of other people's property" (7). The "facts" of the story clearly owe a lot to "fiction": the grandfather's narrative is a hearsay from his daughter, the daughter's interruptions often interpreting simple (or even aggressive) gestures of her husband to be admirable qualities, the grandmother's prosaic ejaculations, the grandfather's scowls at his wife, and evident vicarious enjoyment at the friend's discomfiture create a collaborative "oral" narrative.[9] The contributory character of the story makes it an interactive oral performance presenting a carefully constructed family heirloom for the son to cherish and emulate. That the son is clearly aware of the constructed nature of the depiction is further reinstated by Obama's mention of the Dunham clan's "favorite" stories, the "seamless" nature of their blending, and their claim to veracity by "repeated use" (5).

---

[8] R. L'Heureux Lewis and Maria Johnson cite Barack Obama's 2008 Father's Day speech where he emphasized the personal responsibility of Black fathers by referencing his autobiography in which he compares and contrasts his own childhood with that of children in single parent (with only the mother) families (109, 120).

[9] G. Thomas Couser points out that Obama's citation of oral tradition as a medium of access to his father emphasizes the importance of the oral tradition in African culture (262). I would like to add that the oral stories of the Dunham clan have a contributory character denied to the paternal grandmother's single oral recollection of family history (more in line with African story telling).

Despite the efforts of his mother and maternal grandfather, the father remains an enigma to the son, a fleshed out semiotic signifier at best, a "prop in someone else's narrative." The son concedes an attraction to "the alien figure with a heart of gold, the mysterious stranger, who saves the town and wins the girl" (Obama 26). This connection to a fairy tale scenario is interrupted by the brief meeting between the father and son. In the one visit from his father, when his mother moved back to Hawaii after the separation from her Indonesian husband, the son seems to be still lost in the promises of fairyland, preferring "[the father's] more distant image," one that he could "alter on a whim or ignore when convenient" (63). The father's entry and exit in the son's life is meteoric, a memorable moment in his son's class at school as he speaks of Kenya, and then like a flash he is gone. All that remains, Obama says, is "opaque to me, a present mass," as an emptiness pervades his heart even when he "mimic[s] [the father's] gestures or turns of phrase," for he had never known "their origins nor their consequences"—in other words, despite the visit, he had never known his father (70-71).

Under the circumstances, the only access he has, as the title of the text states, is through the dreams *from* (naturally not *of*) his father. The preposition indicates a virtual transference of dreams, a communication possible in what Obama calls a "chamber of my dreams" (Obama 128). It begins with the son unlocking the padlock of a cell to release a Gandhian figure "with only a cloth wrapped around his waist" (128). Time melts away as father and son exchange positions: "He seemed small in my arms now, the size of a boy." (129) The dream opens up as a space wherein possibly the son tries to deal with the deep sense of abandonment he had felt, projecting on the father his own longings and anxieties,[10] as he speaks of "[a]n implacable sadness" in his father's face as the latter tells him how much he loved his son. The parting that ends the dream leads to the son's realization: "Perhaps for the first time, how even in his absence his strong image had given me some bulwark on which to grow up, an image to live up to, or disappoint." It also leads to his decision "to search for him, I thought to

---

[10] Daniel Stein refers to three sources of "dreams": from Obama's father and grandfathers, the dreams of the American founding fathers and the notion of the American Dream (footnote 11). But I feel this particular dream has a lot more to do with Obama finding himself *in* his father, in his father's past experiences, image, and values of culture even as it deals with other complex psychological issues. Given that dream is a surreal reality, see also Kelley, *Freedom Dreams,* where he discusses surrealism as an area that handles the concept of freedom as a form of self-manifestation.

myself, and talk with him again" (129). The emotionally charged narration, the poetry of the prose, momentarily leads the reader to join the son in this dream till, on reflection, the reader realizes the son's need to "talk" to the father can never be satisfied, as the latter is dead.

But the "need to search" for the man behind the myth takes shape from this point onwards in the narrative. While in Chicago, Obama is visited by his half-sister Auma, one of his father's offspring from his other marriages. He admits "that [the] first contact with Auma altered my life" (Obama 138). She provides him with details of his father's complicated social and political life. The man had married three times in all and fathered a number of children. Politically his career had ultimately floundered because he was an ethnic minority, and he had died virtually penniless and doomed by alcoholism. The effect on the son is devastating: the "single" image, one that he had "sometimes rebelled against but had never questioned," one that he had taken on as his own, now lay shattered. He had "known" the mythical signifier of extraordinary attributes, his father "the brilliant scholar, the generous friend, the upstanding leader," and had sought a "Martin and Malcolm, DuBois and Mandela" in him (Obama 220). Obama had respected the struggle of the everyday black man, "recognizing them as [his] own" but all along had looked for guidance in his father's words: "You do not work hard enough, Barry. You must help in your people's struggle. Wake up, black man!" (220). The clarion now lies mute as, for the first time, the son faces a very flawed human being who was his father. The son's initial disappointment, evident in a barrage of negative questions, is followed by a desperate sense of freedom that speaks of his own ruin but ultimately leads to a tentative effort to decipher the causes of the debacle in his father's life, to lament for the very short time accorded to father and son, a time lost to a skeptical suspicion of the other (Obama 220–221).

Possibly to make up for lost time, Obama, urged by his half-sister, goes to Kenya to get better acquainted with the "home-ground" that raised his father, to connect, if only momentarily, with "where [he] belong[ed], what his father had called 'the sounds of your continent'" (Obama 114, 71). To understand the Obama senior it would be very important to understand his African legacy and lineage. The oral testimony of the younger Obama's paternal grandmother provided him with the much-needed history of his forefathers, complementing the Dunham stories. The two sets of narratives create a comfortable bracketed space for the "son's self-written life" (Couser 262) as it moves from his father, a "fictionalized" character out there, to a very human one. The trajectory is essential to make the transition from the semiotic signifier of Barthes's earlier writing to his final phase of writing in *Camera Lucida*. Gerald Kennedy sees this as "a patently autobiographical search for the vanished landscape and lost community of childhood," a writing that bears witness not by direct reference but by implication (387).

Thus Obama's journey to Kenya and his grandmother's narrative situate his life writing within the parameters of familial and colonial legacy (Obama 394–424). Starting with the great grandfather to the grandfather, it was for Obama "the sound of three generations tumbling over each other like the currents of a slow-moving stream, [his] questions like rocks roiling the water, the breaks in memory separating the currents, but always the voices returning to that single course, a single story (...)" (394). Details about his academically brilliant father, including how he could sweet talk women, his expulsion from school and home, his dropping off his pregnant first wife and son with his mother and leaving for the United States when he got a scholarship, his marriage to Obama's mother and later to another white woman, and finally, his rise to power and ultimate fall from grace, all bring to life a human being riddled with virtues and vices. Through this familial legacy, Obama is given access to his forefathers and their dreams and aspirations as they run through the generations. Through protracted meditation and emotional self-indulgence as he empathizes with his father and grandfather, Obama comes to realize that generational success depends on reinventing oneself (Obama 427–28).[11] A cathartic revelation follows as Obama sits weeping "[b]etween the two graves..." and feels, as he says, "a calmness wash over me. I felt the circle finally close. I saw that my life in America...the sense of abandonment I'd felt as a boy, the frustration and hope I'd felt witnessed in Chicago—all of it was connected with this small piece of earth..." (430). The sense of release is finally achieved from the haunting absence of the father, now a human presence understood and reckoned with.

It is through the interior quest, a reaching back into memory "for the words of [his] father," words that are "irretrievably lost (...) impenetrable... as the pattern of [his] genes" that Obama seeks the reinvention of himself (66). As he points out, "autobiography implies a summing up, a certain closure, that hardly suits someone of my years, still busy charting his way

---

[11] In his Keynote Address at the 2004 Democratic National Convention, Barack Obama cites his grandfather's position as a colonial servant (a virtual slave) as he establishes a connection between his family in Africa and American slavery. See Stein paragraph 11 for more details. By drawing on a "common" lineage, Obama seeks to "reinvent" himself through his forefathers and validate his candidacy for President as son of the American soil.

through the world" (xvi–xvii). In the journey of self-discovery it is the journey that is important, for these journeys are not bildungsroman narratives that move the subject from obscurity to eminence. Barack Obama's autobiography blurs fact and fiction, begins *in medias res*, deals with racial ambivalence and seeks a father he had never known. This purposive and referential narrative, in a Barthesian style, initially attaches meaning (what is signified) to the signifier (the absent father, the representational photographs) and then gradually transforms a physical absence into a very human, albeit flawed, presence. Obama's final act of breaking down at the gravesite signifies a sentimental connection and reminds one of Barthes's grief at his mother's death in *Camera Lucida*. The trajectory of Barthes' writings seems to be encapsulated here: from the abstract structuralist analyses of *Image Music Text* to the more personal discourse of *Camera Lucida*.[12] And as the act of writing makes a very private moment public, it also co-opts the writer of the autobiography into "a perception of his own elemental anxieties and the revelation of his innermost self" (Kennedy 397).

Works Cited

Anderson, Sam. "How Roland Barthes Gave Us the TV Recap." *New York Times*. 25 May 2012.

Baillie, Justine. "From Margin to Centre: Postcolonial Identities and Barack Obama's Dreams from my Father." *Life Writing* 8.3 (September 2011): 317–329. Print.

Baker, Houston, Jr. "Presidential Forum on Multiculturalism: The Task of Literary Representation in the Twenty-First Century." *Profession* 1993. Print

Barthes, Roland. *Elements of Semiology*. Trans. Annette Lavers and Collin Smith. New York: Hill and Wang, 1968. Print.

—. "Photography and Electoral Appeal" *Mythologies*. Trans. Annette Lavers. New York: Hill and Wang, 1972. Print.

—. *S/Z*. Trans. Richard Miller. New York: Hill and Wang, 1974. Print.

—. *Image Music Text*. Trans. Stephen Heath. New York: Hill and Wang, 1977. Print.

---

[12] See Kennedy for a fuller treatment. My reading of Obama's text builds on a similar journey but ends in the very human rather than the humane as in the case of Barthes.

—. *Roland Barthes*. Trans. Richard Howard. New York: Hill and Wang, 1977. Print

—. *Camera Lucida: Reflections on Photography*. Trans. Richard Howard. New York: Hill and Wang, 1981. Print.

Couser, Thomas G. "Filiation in Barack Obama's Dreams from My Father." *Life Writing* 9.3 (September 2012): 259-267. Print.

Dudley, David L. *My Father's Shadow: Intergenerational Conflict in African American Men's Autobiography*. Philadelphia: University of Pennsylvania Press, 1991. Print.

Duell, Jason. "Assessing The Literary: Intellectual Boundaries and Justification in French and American Literary Studies." Web. http://crd-legacy.lbl.gov/~jcduell/papers/Assessing_the_Literary.pdf

Fabre, Michel. *From Harlem to Paris: Black American Writers in France, 1840-1980*. Urbana and Chicago: U of Illinois Press, 1991. Print.

Hakutani, Yoshinobu, ed. Cross-Cultural Visions in African American Literature: West Meets East. London: Palgrave Macmillan, 2011. Print.

—. *Cross-Cultural Visions in African American Modernism: From Spatial Narrative to Jazz Haiku*. Columbus, Ohio: Ohio State UP, 2006. Print

Janis, Michael. "Obama and Africa: "Race" and Reparations." *Critical Essays on Barack Obama: Re-affirming the Hope, Re-vitalizing the Dream*. Ed. Melvin B. Rahming. Newcastle upon Tyne, England: Cambridge Scholars, 2012. 142–163. Print.

Johnson, Michael K. "Barthes and the Politics of Electoral Photography." Web. http://literarytheoryumf.wordpress.com/2008/09/14/barthes-and-the-politics-of-electoral-photography/

Kelley, Robin D.G. *Freedom Dreams: The Black Radical Imagination*. Boston: Beacon, 2002. Print.

Kennedy, Gerald J. "Roland Barthes, Autobiography, and the End of Writing." *The Georgia Review* 35.2 (Summer 1981): 381–398. Print

Lewis, R L'Heureux and Maria S. Johnson. "Barack Obama and the New Black Father." *Critical Essays on Barack Obama: Re-affirming the Hope, Re-vitalizing the Dream*. Ed. Melvin Rahming. Newcastle upon Tyne, England: Cambridge Scholars, 2012. 109–127. Print.

López-Calvo, Ignacio. "Obama's Autobiographical Writing, Critical Race Theory, and the Racializing Gaze." *Critical Essays on Barack Obama: Re-*

affirming the Hope, Re-vitalizing the Dream. Ed. Melvin B. Rahming. Newcastle upon Tyne, England: Cambridge Scholars, 2012. 57–82. Print.

Metcalf, Josephine. "Monster, Dreams, and Cultural Studies: Exploring Gang Memoir and Political Autobiography." *Journal of American Culture* 34.4 (2011 Dec): 391–401. Print.

Obama, Barack. *Dreams from my Father: A Story of Race and Inheritance.* New York: Three Rivers P, 1995. Print.

—. "Keynote Address at the 2004 Democratic National Convention." Boston, MA. 27 July 2004. Speech.

Rahming, Melvin B., ed. *Critical Essays on Barack Obama: Re-affirmimg the Hope, Re-vitalizing the Dream.* Newcastle upon Tyne, England: Cambridge Scholars, 2012. Print.

Ryder, Andrew. "Baudelaire, Rimbaud, Toomer: The Urban Stranger and 'Bad Blood' in French and African American Modernism." *Callaloo* 36.3 (2013): 802–810. Print.

Smithers, Gregory D. "Challenging a Pan-African Identity: The Autobiographical Writings of Maya Angelou, Barack Obama, and Caryl Phillips." *Journal of American Studies* 45.3 (August 2011) 483–502. Print

Stein, Daniel. "Barack Obama's Dreams from My Father and African American Literature." *European Journal of American Studies* 6.1 (Spring 2011): 27. Print.

Whatley Smith, Virginia. "Jean Toomer Revisited in James Emanuel's Postmodernist Jazz Haiku." *Cross-Cultural Visions in African American Literature: West Meets East.* Ed Yoshinobu Hakutani. London: Palgrave Macmillan, 2011. Print.

Expressing Nonsuicidal Self-Injury: Using Creative Writing and Autobiographical Fiction as Self-Care

Belinda Hilton

The last two decades have seen a growing body of research into and awareness of self-injury, culminating in nonsuicidal self-injury being included as a "condition for further study" in the DSM-5 (American Psychiatric Association 803). While there has been a concerted effort to better understand and de-stigmatise self-injury, many who engage in the behaviour continue to remain silent. Because of this, individuals who self-injure need to develop their own systems of self-care as they work towards finding more positive and sustainable coping mechanisms. Considering self-injurious behaviour can be "associated with a sense of urgency and craving" (American Psychiatric Association 804); writing may provide an immediate outlet to express the "negative emotions, such as tension, anxiety, and self-reproach" (American Psychiatric Association 804) that influence self-injury and concededly reveal patterns of problematic thinking that need to be addressed.

The behaviour has long been misunderstood—historically interpreted as a suicide attempt or simply a symptom of Borderline Personality Disorder (Favazza 259), ridiculed as "emo" (Niwa and Madrusiak 12), or attention-seeking behaviour (Favazza xxvi). Accounts of self-injury were rarely discussed or represented in the media before the 1980s (Purington and Whitlock 12). This sense of misunderstanding that surrounds self-injury can result in individuals who self-injure not receiving adequate support from family and friends (Murray and Fox 2) or choosing to keep their behaviour hidden from others (Hill and Dallos 466). Only a small percentage of those who enact deliberate self-harm willingly present themselves at hospitals or mental health services (De Leo and Heller 140). The condition may continue for many years (American Psychiatric Association 804), meaning long term support may be required. While writing may not be a cure at all, there is the potential for writing to provide those who self-injure an additional outlet to enact self-care.

Australian writer and academic Ffion Murphy explores the application of writing as therapy in her novel *Devotion*. Veronica, the protagonist, has stopped speaking after giving birth to her second child. Her psychiatrist, Dr Andrew Moore, tells Veronica: "If you won't talk, then write to me" (Murphy 25). Veronica is given a laptop and begins to write from her hospital bed. She writes: "(…) I lately began carving words, encrypting and sculpting them into an electronic heart. I don't know why, but it keeps me alive" (Murphy 62). Through Veronica's accounts, Murphy addresses the idea that therapeutic writing is simply catharsis: "'Write it out of your system,' Dr Moore says. As though it doesn't lodge still deeper each time it's etched. But what if he's right, what if it changes shape, distorts; with each engraving makes something else, something sweeter?" (56).

The thoughts expressed in this passage highlight concerns that may be raised in relation to writing about self-injury. Might writing about urges or acts of self-injury further reinforce and normalize, 'lodge still deeper' the behaviour or could writing 'distort' and make self-injury 'something else'?

Though *Devotion* is not about NSSI the ideas raised are relevant. Like Veronica, individuals who self-injure may choose to remain silent. Their behaviour may not be discussed with friends and family or health professionals. Despite choosing silence, the desire to express the difficult thoughts and emotions that influence self-injury may still be present. Veronica remains mute and instead explores her thoughts and memories through writing. Dr Moore thinks: "Perhaps she didn't want a flesh and blood listener because she didn't want a response" (Murphy 80). Those who self-injure may remain silent due to fear of the responses they may receive. While understanding of the behaviour is growing there is still much that is unknown, uncertain or unclear.

Most people have an idea of what behaviour may be classified as self-injury, but this idea may vary between individuals. The International Society for the Study of Self-Injury defines self-injury as "the deliberate, self-inflicted destruction of body tissue without suicidal intent and for purposes not socially sanctioned" (ISSS, The International Society for the Study of Self-Injury). There are other commonly used terms that encompass a broader range of behaviours or a less stringent definition. The term self-mutilation, as seen in Favazza's seminal work *Bodies Under Siege*, was dominating throughout the eighties and nineties but is less used now. Self-harm, deliberate self-harm, or DSH are other commonly used terms. Boyd, Ryan & Leavitt state:

> The term "self-harm" is a contested one with no universally agreed upon definition. Some use self-harm explicitly to refer to the specific act of inflicting physical harm on flesh (e.g., "cutting") while others use it to refer to a category of practices that cause the body harm regardless of intention (e.g., "cutting," eating disorders, and suicidal behaviour). (6)

NSSI distinguishes self-injury from behaviours involving the intent to die (ISSS, The International Society for the Study of Self-Injury). It is the term I prefer, and it is also the term used in the fifth edition of the Diagnostic and Statistical Manual. It is important to note, however, that those who engage in NSSI are at an elevated risk to consider or attempt suicide (ISSS). Expectations motivating the engagement in self-injurious behaviour, as listed in the DSM-5's proposed criteria are: "1. To obtain relief from a negative feeling or cognitive state. 2. To resolve an interpersonal difficulty. 3. To induce a positive feeling state" (American Psychiatric Association 803). Favazza states that an individual who practices NSSI "seeks to feel better" (1998, 4). The paradox of self-punishment through self-injury as a way to 'induce a positive feeling' or 'obtain relief' may be theorised as creating "a physical wound that one can care for more easily than one's emotional distress" (Klonsky and Glen 218). Physical pain and damage is seen as a more tangible and acceptable problem. Physical wounds may provide a visible representation of healing, however: "The key to addressing self-harm is not to address the coping strategy, but to address the underlying issues that require coping" (Boyd, Ryan, and Leavitt 27).

Writing holds potential as a method of self-care for individuals who self-injure, in that it can be employed both as a reactive outlet when urges and overwhelming negative thoughts and emotions arise and as a forum for addressing the issues that drive those emotions and actions. I don't want to suggest that writing can be used as a therapy in and of itself for NSSI. While those who self-injure may not choose to seek support or may find it difficult to do so, professional support from a qualified mental health practitioner is vital and should be encouraged. For this reason I am hesitant to use the terms 'therapeutic writing,' 'writing therapy,' or even 'writing for recovery' in relation to NSSI. I believe writing can be beneficial, but as Murphy and Neilsen state: "Writing did not save Plath from suicide, as it has not saved various other writers, including Anne Sexton and Virginia Woolf—or perhaps it is the case that the power of writing to save anyone is limited."

Instead of seeing 'writing as therapy' I prefer to address writing as a tool for self-care: "Self-care means choosing behaviours that balance the effects of emotional and physical stressors (…)" and self-care requires "hard work and perseverance" (Meinecke n. pag.). According to Murphy and Neilsen, "[t]here is a danger in too readily associating writing with healing, for writing might become valorised and overly burdened: claims for its therapeutic value may be overstated and its difficulties elided" (18).

Employing writing as self-care for NSSI should be approached with caution and entails more than catharsis alone. Suggesting in his book *Opening Up: The Healing Power of Expressing Emotions* that writing "should be viewed as a preventive maintenance" (197), James Pennebaker, Professor of Psychology, also notes that "[u]nfortunately, the definition of catharsis has evolved to mean the mere venting of emotion rather than the linking of thoughts and feelings" (28). How, then, can writing be utilised as self-care for those who experience NSSI?

I am a self-injurer (some may prefer to say "an individual who self-injures"). I have consulted with eight different health professionals about my mental health in the past fifteen years and have been medicated with antidepressants on three separate occasions. While some individuals who self-injure may have comorbid conditions and a history of traumatic experiences. I don't have any disorders or diagnosis (that I've been made aware of), and I did not experience any childhood traumas (that I can recall). There have to present been two periods of my life where I have regularly employed self-injury as a coping mechanism, with the behaviour lasting for two or more years each time. The first period was during my late teens and the second began at the age of thirty during my first year of postgraduate study. I began my PhD with an interest in researching how individuals create written representations of the self. When my own identity became complicated by problematic thinking and self-injury, the research I was doing influenced how I tried to make sense of my experiences.

In *Skin Game*, a memoir about self-harm, Caroline Kettlewell writes: "*I can no longer tell if I have/had real emotional troubles or if it is/was merely melodrama*, I wrote in my journal, genuinely uncertain, as always, of the truth or fiction of my own feelings" (138).

When I began self-injuring yet again in my thirties, I struggled with the sense that "I should know better." Like Kettlewell, I was unsure which thoughts and feelings were legitimate and which were fictions. It was health professional number eight who used the term 'stories' to refer to the thoughts that lead me to self-injure. Acknowledging that the dark thoughts that entered into my mind didn't necessarily need to be believed and acted upon gave me a greater sense of agency to re-write my stories of self. My PhD then became a concerted effort to investigate how I could use writing to cope with my coping mechanism.

Once I decided to write about my self-injury, I had to consider which approach to take. There were several concerns that led me to believe writing a memoir would not be the right method. Victor and Klonsky found that individuals with a history of NSSI are highly self-critical and have lowered self-esteem (2) and I can certainly relate to this. Because I was still experiencing NSSI, I was concerned that I might lack the objectivity to reflect on my experiences without allowing a self-negative voice to come through. A first person narrative with a self-critical voice would be counterproductive to self-care. In addition to this concern I still held an entrenched reluctance to discuss my hidden behaviour. This was driven by perceived rejection and a fear that I would be told to "harden up," "let it go," or "just don't think about it," but also not wanting to worry my loved ones. As Victoria Leatham writes in *Bloodletting: A Memoir of Secrets, Self-Harm and Survival*: "The worse I felt, the more I thought I should keep away from people when I was like this: I didn't want to 'inflict' myself on them" (65).

Perhaps the greatest concern was a worry that I could not represent the behaviour accurately, correctly, or appropriately. Could I really create a truthful and trusted account of NSSI? Exploring the idea of readers' perceptions of autobiography Celia Hunt states: "Of course, an autobiography cannot be the literal truth of the writer's self or past" (234). Donna Lee Brien also explores this idea. Brien states that "readers of nonfiction engage with such works principally because they are seeking some truth about the real world that they can believe in" (58). Because I myself was struggling to differentiate fact from fiction, truth from lies, and reality from self-deception, I was not comfortable to explore my NSSI through memoir, autobiography, or creative non-fiction. The best way to tackle my *fictions*, it seemed, would be through fiction.

Celia Hunt writes about the potential for fiction to explore "truths" in her paper "Therapeutic effects of writing fictional autobiography":

> Paradoxically it is this suspending of intentions associated with the truth of the self that makes fictional autobiography potentially a very powerful tool for exploring 'truths' that lie beneath the surface of conscious self-

> knowledge: when people relinquish conscious control over their self-representations, they open up the possibility of thinking about, and experiencing, themselves differently. (234)

For myself, NSSI can be seen as a work of fictionalisation—emotional pain feigned as physical pain. The underlying thoughts that charge self-injury may not be related specifically to the body, yet it is through damage to the body tissue that these thoughts are represented. Concepts of a broken or damaged self are acted out in creating a physically broken or damaged body. Likewise, relief from this thinking may be garnered by seeing the body repair itself and heal, to see the fractured or split become fused and connected. To make the inconceivable, complex and conflicted make sense. If NSSI can be seen as an attempt to make sense of emotional complication, then writing fiction may be a way for me to make sense of this seemingly nonsensical act; to re-fictionalise fictions in order to shift perceived truths towards new possible truths. Hunt states:

> When writers *consciously* use fictional and poetic techniques to tell their story, they suspend the truth-telling intentions inherent in the 'autobiographical pact', and this changes the conceptual frame. Now their primary intention is to use memory or self-experience as a trigger for creative writing with an aesthetic end-product in view. (234)

In essence, by fictionalising my experiences with self-injury, I am actually attempting to address underlying issues of my own self-worth. My NSSI is driven by a problematized self-story, full of fictions. The key objective in using writing as an aspect of my self-care is to clearly identify flawed or inaccurate views of myself and to then rewrite these to reflect a greater sense of worth and agency.

As suggested by Hunt, I began my process by compiling a list of episodes of NSSI and past experiences. This list could then be divided into two categories. One list contained moments that relate specifically to acts of NSSI or reactions to my NSSI. The other list was of moments that highlighted the underlying issues that fuel my self-injury. Through these lists of moments, common themes and feelings that related to the formation of my negative self-view became apparent. These experiences now be repurposed (instead of recounted) as plot points. Some moments could be combined with others to create major plot points and the boiling tensions that will drive the narrative. Other moments can be used as elements of backstory, to drive the reactions of the protagonists to the major plot points. This process of repurposing life events through fictional techniques is the core of Hunt's definition of fictional autobiography (Hunt 231): "It demands of writers that they 'show' (dramatise experience through the minds of participants) rather than 'tell' (report experience from an outsider's point of view), facilitating deeper connection with the emotions" (Hunt 235).

Reaching a deeper connection with the emotions that influence my NSSI is an important part of re-writing my self-story. While self-injury may result in permanent physical scars this does not necessarily mean that the individual can recall the specific motivation for that action. This is certainly true for myself, and is evident also in Caroline Kettlewell's memoir *Skin Game*:

> My scars ought to be a charm bracelet of mnemonics, each a permanent reminder of its precipitating event, but maybe the most disturbing thing I can say about the history of my cutting is that for the most part I can't even remember the whens and the whys behind those wounds. (63)

The process of fictionalising experiences with self-injury may allow for potential connections to be highlighted between trigger and act. The trigger does not activate the act of self-injury but instead puts into action the problematized self-story that gives a perceived reason for the act. Utilising the "show do not tell" approach of autobiographical fiction may enact a greater awareness of the problematized self-story that needs to be addressed.

In addition to the lists of NSSI related moments I have utilised expressive catharsis-writing. This is done through writing down the negative thoughts and self-feelings that enter my mind when the urge to self-injure arises. It is important to note that this process may not stop or delay the act of self-injury. The intention of recording these thoughts is to identify what justifications are being created to engage in the act. The language used to describe myself during this time can be indicative of my problematized self-story. This expressive catharsis-writing can then be reviewed after the urge has passed and I am better able to view myself objectively. The justifications revealed can then be written into the narrative and responded to differently.

Taking an autobiographical fiction approach to exploring my NSSI also requires creating a protagonist who can act as an agent for my own self-reflection. Holly Ringland writes about this process in her paper "Nested Dolls: 'Inner Storytelling' and The Creative Writing Process": "I wrote the women in my stories as an Other I could approach sideways to empathise with her circumstances and explore her emotions by believing they were abstract to mine."

Creating my protagonist *other* is an exercise in writing a character that is likeable despite her own self-perception. The protagonist's past experiences, negative thoughts and NSSI can be addressed as small parts that are not the sum of her whole. Through writing *her* story I can rewrite my own self-story by trying out different reactions—her reactions to experiences and other people's reactions to her. Approaching autobiographical fiction as an act of self-care goes beyond the process of re-writing my self-story, it is a process of reading my self-worth.

Works Cited

American Psychiatric Association. *Diagnostic and Statistical Manual of Mental Disorders*. 5th ed. Arlington, VA: American Psychiatric Publishing, 2013. Print.

Brien, D. "The Power of Truth: Literary Scandals and Creative Nonfiction." *Creative Writing: Theory Beyond Practice*. Ed. Nigel Krauth and Tess Brady. Teneriffe: Post Pressed, 2006. 55–63. Print

Boyd, Danah, Jenny Ryan, and Alex Leavitt. "Pro-self-harm and The Visibility of Youth-generated Problematic Content." *I/S: A Journal of Law and Policy for the Information Society*. (2006): 1–32. Web. 26 May 2014. Print.

De Leo, Diego, and Travis. S Heller. "Who Are The Kids Who Self-harm? An Australian Self-report School Survey." *Medical Journal of Australia*. 181.3 (2004): 140–144. Web. 25 Mar. 2014. Print.

Favazza, Armando R. *Bodies Under Siege: Self-mutilation in Culture and Psychiatry*. 1987. Baltimore: John Hopkins UP, 1992. Print.

Favazza, Armando R. "The Coming of Age of Self-mutilation." *The Journal of Nervous & Mental Disease*. 186.5 (1998): 259–268. Web. 23 May. 2014.

Hill, Kerry and Rudi Dallos. "Young People's Stories of Self-harm: A Narrative Study." *Clinical Child Psychology and Psychiatry*. 17.3 (2011): 459–475. Web. 3 Apr. 2014.

Hunt, Celia. "Therapeutic Effects of Writing Fictional Autobiography." *Life Writing*. 7.3 (2010): 231–244. Web. 16 Apr. 2014.

ISSS. The International Society for the Study of Self-Injury. 2013. Web. 18 Jun. 2014.

Kettlewell, Caroline. *Skin Game*. New York: St. Marin's Griffin, 1999. Print.

Klonsky, E. David, and Glenn, Catherine R. "Assessing the Functions of Nonsuicidal Self-injury: Psychometric Properties of the Inventory of Statements about Self-injury (ISAS)." *Journal of Psychopathology & Behavioral Assessment.* 31.3 (2008): 215–219. Web. 22 Apr. 2014.

Leatham, Victoria. *Bloodletting: A Memoir of Secrets, Self-harm and Survival.* Crows Nest: Allen and Unwin, 2004. Print.

Meinecke, Christine. "Self-care in a Toxic World." *Everybody Marries the Wrong Person. Psychology Today.* 4 June 2010. Web. 6 June 2014.

Murphy, Ffion. *Devotion.* Fremantle: Fremantle Arts Centre Press. 2006. Print.

Murphy, Ffion and Philip Neilsen. "Recuperating Writers—And Writing: The Potential of Writing Therapy." *Text Journal.* 12.1. (2008): n. pag. Web. 20 May. 2013.

Murray, Craig D., and Jezz Fox. (2006). Do Internet Self-harm Discussion Groups Alleviate or Exacerbate Self-harming Behaviour? *Australian e-Journal for the Advancement of Mental Health,* 5 (3), 1–9. Print. pubs.e-contentmangement.com/doi/pdf/10.5172/jamh.5.3.225

Niwa, Kendra D. and Michael N. Mandrusiak. "Self-injury Groups on Facebook." *Canadian Journal of Couselling and Psychotherapy.* 46.1 (2012): 1–20. Web. 29 May. 2014.Print.

Pennebaker, James W. *Opening Up: The Healing Power of Expressing Emotions.* 1990. New York: The Guilford Press, 1997. Print.

Purington, Amanda and Janis Whitlock. "Non-suicidal Self-Injury in The Media." *The Prevention Researcher,* 17.1. (2010): 11–13. Web. 22 May. 2014

Ringland, Holly. "Nested Dolls: 'Inner storytelling' and The Creative Writing Process." *Text Journal,* 17.2 (2013): n. pag. Web. 17 Apr. 2014.

Victor, Sarah Elizabeth, and Klonsky, E. David. "Daily Emotion in Non-suicidal Self-injury." *Journal of Clinical Psychology.* 00.00, (2013): 1–12. Web. 23 May. 2014. Print.

Memory, Trauma, and Resilience:
The Autobiographies of Winnie Madikizela Mandela

Ben Lebdai

Twenty-eight years after the publication of her autobiography *Part of My Soul Went with Him* (1985), Winnie Madikizela Mandela published a diary entitled *491 Days: Prisoner number 1323/69* (2013). Both texts as well as her BBC biopic are signs of her importance.[1] Interestingly, her prison diary sold out within a few days in Johannesburg alone, in December 2013. Indeed, both texts stem from of a special South-African political woman whose autobiographical writings disclose, as I hope to show, an outstanding psychologically strong personality. Her gripping life experience, transcribed through writing, shows her literary qualities and demonstrates a natural sense of communication. I will analyse her impressive capacity to speak her mind in an extremely hostile world. What are the keys to her discourse and her appealing storytelling? What are the sources behind her impressive resilience and resistance? Are they inspired by the culture taught by her father, by her social involvements, by politics or by love? The question that needs to be addressed is whether this whole editorial adventure is a calculated strategy or merely an expression of a set of circumstances which gave a chance to such an outstanding personality to express herself. Considering the powerful personality of her celebrated husband, to what extent does Winnie Mandela stand on her own as a political woman?

The genesis of both publications is a story within history. The young Winnie stood out from the other girls of her age thanks to her genuine personal involvement in helping the poorest in the township of Soweto and by attracting the most charismatic leader of the ANC, Nelson Mandela. Her

---

[1] For her biopic see: http://www.telegraph.co.uk/culture/tvandradio/7085585/Mrs-Mandela-BBC-Four-review.html and http://www.theguardian.com/media/2009/mar/11/bbc-commissions-winnie-mandela-drama.

pugnacity to live her life fully led to the publication of *Part of My Soul Went with Him*, thanks to Anne Benjamin's initiative. She wanted to know more about such a strong resistant woman who struggled against apartheid on behalf of her imprisoned husband. Anne Benjamin's political strategy was to put Winnie in the limelight because her banishment made the headlines and attracted the attention of the ANC. It was hard for the journalist to convince Winnie who was initially reluctant to speak about herself. To put her at ease, Benjamin used oral autobiography through a sound recording, a technique developed in Latin America in the 1950s as discussed in *Le pacte autobiographique* by Philippe Lejeune.[2] The recording was kept secret as Winnie Mandela did not have the right to express herself publicly. Benjamin explains the whole the process: "It is impossible for Winnie Mandela to sit down and write a book. In any case, she dislikes talking about herself (…) she granted me the priviledge of conducting lengthy tape-recorded interviews with her over a considerable period of time."[3] The final publication included the transcripts of the recorded interviews and the correspondence between Winnie and Nelson Mandela. The international impact of such a book was immediate and in France Danielle Mitterand, the French President's spouse, wrote the 1986 foreword of the French version. She encouraged French youth to be inspired by Winnie's commitments.[4] Winnie Mandela's reputation as an anti-apartheid activist grew even more.

The publication of her diary *491 Days: Prisoner number 1323/69* is even more miraculous. After the death of David Soggot, one of Winnie's lawyers when she was in prison, his wife, Greta Soggot, found Winnie Mandela's loose pages while clearing her attic. They were in Soggot's London house during forty-one years! Greta Soggot returned them to Winnie Mandela, who had forgotten all about those pages. The seventy-five-year old Winnie Madikizela Mandela was shocked to receive them and did not want to read them at first: "I was afraid. These memories you keep in a part of your brain; it is part of those things that hurt so much you do not want to remember … this is the truth" (Madikizela Mandela 232). That difficult reading brought back nightmares and fears which are signs of a deep trauma as the critic Cathy Caruth explains: "There is a response, sometimes delayed, to an overwhelming event or events, which takes the form of

---

[2] Philippe Lejeune, *Pour l'autobiographie* (Paris: Seuil, 1998), 19. See Philippe Lejeune, *Le pacte autobiographique*, 338.
[3] Winnie Mandela, *Part of My Soul Went with Him*, London: Norton, 1985, in an editorial note.
[4] Winnie Mandela, *Une part de mon âme*, Paris: Seuil, 1986, 10–12.

repeated, intrusive hallucinations, dreams, thoughts, or behaviours stemming from the event along with numbing, that may have begun during or after the experience, and possibly also increased arousal to (and avoidance of) stimuli recalling the events" (Caruth 152). The first shock was like a boomerang of "Herstory" (History). Then, she took the decision to publish those pages for her daughters and grandchildren without changing a single word or expression. That decision to publish the diary proved to be right as the reaction from the press and the public was positive and enthusiastic.

Chronologically, the diary published in 2013 is about her late 1960s prison days, whereas *Part of My Soul Went with Him* describes her banishment, at Brandfort, her "litte Siberia," in 1977. The recorded autobiography is divided into nine parts where Winnie Mandela speaks about her childhood, her relations with the members of her family, her first imprisonment, and her banishment. She recalls her encounter with Nelson Mandela, a love story which changed the course of her life. The received idea is that she became political thanks to her husband. In *Part of My Soul Went with Him* she proves the opposite in the sense that she was politically aware of the social and political South African milieu before her marriage. In her childhood village, Bizana, her family addressed the issue of racism and apartheid, condemning it. Her father taught her the history of Black people, the story of her roots and her ancestors' struggle against the colonisers, the Dutch and the British. Added to this awareness, there is her personal observation of apartheid society that made her react against injustice. During childhood she had to walk miles, barefoot, to go to school, when the little White girls, well-dressed and with nice shoes, were driven to their schools. Winnie Madikizela wore shoes for the first time when she went to high school, an event that had an impact on her consciousness. She promised herself that she would change the course of history by bringing back justice and wealth to all Black South Africans, something that unveils her revolutionary mind. She also knew very early that the quickest way to be free as a Black woman was through hard studies. Not surprisingly, she became the first Black to be recruited as a social worker at Baragwanath Hospital in Johannesburg. Her commitment to her own people before meeting Nelson Mandela is shown through her involvement with poor and needy Soweto women. In terms of public political commitment, she encouraged women to demonstrate againt the "passlaws." That action led to her arrest and her first imprisonment. It is nevertheless true that her marriage with Nelson Mandela took took her one step further in her commitment to politics. Having been fired from her job, she joined the ANC as a full member. At that point, her life took a new turn as she was arrested under the "Terrorism Act."

Autobiographies generally follow the chronology of a life. For political strategies, Anne Benjamin opened the life story of Winnie Mandela with her arrest and banishment at Brandfort, something that gave the book its full power. In this recorded life story, Winnie Mandela presents the horror of the events imposed by the apartheid police in stark vividness. The use of the first person singular 'I' deconstructs the policy of the apartheid system which systematically refers to Black people as a group, not as individuals. So, the "I" of her storytelling, her name on the cover of the book became part of the "autobiographical pact" (Lejeune 44). It clearly takes a political stand. The life details told in a dramatic way emphasize the harsh treatment of the police towards Winnie Mandela who was arrested in the middle of the night while asleep with her daughter Zindzi. A heavily armed police squad surrounded her house in Soweto as she recalls:

> At about four o'clock in the morning I heard a great noise outside—it seemed as if a hail of stones were dropped on my house and it sounded as if they were falling in the wall—In a fraction of a second there were knocks all over, on the doors, on all the windows, bang, bang, bang-sounds ... Knocking on the door, barking ... I went and opened the dor and of course I saw the whole army inside the yard, chaps in camouflage carrying guns, and members of the Security Branch; they were all heavily armed. (Mandela 2)

The contrast between an unarmed sleepy mother and child and a heavily armed police points to the importance Pretoria gave to Winnie Mandela. This special treatment made her aware of her nuisance towards the apartheid system: "I am a living symbol of the white man's fear" (Mandela 5). The text shows the violence directed against her in the sense that her banishment in Bandfort, under house arrest, is full of sad experiences. Nevertheless, her powerful and sarcastic humour shows her way of avoiding nervous breakdowns and suicide. At Brandfort, the local Black population was advised by the Whites not to come near Winnie Mandela's lodging, not to talk to her or her daughter. The Black population did not obey. With a great sense of irony, Winnie Mandela says: "Once a Black is told by a White man that something is bad, then it must be good and vice versa" (Mandela 5). Despite the harsh orders of the police, Winnie Mandela succeeded in establishing a dialogue with the local population. Her social actions raised the political consciousness of that quiet sleepy town, to the great despair of the local police who did not know what to do with her.

Winnie Madikizela Mandela prison's diary, *491 Days: Prisoner number 1323/69*, is impressive, because despite the suffering she was going through, she had the courage and the stamina to secretly put her thoughts, trauma and pain on paper. Her notes indicate that she has always connected her suffering with that of other women prisoners. She succeeded in hiding her diary despite strict surveillance. Winnie Mandela, the prisoner, jotted down quick notes about key events such as descriptions of her state of mind during the first two difficult weeks of her detention, the development of her attitude throughout her year imprisonment, and the withdrawal of the case by the Apartheid State. Meaningful events such as her mother-in-law's funeral are reported, revealing the horror of the apartheid system. Descriptions of events, like the visits by family members, the food issue, the doctor's visits and the deterioration of her health, are reported with exact dates. Health problems are always described in South African prison diaries, as in Breyten Breytenbach's or Dennis Brutus' prison writings. Ngugi Wa Thiong'O from Kenya or Nawal Saadaoui from Egypt addressed such issues in their postcolonial African prisons.[5] Winnie's daily notes are about her health, the weakness of her heart, her constant bleeding, her thinness, and her disastrous psychologial state of mind due to the fact that her daughter had been left all alone in the outside world. Torture is part of the prison menu. She tells about her strength and fragility and how she once escaped torture thanks to her extreme weakness. She recalls how fainting saved her from another session of torture as she was taken to the hospital in emergency. While the style is elaborate at times, it is often telegraphic due to constant surveillance or extreme illness and weakness. Her tenacity to witness and testify are strong: "Not feeling well again. Feeling nauseous all the time. Starting vomiting after lunch. Reported to Mr Rautenbach—given treatment—white tablets to take after meals. Continued vomiting even after supper" (Madikizela Mandela 66). Her deteriorating health needed up to massive medication every day. Strangely enough those tablets never improved her health.

491 Days: Prisoner number 1323/69 includes letters by Nelson Mandela, and her own letters to her husband are included. This correspondence demonstrates their deep relationship, being today historical testimony of a

---

[5] See Breyten Breytenbach, *The True Confessions of an Albino Terrorist*, New York: Farrar Straus & Giroux, 1985, and Dennis Brutus, *The True Dennis Brutus Tapes*, London: James Currey, 2011.

troubled period. As a prison diary, the most impressive accounts are those written during or after her solitary confinement, which is the most horrific experience she has to go through:

> Being held incommunicado was the most cruel thing the nationalists ever did. I'd communicate with the ants; anything that has life. If I had lice I would have even, I would have even nursed them. That's what solitary confinement does. There is no worse punishment than that. I think you can stand imprisonment of 27 years. You are mixing with the other prisoners, you get you three meals a day, the only thing you have lost is your freedom of movement. Your mind isn't incarcerated that's all but with solitary confinement you are not allowed to read, you are not allowed to do anything, you have just yourself. (Madikizela Mandela 57)

Solitary confinement was difficult for Winnie Mandela. The physical and psychological torture sessions are reported in detail, revealing the impact of such treatments. The great interest of such a diary is that it records the horror of the apartheid brutalities the very day Winnie was experiencing them. The authenticity of the emotions remains intact in such a genre as it conveys the immediacy of the feelings. Harrassment is a means of putting the prisoner in a position of inferiority. Winnie Mandela was constantly harrassed. She comments: "everything is done to make you feel a nobody" (Madikizela Mandela 62). Harrassment could take different forms, such as keeping a strong light on in her cell preventing her from sleeping. This is harsh torture for all women prisoners. Her intimacy is assaulted as she is forced to stay naked for hours, later taking her to a solitary cell, humiliating her even more. The interrogators do not not hesitate to try and make her go mad by telling her that if they had a wife like her they would do like Nelson, this is run away to prison for life. They provided her false information from the outside world to weaken her convictions. One of their tactics was to ask her again and again if she was hearing voices from God: "Do you feel you are chosen by God for the role you are playing amongst your people—the leadership role? Do you hear God's voice sometimes telling you to lead your people?" (Madikizela Mandela 33). The perversion of such questions is that they try to disqualify the ideology of the ANC, dismantling in this way the political agenda of the anti-apartheid programme. The police tried to diminish her revolt and discourage her struggle by reducing it to a mere religious call as if she were a fanatic, a psychopath. Therefore, writing these notes saved her from despair.

Both publications disclose Winnie Mandela's acute and sharp political consciousness. Her commentaries show that she goes beyond the mere description of facts, hence expressing political convictions and proposing an analysis of political issues such as the state withdrawal of the case, which shows her fine analysis of the strategy of the apartheid policy. Besides, she suggests her personal views of how the struggle should be handled. She commits herself as a leader when she develops the idea that South Africa is big and rich enough for everybody to live happily. In order to end the inhuman system of apartheid she claims that socialism is the solution:

> Our future South Africa will be multiracial. It will accommodate all of us. The wealth is enough for everybody. The Freedom Charter is a blueprint of our future government. Whatever adjustments have to be made will be made within that sacred document. It will be a socialist state —there is no other way of sorting out our starvation problems. (Mandela 121).

Her political opinions are stated and she has stuck to them throughout her political life to this day. All her post-apartheid criticisms take their source in the ideological convictions she expressed in the seventies and eighties. Beyond the apartheid ideology, Winnie Madikizela Mandela asserts that the core of the problem is related to the social and economic issues dividing "the haves and the haves-not" (Mandela 121). Her response to the accusation that the ANC militants, including herself, are all communists manipulated by Russia is sharp and uncompromising: "It is not a question of outside agitators or communists from Russia. It is us, the people. We don't have to be told we are hungry. We *are* hungry" (120). The commitment of all South Africans including the Church in the struggle against apartheid is a point about which she has had strong views. Her message to religious authorities is that the church cannot be confined solely to religious affairs. The case of Nelson Mandela's first wife, Evelyn Mace, who saw religion as a way to forget apartheid, is not acceptable. Winnie Mandela argues that religious people "must involve themselves with the community, with politicizing the people" (120). Many churches joined the fight by taking up political issues. Mandela offers an overall historical analysis of colonial times when she declares: "Terrorism was in fact introduced by the white man in this country in 1652" (124). For her, the liberation of the historical leaders of the ANC is the first step towards a solution. History shows that she was right in her analysis. During those years Winnie moved away from being solely Mandela's spouse, to develop into an independent political woman leader whose aim was the eradication of the apartheid system. Such a construction was recognized by Nelson Mandela himself who repeatedly wrote in his letters from Robben Island how proud he was of her. In a letter to his daughters, Zenani and Zindzi, he praised her: "She had held to her beliefs, you will begin to realise the importance of her contribution in the battle for truth and justice and to the extent to which she has sacrificed her own personal interests and happiness" (Madikizela Mandela 106). He always knew that Winnie was as a fighter, a strong – willed woman. The South African police were astonished by her stamina and her determination. The historical leader of the ANC, Ahmed Kathrada, praised her courage during those prison years: "Because of her commitment, loyalty, courage, determination and resilience, Winnie emerged from this log spell in detention unshaken and proud, with her head held high" (Kathrada x). Both compelling texts translate the strength of a revolutionary character who has never been submissive to the apartheid authorities, matrons, interrogators, police officer Swanepoel, or the Security Branch. Winnie Mandela never showed any fear in front of White Afrikaners, something that disturbed them greatly. She knew when to shout at the authority in order to obtain better prison conditions for herself and for all women prisoners. Self-centeredness is surely an ingredient of self-story as analysed by Serge Doubrovski, but Winnie Mandela goes beyond that aspect in stressing that her struggle is for the improvement of prison conditions and for Blacks and women in particular. This is a genuine conviction proved through her official positions held within the ANC as a member of the Women's Federation and President of the Women's League. One cannot to deny her struggle for gender equality:

> Looking at our struggle in this country, the black woman has had to struggle a great deal, not only from a political angle. One has had to fight the male domination in a much more complex complex sense. We have the cultural clash where a black woman must emerge as a politician against the traditional background of a woman's place being at home! Of course most cultures are like that. But with us it's not only pronounced by law. We are permanent minors by law. So for a woman to emerge as an individul, as a politician in this context, is not easy. (Mandela 73)

Winnie has always claimed that women had to fight both the colonial enemy and Black male chauvinism in the townships. A detail reported in *Part of My Soul Went with Him* when she remembers her mother praying to have a son is very symbolic, as it shocked her. She promised herself: "I will prove to her that a girl is as much of value to a parent as a son" (Mandela 29). Her commitment for Women's Rights struggle is definitely not a posture, but rather a conviction that goes back to her childhood.

Winnie Mandela's political consciousness in both texts confirms her sense of liberty and demonstrates that she is articulate in terms of form, depth and convincing in terms of content. Her qualities lie on her great sense of humour and her sense of derision that underlines her resilience. Her sense of repartee, the talent that is obvious when she expresses herself in public, has surely played a major role in advancing the cause of the ANC, keeping the name Nelson Mandela alive during his twenty five years at Robben Island. In courts of justice, in the Townships, through public speeches, she knew how to defend the struggle of the ANC and the cause of women. There are gaps in both texts which reveal her difficulty to speak and write about her most intimate emotions. Conversely, they are expressed in her personal letters included in both publications. Indeed, her words are not words of tenderness, but express a deep trauma. Her autobographical texts are a contribution to the prison writing genre particularly in South Africa as they express distressing times of imprisonment through a highly political lens. Her writing is slightly different from Breyten Breytenbach and Dennis Brutus's prison writings which instead focus on the physical and material disturbances of such experiences. The people of South Africa got to know her better through these texts. Many disagree with some of her actions as various allegations shadow her reputation, the sulfurous private life she is supposed to have had. Here again those moments of her life are never mentioned. Her divorce from Nelson Mandela shattered the ideal image of the perfect revolutionary couple, but it also showed her humanity and her womanhood. Nevertheless, when Nelson Mandela passed away, it was in her arms, December, 12th 2013, something that points to the depth of their relation despite the trials and tribulations of life.[6] Within the world of political memory against racism and colonial injustice, her emblematic figure stands out among leading women protesters such as Angela Davis in the USA or Djamila Bouhired in Algeria, all icons of courage and determination. Her complex personality is both fascinating and disconcerting, almost resembling a "fictional character." At the age of 76, her moves and

---

[6] Winnie Madikizela Mandela describes Nelson Mandela's last moments on the ITN channel:
http://www.telegraph.co.uk/news/worldnews/nelson-mandela/10514814/Winnie-Mandela-describes-Nelsons-death-Then-he-drew-his-last-breath.-He-was-gone.html

official statements are still reported and commented by journalists. She is still critical of political issues as in the epilogue of *491 Prisoner number 1323/69* written in November 2012: "Right now, people like myself who come from that era become petrified when we see us sliding and becoming more and more like our oppressive masters. To me, that is exactly what is happening and that is what scares me."[7] Both autobiographical texts confirm that this South African icon will never be silenced, until her last breath.

Works Cited

Breytenbach, Breyten. *The True Confessions of an Albino Terrorist.* New York: Farrar Straus & Giroux, 1985. Print.

Brutus, Dennis, *The True Dennis Brutus Tape.* London: James Currey, 2011. Print.

Caruth, Cathy. *Trauma, Exploration in Memory,* John Hopkins UP, 1995. Print.

Kathrada, Ahmed. In Madikizela Mandela, Winnie. *491 Prisoner Number 1323/69,* Johannesburg: Picador, 2013. Print.

Lejeune, Philippe. *Pour l'autobiographie.* Paris: Seuil, 1998. Print.

—. *Le pacte autobiographique.* Paris: Seuil, 1996. Print.

Nelson Mandela, *Long Walk to Freedom.* 1994. London: Abacus, 2013. Print.

Mandela, Winnie. *Part of My Soul Went with Him.* London: Norton, 1985. Print.

Madikizela Mandela, Winnie. *491 Prisoner number 1323/69.* Johannesburg: Picador, 2013. Print.

---

[7] Winnie Madikizela Mandela, *491 Prisoner number 1323/69*, op-cit, 239.

Autobiography and the Scene of Speech in Gertrude Stein's *Everybody's Autobiography*

Christine Savinel

In *The Autobiography of Alice B. Toklas* (1933), Gertrude Stein experimented with a playful and transgressive form of "heterobiography," to use Boldrini's term (Boldrini 2012), as she wrote in the name and voice of her companion, Alice Toklas. With that book, she encountered for the first time a form of popular success, which made her partly unrecognizable to herself—blurring her image of self as avant-garde "difficult" writer. She spent the next four years working out the issues of self and audience, of inside and outside recognition, which are at the core of *Four in America* or *The Geographical History of America* (1936), and the very subject of many lectures she gave during her triumphal tour of America in 1934–1935. When her publisher asked her for a second autobiography, hoping for a duplicate success, she rather readily complied, with a new experiment in narrative of self, *Everybody's Autobiography* (1937). While *Toklas* was an account of roughly three decades, from the turn of the century to 1932, *Everybody* covered only the short period since the publication of *Toklas*. Ironically enough, this second innovative autobiographical text was not met with great public success. It nonetheless enabled Stein both to come to terms with the idea of being a difficult or a popular author, and to address questions of singularity or generality of one's voice.

She achieved such coming to terms through discourse staging and reflexivity. *Everybody's Autobiography* opens with a conversation between Stein and Toklas on the very subject of autobiography and authorship: "Alice B. Toklas did hers and now anybody will do theirs. Alice B. Toklas says and if they are all going to do theirs the way she did hers" (1). Irony reaches a point of delightful nonsense when the logical ground for anybody being capable to write "their" autobiography seems to be the fact that

Toklas wrote hers, while of course she never did—in a letter to Stein, Thornton Wilder called her "the Autobiographer-*malgré-elle*" ("in spite of herself"; September 1937, 180). The "fun" is based here on a loosening of all categories: if anybody can write for anybody else, then biography and autobiography are one, signature proves aleatory, and so do whatever autobiographical tenets or contract. Since everybody can speak for himself or herself as anybody else, or as everybody, what comes to predominate is the powerful performance itself.

Indeed, in Stein's works there is always, and more so after *Toklas*, something close to a "Listen to me" appeal or claim. *Listen to me* is the very title of a play she wrote in 1936, in which "three characters" disappear at first behind a common soliloquy:

> And so no longer three characters but all who are there say this. Listen to me.
> A soliloquy (*Last Operas and Plays* 387)

The three characters reappear later in the play, in a variable configuration, which confirms their being but numbers representative of a totality ("all who were there") or of a generality, that can just as well become any singularity as each one says "Listen to me." The appeal or injunction is recurrent in her texts: it encapsulates and dramatizes some central Steinian issues, being the power relationship between author and audience, and the tension between inside and outside attention. A "listen to me" request is indeed inherent in the very theatrical quality of her writing. There are two versions of it which alternate in all her portraits, lectures, poetry and autobiographies. The first one could be phrased as "Listen to me existing," or, in an even more Steinian form, "Listen to me being existing" ("Now I am writing about what is which is being existing." *Everybody* 258). The phrase constitutes a rather "pure" existential definition of autobiography, while it also exemplifies Stein's idiom (the "Steinese"). Indeed, the Steinian grammar as she practices and defines it in "Poetry and Grammar" (1935), for instance, is itself characterized by its "existing" quality. She prefers words that "do something" so that they can "keep alive" (*Lectures* 214): hence her fondness for verbs or conjunctions as opposed to static adjectives. Thus does Stein dramatize both "the active life of writing" (220) and her own active writing life as part of her "existing." The second "Listen to me" form could be "Listen to me thinking," or eventually, as she formulates it in "Grant": "Listen while I think again" (*Four in America* 46). In *Everybody*, Stein achieves her own autobiographical mixed genre, as that very conjunction of narrative and thinking, part commentary on her own life and works, part general meditation in progress.

Here the reader may be struck by certain analogies with Nietzsche's *Ecce Homo*. Not least of all the latter's famous address in the Preface: "Listen to me for I am such and such" (Nietzsche 93).[1] Central to *Ecce Homo* is the very principle of commenting on one's works and revisiting them, and that is also present, though less exclusively, in Stein's autobiographies. Nietzsche's "Why do I write such good books" (130) seems to be mirrored in Stein's why and how did I write such innovative books. Both authors declare likewise the unlimited scope of their writing in time: to Nietzsche's last chapter of *Ecce Homo*, "Why I am a destiny"—"There will come a time when my name will be associated with the memory of something prodigious" (Nietzsche 187)— echoes Stein's "slowly I was knowing that I was a genius" (*Everybody* 79). Whatever obvious differences in context and perspectives, the forms of self-praise and self-confidence make for striking parallels.

Indeed, whatever the anxiety of identity Stein experienced in between her two autobiographies, *Everybody's Autobiography* is characterized by extreme authority and self-confidence of voice, even as it narrates her doubts. Such authority is best demonstrated by Stein's bold offhanded treatment of narrative practices, all her disruptive and digressive moves. Though at first sight, the general pattern of the book corresponds to plain narrative, as wished by Stein, who wrote to Thornton Wilder: "I am writing the narrative book which we talked about (...), it goes slowly and simply perhaps too simply, I always want to be commonplace perhaps I have managed it this time (...)" (October 26 1936, 124). Some parts of the book do have plainly narrative titles, such as "Preparations for Going to America," "America," and "Back Again." Some others sound more meditative, as "What was the effect upon me of the Autobiography [meaning *Toklas*]." In fact, all five parts combine narrative and thinking, evocations and meditations—nothing unusual in an autobiography. More specific, though, is the way narrative and meditative modalities do not so much interact as they interrupt each other. The autobiographical form is made to distribute heterogeneous discourse, with constant shifts of temporality or topic. Unlike *Toklas*, *Everybody* proves rather resistant to sequence in general, and its form of discourse more associative than sequential. Stein does follow a general chronological pattern of the three years under survey, but it comes to disruption, and then into conjunction with a field of vertical

---

[1] All translations mine, unless otherwise specified.

associations. Any memory triggers a system of associations, sometimes taking the extreme form of a list of analogous experiences. Such cross-interfering movements of sequence and association often transform the flux of the autobiographical narrative into a temporal vortex from where the self gets reinforced, through its multiple staging, then and now and at all times. Basically, following the category principle, the mention of a servant, a friend or a photograph almost never fails to evoke others, which systematically disrupts the narrative, rechanneling it through analogy and difference. The book is a succession of rather long periods, each cycle including narration, evocation, multiple associations, and a final movement back to narration. One typical example can be found pages 122 to 126. The cycle starts with "So the winter after I wrote the Autobiography [meaning *Toklas*] was almost over and I had almost thought I would go to America to lecture." (122) In the next five pages, Stein evokes topics ranging from writing and forgetting about people, Soviet Russia, being a genius, and popular writing, to the passing of civilizations. And the period ends with this theatrical move back to track: "I detach myself from the earth being round and mechanical civilizations being over and organization being dull although nobody knows it yet but they will and go on with what happened the summer before we went to America." (126). Using a both immediate and general present ("I detach myself") to describe what is taking place on the stage of writing, she dramatizes her wrenching herself from all analogies, associations or digressions (ironically presented, it seems, as bordering on dispersion and logorrhea, with the breathless "and" structure), and her coming back to plain narrative.

As to structures of dispersion and divergence, Stein could declare, with Sterne, that "Digressions are the sunshine." They are the stimulus of this work and its central object too. *Everybody* is also about visiting back in America, a digression from her usual ways, as she never crossed the Atlantic back to her native land since she settled in Paris in 1903. But that is a counter-digression to her initial departure, the original wandering away, the self-founding one. With the exception of the English language, from which she never swerved, and which remained her constant place, Stein's defining gesture is a diverging one. The all-inclusive monologue that came to be her signature after *Toklas* is characterized by all kinds of departures—from genres, from forms and from the main track of discourse, while digression comes to be the formal transcription of the free course of the mind. In *Everybody*, they structure the text from beginning to end. Speech markers that signify reintegrating the main line, such as "Well anyway" (159, 160),

"All right anyway" (199) or "But to come back to" (200) punctuate the periods. The very opening of the book installs digression as an essential mode: "That is the way any autobiography has to be written which reminds me of Dashiell Hammett. / Before I am reminded of Dashiell Hammett I want to say that just today I met Miss Hennessy (...)" (1). Digression thus repeatedly stages the intersection of time and possibility, extending the free scope of the autobiographical domain, including both the time of existing and that of writing. Here too, the extensive use of digression reflexively emphasizes the all-power of the voice staging its operations and choices. In *Everybody*, some passages present such a succession of interruptions, instant changes or branching that the reader may experience an impression of a *cadavre exquis* (exquisite corpse) pattern, hence of being played with or playing. Such constant disruptions and shifts, as well as the general heterogeneity of discourse cannot but reinforce the predominance of voice. There is, besides, in Stein's writing the almost hypnotic quality of her performing voice.

While she did not enjoy watching performances of her plays, Stein did enjoy watching herself performing writing. The degree of reflexivity here entails the sensation of an almost split instance of self. In "The Subject of Nietzsche's *Ecce Homo*," D. J. Wright says that in that text "the ghost of the anxious author haunts the production of his textual namesake." (Wright 224). If "haunting" does not sound exactly relevant for Stein's modality of self-duplication, the staging of self in *Everybody* is such that the reader has to be aware of a "Stein" existing, writing and thinking, apart from the author Stein, under whose eyes or at least in whose voice she performs. The (fake) performance of two in *Toklas* persists in a way in *Everybody*, through the substantial distance between Stein and "Stein," as represented or performing. Obviously, autobiography offers a privileged stage for the obsessive questioning and testing of identity Stein is carrying on in all her texts at the time. She enjoys multiplying images and reflections of her "self." She playfully emphasizes, for instance, the inevitable discrepancy between present and past selves:

> And identity is funny being yourself is funny as you are never yourself to yourself except as you remember yourself and then of course you do not of course you do not really believe yourself why should you, you know so well so very well that it its not yourself, it could not be yourself because you cannot remember right and if you do remember right it does not sound right and of course it does not sound right because it is not right. You are of course never yourself. (70)

Inscribed within the scope of what Stein calls "funny," meaning both fun and disquieting, the idea of being oneself demonstrates its absurdity and its ultimate impossibility through a series of negative deductions, in such a fast succession that it emphasizes the gap between "yourself" and yourself. In *Le triangle d'Hermès* (*Hermes's Triangle*), Jean-François Côté evokes "the essential motivation of a writing immerged in the question of individual identity: the indispensable passage through the 'I,' or better, the gaze being transfixed in the specular reflection between 'I' and 'self' conveys exactly the myth of Narcissus to which we figuratively associate here the aesthetic position of Gertrude Stein" (Côté 96). This symbolic and aesthetic narcissistic structure, however, must be qualified, as of a general value, either through the reflection of self to self being a "relationship of universal specificity" (Côté 106); or through the idea of a universal narcissism assuming variable forms, as seen by Derrida: "There is no such thing as narcissism or non-narcissism; there are more or less wide, open, generous, comprehensive narcissisms [...]" (Derrida 1992, 212). Whether such universal dimension of narcissism must be linked with the mirrored image of self or with the intrinsic structure of narcissism, it tends to dissipate the confusion between self and ego. In *Everybody* Stein evokes the puppet-play about identity she wrote for Donald Vestal[2]: « And that is always with me, there is me myself and there is identity my identity and so I wrote a marionette play for Donald Vestal about identity. (...) He sent me photos of it and they are rather touching, there are two Gertrude Steins and they are rather touching" (211). Two "Gertrude Steins" on that other marionette stage evoked by Stein, added to the two already on the autobiographical stage there, that makes four figures of "Stein" in fact, on that very borderline Derrida says in *Otobiographie* is the "*dynamis* (...) between 'work' and 'life', system and 'subject' of the system" (Derrida 1984, 40). Multiplying those sakes or figures of self on the autobiographical stage contributes to make of her 'I' a general instance of self.

It also enables her to go beyond the quandary of identity and to get back a feeling of unified voice. In *Everybody* and in *The Geographical History of America*, she works out the question of interior and exterior identity. And famously so through the motif of her little dog's identifying power: "I became worried about identity and remembered the Mother Goose, I am I because my little dog knows me and I was not sure but that only proved the

---

[2] Donald Vestal, a puppet-master Stein met in New York in 1934, for whom she wrote *Identity or I Am Because my Little Dog Knows Me* (1934–36).

dog was he and not that I was I" (*Everybody* 306). Obviously, the little dog represents the possible power of the exterior world, that is of the public, over the author's identity. Here is another common point with Nietzsche, what Wright terms "public vulnerability," asserting that "the 'Nietzsche' of *Ecce Homo* suffers from an even greater dependency on others than his author does" (Wright 224). The feeling is more transient with Stein, but in those 1934-1936 years, she keeps returning to the point of her sudden vulnerability to public reaction, through recurrent meditations about contingency of "self," around transference figures as varied as the little dog, the little boy who cannot fail to grow up, or Henry James who could not know that he would become Henry James—again a variation of the Nietzschean becoming what one is. The last two motifs are most present in *Four in America*, but *Everybody* does stage an ongoing meditation on the contingency of her own genius and the unity of her author's voice, as tested through her American experience too.[3] One further interest here is that she can inscribe her meditations within the very same autobiographical genre that had been at the origin of her success, and hence of her identity anxiety.

The way she treats the genre, revisiting and commenting on her own "existing" experiences, as well as her writing and listening practices, and giving voice to so many individuals (friends, famous people in America and France, neighbors, servants), she transforms autobiography into a scene of speech, a stage for the plural-singular voice. She works out a form of narrative-meditative monologue that includes all and everyone in its ongoing flux.

To what extent can Stein's scene of speech be seen as sophisticated transcription of an oral form of reporting or thinking deserves a wider scope of analysis than this brief essay. It was one of her own recurrent concerns. She reports in *Everybody* her famous answer to some students at Berkeley: "(...) the only thing I remember is their asking why I do not write as I talk and I said to them if they had invited Keats for lunch and they asked him an ordinary question would they expect him to answer with the Ode to the Nightingale" (301). Beyond the sally, she reveals her concern for that partition between speech and text, which duplicates, differently, the tension between inside, experimental and difficult on the one hand, and outside, easy and popular on the other one. This book in particular strikes a middle way, and if she worries at times about its being written in a too

---

[3] Such is not my subject here, but it must be noted that the —always already semiotic— American place helps Stein regain a sense of inside meaning.

simple form, it actually seems to operate a form of salvaging of the common, retrieving it from the idea of easy success, to the benefit of the commonplace as common voice, and universal self.

Stein's voice in *Everybody* is then that singular generality, a singular society of speech. Even though she is never off stage, the endless digressions, the multiple sakes and characters, the lists, and the associative vortexes make her voice as singular as it is general. The seemingly endless flux of speech contributes its effect of a common discourse. Maurice Blanchot shares with Stein the idea that speech should go on forever. Stein writes in "Poetry and Grammar" "(…) when I first began writing, I was completely possessed by the necessity that writing should go on (…)" (217); Blanchot develops his project of *L'entretien infini* (*The Infinite Conversation*[4]), in which speech becomes impersonal, that is for him "Everybody's speech" (26). "Everybody's speech" proves relevant for Stein indeed, but to the notion of impersonality I would prefer that of generality. For all her use of indefinite quantity and quality forms, for all the suppression of punctuation and of any form of hierarchy (between times, subjects, people), I do not think Stein aims at an impersonal or a neuter voice.[5] If non-differentiation is a principle of structure with her, she tends to create an effect of a large, common, but highly singular voice. Behind the provocative proposition that "(…) autobiography is easy for anyone and so this is to be everybody's autobiography" (4), we discover the both anguished and playful attempt at reconstructing voice and image of self, salvaging them from the commonality of popular success, but retaining the power of generality. She does not cast off the personal; she embraces the general.

On that open scene of speech, she was able to sort out delicate points of identity and discriminate between inside and outside, public opinion, and private author's self. She was also able to free herself from contingent success through reinstating and staging the author's arbitrary power. Writing *Everybody's Autobiography* was part of a process of a both anguished and playful reconstruction of her singular voice and image of self, as her interruptive and digressive system shows—which may disintegrate the autobiographical narrative line, but never dissolves the voice, dramatizing, to the reverse, the author's power. Likewise, Stein retrieves here the common, to the benefit of a singular generality, evolving a form of general lyricism. An echo to such a tension between the general and the singular we can find

---

[4] Title translated by Susan Hanson.
[5] I do not follow Ulla Dydo here, when she suggests Stein might be "a master at neutralizing the language" (Dydo 6).

again in *Ecce Homo*: "Listen to me for I am such and such. But pray do not confuse me with somebody else" (Nietzsche 93).

Works Cited

Blanchot, *L'entretien infini*. Paris: Gallimard, 1969. Print.

Boldrini, Lucia. *Autobiographies of Others, Historical Subjects and Literary Fiction*. New York: Routledge, 2012. Print.

Côté, Jean-François, *Le triangle d'Hermès, Poe, Stein, Warhol, Figures de la modernité esthétique*. Bruxelles: La lettre volée, 2003. Print.

Derrida, Jacques, *Otobiographies, L'enseignement de Nietzsche et la politique du nom propre*. Paris: Galilée, 1984. Print.—. "Il n'y a pas le narcissisme » (1986) in *Points de Suspension*. Paris: Galilée, 1992.

Dydo, Ulla E., *Gertrude Stein: The Language That Rises 1923–1934*. Evanston, Ill.: Northwestern UP, 2003. Print.

Nietzsche, *L'antéchrist*, suivi de *Ecce Homo* (1888). Paris: Gallimard, trad. fr. J.-C. Hémery, 1974. Print.

Stein, Gertrude, *The Autobiography of Alice B. Toklas* (1933). New York: Library of America, vol. 1. 1998. Print.

—. *Four in America* (1933). New Haven: Yale UP, 1947. Print.

—. "Poetry and Grammar," *Lectures in America* (1935). London: Virago, 1988. Print.

—. *Listen to Me* (1936), *Last Operas and Plays*. Baltimore: Johns Hopkins UP, 1949. Print.

—. *Everybody's Autobiography* (1937). Cambridge, MA: Exact Change, 1993.

The Letters of Gertrude Stein and Thornton Wilder, ed. Edward Burns, Ulla Dydo, with William Rice. New Haven and London: Yale UP, 1996. Print.

Wright, D. J. "The Subject of Nietzsche's *Ecce Homo*" in *Autobiography as Philosophy, The Philosophical Uses of Self-Presentation*, ed. Thomas Mathien and D. G. Wright. New York: Routledge, 2006. Print.

When Worlds Collide:
(Auto-)Biography, Truth, Identity, and Normalcy in the Case of Elias Canetti

Claude Desmarais

The simple act of comparing an autobiography (1981 Nobel Prize for literature recipient Elias Canetti's three-volume work) and the biography of Elias Canetti (published by Sven Hanuschek in 2005) might seem like a fool's game, as both have quite distinct modes of narration. Yet beyond genre differences, Helene Cixous's remark that "all biographies like all autobiographies like all narratives tell one story in place of another" (qtd. in Anderson, *Autobiography*, 1) points to the struggle for narrative supremacy between two such life-writing texts. By what means, then, does each of these texts make its mark, particularly in relation to the other? My framework for comparing these life-writing texts stems from John Paul Eakin's discussion, in *Living Autobiographically*, of how such texts are bound by expectations about truth, identity, and normalcy. Eakin's "terms of autobiography," as I call them, will provide a measuring stick for examining Canetti's self-portrayal and portrayal of others. In the process, it will become apparent how these two life-writing texts tell sometimes complementary, sometimes contradictory stories as they seek to meet such expectations, at risk of finding themselves to be the story replaced by another.

Canetti's three volumes of autobiography published between 1977 and 1985 tell the story from his early childhood to 1937, the year of his mother's death. Generally, the autobiography has been characterized as Canetti's retreat to a more traditional narrative, to be contrasted with his novel *Die Blendung* (1935) or his travel narrative *Die Stimmen von Marrakesch* (1968).

Hanuschek, for his part, sees the autobiography as a highly constructed account that has, at times, a problematic relationship to autobiographical truth and that seeks to territorialize Canetti's early life. One of many aspects that Hanuschek criticizes is how, as time goes by in the autobiography, readers are more and more subjected to a cavalcade of figures, rather than any further or deeper insight into Canetti. This leads Hanuschek to comment that Canetti's autobiography becomes, as the narrative proceeds, "eine Autobiographie ohne autobiographisches Subjekt" (an autobiography without an autobiographical subject, 24). Moreover, in a roundabout way to his own frustration as biographer, Hanuschek admits how much of the information of the autobiography could not be checked: "die Recherchen sind hier zu hohen Graden auf die Lebensgeschichte angewiesen, die es doch gerade zu überprüfen gälte" (research here is dependent, to a high degree, on the life-story, that really should be examined, 20). Hanuschek comments further, within a wider discussion of Canetti's numerous reservations about, and attitude towards the genre of biography, how the autobiography exercises control over biography, a general process which Hanuschek sees continued in Canetti's use of time lines for the release of archival material, and even for the permission to write biographies.[1]

Hanuschek's biography, for its part, covers the period from Canetti's birth in 1905 until 1994, the year of Canetti's death on August 14th (Hanuschek, 687). Thus, the biography adds the story of roughly sixty years of Canetti's life to Canetti's life-text (what I consider to be the combined narrative of all Canetti life-texts). In addition to this, the texts are marked by the generational differences between the authors, as well as by major shifts in societal attitudes, which also help explain some of the divergence between autobiography and biography. This difference is most noticeable, in one, the extensive discussions of Canetti's brother and his letter-writing with Elias and Veza Canetti, which Hanuschek describes as a "triad" (350–53); two, the sections on Canetti's romantic relationships in the early London years; and, three, on Canetti's marriage to Hera Buschor in his later years.

Hanuschek further differentiates his biography from Canetti's autobiography because his text is written as a *Dokumentarbiographie*, that is, a biography where documentation determines whether material can be included; even if, as Hanuschek clearly states, his work will have recourse to literary techniques. Hanuschek further elaborates on his notion of *Dokumentarbiographie* when he notes the impossibility of providing a complete or well-rounded portrait of someone's life, instead arguing that

---

[1] "Schon das Verfassen der großen Autobiographie ist ein Akt des Kontrollzwangs, die präzise Regelung des eigenen Nachlasses bis hin zu Fristen für mögliche Biographien sind weitere Akten dieser Art" (21).

what he presents are facets of a portrait ("Facetten eines Bildes") and broken (paint) strokes ("durchbrochen [...] Strichen" 25).

In contrast to Hanuschek's notion of documentary biography as the *contrat de lecture* of the biography, Canetti uses memory as the basis and foundation of his autobiography's truth claim. In this context, Hanuschek discusses Canetti's oft-cited truth incantation, a passage on memory; Canetti's *Glaubensbekenntnis* states that memory should be spared modern surgical interventions, by which Canetti meant, for instance, psychoanalysis (Hanuschek 93). Hanuschek critiques Canetti for the way he uses memory to protect its veracity vis-à-vis research-based objectivity, or from attacks that see it as a constructed fictionality,[2] yet the biographer does not "fault" Canetti for the constructedness and changing nature of memory. This, Hanschek states, is a result of the connection between memory and life narratives itself, and their ability to change each other; as has been shown by the recent research in a variety of fields of inquiry (99). Thus, though he removes in a sense fault from Canetti for relying on memory, at the same time Hanuschek reserves the right to critique other aspects of Canetti's self-representation, and of the portraits he draws of others in the autobiography.

In examining the portraits of Canetti's parents in the autobiography and in the biography, we are faced with the two characters where Hanuschek was largely dependent on the autobiography for information. As Hanuschek notes, Canetti's portrait of his father stands in stark contrast to the "Vater-Bearbeitung" of the late 1960s and early 1970s, when many wrote critically of their fathers and their roles in National-Socialism (94). Canetti's father, Jacques, died at the breakfast table in Manchester, England, when Canetti was seven. Canetti's much longer relationship with his mother, who did not die until Canetti was in his early 30s, is depicted as a much more tormented affair, marked by extreme jealousy and constant struggle over Canetti's, and his mother's right to self-determination. The three-volume autobiography's closing passage depicts his mother's death as a difficult yet successful resolution of their conflicts, and functions as a final autobiographical moment incarnating Canetti's struggle against (her) death.

All in all, the autobiographical stories about Canetti's parents seem to meet the standards of truth set out by Eakin, something that is tied both to narrative coherency—for example the acceptance of Frank McCourt's long dialogue passages from his youth as being "truthful," but in a way that is

---

[2] "Canetti behauptet hier nicht weniger, als daß er sich recherierbarer Objektivität ebenso verweigere wie konstruierender Fiktionalität" (93).

different from a transcript of such conversations, if such a thing ever existed—and to not lying (see the James Frey memoir case as discussed in Eakin, 20). These parental portraits also seem to meet Eakin's concepts of how they help to foster both identity (Canetti's sense of self as shown to stem from his parents), and normalcy, "a comfortable sense of being a good, socially proper, and stable person" (Charlotte Linde, cited in Eakin, 29). This notion of normalcy could also be fulfilled by how Canetti's autobiography does not speak ill of the dead, and honours his mother and father.[3]

Hanuschek generally accepts these portraits, but makes a number of factual corrections that at least partially rewrite the narrative and indicate how Canetti idealizes his father, and plays down conflict with his mother. As part of the idealization of the father, Hanuschek cites how Canetti narrates the scenes of his father introducing him to reading, and promising his son Elias that he could freely choose his profession. But a more important point underlies Hanuschek's reading of Canetti's idealization of the father. Thus, whereas Canetti claims that his father died while reading the *Manchester Guardian* headline that Montenegro had declared war on Turkey, Hanuschek shows how this headline appeared the day after the father's death, that is, on the 9th of October, 1912, and not on the 8th (51). Whereas Canetti takes this connection between the declaration of war and the threat it poses to all the Canetti relatives living in Bulgaria as a sign that his father is the first great victim of Canetti's struggle against death (his lifelong *Todesfeindschaft*), Hanuschek demonstrates how this narrative, so important for Canetti's narrative identity, is faulty, a construct that does not correspond to historical reality.[4] Though the autobiography does provide a number of different possible reasons for his father's death, and thus Hanuschek's correction should not shatter readers' belief in the truth of Canetti's narrative, it does make clear how the autobiography plays along the borderline between truth and fiction at times. The accumulation of such corrections, moreover, would definitely make readers more liable to place greater trust in the documentary biographer Hanuschek. This is, moreover, a general reader reception of biography; readers expect, generally, both a

---

[3] Eakin's discussion of normalcy takes a very different view of its meaning, shifting focus from the "obligations of those who perform self-narrations to the responsibilities of those who receive and judge those performances," 43ff.

[4] Hanuschek also notes that Canetti's father was not a partner in the Manchester family business, and so his social and economic situation did not make him a "free" man, and that this might have contributed to the father's death (49).

greater veracity about the subject matter compared to an autobiographical text, and a more expansive view of the material.

In the case of Canetti's mother, Hanuschek demonstrates how Canetti plays down the at times severe nature of their interpersonal conflict using unpublished documents from the Canetti archives in Zurich. One instance of such conflict that is mentioned, and which acts as proof for Hanuschek's assertion, is when Canetti's mother claims there is no money for him to take a long-planned vacation; a humouristic send-up of common-sense masking as Freudian psychology, ensues. After Canetti has filled out reams of paper with the word "Geld" (money), the doctor that makes a house-call tells Canetti's mother to send her son on this vacation as it will be good for his "Ödipus" (*FO* 160). This narrative, with its comical point, masks the severity of the situation in Hanuschek's view, while, as the biographer shows, other severe confrontations go unmentioned. Thus, though Canetti had broken off all contact with his mother for several years before her death, the closing passage of the autobiography only relays the process of revalorizing the mother that took place after her death (279). In both of these instances, Hanuschek also sees a process of aestheticization at work, which allows him to at least partially question the veracity of the autobiography and Canetti's claim that his memory should go unquestioned; such narrative techniques, in Hanuschek's view, seek to cover over some problematic aspects of the autobiography.

A number of other factors also lead Hanuschek to question the autobiography's value vis-à-vis documentary biography, but in terms of the general trend, Hanuschek's critique of the portrait of the mother and father continues throughout the autobiography. The effect of this critique, moreover, is amplified through Hanuschek's use of the archival material to discuss those characters who, unlike Canetti's parents, lived on beyond 1937.[5]

A similar instance of playing down conflict is dealt with at length in Hanuschek's discussion of Canetti's youngest brother, Georg. This also involves an issue that can be understood as having two factors: one, Canetti avoiding a topic that has since become socially acceptable or two, his respecting personal space: it is dealt with at length by Hanuschek.[6] Namely, Hanuschek shows how Georg, a Paris-based tuberculosis doctor (himself a tuberculosis patient) who cared for the mother up to her death in 1937,

---

[5] *Party im Blitz: die englischen Jahre* (2003), which covers his years in England, was released posthumously.
[6] See Eakin's discussion of Kathryn Harrison's *The Kiss* (1997) for the perils of speaking ill, particularly of family, even when the narrative is truthful (40–42).

receives a very minor role in the autobiography, despite his strong ties to Elias Canetti, and his more extensive correspondence with Veza Canetti. Apparently, both because of his respect of his brother's personal space, and in an effort to avoid a topic that has since become more socially acceptable, Canetti's autobiography does not mention his brother Georg's homosexuality. Of course, it is hard to decide which of these two attitudes dominated Canetti's thinking. What is clear though, is that his brother Georg's larger life was not fit into the autobiographical construct.

A quick perusal of the figures from the cultural and literary world that are presented in the autobiography shows that here too, Hanuschek's process of documenting his biography involves questioning the veracity of portraits, either because Canetti downplays his conflict with certain figures, or overemphasizes his connection to others, or, a third option, attempts to aestheticize a personal conflict. For instance, Hanuschek cites the autobiography's negative depiction of Brecht as a moral "Gegenbild" (counter-image), versus Canetti's personal notes that reveal how Canetti felt that Brecht "einen sehr guten Einfluß auf mich hatte" ([Brecht] had a very good influence on me, 162). Likewise, Hanuschek criticizes Canetti's portrait of Hermann Broch as a flawed portrait that encumbers the narrative voice and balance, precisely because Canetti did not express his very critical opinion of Hermann Broch as found in Canetti's notes (204). Finally, Hanuschek argues that Canetti excoriated and wrote Ernst Fischer, a life-long communist and editor of the left-wing *Arbeiterzeitung* (Workers' newspaper) in the 1930s, out of the autobiography for two reasons (Hanuschek 196). First, because he was a communist—which might, via guilt by association, harm Canetti's reputation and book sales[7]—, and most importantly, because he revealed Veza Canetti's disability (Hanuschek 197).[8]

This issue of disability and its representation, or lack thereof, brings us to the portrait of Veza Taubner-Calderon, later Veza Canetti, and again touches upon what Hanuschek terms Elias Canetti's sense of discretion.

---

[7] I would add that readers' ability to easily categorize Canetti as a communist or communist sympathizer might also hamper their willingness to consider Canetti's notion of his *Todesfeindschaft* or of *Verwandlung* (transformation) as anything more than utopian thinking.

[8] In Fischer's autobiography, *Erinnerungen und Reflexionen*, (Memories and Reflections, 1969), it was not necessarily the characterization of Canetti as an "attractive diable boiteux," but the mention, six years after Veza Canetti's death in 1963, of her disability (Veza was missing the lower part of her left arm), something which Canetti hid from the public even after Veza's death. Canetti never forgave Fischer for this, breaking off relations completely (Hanuschek, 196).

Veza Canetti, herself a writer, banned all discussions of her disability, apparently to avoid discrimination. Elias Canetti, as Hanuschek shows, fiercely held to this, including long after Veza's death. For readers of Canetti's portrait of Veza in the autobiography, the revelation of such a lacuna can come as shock, leading either to a greater appreciation of the portrayal as respectful, or a questioning of the autobiographical portrait for leaving out such an important detail; and it was a decision about which Canetti had his doubts (Hanuschek 263).

Whatever the case may be, not mentioning Veza's disability again fits Hanuschek's notion of the autobiography as a story that does not tell the whole story, which rounds out the edges, and removes the deeper valleys. So while Canetti's autobiography seeks to meet a sort of normalcy that is about discretion, and is perhaps most apparent in how the autobiography deals with Canetti's sex life by aestheticizing it, Hanuschek's biography seems to adopt Eakin's notion of normalcy, whereby readers are called to possess the maturity to see Canetti in his many lives, and his many, at times contradictory actions.

The deeper valleys I allude to here is the mental anguish that at times resulted from or in the relationship between Veza and Elias, whereas in the autobiography any conflict is usually aestheticized in conflicts over literature (133), a phenomenon tied to the "Literarizität" of Canetti's autobiography, as noted by Martin Bollacher (22). In the autobiography, Veza is portrayed as being quite different from Canetti's mother, and Hanuschek shows not only that Veza and Canetti's mother knew each other, contrary to the autobiography's claim that they had never seen each other, but that they were culturally at least, of one mind, both well-read and interested in music (109). As Hanuschek portrays the relationship, Veza was, even when she and Canetti were still romantically involved, a sort of mother figure; Canetti clearly moves away from his mother once he starts a relationship with Veza, particularly once they marry (278).[9]

Hanuschek focuses on how Elias Canetti characterizes Veza as a *Rabe*, the bird of death that has been transformed into a Spanish woman in the autobiography, because her favourite poem was Edgar Allan Poe's "The

---

[9] Hanuschek sets as the date of Veza's role in the relationship changing into a sort of mother-sister one as the summer of 1932, when she lost a child at birth (268). Without going into much detail, and thus maintaining a sense of propriety and avoiding any possible libel action, Hanuschek thus follows the trend of most Western biography writing by discussing the sexual life as part of a biographical narrative. See Nigel Hamilton for some of the more explosive biographies to deal with sexuality in the 1960s and 1970s in *Biography. A Brief History*, "The Miner's Canary," 251–278.

Raven." Death and the raven, as one of Veza's comments on the Rax Mountains in Austria demonstrates, stood both for the terror of death, and the attraction it held for her (Hanuschek, 111). This aspect of Veza's character, and the role it plays it in her relationship with Elias Canetti, is described at length by Hanuschek (283), particularly for the years of their exile and after WWII in England, years not covered in the autobiography. Nonetheless, it is clear that Veza's preoccupation with death does not make its way into the autobiography except under literary code (the raven). This mirrors how personal conflicts are aestheticized, such as an episode where love letters are hidden in a tree (the locus amonae), or another which involves Veza "keeping" Büchner's *Woyzeck* secret from him. Hanuschek does not contradict these accounts in the autobiography, but he does wonder why Veza's pre-occupation with death and suicide, and Canetti's own periods of mental anguish, including one specific mental breakdown into a state of paranoia in 1936 (282), go unmentioned. No doubt part of Canetti's unwillingness to dwell on such moments has to do with his *Todesfeindschaft*, as well as his disdain for psychology, particularly the popular Freudian kind.

Whatever allowances readers make for the autobiographer, all of the examples mentioned to date, if they do not discount the autobiographical story somewhat, at least set up some contrast between the autobiography and the biography, if not a counter-narrative in the biography.

Which leads me to my final point: Hanuschek's balanced and fair-minded criticism of Canetti, no doubt tempered by a genuine attempt to understand and represent the author, suits the genre demands of biography. However, his approach does, in my estimation, damage the literary text; in terms of how various portraits and moments are narrated, but also in terms of how the biography affects the general literary thrust of the autobiography. Before developing this criticism, it should be stated that Hanuschek in no way practices outdated historiographical processes, described by Dagmar Günther as the literal and highly selective use of life-writing, as [a] "provider... of fact" (cited in Woods, *German Life Writing*, 6). Instead, he can be said to focus on "biographische Sinnkonstruktionen" (biographical constructions of meaning) rather than argue for the fictionality of Canetti's text. Yet, by making use of the biographer's tools, Hanuschek's text necessarily and nonetheless must write over the text it both mirrors and questions. Hanuschek even hints at this process when he declares that in writing

Canetti's life-story he wishes to make many of Canetti's secrets visible, and leave others open to interpretation.[10]

Whether Hanuschek consciously references this word ("Lebensgeschichte," life story/history) from the subtitles of Canetti's second and third volume, *Die Fackel im Ohr* (*The Torch in my Ear*) and *Das Augenspiel* (*The Play of the Eyes*), cannot be known, as the term is the common one for describing life-writing in German. But a concrete example of this writing over Elias Canetti's autobiography, a process which I am now partially replicating in relation to Hanuschek's biography, can be found in Hanuschek's discussion of the opening passage of the autobiography, a chapter entitled "Meine früheste Erinnerung" (my earliest memory) in *Die gerettete Zunge* (*The Tongue Saved*).[11] In the actual passage, the story is told, nominally, twice: first from the perspective of the 1st person narrator as a child, then from the perspective of the mother. Yet while the first story goes from the child's perspective and expands into a timeless repetition of the threat, the mother's story, a factual retelling, reduces this existential moment into a maudlin affair. The young girl caring for Canetti was having an affair with the young man across the hall who would playfully threaten Canetti to keep him from telling. Just how keen the second narrative, the mother's, is on erasing the first is emphasized by the repetition of the word "muss" (must have) in two consecutive phrases: "auf diese Art müssen sie sich zuerst begegnet haben, so muß es begonnen haben" (that's how they must have met, that's the way it must have started, *GZ*, 10). At the very end of the mother's narrative, the text makes a statement that troubles any reader who has too simply accepted the mother's narrative as the truer story: "Die Drohung mit dem Messer hat ihre Wirkung getan, das Kind hat zehn Jahre darüber geschwiegen" (The threat with the knife worked, the child quite literally held his tongue for ten years, *GZ*, 10).

Hanuschek's rewriting of the "earliest memory" focuses on the colour red as exemplifying the scene's violence, later commenting how it symbolizes the "heillosen 20. Jahrhundert" (the terrible [or hopeless] twentieth century, 31–32). Hanuschek then mentions that the mother recognizes the Carlsbad Pension because of the colour red, and then cites,

---

[10] "Elias Canettis Lebensgeschichte enthält weiterhin eine Fülle von Geheimnissen, die mit diesem Buch offen gelassen, zum Teil auch erst als Geheimnisse sichtbar werden" (Hanuschek 16).

[11] English translations from Joachim Neugroschl's translation of *Die gerettete Zunge*, *The Tongue Set Free. Remembrance of a European Childhood* (1979).

cuts, and in my opinion, rewrites, reduces and diminishes both the opening passage, and thus the autobiography as a whole:

> Die "früheste Erinnerung," "in Rot getaucht," ist von exemplarischer Gewalt; am Rot überall soll die Mutter die Karlsbader Pension erkannt haben: "Auf dem Arm eines Mädchens komme ich zu einer Tür heraus, der Boden vor mir ist rot (…) Er sagt: 'Jetzt schneiden wir ihm die Zunge ab.' (…) Im letzten Augenblick zieht er das Messer zurück, sagt: 'Heute noch nicht, morgen.' Er klappt das Messer zu und steckt es in seine Tasche (9).[12]

Though I do not disagree with Hanuschek's interpretation of the color red, and realize that any literary text can receive, as this one has, numerous literary interpretations, Hanuschek's presentation of the passage involves a number of surgical operations that rob it of one literary connotation, which I call narrative agency. For instance, the last line is not the one that ends the cited passage above ("Er klappt das Messer zu…"), but rather a whole paragraph, that starts with "Jeden Morgen" (every morning) and relates how the man is going to cut off his tongue. The final two lines of this paragraph, the most telling for my interpretation, are: "Ich weiß, daß er sie mir abschneiden wird und fürchte mich jedesmal mehr. Der Tag beginnt damit, und es geschieht viele Male" (I know he's going to cut it off, and I get more and more scared each time. That's how the day starts, and it happens very often, GZ, 9). With these lines, the passage's existential nature, if not the only interpretation, at least becomes possible. Likewise, Hanuschek places part of the mother's explanation for the memory, "am Rot überall soll die Mutter (…) erkannt haben" (She could tell because of the ubiquitous red…) before his citation of the first part of the opening passage, which he starts with "Auf dem Arm eines Mädchens komme ich zu einer Tür heraus…" (I come out of a door on the arm of a maid…). Whereas in the autobiography these two versions of the story, Canetti's and his mother's, are told one after the other, and were separated by a space so that each stands on its own, in Hanuschek's rendition, the narratives are intermeshed so that the "historical" narrative, the one with place names and easily definable reasons, wipes out the ahistorical narrative with its existential meaning.

---

[12] "The 'earliest memory', 'dripped in red' is of exemplary violence; the mother is said to have recognized the Carlsbad Pension because of the colour red: "On the arm […] He claps the knife shut and puts it in his pocket."

Now, *pace* Hanuschek, even an accomplished biography cannot be a duck, that is, cannot be a thorough literary analysis of an autobiographical text. So though I find no real problems with Hanuschek's biography for fulfilling genre expectations, and what Eakin posits as readers' expectations around truth, identity and normalcy, it nonetheless appears that Cixous was prescient about the effect of one narrative on another, when worlds collide.

Works Cited

Anderson, Linda. *Autobiography*. New York: Routledge, 2007. Print.

Bollacher, Martin, and Bettina Gruber, eds. "Die Gegenwärtigkeit des Vergangenen. Elias Canettis autobiographische Erzählung *Die gerettete Zunge. Geschichte einer Jugend*." In: *Das erinnerte Ich: Kindheit und Jugend in der deutschsprachigen Autobiographie der Gegenwart*. Martin Paderborn: Bonifatius, 2000. 15-36. Print.

Canetti, Elias. *Die Gerettete Zunge. Geschichte einer Jugend*. München: Carl Hanser, 1977. Print.

—. *Die Fackel im Ohr. Lebensgeschichte 1921-1931*. München: Carl Hanser, 1980. Print.

—. *Das Augenspiel. Lebensgeschichte1931-1937*. München: Carl Hanser, 1985. Print.

—. *The Tongue Set Free. Remembrance of a European Childhood*. Translated by Joachim Neugroschl. New York: Seabury: 1979. Print.

Eakin, Paul John. *Living Autobiographically: How we Create Identity in Narrative*. Ithaca: Cornell UP, 2008. Print.

Hamilton, Nigel. *Biography. A Brief History*. Cambridge: Harvard UP, 2007. Print.

Hanuschek, Sven. *Elias Canetti. Biographie*. München: Carl Hanser, 2005. Print.

Woods, Roger, Dennis Tate, and Birgit Dahlke, eds. "Introduction: The Purposes and Problems of German Life Writing in the Twentieth Century" In: *German Life Writing in the Twentieth Century*. Rochester: Camden House, 2010. 1–24. Print.

'It's Our Shared Memories… The Stories We Tell…':[1]
Politics and Identity in Two Memoirs by Hungarian-Canadians

Dagmara Drewniak

According to Donald J. Winslow, memoirs by nature rely on "centering more upon social and historical background, less upon private life" (1995 [1980]: 39–40). This interplay between the personal sphere and the socio-historical panoramic view is often a foundation for memoirs and other life-writing genres. This particular connection is pertinent to the two memoirs analyzed in this text: Anna Porter's *The Storyteller. Memory, Secrets, Magic and Lies. A Memoir of Hungary* (2001 [2000]) and Elaine Kalman Naves's *Shoshanna's Story. A Mother, a Daughter, and the Shadows of History* (2006 [2003]). Both texts offer sketches of personal stories in light of the important events in the history of Hungary which have definitely contributed to the identities of the authors of these memoirs. According to Nancy Miller, a memoir is a genre which "hesitates to define the boundary between public and private" (Miller 2) and as such, this definition becomes of substantial importance for the study of selected memoirs which blur the clear-cut boundaries between what originates from the public and history and what stems from the entirely private and emotional. I argue here that both texts offer an account of Hungarian history which greatly influenced the fates and identities of the main protagonists (and authors at the same time). While the abolishment of these boundaries may locate these texts at the crossroads of a memoir and an autobiography, it is still necessary to acknowledge that their fragmentary and inexhaustible nature would support their categorization as memoirs, which, according to Marlene

---

[1] The quotation used in the title comes from Anna Porter's *The Storyteller. Memory, Secrets, Magic and Lies. A Memoir of Hungary* (55).

Kadar "take their lead from the historical circumstances and personages that have influenced the memoirist's recollections" (663). Thus, as Smith argues "the moment of self-narrating" (108) is a crucial one in the construction of the self in such historically and politically based life-writing discourses. This very blending of the personal and socio-historical dimensions is highlighted in the subtitles of the memoirs. In the case of Anna Porter's *The Storyteller. Memory, Secrets, Magic and Lies*, the subtitle reads *A Memoir of Hungary*, which suggests the permeation of personal storytelling, family secrets, and lies with a wider background of Hungarian history. Elaine Kalman Naves's *Shoshanna's Story* is subtitled as *A Mother, a Daughter, and the Shadows of History*, which again emphasizes the interconnection of these two aspects.

The personal sphere in the texts selected in this paper is a basic story, the groundwork onto which the shadows of history are laid. In this way, the lives of the families and main protagonists (being the authors at the same time) are shaped through the experience of Porter's family's long history with a special emphasis put on the Second World War, then the following years and cumulating in 1956—the year of the Hungarian Revolution. In the case of Kalman Naves's text, the political dimension consists of the Holocaust, its aftermath for Jewish families, and the subsequent emigration, all of which shadow the lives of the family members. As a result, these memoirs, while still recalling the private, family story, fall close to the category of political memoirs, giving an account of the history of Hungary, with its politicians, political tensions the families suffered from, and finally political declarations of their homeland which were not always supported by its citizens. As has been stated by Michael Ondaatje, "history enters us" (18) and therefore largely shapes our personages but such generational memoirs also contribute to the Canadian literary scene "translat[ing] foreign experience into claims on a homegrown culture" (Egan and Helms 220).

Anna Porter was born in 1944 as Anna Szighety in Budapest, where she spent her early childhood years before her family emigrated to New Zealand in 1956. She graduated from university there and in 1969, she emigrated to Canada where she started a career as a publisher, editor, and writer. She established Key Porter Books and has written a few books: crime stories, and more importantly non-fiction among which are *The Storyteller: A Memoir of Secrets, Magic and Lies*, *Kasztner's Train: The True Story of Rezső Kasztner, Unknown Hero of the Holocaust*, which won the 2007 Writers' Trust Non-Fiction Award and the Jewish Book Award for Non-Fiction, and *The Ghosts of Europe: Journeys through Central Europe's Troubled Past and*

Uncertain Future published in 2010, which received the 2011 Shaughnessy Cohen Prize for political writing (Anna Porter's Profile; the cover of *The Ghosts of Europe*).

Her memoir *The Storyteller* was published in 2000 in Canada and is the story of Porter's grandfather Vili Rácz who in the first decades of the twentieth century was a multi-skilled Olympic athlete, took part in other championships and held several records in various disciplines but who was predominantly a Hungarian patriot witnessing the most important historical events in the first fifty years of the twentieth century in Hungary. As has been stated in a recent interview, Porter's initial intention was to write a story which would be entirely concentrated on him as a prominent figure and would be devoid of the personal layer referring to Porter herself (Richards no date of publication given). It was only in the subsequent drafts of the book that Porter inscribed herself into the story, having noticed the inextricable connections between her being her grandfather's favorite grandchild, the stories she listened to for many years and the impact they had on her. On the one hand, it proves the strong bonds between the genre of the memoir with that of the biography as Porter's aim was at first to actually write a biography of Vili Rácz in the Hungarian socio-political scene and thus demonstrate the necessity immigrants to Canada experience of "[r]emembering their forebears (...) [and] by inserting their extended relationships into the history of their times and places, combin[ing] the autobiographical with biographical" (Egan and Helms 223). On the other hand, it also exhibits the ways in which Porter herself is made of history; how inseparably her life has been tied to the generations that precede her and how important their stamp becomes in the formation of her own identity as a Hungarian-Canadian.

The Storyteller portrays Vili Rácz as the patriarch of the Rácz family exerting a tremendous influence on his three daughters' lives and numerous friends, lovers and other people who worked with him and also, more importantly, as a powerful storyteller confiding his recollections and legacy to his favorite granddaughter—Anna Porter. Although Vili as a storyteller goes back to the bygone eras of the Huns' invasion and the Magyar tribes, the main storyline concentrates on the turn of the nineteenth and twentieth centuries and the first half of the twentieth century until the Hungarian Revolution of 1956 (this event was also experienced by Porter herself), which made the Ráczs leave their country. The story of the Ráczs' family presented in the book mainly revolves around the first half of the twentieth century which is one of the most turbulent periods of Hungary's history but

Vili gives a historical background to it. The country witnessed the decline of the Austro-Hungarian empire, the rise of independent Hungary, the loss of "two-thirds of its land and three million of its people to Romania, Serbia and the newish state of Czechoslovakia" (Porter, *Storyteller* 26). The book also widely discusses the political consequences of the alliances Hungary made during the two World Wars as well as the Communist regime, which later held the country in its grip.

Throughout the book, Porter recalls the stories she listened to and inherited from Vili Rácz and tries to analyze them from her own Canadian perspective. Vili's stories have become so formative in Porter's life due to the fact that she hardly knew her father and Vili took the role of a mentor who sparked her interest in Hungarian history, exerted a strong influence on her, demanding promises to study hard, never to marry (a promise which she later broke), and to visit the region of Transylvania, known in Hungary as Erdély, where his ancestors came from. The legacy he entrusted her with comes in the form of a wide existential definition. He said: "Life is … a succession of loose ends, roads leading nowhere in particular, tales unfinished, so many left unexplored, endless possibilities lighting the way you travel. Often we don't even know what happened until the train we should have taken has already passed by. Whatever you do, grab the rail, jump on. Don't live a half-lived life" (Porter, *Storyteller* 370). These words have made Porter reminisce on Vili's stories and collect them in a book. Her grandfather's words have also encouraged her to find her father, who managed to escape to Vienna, leaving her mother and the young Anna behind.

Even though Vili was a descendant of the Hungarian nobility, owning lands and vineyards and during the short interwar period of Hungary's independence a respected persona in the country, he was treated as an enemy of the nation after the Second World War. Although he still managed to establish a series of movie magazines and cherished the brief moment of freedom during the first three post-war years, in the years to follow, he was arrested and convicted to many months in prison and hard work for being a *kulak* and a capitalist entrepreneur. Released from prison after a few years thanks to his daughter's—Pucci—Porter's mother—marriage of convenience to a Party comrade Jenő, he came back silent, broken and devoid of hope for Hungary but still treasuring his love for the country. For Vili, the most fortunate historical period was always "the brief moment of euphoria that began on March 15, 1848. His last heroes included Count Stephen Széchenyi, Lajos Kossuth, Sándor Petőfi, Mór Jókai and a range of generals who died in the last defence of independence from the marauding Austrians in 1849" (Porter, *Storyteller* 150, spelling original). These were the heroic people whom Vili talked about endlessly whose deeds of heroism he wanted Porter to remember. This historical layer is continually intertwined with the more personal account of how the stories have influenced Porter's identity. Alongside dates and names as well as the pictures of Vili in his Hussar uniform which are in the book and on its cover, Porter acknowledges that she has become more aware of the importance of memories. Vili told stories not only to teach his granddaughter about the long and painful history of Hungary but also to guarantee that she becomes an upholder of Hungarian identity: "he explained that, being who we were, we had a number of obligations he took seriously, and he expected me to do the same. 'The old families,' he said, 'are responsible for keeping the memories. It's our shared memories that make us a country. The stories we tell and our language. Stuck between the Slavs and the Germans, and a thorn in both their sides, we have endured" (Porter, *Storyteller* 55). This quote evokes all the painful moments in the history of Hungary and Europe which destroyed countries, governments and alliances, but Vili's lesson for his confidante is to remember, as a memory preserves national and personal identity. For the small country which Hungary became after the Second World War, for a country speaking a difficult language that does not belong to any neighboring language families, memories are a warrant of survival. Furthermore, Vili stressed the importance of language: "language, you see, is what makes us who we are" (58).

In her memoir, Porter admits that she questions her identity as a Canadian of Hungarian origins (343) but she ascertains that her daughters, being true Canadians, although devoid of her own doubts, remain indebted to the legacy Vili believed in. As Porter claims: "Still, the old stories that filled my childhood have made their way into theirs" (343). Not only do they accompany Porter in her visit to Hungary and Transylvania, which was only possible after the fall of Communism in both Hungary and Romania, they also take part in a traditional event of a Hungarian diaspora in Toronto (e.g. the annual Toronto Helicon Ball). Despite the fact that Vili remained in New Zealand till his death in 1975, he never fully recognized himself as an immigrant living in another country (Anna Porter left him in 1968 to go to England and then to settle down in Canada). He abided by his old stories and his dreams of a free homeland as "he never thought of [New Zealand] as home. It never changed who he had been. He didn't apply for citizenship. He didn't even see himself as an immigrant. When he talked of the great Rákóczi in exile to the end of his life, never able to return home, I know he was thinking of himself" (342).

Revising her past in the book, Porter brings back the memories of her ancestors and becomes the one who by guarding them pays her debt to the old tales and her grandfather who has shaped her own identity. Anna Porter, while retelling the stories, subjects herself to what de Certeau understood as speaking "in the name of the 'real'" and thus her memoir "makes itself believable by saying: 'This text has been dictated for you by Reality'" (de Certeau 148). According to Sidonie Smith, "narrative performativity constitutes interiority. That is, the interiority or self that is said to be prior to the autobiographical expression or reflection is an *effect* of autobiographical storytelling" (Smith 109). Ultimately, Anna Porter's self is created through, and simultaneously is an effect of, performing an autobiographical narration in her memoir. It therefore becomes, an expression of her identity formed in response to the recreation of the history of Hungary.

Elaine Kalman Naves, born in Hungary in 1947, grew up in Budapest, from which her family emigrated to London, and then in 1959 to Montreal. Kalman Naves is a freelance columnist, editor and writer. She has written several books including two memoirs *Journey to Vaja: Reconstructing the World of a Hungarian-Jewish Family* (1996) and *Shoshanna's Story: A Mother, A Daughter, and the Shadows of History* ([2003] 2006). She has been awarded the Quebec Writers' Federation prizes for non-fiction and two Jewish Book Awards for Holocaust Literature for both memoirs. (Elaine Kalman Naves's Profile)

Elaine Kalman Naves's *Shoshanna's Story. A Mother, a Daughter, and the Shadows of History* ([2003] 2006), selected for a discussion here, is a book whose title also suggests the coexistence of history which explores the fates of Hungarian Jews making their way to Canada and at the same time a private story of a mother-daughter relationship shadowed by the history of Second World War Europe. Despite the initial stipulation concerning the change of certain names in the text, Kalman Naves concludes that her memoir is her "rendering of real events, [her] version of truth" (Kalman Naves, *Shoshanna* xi). On the level of content, Kalman Naves's family memoir consists of retracing the history of her mother, Shoshanna, who having survived a concentration camp, comes back to her hometown to find work in an orphanage where she is found by her remote friend from the past—Gusti. At that time Shoshanna was twenty-seven and Gusti was forty; both of them had been married before, but Shoshanna's husband Márton had disappeared during the war and was considered to be dead whereas Gusti's wife and daughter had died. The text is, however, mainly the story of their, for they got married and had a child—Ilushka/Elaine, painful decision to leave Hungary in 1956 and the reasons behind this decision and emigration to Canada where they had to reconsider their Jewishness again.

The very first instance of a complicated family fate lies within the grand history of the Second World War and its consequences for the identities of all of the characters. It concerns the tangled story of Shoshanna's marriage to Márton. As a soldier, he was sent to the Russian front in 1942, a mere eight days after marrying Shoshanna, and did not return or even write home for the next five years. When the war was over and he still did not come back until 1947, Shoshanna thought he had died. Kalman Naves in her memoir explores the whole sequence of 'ifs' studying the chances of reversed fates of these two people. But Shoshanna's story has to be placed in the right proportions of an orphaned, young girl, devastated after the release from the camp in 1945, coming back to find that no close relatives have survived the war and feeling certain about her husband's death in Russia. History shaped Shoshanna's and Gusti's lives, a history in which they involuntarily had to participate.

The Revolution of 1956, which for Kalman Naves's father, Gusti, was a mere continuation of the past war, also took its toll on the family. Speaking of this prolonged unrest in Hungary, she notices: "the war never ended for my father. Twelve years later, when the Revolution broke out, the wounds were ... fresh" (101) and

> [f]alse charges, in fact, were the order of the day. Hundreds of thousands were arrested as enemies of the state or as wealthy kulaks, thousands were tortured, sent to internment camps, or murdered. In another popular joke, two prisoners are talking about their sentences. One asks: 'What did you get?' The other replies: 'Fifteen years.' 'For what?' 'For nothing.' 'Impossible,' says the first. 'For nothing you get only ten. (104)

This, together with the fact that it soon became too dangerous to live upstairs and the family moved downstairs to a crowded cellar, because of the regular fights and shooting, has shaped their lives in Revolution-torn Budapest. Despite the terrible stories the family heard about people shot on the spot while crossing the border with Austria illegally, Kalman Naves's family started to consider emigration. This was also the step advised by the small circle of friends who knew that Shoshanna had a sister already living in Canada. It was also a time of intense discussions that Shoshanna had with her husband about the future of Hungary, which frequently finished with accusations thrown at Gusti: "You love this accursed country despite everything. You have no intention of leaving" (121). Gusti, however, decided to apply for an official leave, and he succeeded. They were in a lucky position because of that, although they were not happy at all as "once we surrendered our Hungarian identity papers at Hegyeshalom and were left with only the *laissez-passer* stamped with the dreary letters that spelled out 'stateless,' he turned to my mother with an expression of mournful gravity. 'Thus far, I have brought you myself. To the edges of my world. From here on, you're our captain'" (122–23).

Considering the fact that at the moment of emigration Shoshanna was thirty-eight and Gusty fifty-one, it was Shoshanna who was supposed to face the accommodation to the reality of London first, and then Montreal. London was a friendly place and a successful stay but the shadow of history also prompted their decision to move on to Canada. Once in London, the family was asked to merge into the Protestant English society, which they did and Kalman Naves remembers that period as a nice phase for a child, as she did not differ from others. On the contrary, in Canada the family wanted to restore their Jewish identity, which Elaine Kalman Naves strongly objected to. Her identity was questioned once again and as a stubborn girl, she exclaimed "I could be a Jewish child at home! (...) I could be a Jewish child in private" (176). The prospect for the Jews emerging from post-WWII Europe, which they met in Canada, was a novelty. When Elaine was registered at school, the head teacher said: "This is not Nazi Germany, Mrs. Kalman. You've come to a free country. (...) No one will ever persecute your child here" (177). The school principal did not know that it was not really the persecutions Elaine was afraid of, but rather that her personality had been formed in such a way that she wanted to be in the mainstream and that her identity had already been shaped by the family's reluctant religiousness.

Finally, due to the political atmosphere in Montreal in the 1960s, the family restored their Jewish traditions, and Kalman Naves says that "all became clear for me and my Jewish identity fell firmly into place" (205) although it meant for her father to speak "about his great respect for the man from Galilee, a notable Jewish reformer and rabbi" (205) and for the family to have "a Christmas tree and Christmas presents to celebrate the birth of a great Jew" and to kindle "the Hanukkah menorah at the same time as the Christmas lights winked in our window" (205). Complicated as the family's past is, it has always been closely connected to history. Even, when in Canada, the family witnessed the Six Day War and the inclusion of Jerusalem into Israel, the family feasted it as their own victory, which for the young Kalman Naves meant to reconsider her identity: "I could choose to regard the Jewish star as a tattoo of shame or a badge of courage. Either way, it was mine" (206).

Shoshanna's Story finishes with a chapter entitled 'History.' It is interesting to note that apart from the partial change of names, Shoshanna alongside recounting her history, inserts convictions of the following type: "a veil of discreet obscuring settl[ed] over the past" (212) and the memories Kalman Naves's mother offers as family history become rather "tales" which even have "subtexts" (213). Kalman Naves's book becomes yet another example of a whole range of memoirs, autobiographies, life narratives which are classified as non-fiction although her text has bordered storytelling (the domain of fiction) where a storyline intertwines with history. Poignantly, she concludes:

> I chafe under the burden of the stories I've been listening to all my life with a petulance that I know ill befits a mature adult. As if, were she [Shoshanna] able to keep quiet, it would all go away somehow. The truth is that I have to recognize that the bony outline of Shoshanna's stories is my bedrock. It is what I am built on. Willing to disappear would be to risk disappearing myself. In the end, is what Shoshanna has asked of me so terrible? She has made me into her audience, subjected me to a chain of words linked one to another. What I heard were anecdotes, attenuated memories—many I would rather have shut out—but still only stories. Yet the stories weren't stories when she lived them. They were real life, her life, demanding to be remembered. (261)

In conclusion, the study of the two exemplary Hungarian-Canadian memoirs undertaken in this project aims to address political and historical storytelling and thus the legacy the older generations pass onto the younger ones as a factor determining one's identity seen as an outcome of inherited memories, preserved stories, and family bonds. Both Anna Porter and Elaine Kalman Naves have been formed by the memories their families bestowed upon them. These shards of memories have been family stories but also political stories as both their families have been influenced by the events of the first half of the twentieth century and predominantly the 1956 Revolution in Hungary, which when bloodily quenched, was a point of departure for the families' emigrant histories. The narrative retracing these histories proves necessary to the formation and epistemology of one's identity as, according to Benedict Anderson, it is "a conception of personhood, *identity* ... which, because it cannot be 'remembered,' must be narrated" (Anderson 204 as qtd. in Smith 108).

This research was supported by grant UMO-2012/05/B/HS2/04004 from the Polish National Science Centre (Narodowe Centrum Nauki).

Works Cited

De Certeau, Michel. *The Practices of Everyday Life.* Tr. Steven F. Rendall. Berkeley: U of California P, 1984. Print.

Egan, Susanna and Gabriele Helms. "Life writing." Kröller 216–240. Print.

Kadar, Marlene. "Life Writing." New 660–666. Print.

Kalman Naves, Elaine. Shoshanna's Story. A Mother, a Daughter, and the Shadows of History. Lincoln: U of Nebraska P, 2006. Print.

Kröller, Eva-Marie, Ed. *The Cambridge Companion to Canadian Literature.* Cambridge: Cambridge UP, 2004. Print.

Miller, Nancy. 1996. *Bequest and Betrayal. Memoirs of a Parent's Death.*Bloomington: Indiana UP. Print.

New, W.H., Ed. *Encyclopedia of Literature in Canada.* Toronto: U of Toronto P, 2002. Print.

Ondaatje, Michael. *The English Patient.* London and Basingstoke: Picador, 1993. Print.

Porter, Anna. *The Storyteller. Memory, Secrets, Magic and Lies. A Memoir of Hungary.* Toronto: Anchor, 2001, Print.

—. *The Ghosts of Europe. Journeys Through Central Europe's Troubled Past and Uncertain Future.* Vancouver and Toronto: Douglas&McIntyre, 2010. Print.

Richards, Linda L. "Interview with Anna Porter." *January Magazine.* http://www.januarymagazine.com/profiles/aporter.html. 15 July 2014. Web.

Smith, Sidonie. "Performativity, Autobiographical Practice, Resistance." Smith and Watson 108–115. Print.

Smith, Sidonie and Julia Watson. Eds. *Women, Autobiography, Theory. A Reader.* Madison: U of Wisconsin P, 1998. Print.

Winslow, Donald J. *Life-Writing. A Glossary of Terms in Biography, Autobiography, and Related Forms.* Honolulu: U of Hawaii P, 1995. Print.

From Autobiography to Storytelling: The Works of C.S. Lewis

Daniel Warzecha

C.S. Lewis (1898–1963), the famous mid-twentieth century Anglo-Irish Christian apologist and novelist, was a prolific writer. He wrote about 12,000 pages. He did not fit in a pigeonhole: he was a poet, a scholar and don, a literary critic, an apologist, a lecturer, a novelist, and a letter writer. He was a passionate Christian apologist who was in love with books, words, and stories. He was also a rigorous thinker who could have been a philosopher.

Interestingly enough, Lewis's literary works unfolded within a dense, diverse and continuous autobiographical space. Autobiography was part and parcel of his aesthetic and apologetic stance, approach and strategy. As soon as he became a new convert to Christianity he started his career as a writer with an allegorical confession and defence of Christianity justified theologically and philosophically. He wrote a palimpsest of John Bunyan's Pilgrim's Progress which Lewis entitled *The Pilgrim's Regress: An Allegorical Apology for Christianity, Reason and Romanticism* (1933). Twenty three years later the confirmed novelist felt the need to revisit his childhood and youth from aesthetic and spiritual viewpoints while paying tribute to all the thinkers, writers, and mentors who had impacted on him, and he wrote *Surprised by Joy: The Shape of my Early Life* (1955). At the end of his life, devastated by his beloved's death, the old apologist meditated on the psychological and spiritual repercussions of death. Under a pseudonym he wrote *A Grief Observed* (1961).

Autobiographical material (also to be found in his numerous letters) became the source out of which Lewis wrote his fiction. To understand the writer, one must bear in mind that important things happened in his life, and he felt a compelling need to share them with his friends, students, pen friends, and an increasing number of readers. Lewis pondered on what happened to him and theorized about some of the essential events and intellectual influences that shaped his mind and contributed to making what he was to become as a person and as a writer. He theorized about some ideas and causes that were to become the key-themes he developed in his essays that were and fictionalized in his novels and stories. For example, education is a case in point. Several chapters in *Surprised by Joy* are devoted to Lewis's education. He attended public schools in Northern Ireland and England but finished his secondary education with a private tutor. And he analyzed the pros and cons of both systems. When he was young, Lewis was particularly influenced by the imaginary world of William Morris, John Milton, and George MacDonald who "baptized his imagination" (*Surprised by Joy* 140). Lewis then developed the idea that 'good' and 'bad' literature will influence young people positively or negatively. He criticized what he considered as alienating education (in a famous essay called "The Abolition of Man") and he illustrated the same idea in *That Hideous Strength* through the Studdock couple who had been distorted in their minds because of the 'wrong' and 'bad' books they had read as children. The same remark could be made about Eustace, the main hero of *The Voyage of the Dawn Treader*. Straight away he is depicted as an unpleasant character because of three factors: family background, school, and books. His parents "were very up-to-date and advanced people. They were vegetarians, non-smokers and tee-totallers" (7). He went to the wrong kind of school ('model schools') and read the wrong books ('books of information', 7). So as a storyteller Lewis considered that it was his duty to 'irrigate the deserts' of his young readers by telling them exciting, captivating, and edifying stories.

From all the major decisive influences and events that are to be found in his autobiographical books and illustrated in his fiction, the most decisive one is his religious conversion.

One must bear in mind that Lewis's career as a writer, thinker and storyteller really coincided with a founding experience which had a resounding effect throughout his life, i.e. Lewis's (re)conversion to Anglican Christianity in the late 1920s. What did that experience consist in? Conversio in Latin means "a reversal, a turning back, a change of direction." The word stems from two Greek words with a different meaning: epistrophê means that one takes a new direction (a return to the origin or to oneself) and metanoia means changing one's thought, repentance. It implies ideas of change and new birth. Thus epistrophê implies a new lifestyle whereas metanoia implies a new mindset.

Unlike Saint Augustine or Saul of Tarsus on his way to Damascus, Lewis did not undergo a subita conversio ('sudden'). Rather, it was a long, deep and complex process involving simultaneously an aesthetic and spiritual preparation and quest and intellectual debates with himself and his friends. But paradoxically enough, feelings were strangely absent in his conversion process. Or so are we told because in autobiography any writer sheds a retrospective light on some aspects of his/her life that he/she has carefully chosen to disclose while leaving other parts of his/her life in the shade.

Although he was brought up in the Anglican Church when he was a child, in his teens Lewis turned to a sort of agnosticism. That period lasted till he was in his late twenties. In 1929 the young don had a few good friends and colleagues who turned out to be Christians. They questioned his atheism and influenced him. Eventually Lewis gave in, reluctantly. As he puts it in his second spiritual autobiography:

> You must picture me alone in that room at Magdalen, night after night, whenever my mind lifted even for a second from my work, the steady, unrelenting approach of Him whom I so earnestly desired not to meet. That which I feared had at last come upon me. In the Trinity Term of 1929 I gave in, and admitted that God was God, and knelt and prayed: perhaps, that night the most dejected and reluctant convert in all England. (*Surprised by Joy* 178)

At that time, Lewis became a theist. Two years later as he was going to a zoo, he became a Christian. He reported the event in a factual, unemotional way: "When we set out I did not believe that Jesus Christ is the Son of God, and when we reached the zoo, I did" (184–5).

The description of the inner process is well illustrated in *The Pilgrim's Regress*. Like St Augustine in his *Confessions*, Lewis felt the urgent need to explain and justify his renewed faith but he chose to tell it in an allegorical way. The book is a mix of autobiography, poetry, fiction, philosophy, theology, and biblical exegesis.

He fictionalized his conversion experience by describing the story of John the pilgrim who, like his archetype, Christian, in Bunyan's *The Pilgrim's Progress*, journeys from his homeland called Puritania seeking an island and unconsciously returning home, his journey describing a full circle. But during the journey while John meets a lot of allegorical figures with whom he talks (Reason, Wisdom, History, Contemplation (for poetry), Mother Kirk (standing for the Church in its broad sense), a man (standing for Christ), he becomes a Christian.

Besides, *Pilgrim's Regress* functions as a matrix-book in which one finds all the key-ideas, leitmotivs, themes and metaphors that will be developed throughout Lewis's succeeding works.

Explaining it that way was probably not fully satisfying. It satisfied one's intellect but did not account for the emotional dimension of the conversion process. Moreover, allegory and metaphysical and intellectual debates could only appeal to a limited number of intellectuals and educated people. Lewis resorted to two other ways of writing about himself: a more conventional autobiography and fiction. In *Surprised by Joy*, Lewis warns: "The book aims at telling the story of [his] conversion and is not a general autobiography, still less 'Confessions' like those of St Augustine or Rousseau" (p. ix). Yet, interestingly enough as St Augustine's *Confessions* is fundamental for an understanding of its author's turn of mind, in the same way Lewis's aesthetic and spiritual autobiographies are retrospectively fundamental as they shed light on his state of mind as a fiction writer.

So another way of understanding that major event of conversion seen from a phenomenological point of view was to describe and illustrate it through fiction. The most striking and graphic example is Mark and Jane Studdock, the main protagonists of *That Hideous Strength*. They happen to be involved in two opposite camps: Mark gets employed by the N.I.C.E., National Institute of Co-ordinated Experiments, a so-called scientific institution which really prepares a kind of dictatorship, whereas his wife, Jane, gets involved in the opposite organization (the Pendragon led by Ransom, a kind of Arthurian, Christ-like figure). But both Mark and Jane undergo a complete change of state of mind. Mark finally understands the real purpose of the N.I.C.E he has been working for and turns from atheism to deism. His conversion is more intellectual. His wife becomes a Christian as well but her conversion is more emotional. What happens inside them is compared to an inner cataclysm, a kind of earthquake. Something has been 'shaken,' 'unmade' or 'overturned,' words used by the writer to describe the state of mind of three female characters who went through an inner transformation: Jane Studdock (*That Hideous Strength*), Orual (*Till We Have Faces*) and Camilla Bembridge (*The Dark Tower*).

Conversion is a complex process comprehending heart and mind, emotions and intellect. Furthermore, conversion can be accounted for by various factors or parameters: childhood, literary influences, determining encounters and places.

Childhood

For Lewis, childhood was a time of happiness and blessings, filled with enriching aesthetic discoveries and emotions. That is why all his life he remained in love with childhood and could bequeath unputdownable children's stories to generations of young readers. As George Sayer, one of his biographers wrote, "without this ability to recall and live imaginatively in the world of childhood, Jack could never have become a great writer of stories for children" (*Jack* 139). His awakening to beauty occurred as he discovered what he called *joy*, a word borrowed from Wordsworth. For Lewis it was a strong aesthetic and spiritual feeling that became a quest and a leitmotiv as recalled in *Surprised by Joy* and in *The Chronicles of Narnia*. *Joy* was first triggered by a toy garden his brother Warren had made for him. The toy garden brought about an intense poetic sentiment in the child's imagination. That feeling was then reinforced after reading Beatrix Potter's *Squirrel Nutkin* and above all after seeing the Arthur Rackham's picture of *Siegfried and the Twilight of the Gods*. It brought about a fascination for 'northernness,' not so much a geographic place but a strong poetic emotion for an imaginary world. Lewis explored and amplified that leitmotiv in some of Narnia stories. From childhood, Lewis did not only inherit unforgettable memories but also immeasurable suffering with the death of his mother when he was nine. He did not mention it at all in *Pilgrim's Regress*. He discreetly referred to it in *Surprised by Joy*. He revisited the tragic event by incorporating it as an element of the plot in *The Magician's Nephew*, the first story of the Chronicles of Narnia. Digory Kirk rescues and heals his dying mother by bringing a magic apple from Narnia. Although the event is dealt with poetically and fictionally, it functioned as a kind of therapy for the writer.

Literary Influences

Lewis's scope of reading was vast, his library was enormous, and his taste eclectic. It ranged from thinkers of antiquity, Church fathers, medieval writers to seventeenth-century metaphysical poets, nineteenth-century romantics and twentieth-century theologians and apologists. In addition, Lewis could simultaneously enjoy German philosophers and children's tales, science-fiction novels and railway station literature. It would be impossible to mention all his literary influences. In what follows I will just mention the most determining ones, those that prepared his mind and psyche to receive the Christian message again.

In his late twenties Lewis had read or re-read Milton's *Paradise Lost* (1674). Lewis was fascinated by "Milton's 'enormous bliss' of Eden" (*Surprised by Joy* 11). He was struck by the beauty and power stemming from of the poet's verses as he evoked spiritual realities: heaven, hell, evil, angels, mankind lost and redeemed.

William Morris (1834–1896) books played a determining role in shaping and influencing Lewis' imagination. He had read all of his works. He compared the reading experience of William Morris to a 'revival'. It contributed to reactivate the 'joy' and the 'magic' he had already discovered elsewhere.

In April 1918, Lewis was in a French hospital recuperating from a wound in his lung received in the trenches. He discovered Chesterton's essays.[1] Even though Lewis did not support or accept the content of his books, he was immediately seduced by the famous English apologist, more precisely by his style and humour. He qualified the discovery as 'providential':

George Macdonald's *Phantastes, a Faerie Romance* (1858)[2] exerted perhaps the most decisive influence on Lewis's psyche. He picked it up at a railway bookstall. The fantasy book encapsulated all that Lewis had enjoyed elsewhere; he found again the 'joy' he had been seeking. The book conjured up memories of his mother and baptized his imagination. Lewis encountered holiness.

The reading process cannot be dissociated from the writing one. All Lewis' ideas, mental pictures extracted from his readings, dreams or fantasies were bubbling up inside him trying to get out and eventually took different forms: poems (not very successful), essays, novels, children's stories, scholarly studies, and letters (real and fictionalized). Fiction is probably the most significant form. Similarly, just as Lewis' imagination was baptised, he wanted to 'baptise' his reader's imagination by creating an intellectual, imaginary and spiritual atmosphere so as to prepare him, too, to receive the Christian message. His works functioned as a *preaparatio evangelica*.

---

[1] Gilbert Keith Chesterton (1874–1936) was a poet, a journalist, a biographer, a novelist and a Christian apologist. Father Brown, the main character of his police novels, made him famous.

[2] George Macdonald (1824–1905) was a Scottish author, poet, and Christian minister. He was a pioneering figure in the field of fantasy literature.

Determining Encounters

In *Surprised by Joy* three chapters are devoted to determining encounters, life-long friendships and enriching relationships. One chapter, entitled 'The Great Knock,' is devoted to his teacher Kirkpatrick, a great intellectual figure who shaped the young boy's intellect by his rigor. Kirk, as he was nicknamed, never took anything for granted. He used to put reason above all things. In the *Pilgrim's Regress* reason is allegorized as a woman. She delivers John who is captive in a prison kept by a giant. Lewis also revisited his teacher Kirkpatrick through some well-depicted characters: Professor Kirke in *The Magician's Nephew* and some scholars in *That Hideous Strength* whose function was to question reality and discover what lies below the surface of things.

Lewis had life-long friends among whom his own brother. Warren was his best friend. From an early age onwards, the two brothers shared the same joys, hardships and suffering. As Lewis became a famous novelist and apologist, Warren was his secretary who typed all his brother's letters. Most of them have now been archived in *The Lewis Papers*. Arthur Greeves, Lewis's neighbour in Northern Ireland, comes second. Their friendship lasted for 50 years. He was one of his most faithful pen friends. Arthur was, as Lewis put it, his *alter ego*. They shared the same taste for Northern mythology. Arthur taught him what Lewis lacked: simplicity, humility, and homeliness (a mixture of ordinary things and holiness). Arthur's homeliness provided Lewis with a source of inspiration in his fiction in which he 'glorified' ordinary and down-to-earth people who turned out to be unlikely heroes.

In the list of determining encounters, Owen Barfield (1898–1997) came third. He was the opposite of Lewis who called him the 'anti-self.' They used to argue about philosophical and metaphysical issues. Barfied was an anthroposophist and a spiritualist who also played an important role in Lewis' mental and intellectual evolution even though he did not share his friend's taste for the occult. Barfield helped him to accept spirituality.

Among all his peers, some figures are worth mentioning: Charles Williams (1886–1945), Nevill Coghill (1899–1980), Hugo Dyson (1896–1975), and J.R.R. Tolkien (1892–1973). All these dons and writers whom Lewis regularly met for years happened to be Christians too, Christians from different denominations. J.R.R. Tolkien drew Lewis's attention to one relevant question related to myth and mythology. He asked him why he could accept the idea of dying gods like Adonis or Balder and at the same time refused the idea of a dying Christ. The argument hit the target. The myth issue was central in Lewis' understanding of Christianity. Indeed throughout his apologetics Lewis developed the idea that Christ is the great Myth 'incarnated' in human history. The factual and historical event had been already prepared, prefigured and announced in pagan mythology. As *The Pilgrim's Regress* put it "even Pagan mythology contained a Divine call" (189). In the last chapter of *Surprised by Joy*, Lewis claims that "Paganism had been only the childhood of religion, or only a prophetic dream" (183). By Lewis' question, "where has religion reached its true maturity?" (183), the reader is led to understand that Christianity is religion in its true maturity.

Places

One could mention several places that marked Lewis's personality and influenced his works: Ireland with its beautiful landscapes, but also many places in England among which Oxford where so many good things happened to Lewis. He spent almost all of his adult life there. He met his peers and friends on a regular basis during World War II within the Inklings, an informal literary society. When he got a permanent post at Oxford University, Lewis eventually bought with his brother a property called 'The Kilns' in the suburbs of Oxford. He lived there for over 30 years.

More generally, Lewis delighted in the countryside (as opposed to the town). He would take long walks in the Irish, Scottish and English countryside alone or with friends during the school or summer holidays. Each time it would cause ecstatic feelings. Lewis loved to behold landscapes for a long while. He would then transpose these mental descriptions into poetic verse, or poetic prose embedded in his autobiographical or fictional works.

Throughout Lewis's fiction one is struck by the predominance of nature with all sorts of varied landscapes. But these natural scenes do not function as a mere backdrop. In Lewisian fiction nature operates in four directions: it co-operates in God's Providence as an accomplice, so as God's servant it reveals, it warns and it takes revenge. As the protagonists (like the children in *The Chronicles* or Ransom in Malacandra or John in *The Pilgrim's Regress*) evolve in the middle of these landscapes, something happens to them and in them. For example, in *The Pilgrim's Regress* nature is clearly depicted as the accomplice of a divine plan. That is why it "deceives" the pilgrim who is attracted and seduced first by the sight of an island and secondly by the sight of mountains which appear to be a decoy, a delusion. But they kindle his desire and fuel his quest. But eventually nature brings John back to Puritania and to the Landlord without his knowing it. Moreover, as testified in many Lewis's letters, nature gives rise to aesthetic experiences which prepare the awakening of the spiritual (like spiritual foretastes). Nature functions as a pointer to what is happening inside the poet.

In a nutshell, like for seventeenth century's metaphysical poets (Herbert, Donne, Traherne), nature functions as a book. It is meaningful. It conveys and delivers messages to the pilgrims (*The Pilgrim's Regress*), to the poet during his long walks and to the protagonists in his fiction. There is a consubstantial relationship between nature and what they experience. This idea stems from a theological notion that nature, being God's creature, participates in God's will either as a tool, as a pointer or even as a weapon (with which God will punish the wicked).[3]

Conclusion

Most of Lewis's fiction was devoted to an exploration and illustration of the idea that culture (literature, paintings, music, arts) provides indicators of something greater and higher. The quest for 'joy' in *Surprised by Joy* is a metaphor of that. At the end of his second autobiography, Lewis confessed that "the subject has lost nearly all interest for me since I became a Christian (…) it was only valuable as a pointer to something other and outer" (185).

In an essay called *Christianity and Culture*, Lewis wrote that even though "culture is not everyone's road to Jerusalem (…) "culture has a distinct part to play in bringing certain souls to Christ. Not all souls (…) "(29). Lewis was one of those souls. He continued: "Has [culture] any part in the life of the converted?" For him it happened to be true. How?

> If all the cultural values, on the way up to Christianity, were dim antepasts and ectypes of the truth, we can recognize them as such still. And since we must rest and play, where can we do so better than here— in the suburbs of Jerusalem? It is lawful to rest our eyes in moonlight— especially now that we know where it comes from, that it is only sunlight at second hand. (29)

This paragraph metaphorically encapsulates Lewis's conception and vocation as a writer and apologist. 'Joy' (as explained in *Surprised by Joy*) was the foretaste of something greater and higher. Mythology (largely developed in *The Pilgrim's Regress*) was the copy of the original, which is greater and

---

[3] Feverstone is a case in point. He experiences a descent into hell. The earth literally swallows him (*That Hideous Strength* 736).

higher. So Lewis considered it to be his 'mission' in his fiction to point to these foretastes, to highlight these copies, and emphasize these marks. His literature functions as 'a pointer to something other and outer'. But it would be unfair to qualify it as propaganda. The reader is free to 'rest and play' there. He can enjoy the stories for themselves. *The Chronicles of Narnia* are above all 'good' stories. The same could be said for the Cosmic Trilogy. *The Screwtape's Letters* is a very enjoyable book. The reader can choose to stay in the 'suburbs of Jerusalem in other words approach the Divine. But coming nearer is not necessarily encountering. To use another metaphor expressed by Aslan in the last pages of *The Last Battle*, the reader is invited to "come further in and further up" (165). But here literature ends and life begins.

Works Cited

Lewis, Clive Staples. *The Pilgrim's Regress, an Allegorical Apology for Christianity, Reason and Romanticism*.1933. London: Fount, 1998. Print.

—. *The Dark Tower*, 1938. [Unfinished by Lewis]. Ed. Walter Hooper. London: Collins, 1977. 17–91. Print.

—. *The Screwtape's Letters: Letters from a Senior to a Junior Devil*. 1942. London: Harper Collins, 1998. Print.

—. 'Christianity and Culture' (1940) in *Christian Reflections*. London: Fount Harper Collins, 1998. 14–45. Print.

—. *The Abolition of Man or Reflections on Education with Special Reference to the Teaching of English in the Upper forms of School*. 1943. Nashville: Broadman & Holman, 1996. Print.

—. *The Magician's Nephew*. London: Bodley Head, 1955. Print.

—. *Surprised by Joy, the Shape of my Early Life*. London: Geoffrey Bles, 1955. Print.

—. *Till We Have Faces: A Myth Retold*. London: Geoffrey Bles, 1956. Print.

—. *The Last Battle*. London: Geoffrey Bles, 1956. Print.

—. *A Grief Observed*. London: Faber & Faber, 1961. Print.

Sayer, George. *Jack: Lewis and His Times*. San Francisco: Harper & Row, 1988. Print.

Avoiding Self-Centered Fairytales:
Autobiographies by Female Singer-Songwriters

Daniela Chana

Singer-songwriters claim authenticity. This is underpinned by personal statements in interviews, for instance, when Tori Amos explains that most of the songs on her album *From the Choirgirl Hotel* (1998) have been inspired by the pain after her sad experience of miscarriage (Pareles, "At Lunch with Tori Amos"). As the audience at a concert knows that the artist onstage has written and composed the songs herself or himself, an intimate feeling is created. While this does not necessarily mean that all the songs are autobiographic, or that the artist might not have followed market interests, it still appears more authentic if the audience at a concert is able to look into the face of the person who wrote the words.

If thoughts and feelings are to a large extent shared with the audience through the music already, what is the real task of an autobiography? Moreover, how can the danger of self-centrism be avoided? Tori Amos and Patti Smith have both found ways to deal with this issue. Although their books address very intimate autobiographic details, they lack chronological accounts of a life-story or a career path. Amos' *Piece by Piece* (2005) and Smith's *Just Kids* (2010) are innovative in form and content, so that readers may even hesitate to call these books "autobiographies." In this paper, I will discuss both books in detail and point out the strategies both artists use in order to avoid self-centrism.

Tori Amos, born in 1963, is an American singer-songwriter who combines sophisticated piano compositions with complex lyrics. Her songs often show references to various mythologies (mostly Greek archetypes) and literary classics. They examine the role of women and men in different cultures, the dark sides of relationships, various facets of sexuality, violence, and religion. Among her work are several concept albums, such as *Boys for*

Pele (1996) or *Scarlet's Walk* (2002), in which one dominant topic can be traced throughout the songs of the record. Being open to artistic experimentation, she also recorded an album with variations on classic composers called *The Night of Hunters* (2010), and she is the author of the musical *The Light Princess* (2012). Her live performances are extraordinarily intense and emotional as Amos is hammering and beating the piano while she screams, whispers, and moans. In 2005, she published her autobiographical book *Piece by Piece*, co-written with music journalist Ann Powers.

Piece by Piece is not structured like a narrative but rather like a compendium. It assembles fragments of conversations between Tori Amos and music journalist Ann Powers, essayistic and philosophic reflections by the artist, comments on the origins of song lyrics, quotes from people who are close to her, photographs, and artwork. Eight chapters divide the book into thematic sections, like an encyclopedia. Each of them has its own focus: genealogy, sexuality, composition, motherhood, the act of creation, life on the road, fame, and the music business. These topics are approached in an essayistic way as Amos and Powers are throwing light on them from different angles. The artist shares her thoughts and explains her autobiographic connection to them, while her voice is continuously interrupted by snippets of conversations with Ann Powers and quotes from her friends and relatives. As a result, the focus shifts from a self-centered artists' biography to a complex philosophic discussion by myriads of voices.

Although *Piece by Piece* is no genuine autobiography, it contains several very intimate insights into Amos' life. One particularly touching passage is the chapter in which Amos talks with surprising openness about her miscarriages. A long passage is written by her doctor who explains in detail the medical reasons for these horrible experiences (*Piece* 174–76). Afterwards, Amos describes how her Native American roots helped her to cope with her enormous grief. We learn that after her second miscarriage, she lay down on the beach and remembered that the Native Americans regarded Earth as a mother. "I laid myself on the earth and the message came to me. The earth said, "Surrender this to me. You've lost a few babies. I lose babies every day. I understand this pain. So trust me. Give this to me." And I almost felt as if the earth and I became blood sisters" (171).

Whenever Amos tells a personal story in her book, it is not for exhibitionistic purposes but for a deeper reason. It is important to note that this account of her dialogue with Mother Earth can be used as a key to understand Amos' music. Many of the songs she released throughout her career show tongue-in-cheek references to her "Indian blood"[1] or draw on this close bond to nature as a heritage from her Native American roots. The most recent example is the song "Oysters" which has been released on Amos' 2014 album *Unrepentant Geraldines*. It tells the story of a woman who can confront her deep pain and despair only by turning oysters in the sand and finding that "not every girl is a pearl." The resemblance to the autobiographic scene Amos described in *Piece by Piece* is striking. After having read the book, the deeper philosophic meaning of "Oysters" is much easier to grasp.

In *Piece by Piece*, Amos shares her detailed thoughts on some issues which are reoccurring and crucial in her songs as well. One dominant topic in her songwriting from the beginning of her career until today is the suppression of female sexuality in Catholic societies. An early song of hers, "Icicle" from her second album *Under the Pink* (1996), for instance, tells the story of a girl who is masturbating during an Easter celebration. The lyrics of "Icicle" contain a harsh criticism of patriarchal structures when referring to the Bible as a book that is "missing some pages." In *Piece by Piece*, Amos explains in more detail what these missing pages are: She expresses her uneasiness about her impression that any hint at female sexuality has been erased from the Scripture (68–69). According to her, this is one of the reasons why women are lacking power in Christian societies until today: being ashamed of their sexuality, they suppress any drive that could make them strong and self-empowered in other contexts as well (68–69). In order to underpin her arguments, Amos explains the autobiographical background of "Icicle," admitting that she herself had erotic fantasies about Jesus in her early youth (68–69). This revelation as well serves a higher end as she in the following uses the example of Jesus to illustrate her idea of the ideal husband, "a guy who wants a complete partnership with a woman" (71). Her personal statement thus is embedded in a socio-critical context, serving as a comment on the relationship between men and women.

Amos also writes about Greek mythology which is an important point of reference in her song lyrics. Already in her early works, like the album *From the Choirgirl Hotel* (1998),[2] as well as on more recent records, like *American Doll Posse* (2007), Amos examines the female archetypes that are repre-

---

[1] One of the many examples is: Tori Amos. 'Scarlet's Walk', from *Scarlet's Walk*. © 2002 by Epic, Sony Music Entertainment Inc., 5087829. Compact disc.
[2] The most obvious example on this record, as the reference is already made in the song title, is certainly 'Pandora's Aquarium', from *From the Choirgirl Hotel*. © 1998 by Atlantic Recording Corporation. 7567830952. Compact disc.

sented in Greek goddesses.[3] She uses them as a source to understand today's complex relationships between men and women. In her book, she expresses her belief that the old archetypes are still active today. In her view, women define themselves according to the myths and take on the roles of, for instance, Demeter or Persephone, even if they are not consciously aware of them (*Piece by Piece* 6–7) In *Piece by Piece*, Amos uses herself as an example and talks about past relationships (72–74) in order to illustrate her philosophic ideas. Hence, private facts and intimate details are only given when they contribute to the understanding of Amos' songs and reflections.

Apart from disclosing the philosophical background of her lyrics, she also dedicates long passages of her book to the process of composition and the hard work it includes. She is very honest about the difficulties as well as the coincidental aspects of the process:

> There are times when I'm doing lots and lots of research, and I'll start gathering words and phrases form various sources—books, conversations, visual art. I'll start pulling my references out, and I have no idea which ones will prove useful. I'll just start jotting down ideas. I can do that for hours, but a lot of it is a load of crap. I can play piano for myself for hours. It's nonsense, most of it. [...] Within a few hours, maybe a rhythm pattern will arise. (107–108)

In addition, Amos emphasizes that songwriting does not start with creation but rather with the opposite: taking something in.

> [T]he songs are separate from me. Yes, I write them; I gather the elements. But I do so by going around and listening to other people's stories. I watch the audience; I study how people react to what I've already created, and that also goes into new songs. It's like being a chronicler, instead of being just somebody who invents. (2)

This modesty can also be found in Patti Smith's book *Just Kids* (2010). Smith (born in 1946) is an American poet and singer-songwriter who combines a rock and roll sound with self-revealing and confessional lyrics

---

[3] More detailed reflections on Amos' game with archetypes on the album *American Doll Posse* can be found in several other papers of mine, for instance: Daniela Chana, 'Celebrating the Pain—Female Singer-Songwriters and the Beauty of Gloomy Images', Paper presented at the *4th Global Conference: Making Sense of: Pain*. (Michna Palace, Prague, 9–11 May 2013), URL: http://www.inter-disciplinary.net/probing-the-boun daries/making-sense-of/pain/conference-programme-abstracts-and-papers/session-8-voices-managing-coping-with-and-celebratingpain/, 13 June 2014. Web.

influenced by classic poets, such as Arthur Rimbaud (Smith, *Just Kids* 23). In her songs, she often uses religious imagery next to a naughty vocabulary while dealing with sexuality,[4] love, or precarious life and working conditions.[5] She is a charismatic performer and had one of her biggest hits with the single "Because the Night," a duet with Bruce Springsteen in 1978.

Unlike Amos' *Piece by Piece*, Smith's book follows the structure of a narrative. It begins *in medias res* with the death of her close friend Robert Mapplethorpe in 1989. Right from the start, Smith uses a very sentimental language that illustrates the deep pain of this loss. In the foreword, for instance, she describes how she woke up from her sleep and felt that Mapplethorpe had died already shortly before she received the message of his death (*Just Kids* XI). This is typical for the spiritual and emotional tone she keeps throughout the book. Hence, it is clear already from the first pages that the aim of this narrative is not self-praise or self-aggrandizement. Instead, it focuses on the story of the relationship between two human beings, two artists.

In the following, we find a brief account of Smith's childhood and early youth. Even these passages are not self-centered. Rather to the contrary, they emphasize her strong religious belief (4–5), her upbringing and education (4–12), and the special conditions of life for a teenage girl in America in the 1960s. When Smith, for instance, talks about the horrible consequences of an unwanted teenage pregnancy (17–18), there is an obvious focus on the socio-cultural dimension. Tension is created by a few facts about Robert Mapplethorpe's youth and family background which are woven into the narrative at several points. Hence, in this first chapter of the book, both artists' early years are narrated simultaneously as in a double biography. Since the readers know that at some point these two still separate lives will meet, there is a certain sentimental or even romantic dimension, indicating that Smith is not the only protagonist of this story. She is just one half that will find the second half as the narrative continues. Already in these passages at the beginning, Smith directly refers to Mapplethorpe's early experiments with drugs during his teenage years (20–21). As a result, his appearance in this book right from the start is connected with danger and death, giving him the appeal of a very romantic and tragic character.

---

[4] For instance: Patti Smith, 'Dancing Barefoot', from *Easter*. © 1996 [1978] by Arista Records, Inc., BMG Entertainment. 07822188262. Compact disc.
[5] For instance: Patti Smith, 'Piss Factory', from *Land (1975–2002)*, Disc 2, © 2013 [2002] by Arista Records, Inc., Sony Music Entertainment. 88883772352. Compact disc.

Their chance encounter in 1967 is described in a very romantic way. Mapplethorpe appears as a savior who enters her life as she is homeless and almost starving because she does not have enough money to pay for food. They meet in the bookstore in which Smith has found a job. As he is about to buy the Persian necklace that Smith would have liked for herself, they start a conversation (36–37). The very same night, they coincidently meet again in the street, and Mapplethorpe saves her from a man who pesters her (38). Soon they discover their shared interest in art and poetry and how they are both driven by the ambition to create something that will last. As they are both sensitive, creative, and full of high hopes, they are immediately drawn to each other. Although he is poor and jobless himself, Mapplethorpe knows a place where they can share a room (39).

They live together like a couple for six years, although Mapplethorpe soon becomes aware of his homosexuality (77). The close bond between them remains even as they go their separate ways in the 1970s as Smith is getting married, founding a family and becoming a successful musician while Mapplethorpe follows his career path as a photographer. Nevertheless, the narrative breaks off when they are moving into separate apartments in 1972 and is only taken up again in 1986 when Smith is pregnant with her second child and learns about Mapplethorpe's infection with HIV (265). Almost nothing is said about the progress of Smith's career as the leader of a world famous rock and roll band in the meantime. As indicated above, *Just Kids* is a book about a deep, life-long friendship, and not about a star, or about a career. The closing chapter focuses on the last encounters between both artists before Mapplethorpe dies from AIDS in 1989. An appendix assembles photographs and a few poems Smith wrote in memory of her friend.

Throughout the book, we find Smith hiding behind Mapplethorpe. The black-and-white cover photograph of the British edition shows Smith and her friend side by side. They are so close together that their heads are touching. The choice of this picture emphasizes the book's focus on the relationship between the two artists as well as their equal status. As they are both holding their heads in a similar angle, they almost appear like twins. On the back cover, we see them kissing. In the kiss, both faces become one, which makes the individual only half visible.

In the narrative of the book, Smith shows enormous respect for her friend and often seems to politely take a step back. While she constantly emphasizes her own insecurities and self-ascribed lack of talent (12), she turns Mapplethorpe into a legend. She presents him as the bigger artist, the one who is more haunted by a creative force. "We were both dreamers, but

Robert was the one who got things done. I made the money but he had drive and focus. He had plans for himself but for me as well" (127).

In addition, Smith is very modest and generally describes her career as something that happened to her rather coincidentally. She emphasizes that the creative process is not a one-woman-show. Mapplethorpe in this context almost takes on a parenting role: "Everything distracted me, but most of all myself. Robert would come over to my side of the loft and scold me" (152). Her friend is portrayed as the one who provides stability when she is paralyzed by insecurities and crisis:

> Why commit to art? For self-realization, or for itself? [...] I wondered if anything I did mattered. Robert had little patience with these introspective bouts of mine. He never seemed to question his artistic drives, and by his example, I understood that what matters is the work. (65)

Her modesty goes so far that she even expresses feelings of guilt in connection with her success. About her first poetry reading which brought her many offers for further readings and publications, she writes: "It came, I felt, too easy. Nothing had come to Robert so easily." (182) As indicated above, the years of Smith's biggest success as a musician in the 1970s are completely missing in the book.

Smith's book serves as a very detailed and vivid description of the art and music scene in New York City in the 1960s and 1970s. The readers are drawn into a realm of young and creative people who are struggling to survive under difficult circumstances in a dangerous environment. At the beginning, Smith is introduced to us as a 20-year-old woman sleeping on the street, unable to afford buying food, and willing to do almost any job (26). She finds work in a bookstore, but still can't afford an apartment, so she takes to sleeping in the store (37). Later, when she lives with Mapplethorpe, they struggle enormously in order to afford food and art supply:

> Often we'd stand in the cold on the corner of St. James Place in eyeshot of the Greek diner and Jake's art supply store, debating how to spend our few dollars—a toss-up between grilled cheese sandwiches and art supplies. Sometimes, unable to distinguish the greater hunger, Robert would keep nervous watch in the diner while I, filled with the spirit of Genet, pocketed the much-needed brass sharpener or colored pencils. (56–57)

New York in the 1960s is depicted as a rather wild and dangerous place. Smith vividly describes how one day, a young man gets murdered in front of their apartment (85). When Mapplethorpe suffers from a serious infection with high fever in 1969, they are not able to afford proper medical treatment and are lucky to find a doctor who allows them to postpone the payment (95).

As has been shown in this paper, Tori Amos and Patti Smith both find ways to avoid self-centered fairytales as they focus on thoughts and emotions. Both refrain from giving a chronological account of their career paths. Instead, they discuss philosophical or socio-cultural issues and put other people in the fore. Nevertheless, *Piece by Piece* as well as *Just Kids* allows intimate insights into both artists' lives. Although they contain autobiographic passages, it would be far too simple to call them "autobiographies."

Works Cited

Amos, Tori and Ann Powers. *Tori Amos: Piece by Piece. A Portrait of the Artist: Her Thoughts. Her Conversations*, London: Plexus, 2005. Print.

Amos, Tori. "Icicle." *Under the Pink*. © 1994 by East West Records, Warner Music UK Ltd. 7567-82567-2. Compact disc.

—. Oysters. "*Unrepentant Geraldines*. © 2014 by Mercury Classics, Decca Music Group Ltd., Universal Music Group, 0028948109029. Compact disc.

—. Pandora's Aquarium." *From the Choirgirl Hotel*. © 1998 by Atlantic Recording Corporation. 7567830952. Compact disc.

—. "Scarlet's Walk" *Scarlet's Walk*. © 2002 by Epic, Sony Music Entertainment Inc., 5087829. Compact disc.

Chana, Daniela. "Celebrating the Pain—Female Singer-Songwriters and the Beauty of Gloomy Images." Paper presented at the *4th Global Conference: Making Sense of: Pain*. (Michna Palace, Prague, 9–11 May 2013), URL: http://www.inter-disciplinary.net/probing-the-boundaries/making-sense-of/pain/conference-programme-abstracts-and-papers/session-8-voices-managing-coping-with-and-celebratingpain/, 13 June 2014. Web.

Pareles, John. "At Lunch with Tori Amos, Disclosing Intimacies, Enjoying the Shock Value." *The New York Times*, 23 April 1998, URL: http://www.yessaid.com/toriamos.html, 16 June 2014. Web.

Smith, Patti. "Dancing Barefoot."*Easter*. © 1996 [1978] by Arista Records, Inc., BMG Entertainment. 07822188262. Compact disc.

—. *Just Kids*, Bloomsbury: London, 2012. Print.

—. "Piss Factory." *Land* (1975-2002), Disc 2, © 2013 [2002] by Arista Records, Inc., Sony Music Entertainment. 88883772352. Compact disc.

Four Moments of Self-Recovery:
Postcoloniality, Odia Identity and Autobiography

Dipti R. Pattanaik

While discussing autobiographies that articulate native and indigenous consciousness, Gillian Whitlock in *The Intimate Empire* poses an important question about the genre of autobiography: "When does autobiography become active in the politics of identity? A discursive threshold must be reached before autobiographic writing appears as an agent. This is clearly not the case for each individual autobiographic act" (146).

This paper seeks to analyse four autobiographies in Odia, which to my mind have reached that discursive threshold and are accounts of self-recovery under a colonial/ postcolonial dispensation. Their authors were active cultural agents who played significant roles in the identity politics of Odia society thereby transforming the polarity between personalism and communalism. These autobiographies are Fakirmohan's *Atmacarita* (2010), the first of its kind in the Odia language, *Atmajibani* (1978) by Gopal Praharaj, Panikabinka *Atmakahani* (1985) by Baishnab Pani, and *Kalakarara Kahani* (2011) by Dinabandhu Das. I would like to argue in the course of the following essay that these four autobiographies represent four important personality traits that were manifested in the native subjects because of their interactions with colonial forms of knowledge and power. In my argument I have made the following assumptions: that autobiographies are a 'kind' of literature (Fowler 4) especially after Gusdorf's 1956 essay outlining the "Conditions and Limits of Autobiography"; that autobiographies are a construction like any other 'kind' of literature like the novel, epic, or essay; that writing of autobiography like that of history involves the selection of so-called 'facts', and 'events'; that this selection and narration is regulated by the interaction between the reigning belief system of the society concerned and the ideoloy of the autobiographer. Hence an assessment of the interaction between the social background and ideological imperatives underpinning the 'truths' depicted in the autobiographies can be made by deconstructing their structures.

By analysing the structures of autobiographies written in Odia, an attempt has been made in this paper to explain the sociological processes of Odia society in the twentieth century. Only four autobiographies with some degree of similarity among them have been analysed but the broad framework of my analysis can be employed in the reading of other Odia autobiographies as well. One link that connects these four autobiographies is their confessional tone. The other link about which I have hinted earlier is their authors' involvement in some way or other in the identity politics of the region. However, the most important thread that connects all of them is their response to the intrusion of colonial modernity in Odisha. It is a fact that autobiography as a literary genre in Odia, and confession as an aesthetic strategy in a written discourse received social sanction because of colonial transactions. Of course, confessional narratives can be found earlier in Odia written literature here and there as in *Dardhyata Bhakti* or *Bilwamangala Gatha*. The narrators in these poetic utterances are voluble about the worthlessness of their earlier sinful lives. The main purpose of these confessions was to highlight the radical difference between the authors' past sinful life and their present reformed life. The ideological imperative of all these confessions is the construction of a belief system which implies that even a fallen being caught in the web of sin and delusion can transcend himself and find divine life by opting for *bhakti* and spiritual knowledge. According to a powerful Hindu world-view that nurtures this belief system, every situation is the effect of a particular *karmic* configuration. According to this view conscious beings have free will and are free to choose their actions. The Divine is not a judge who dispenses punishment but an enabler in man's temporal and spiritual enterprise. Such an ideology might in all probability have inspired Fakirmohan, the first autobiographer in the Odia language. However, apart from that, the other most important inspiration, which has shaped the Odia episteme in early twentieth century, was colonial modernity.

Colonial modernity had a surreptitious entry into Odia episteme on the back of proselytizing enterprise of Christian missionaries after various parts of Odia speaking tracts were occupied by the colonial administration in the late eighteenth and early nineteenth centuries. The missionaries in order to spread the Words of God, encouraged literacy by establishing modern schools, printing press for the wide dispersal of the Words. They also introduced translational process to make those words available in the native language of Odia; they tried to systematise the native language by codifying grammatical principles, they also tried their hands at lexicography and so on.[1] Although they were more interested in proselytizing activities than in developing Odia cultural life, the introduction of these instruments of modernity galvanised the intellectual and literary life in Odisha. They were, however, marginally successful in their primary goal of converting people into Christianity although some of their broad principles became part of the public consciousness. The other powerful inspiration apart from the religious one, which the contemporary western life and social system exercised, was the democratic impulse.

On the one hand, the monocultural impulse and the so-called civilising mission was at the root of a hegemonic structure like colonialism and, on the other, the democratisation of power destabilised the foundations of old-world privileges. The traditional societies like Odisha which came under British colonial rule in late eighteenth and early nineteenth centuries were impacted by this many-layered modernity. The autobiographies under discussion repeatedly lay bare the complex relationship between tradition and modernity.

It has been hinted earlier that the first Odia autobiographer Fakirmohan might have been influenced by the confessional accounts of traditional Odia poetry like *Dardhyata Bhakti* and *Bilwamangalgatha*. But, more importantly, his autobiography is also, in its choice of subject matter, corpus of information and narrative style, a testament of the above mentioned complex interaction between tradition and modernity. In an earlier essay we have demonstrated how Fakirmohan's entire literary oeuvre is a balancing act between the acquired modernity and an inherited tradition.[2] From the point of view of that essay Fakirmohan's autobiography, which was penned at the very end of his literary career, can be seen as an effort to further his political and literary ideology.

The idea that the identity of a human being, whatever station in society he might have hailed from, is important in its significance for the larger corporate life is a sign of the democratisation of the society. Such an idea

---

[1] For more details about the process see Dash, Debendra K. & Dipti R. Pattanaik. "Missionary Position: The Irony of Translation Activism in Colonial Orissa" in *TTR* Vol. Xviii No. 2. Montreal (2005).

[2] For more details see Debendra Dash and Dipti R. Pattanaik. "The Tradition-Modernity Dialectic in Six Acres and a Third" in *Colonialism, Modernity and Literature: A View from India* (Ed. Staya P. Mohanty). New York: Palgrave Macmillan, 2011. Print. pp. 207–228.

might have been one of the sources of inspiration for the proliferation of the autobiography genre in Odia in the twentieth century. It is true that colonisation had redrawn the power equations in traditional society. The traditional system of access to power and privilege by birth and lineage was constricted. Along with that, another group, either through its merit, shrewdness or through the ability to compromise with the colonial structures, had usurped the positions of power. Most of that group had internalised the western mode of education and cultural mores. Often they exercised their power over the common folk as sub-colonial hegemonists. The oppression of Odisha at the hands of the Bengali elites from the nearby province is a manifestation of such a process. Fakirmohan's autobiography is a representation and a radical critique of that process. On the one hand Fakirmohan criticised the sub-colonising attitude of the neighbouring Bengalis and the British colonialism, which spawned it in the first place and, on the other he, himself, became in several instances an instrument of those very forces he attacked, in his quest for identity and a stable selfhood. This contradiction is at the bottom of the confessional tone permeating his *Atmacarita*. Fakirmohan himself, in his own struggles in life, was able to climb from the social margin to the centre in the colonial structure of power. However, in the course of his rise he had to make several ethical and moral compromises for the benefit of the complex social forces unleashed by colonialism that regulated power and used him as an instrument. His autobiography can be read as a successful attempt to recover his badly battered self and the so-called pure individual identity.

In *Atmacarita* Fakirmohan created such an impression about the Bengalis at the power centres of Odisha. The ideology of this new hegemonic group is to acquire power by being both submissive and shrewd in their relationship with the colonial rulers and believing that their empowerment somehow contributes to the general welfare of the public at large. The much-maligned Kantichadra Bhattacharya wrote the essay, "Udia Ekta Swatantra Bhasha Nahe" (Odia is not a separate language) in the belief that he was doing good to the common Odia people.[3] A similar ideology—that British colonial rule is beneficial for savage Indians—served as the moral and ethical justification for the imperialist agenda. While protecting the

---

[3] Kantichandra, like many Bengali intellectuals of the time, believed that Odia is only a dialect of the Bengali language. Since there were not enough textbooks in Odia, promoting the dialect would ultimately harm the Odia people. See Kantichandra, "Udia Ekta Swatantra Bhasha Nahe" 5–9 qtd. in Dash, G.N. *Odia Bhashacharchara Parishad* (1983).

interests of the native rulers under whom he served on many occasions and even while opposing Bengali hegemony, Fakimohan might have been guided by such an ideology, which had everybody's good as its goal. This ideology was also responsible for the creation of a regional elite group, which was successful in opposing the rapacious Bengali hunger for power but acted as an obstacle for the liberatory aspirations of the common Odias. This contradictory condition is the result of the social system spawned by colonialism.

In his book *The Intimate Enemy* (1983), Ashis Nandy has indicated how colonialism brings about an irreversible change in the character of both the ruler and the ruled. Fakirmohan's *Atmacarita* is a construction of such a colonised subject and selfhood. It has been hinted earlier how the colonised subject is at the same time both shrewd and submissive towards the master race. In many places in *Atmacarita* Fakirmohan demonstrated these self-contradictory tendencies of his character. By duping his British superior officer, Collector John Beames, during a rainy morning (117–118), by betraying his captor Dharani (225–29), by cheating the common public about the modus operandi of a printing press (75), the self Fakirmohan has recovered from the complex social processes of his times is designated by Swapan Chakroborty as the 'Civil and Sly' character of the colonised subject.

This self, driven by social necessity, however, was in perpetual conflict with Fakirmohan's traditional 'mahat'—the repository of ethical and spiritual values of the community. The presence of the communitarian super ego in the individual's subconscious influences his value system and conscience. In the dubious manner Fakirmohan represented a few incidents of his life in *Atmacarita*, probably because they fail to get approval of his conscience and the traditional 'mahat', lay bare the structural principles that organise his autobiography. For example, he did not categorically state whether his first wife was alive when he married for the second time. In the bowdlerised version of *Atmacarita* that his son published after Fakirmohan's death, it is mentioned that his second marriage took place after the death of his first wife. However, in his editorial note, Debendra K. Dash, the editor of the most recent version, has argued convincingly that providing specific dates was foreign to Fakirmohan's nature. He argues that Fakirmohan's first wife was still alive when he married for the second time. It is strange that Fakirmohan himself is so casual in his narrative about such an important event in his life like marriage.

He also writes just one sentence about another very important incident in his life. This relates to the criminal charges against the brother of his second wife. His brother-in-law was apparently a drunkard like many educated Odia elite of those times, including Fakirmohan himself. Apart from being a drunkard his brother-in-law used to beat his wife. On one occasion, the brother-in-law killed his wife in the course of his beating. Fakirmohan had to use his personal influence and money to rescue his brother-in-law from the dragnet of the British police and judicial system. The oblique one-liner about the incident was later weeded out from the bowdlerised version published by his son Mohinimohan. It is natural for Mohinimohan to edit this portion in order to protect the reputation of his maternal uncle's family. Scholars have since retrieved the details around this incident from the periodicals of the era stored in archives. This information provides an insight into the moral rut to which Odia elites had descended and justifies why Fakirmohan in several of his writings was so critical of the forces colonial modernity had unleashed. It is ironical that, although he blames the educated mimic men who ape cultural mores of their colonial masters and allow themselves to go astray, he uses his own proximity to the structures of colonial power to save his criminal brother-in-law from being convicted as a murderer. In later life he blames himself, albeit in a muted manner, for coming to the aid of his in-laws' family but only after his brother-in-law betrays him in his hour of need.[4]

About his other lapses, however, like his alcoholism, adopting Brahmo religion, temptation to be converted into Christianity, etc., he is relatively more frank and voluble. He blames his own weak character for violating the 'mahat' in these cases, but he also delineates in detail the social atmosphere that aids and encourages such transgressions. In the twelfth chapter of *Atmacarita* entitled "The Changes in Social Mores," he indicated how modern education and western culture brought about a moral crisis in the organic community of Odias. This happens not only in youth thinkers his autobiography, his entire oeuvre is a committed response to the challenges of the multi-layered modernity. Can we read the confessions of *Atmacarita* as the dialectical exchange between his imaginary ideal and pragmatic self?

Among the several inspirations behind the penning of the *Atmacarita* one important concern was the recovery of Odia identity. The challenge neighbouring Bengalis and colonial social structures had posed against Odia

---

[4] For more details see Debendra K. Dash and Dipti R. Pattanaik. "Filial Censoring: Cultural Politics Behind the Bowdlerisation of Fakirmohan's Autobiography." *Samas*, Vol I, No. I, Monsoon, 2001. pp. 56–74.

identity was adequately responded to by Fakirmohan in his autobiography. One of the reasons why he set about writing his autobiography was because there was hitherto no such autobiography in Odia. An admirer, Ashraf Ali Khan, in a letter published in *Sambalpur Hiteisini*, specifically pointed this out to him on 19 December 1914 (Dash 295-99). Mr. Khan had hoped that Fakirmohan's autobiography would inspire many more in later times. In fact, in eighty years after the first one, more than one hundred eighty autobiographies have been written in Odia language. The closest to Fakirmohan's style and genius could be Gopal Chandra Praharaj's mutilated autobiography. Not only that, Praharaj's life contains many of Fakirmoan's fears about colonial modernity.

Fakirmohan had only anticipated in his autobiography that the traditional moral fibre of the society would be destroyed under the impact of the foreign culture. But Praharaj seems to have worked them out in his own life. Fakirmohan blames the modern life-style for encouraging his alcoholism. But, using the freedom provided to him during his college days, Praharaj indulges in many socially disapproved activities like visiting prostitutes and sleeping with the wife of his friend with the active encouragement of the said friend. He contracts venereal diseases. His social status is compromised. In his confessions, he blames himself for these lapses. However, how far he was sincere about his confessions is a moot point. Perhaps a sense of guilt might have haunted him while facing his father with the consequences of his actions. It is said that those who love sin are prone to confessions. The activities of his later life, including his affair with Pitambari Debi, the younger sister of his wife who was a child-widow, expose the insincerity of his confessions.

There are strong reasons to believe, as many researchers of Praharaj's work do, that Praharaj's more complete autobiography containing explosive details about the contemporary life has been partly destroyed by people close to him in order to protect the honour of the family and those involved in his life (Dash, *Gopal* 9). The recently published autobiography (2013) of Santanu K. Acharya, a close relative of Praharaj and a famous Odia writer of fiction, gives credence to many rumours about Praharaj's later life, which have been doing rounds in the elite circles of Odia society in the 20th century. One such is that Praharaj got his own wife raped and murdered by a hired goon because she disapproved of his relationship with Pitambari Debi. He himself later fought in the British courts to get the rapist and murderer released. He razed to the ground the palatial building he had built for his wife in his ancestral village. He became extremely agitated and severely reprimanded Pitambari Debi for her sexual indulgences with other men. Vexed by this, Pitambari Debi poisoned him to death. She squandered the vast property of Praharaj in trying to extricate herself from the legal proceedings following Praharaj's death. Praharaj's dramatic death was some kind of poetic justice life administered him. But before that, he had established himself as an intellectual leader of his times, painstakingly compiling an Odia encyclopaedia, giving Odia belles-lettres a maturity hitherto unachieved, compiling folk-tales which became a handbook for every educated Odia and so on. Apart from contributing immensely to the growth of modern Odia literature, he acquired for himself a social prestige by serving as a bridge between the common folk and the social elites, including the colonial masters.

Even if we restrict our enquiry to the published portion of his autobiography, we are confronted with some basic questions about the moral turpitude of the society. Is the moral degeneration referred to in Praharaj's oeuvre really a consequence of foreign impact as Fakirmohan had diagnosed? Of course, analysing the moral degeneration of the Bengali youth, thinkers and social activists in the neighbouring Bengal of the period had harboured such a thought. There were allegations that English-educated youth were encouraged to eat beef and drink alcohol. Even teachers like Henry Derozio were victims of such canard although there was no evidence that Derozio was encouraging such activity. The truth of the matter is that the opportunistic class of elites was indulging in various immoral activities under the protection of colonial administration. Niranjan Dhar's *Vedanta and Bengal Renaissance* (1977) documents in detail the class character of Bengali elites. Dhar even implies that there was a business interest behind Rammohan Roy's so-called progressive enterprises. Modernity in the hands of those elites was like a shield to cover their lechery and self-aggrandisement. Fakirmohan also describes how the modern Brahmo religion provided a moral support to many in Odisha for drinking alcohol. In his autobiography *Swabhaba Niyata Jibana Yudha* (1960), the social reformer Bairagi Mishra provided probably the most rational explanation for the moral degeneration of the power-elite of the then society. According to him, since the Brahmins were enjoying all privileges and power without any labour they were prone to many wrongdoings. Under their active encouragement, immorality had spread widely in the society. The elite class probably wanted to resist change by branding western modernity as the most visible cause of moral downfall, even as they benefitted most from those changes. Propaganda against modernity was one of their strategies to perpetuate their hold on centres of power.

Praharaj hailed from such an elite class in Odisha. It has been noted earlier how a colonised native elevate himself to a hegemonic class through 'the Civil and the Sly' strategy. Like Fakirmohan's ascent to positions of power in an earlier generation, Praharaj's forefathers had acquired an elite status by using the colonial administration (Praharaj, *Atma* 1). There seems to be a wide gap between the ideals of the organic community like faith in God and morality on the one hand and contemporary daily life on the other. Was he trying to record the hypocrisy and dishonesty of the corporate life of his times through his confessions? The following narrative supports such a conjecture:

> Honesty and faith in the Divine—I would like to record one fact here. From my own experience, I have felt that we do not have much commitment towards truth. Such a remark from a westerner is sure to incense many a respectable Indian. But speak truth always—this remains only a bookish lesson in our domestic atmosphere. What I encountered as a child at home, and as a student in school has confirmed my belief that we are made up of the metal of falsehood and in consequence have lost the firmness of the resolve for truth. Unless the domestic, familial and social atmosphere in which we grow up is changed, our faith in truth and the Divine will not be firm. (Praharaj, *Atma* 20, my translation).

It is interesting to note here that the colonising rulers too harbour such a view about the native 'other,' in order to justify their 'civilising mission' morally. The colonised subject also adopts this so-called mendacity and double-speak as a self-preserving strategy. In *Atmacarita* Fakirmohan explained his fraudulence both as a tactic for survival and as a tool for the greater good. When there is a consolidation of individuation and democratic values even within a colonial society another ideology takes shape which can be termed as the attitude of a 'critical insider.' A critical insider puts a premium on eliminating personal and communal shortcomings that stand in the way of the formation of a glorious personal and national identity. The strands of this ideology we come across in his autobiographies can be deciphered more or less in all his literary and intellectual ventures.

Despite their overt and covert criticism of the colonial power structures, both Fakirmohan and Praharaj were active participants and direct beneficiaries of the prevailing system. However, Baishnab Pani remained at the margin of that power circle all his life. He only had a working relationship with the elite class in order to promote his art. Whatever acceptance he gained among the elites was through the power of his literary skills. He never felt the urge for allegiance to the ideology of the elites, their value system and moral framework. In his autobiography, therefore, we encounter a celebratory tone about his own so-called sins. Even the temporary guilt Praharaj demonstrates while confessing his adultery and visits to brothels is absent altogether in Pani's confessions. He did not even baulk at confessing actions which are criminal in nature. He kidnapped women from villages, sold them in brothels, and led the life of a hired goon. He shows absolutely no remorse while narrating such actions. However, at the same time he punished one of his own teachers violently when he discovered his homosexual exploitation of a fellow-student. Can we read Pani's naked truthfulness as a reaction against the hypocrisy of the elite class about which Praharaj narrated in his autobiography? Was he able to banish all kinds of mendacity and hypocrisy from his life since he remained all along in the social margins and had no inclination to rise to the centres of power?

Apart from getting encomiums from elite literary and political establishments Pani was widely accepted among the masses for his genius. This mass acceptance might have given him the strength to come clean so boldly in his autobiography. I have earlier argued how modernity willy-nilly ends up democratising even a colonised society. In democratic society people attempt to free an artist from much social bondage by patronising him which in turn widens his scope for the search of his individual identity and selfhood. In order to assert this individualism, Pani married a washerwoman, even though he was a Brahmin and his first wife was still alive. His action at that time was a radical challenge to the traditional caste-system and the notion of respectability. He was forced to reside with his untouchable wife outside the village premises, outside the ambit of the respectable community. If we do not take into account the suffering of his first wife, his step would appear to be such a progressive one in the social milieu of his times. However, no ideological mission like eradicating caste discrimination in society seems to have driven his action. Maybe he was disdainful of the moral laws of the society and the so-called notions like Brahminical purity and respectability, but he was not free from the patriarchal mindset, which believed that woman was an object of sexual enjoyment. In order to justify his habit of rampant womanising, he often subverts and misrepresents traditional value system. One such misrepresentation is that since he was a bhakti-poet this lechery and promiscuity would not affect him:

> There is no place for sin in the person from whose mouth hundreds of devotional songs are emanating. (Pani 9, my translation)

Further, he seeks to justify his second marriage as a source of inspiration for his creativity:

> Love is of two kinds. One is with one's own wife and the other is with another woman. Making love with the other woman is superior to the lovemaking with one's own wife. Just cast a glance at the lovemaking of Radha and Krishna. Radha became Krishna's source of energy only through illicit love. (Pani 50, my translation)

The kind of arguments Pani offers as a matter of self-justification are extremely weak. But the fact that he is able to confess his anti-social activities so freely is indicative of a new social process. It should be noted here that the very society whose disciplines and morality he flouted with abandon, accepted him whole-heartedly and celebrated him as a poet of the masses. Although his so-called truthfulness was a threat for the social system, it was more acceptable than the hypocrisy and falsehood of the elite class. In Praharaj's autobiography, we witness the point of view of an emergent individual critical insider. The mass acceptance of Pani's autobiography is indicative of the wider spread of that point of view and its socialisation.

The more a society becomes democratic, the more receptive and tolerant it becomes. Not resisting the hegemonic oppression of outside forces is not the real test of that tolerance. But to recognise and respect the challenges coming from internal differences and from the margins of the society are the true signs of a modern democratic society. The cultural iconisation of Baishnab Pani is a new chapter in the evolution of Odia society. Although he belonged to a high caste, his autobiography is the narrativisation of sympathies for the social margin. Such sympathy we encounter again in Dinabandhu Das's autobiography *Kalakarara Kahani* (KK). KK is different from the other three autobiographies in many respects. The three autobiographers concerned were litterateurs. Consciously or unconsciously, they might have tried to lend aesthetic beauty to their narrative style. In KK we do not come across much awareness of aesthetic traditions. The earlier autobiographers either belonged to the elite class or were patronised by them. Dinabandhu Das was oppressed and exploited by the elites all his life. On the one hand, he was ignorant of the literary conventions of the elite class and, on the other, he had a glimpse of elite life-style from a distance.

As luck would have it, his reputation as an actor inspired him to write an autobiography. His confession is rightly the harbinger of a new voice in the Odia society, the voice of the subaltern. This subaltern voice, freed from the rhetorical devices of conventional literature, was more down to earth and honest.

In Pani's autobiography, we encounter the map of cultural iconisation of the man from the margin. We ascribe the widening responsiveness and tolerance of Odia social life as the reason of such iconisation. In KK we witness another dimension of that tolerance, for KK is a daring attempt to unmask the socially approved Odia cultural icons of the middle decades of twentieth century. After being canonised Pani had an easy cohabitation with other cultural icons of his times. Although harassed by envious contemporary cultural leaders, Fakirmohan remained silent about those incidents and personalities. Praharaj did not attack his contemporary elites directly. But having looked at the elite class from the point of view of an exploited subaltern all his life, Dinabandhu Das was very naturally able to unmask all kinds of hypocrisies of that class. The way he represented such powerful cultural figures of the time like Kalicharan Patnaik forces us to hate the latter as a human being. Das' autobiography underscores the wide gap between literary ideals and practical life and between moral values and their real-life practice. The artless manner in which he parades his frustrations, suicidal tendencies and exploitations at the hands of the powerful cultural pimps draws one's sympathies automatically towards his plight. Although he himself was an actor, by exposing the promiscuity, dirt and exploitation behind the stage and his own willy-nilly participation in them, he razed the foundation of social structure to the ground. He pointed out the dearth of human responsiveness in the process of cultural iconisation in Odia society. At times, he expressed his scepticism about socially acquired values. For example, in stage tradition a lot of respect is accorded to one's mentor. Because of such an ideology, he was not able to extricate himself fully from the exploitation this tradition entails. KK is a candid document of how an ideology can be a fetter for the exploited. Not having mastered a narrative skill Das often provides a freshness of approach, but the repetitiveness of facts in his autobiography, the saddling of unconnected and unnecessary details in the course of the narrative might be a drag on the reader.

However, autobiographies are valuable not only for their literary worth but also because the confessional and narrative elements they contain can be interpreted as parts of a social process. The four autobiographies have been designated as four different stages of the evolution of Odia social life.

Those four stages are the construction of the identity and selfhood of the colonised subject within a colonial set up, the insight of a critical insider in an increasingly democratic society, the challenge from the margin and the voice of the voiceless subaltern.[5] In every autobiography discussed here, strands of such ideological configurations were present in various degrees. These configurations are the responses of Odia society to the challenges of a multi-layered modernity. For the convenience of the narrative only, I have tried to indicate these responses as separate from each other.

I am grateful to Mr. Sher Khan, Research Scholar, BHU, Varanasi, for providing valuable suggestions in the course of writing of this paper.

Works Cited

Acharya, Santanu K. *Mo Jiban: Anya Eka Upanyasa*. Cuttack: Grantha Mandira, 2013. Print.

Bhattacharya, Kantichandra. "Udia Ekta Swatantra Bhasha Nahe" as cited in Dash, G.N. *Odia Bhashacharchara Parishad*. Cuttack: Odia Gabeshana Parishad, 1983. Print.

Chakravorty, Swapan. "The Civil and the Sly." *New Straits Time* 02 June 1999. http://news.google.com/newspapers?id=zcwyAAAAIBAJ&sjid=yBQEAAA AIBAJ&pg=6656%2C261494 28 July 2014. Web.

Das, Dinabandhu. *Kalakarara Kahani*. Cuttack: Kahaani, (2000), 2011. Print.

Dash, Debendra K. Ed. *Atmacarita* by Fakirmohan Senapati. New Delhi: NBT, 2010. Print.

Dash, Debendra K. & Dipti R. Pattanaik. "Missionary Position: The Irony of Translation Activism in Colonial Orissa." *TTR* 18.2 (2005). Print.

—. "The Tradition-Modernity Dialectic in Six Acres and a Third" in *Colonialism, Modernity and Literature: A View from India* (Ed. Staya P. Mohanty). New York: Palgrave Macmillan, 2011. Print. 207–228.

—. "Late 19th Century Literary Discourse and Oriya Identity." *Utkal Historical Research Journal*, 8 (2004): 108–19, Print.

---

[5] For the convenience of the structure of the essay, these four ideological imperatives were presented in a linear continuum of evolution, but these character traits of the colonial/postcolonial subject can coexist in any particular time or society or even in a single individual.

—. "Filial Censoring: Cultural Politics Behind the Bowdlerization of Fakirmohan's Autobiography." *Samas*, 1.1 (2001): 56–74. Print.

Dash, Gouranga C. (Intro.) *Gopal Chandra Praharaj*. Bhubanneswar: Odisha Sahitya Akademi, (1995), 2008. Print.

Dhar, Niranjan. *Vedanta and Bengal Renaissance*. Minerva Associates Publication, 1977. Print.

Folwer, Alastair. *Kinds of Literature*. Oxford: Oxford UP, 1982. Print.

Gusdorf, Georges. "Conditions and Limits of Autobiography" (Tr. From French by James Olney) in *Autobiography: Essays Theoretical and Critical*. (Ed. James Olney). Princeton: Princeton UP, 1980. Print.

Mishra, Bairagi. *Swabhaba Niyata Jibana Yudha*. Cuttack, 1960. Print.

Nandy, Ashis. *The Intimate Enemy: Loss and Recovery of Self under Colonialism*. Delhi, 1983. Print.

Pani, Baishnab. *Atmakahani*. Cuttack: Subash Sahoo, 1985. Print.

Satpathy, Nityanand. Ed. *Atma Jibani* by Gopal Chandra Praharaj. Cuttack: Pujyapuja Sansad, 1978. Print.

Senapati, Fakirmohan. *Six Acres and a Third: The Classic Nineteenth-Century Novel about Colonial India*. Berkeley: U of California P, 2005. Print.

Whitlock, Gillian. *The Intimate Empire: Reading Women's Autobiography*. London and New York: Cassell, 2000. Print.

Writing Me, Raising Me, Beating the Drums Louder: Fictional Autobiography as a Feminist Tool for Expression in African and Diaspora Women's Writing

Ebere Nnenna Agugbue Nweze

This paper discusses autobiographical elements in the selected fictional writings of two women writers; one from Anglophone Africa, Buchi Emecheta and the other from Anglophone Caribbean, Zee Edgell. It attempts to highlight how they have used the literary genre of autobiography as a successful tool for expression in the selected novels.

The fictional autobiographical writings discussed in this paper tell stories of human development, and progression. They create living characters with events and activities that afford the characters or tellers immense opportunities for self-definition and assertion. Thus in line with their feminist goal of self-definition, voice, and consciousness-raising, African and Diaspora women writers find the genre of fictional autobiography an essential tool for expression in their writing. The fictional autobiographical novel establishes the being of the protagonist in the novel. Thus, when black women writers use the form, especially when their protagonists are girls or women, they tend to subvert the notion of voicelessness and invisibility of the female in black society and literature. They make the female character come alive; thereby forcing readers and critics to reckon with her development as a living human being within the society. Their approach enables the reader to trace the growth of the female characters as the latter encounter several obstacles that they eventually overcome.

Feminist writing craves the indulgence of the assertiveness evident in fictional autobiographical writing. Assertiveness and woman centredness are germane to recognition and acceptance of women in most societies, especially in the largely patriarchal African and Diaspora societies. In the light of the layers of patriarchal obstacles women have to surmount in order to be heard, women writers try to write assertiveness into their characters. The life stories of the female character create a paradigm for success and achievement as Florence Stratton notes:

> In certain important aspects, the female Bildungsroman stands in opposition to the entire African [Black] male literary [cultural] tradition; a tradition to which the very notion of female development is alien. For it is a form, which by its very definition, characterizes women as active and dynamic; as developing. Women are, in other words, conceptualized not as the other but as self-definitive. Furthermore, their status as historical subjects is given due recognition. (107)

There are two identifiable categories or essential elements of autobiographical writing; the promotion of assertive individualism and the image of the self as a representative of the group. Writings portraying the struggles and successes of female characters are held up as beacons of hope to women saying that they can and will succeed if they are willing to fight for their place within male-dominated societies. Thus the female character that succeeds represents not just an isolated case but the collective success of all women. This connects to the tendency of the protagonist of fictional autobiographical writing to function as representative of the image of a group as Oriaku notes:

> There is the image of self as a representative figure but this outstanding kind of representativeness whereby the individual gathers into his being the major or significant attributes and experiences of his group. Both types recognize the primary influence of the environment or society on character formation or personality development; the protagonist is often shown to be what he is because of the environment or despite it. In addition the life of an individual has significance only inasmuch as he [she] is a member of a community or group and has some special relationship with his fellows. In one case the subject sets himself up as a model for others to emulate and in the other the community is seen in the self, its miniature and symbol. (10–11)

Rosalind Coward also notes how most female-authored autobiographical novels tend to portray the female protagonists as representing women as a collective, "For the autobiographical voice of most of these contemporary women-centred novels often appeal to a collectivity. I am, but I am a representative of all women. The history of my oppression is the history of all women's oppression" (35).

I will now turn to a discussion of the autobiographical nature of the selected works of the two writers. The Nigerian-born, British based writer, Buchi Emecheta's novels: *In the Ditch, Second Class Citizen, The Slave Girl,* and *Double Yoke* are all fictional autobiographies. Her use of this genre enables the reader to trace the growth of her female characters as they encounter several obstacles that they eventually overcome. In an earlier work on autobiography James Olney acknowledges:

> Autobiography is the literature that most immediately and deeply engages our interest and holds it and that in the end seems to mean the most to us because it brings an increased awareness, through an understanding of another life in another time and place, of the nature of our own selves and our share in the human condition. (vii)

Emecheta truly takes the reader through different stages in the life of Adah, the protagonist of two of her novels *Second Class Citizen* and *In the Ditch.* The reader follows Adah's life journey as she grows from an unwanted girl child, to an assertive young woman who is able to define what she wants and pursue it in both patriarchal and racist societies that seek to submerge her personality under the rubric of sexism and racism in both novels. The reader is made to follow Adah's development from a point of naivety to that of sophistication. Abioseh M. Porter points out how this journey plays out, "As a novel of development, *Second Class Citizen* is quite successful in the depiction of Adah's growth from the initial stage of naivete and ignorance to her final stage of self-realisation and independence" (126). In her own autobiography, *Head Above Water,* Emecheta acknowledges a parallel between her own life experiences and that of Adah, the protagonist of both *In the Ditch* and *Second Class Citizen:*

> I decided to use the fictitious African name of Adah meaning 'daughter.' Well time proved that to be a vain hope. People could tell straight away that Adah's life was over fifty percent mine. I wrote the story of my life as if it were somebody else's ... Reading my first novel ... years later, I saw that using the fictitious name Adah instead of Buchi gave the book a kind of distance, and the distance gave the book the impression of being written by an observer. I was writing about myself as if I were outside me, looking at my friends and my fellow sufferers as if I was not one of them. (58)

In the novel, *The Slave Girl*, Ogbanje Ojebata, the protagonist of the novel not only matches the description of Emecheta's mother but in fact, bears the same Igbo name as Emecheta's mother. The meaning of the name, 'she who returns home after wandering away from home' describes the experience of Emecheta's real mother who was sold into slavery. Emecheta discloses this parallel in *Head Above Water*:

> My mother, Alice Ogbanje Ojebata Emecheta, that laughing, loud-voiced, six-foot-tall, black glossy slave girl ... who forgave a brother that sold her to a relative in Onitsha so that he could use the money to buy *ichafo siliki*—silk head ties for his coming of age dance ... my mother, that slave girl who had the courage to free herself and return to her people in Ibusa, who still stooped and allowed the culture of her people to re-enslave her. (3)

Perhaps by writing the story about her mother, Emecheta intends to enlighten women about the different levels and layers of oppression that they need to watch out for.

Emecheta also acknowledges that her experiences at the University of Calabar, Nigeria influenced her novel *Double Yoke*. The dearth of female students in her creative writing class spurred her to create a character like Nko whose life subverts the male notion of responsible womanhood. Nko is able to write her own "herstory" in which the reader is invited to judge the appropriateness of her actions in the light of the realities of the university. Nko is an undergraduate student in her final year. She has a boyfriend who wants to marry her when she graduates. Her boyfriend is also a classmate. However, her professor wants a sexual favour from her in order for her to pass his course. If she dares refuse his advances, she will fail his course and will not graduate with her mates. She tells Ete Kamba, her boyfriend, about this dilemma. He becomes upset and begins to doubt her faithfulness and loyalty to him. He becomes very distant and threatens to end their relationship. She had hoped that Ete Kamba would give her some moral support but she was no longer sure that their relationship would continue. Thus Nko finds herself in a double bind relationship with both Ete Kamba, her student lover, and the professor, her teacher pulling her in different directions with different expectations. But she is sure that she wants to graduate. She decides to oblige her professor. After all she reasoned, she may still meet someone else in the future who may not know her past or may even understand her predicament if he knew. The reader cannot but admire her pragmatism in handling the situation especially as she reconciles with Ete Kamba towards the end of the novel.

When asked why her novels' settings and stories resemble her real life African/Nigerian/Ibusa background, Emecheta, a sociologist by training, attributes the prevalence of social realism in her work to one of the attributes of literature which is to use life's experiences as its raw materials. Thus, the distinction between life presented factually or modulated by the imagination becomes thin and often indecipherable. One can also say that with the propagandist stance of feminist literature and minority literature, social realism is a very important tool for expression in consciousness-raising fiction.

The Caribbean writer, Zee Edgell also uses the fictional autobiographical mode of expression to foreground issues concerning women in her works. Some of her novels trace the development of the female protagonists as girls from relative ignorance and immaturity to adulthood, awareness, and maturity. The development of her female characters can be said to be parallel to the quest for independence of her nation, Belize. For instance, the triumph of Beka, the protagonist of her first novel, *Beka Lamb* (1982) over the habit of lying is shown side by side with the struggle for independence of Belize. Roger Bromley points to this relationship between the personal life of Beka, the protagonist and the political development in Belize in his analysis of *Beka Lamb*:

> [T]he meanings of the private and the socio-political are never really separable. At every point in the novel, yet not polemically or obtrusively, the personal and the historical intersect as the dominant themes of gender and politics assume the form of a cultural mediation of the making of Belize. (10)

Edgell is careful to write a novel of development because as the first literary voice from independent Belize, her angle of vision is crucial in assessing both the literature and socio-political environment in Belize. As a woman writer too, she wants to foreground issues concerning women and the family in her writings. In an interview with Gay Wilentz, she admits that her point of view is important in her fiction:

> I wanted to record my point of view from the writer's perspective; what I thought I had seen. Not necessarily what was, but what I thought I had seen. It was there. We don't have a history written by Belizeans yet, so

that I wasn't in any position to write a history, but I felt that history was sufficient to write a novel. (185)

Thus in writing an autobiographical novel that seems to be parallel to Belize's socio-political history, she is aware that she is looked upon as a pioneer in her country's literary history.

Egdell's second novel, *In Times like These*, continues the autobiographical explorations of socio-political events in Belize started in *Beka Lamb*. In the same interview with Wilentz, she acknowledges the link between the two novels, "People don't realize that although this novel is set in a certain year, many of the events, flashbacks deal with *Beka Lamb*" (185).

This story which combines history, politics, and romance portrays the struggles and triumphs of a young woman against the sexist socio-political and economic forces that act as debilitating agents against women in Belize and other Caribbean societies. The story starts with Pavana Leslie as a fully-grown woman. However, in a series of flashbacks the reader follows her development from a naïve young student in London to a mature woman who is able to make her own choices. Edgell's concern in this novel is to project all she wanted Belizean and Caribbean women to be in Pavana. She touches on many issues affecting women in Belize including motherhood, relationships with men, economic instability, political ignorance and marginalization. Through the choices her protagonist makes, Edgell tries to redefine the image and role of women in Belize. For instance, Pavana refuses to be cast in the mold of the Caribbean concubine or common law wife when she becomes pregnant. She also refuses to have an abortion as suggested by Alex. Instead, she chooses to have her children and refuses to be weighed down by them. She refuses to give up her career in order to be a full time mum. The strong woman who emerges at the end of the novel is a far cry from the naïve young woman the reader meets in London at the beginning of the novel.

Pavana's struggles with and triumphs over her corrupt male colleagues in her job as the head of the country's Women's Unit is a message from Edgell that women need not succumb to victimization and oppression. Her eventual resignation from the Unit is an indictment of a government that pays lip service to women empowerment. There is no doubt that there are strong autobiographical elements in this novel for indeed Edgell served at some point as Director of the Women's Bureau in Belize.

Edgell's third book, *The Festival of San Joaquin* is also a Bildungsroman of some sort. This novel tells the story of a woman who is being tried for the murder of her common-law husband. Adele S. Newson tells of the authenticity of Edgell's social vision in foregrounding issues concerning women. *The Festival of San Joaquin* is based on a real incident, the arrest of a woman for the murder of her common-law husband (199).

Luz Marina, a poor woman of Meztiso descent, marries Salvador, the son of a wealthy woman of Indian background. In a series of flashbacks, Edgell traces Luz Marina's relationship with the Casal family. The racial and ethnic conflict prevalent in Caribbean society can be seen playing out in this novel. Luz comes into the family as a maid and companion to the elderly Mrs. Casal, Salvador's mother. However, when Salvador falls in love with her, the family refuses to give their consent to a legal marriage. They can relate with Luz as a maid but not as a family member. Thus, Luz and Salvador settle for co-habitation or common-law marriage. Eventually, Salvador who is given to drinking and violent displays of anger starts abusing Luz. One day, during a domestic brawl, Luz mistakenly kills Salvador in self-defense. The family drags her to court for murder. However, in a society that sanctions male violence but frowns at women's defense, Luz is passed off as insane and recommended for therapy. As the readers follow Luz Mariana's struggles to be re-integrated into the society, they are impressed by one woman's determination to carry on with her life or what is left of it despite the many forces that are working against her resolve. The bond that exists between Luz and her mother underscores the need for bonding between women. Both women are victims of domestic violence from the men they love. Luz's mother is nursing a near invalid husband who batters her whenever he got into drunken rages while Luz is also battered by Salvador.

Luz is eventually discharged and acquitted for Salvador's murder. She also gets the custody of her children thereby affirming that she is whole again and capable of performing a nurturing role in the society. Luz's victory over the Casal family is not only a triumph for the poor and powerless against the rich and powerful but is also a triumph for women in the Belizean society that sees women as docile and subservient. In an interview with Renee Hausmann Shea, Edgell explains that Luz Marina's story has connections with her own family's ethnic and racial background.

In the three novels discussed in this paper, Zee Edgell makes a point of tracing the development of her female characters from positions of weakness to strength. In making these women triumph, she inscribes her vision of gender empowerment for women in spite of all the odds that seem to militate against them. Women too have a choice to either collaborate with or reject the forces that subjugate them. As her female characters lead the way, she expects other women in Belize and indeed all black societies to follow.

In essence then, when African and Caribbean women use the fictional autobiographical mode of expression, they seem to be deliberately setting out to inscribe the presence of the other sex as well as highlight her plight in society. They heed Trinh T. Minh-ha's definition of committed writing, "To write is to communicate, express, witness, impose, instruct, redeem, or save at any rate to *mean* and to send an *unambiguous message*. Writing thus . . . may be used to orient toward a goal or to sustain an act" (16).

One of the major purposes of the fictional autobiographies discussed in this paper seems to be the presentation of the triumphs of individual women on the one hand and to point to them as examples to other women on the other hand. The success stories of these female protagonists can translate to success stories to other women who dare to negotiate for their space in patriarchal societies. Femi Ojo-Ade captures the way this method of presentation affects even the reader in this summation; "When a piece of writing is autobiographical ... the reader knows that he is going to be a fellow traveler in a journey through the night into the dawn of a new day" (13).

Feminism arguably is a protest theory, and in feminist novels, some writers tend to employ the points of view that will best convey their protest. Embedded in this protest is a determination to foreground the issues of womanhood making her visible and strong in the fictional world of the writers against the perceived notion of women's invisibility and voicelessness both in the real and fictional world of men. Thus, some fictional autobiographical novels are written in the first person narrative point of view where the 'I' becomes a living person, the name of a person that readers can identify with. As readers trace the development of 'I', they tend to empathize with her in her travails and at the same time identify with her achievements. Yet others are written in other points of view with the author often speaking and espousing her ideology through the characters. The third person omniscient point of view is used to best express the writer's ideology through the characters. This particular point of view enables the writer to know the inner thoughts of the characters. The writer can then manipulate these thoughts in order to achieve her or his purpose as she or he is able to go in and out of the characters' minds at will. Trinh T. Minh-ha points out the all-knowing tendency of this point of view:

> The writer is necessarily either God or priest ... God and priest form an inseparable pair; the two often merge since the priest represents God and rarely hesitated to assert her/his claims to God's message. Thus no matter how novel her work may appear to be, the woman who writes about herself/others from the standpoint of the one-who-knows deliberately/involuntarily carries on the conventions of the Priest-God scheme. Omniscient and omnipresent, she is everywhere and understands everything at the same time; she follows her own or her characters' outer expression and inner conscience simultaneously; she sees the present, past, and future of all events; and above all, she has the power to dissolve the opacity of life ... Charged with intentionality, writing is therefore disclosing (a secret), and reading is believing. (29-30)

The two female writers have used a mixture of the first person point of view and the third person omniscient point of view in the selected novels discussed in this paper. The different points of view used together with other literary devices no doubt combine to achieve the goal of the writers, which is the foregrounding of the issues concerning women.

Works Cited

Belsey, Catherine, and Jane Moore, eds. *The Feminist Reader: Essays in Gender and the Politics of Literary Criticism*. Malden, MA: Blackwell, 1997. Print.

Bromley Roger. "Reaching a Clearing: Gender and Politics in *Beka Lamb*." *Wasafiri*, 1.2 (1985): 10–14. Print.

Conde, Mary, and Thorunn Lonsdale, eds. *Caribbean Women Writers: Fiction in English*. London: Macmillan, 1999. Print.

Coward, Rosalind. "How I Became My Own Person." In Belsey and Moore 26–35.

Edgell, Zee. *Beka Lamb*. Oxford: Heinemann, 1982. Print.

—. *In Times Like These*. Oxford: Heinemann, 1991. Print.

—. *The Festival of San Joaquin*. London: Heinemann, 1997. Print.

Emecheta, Buchi. *Second Class Citizen*. Glasgow: Fontana/Collins, 1974. Print.

—. *The Slave Girl*. London: Allison and Bushby, 1978. Print.

—. *In the Ditch*. London: Heineman, 1994. Print.

—. *Double Yoke*. London: Ogwugwu Afor, 1982. Print.

—. *Head Above Water*. London: Heinemann, 1986. Print.

Minh-ha, Trinh T. *Woman, Native, Other: Writing Postcoloniality*. Bloomington: Indiana UP, 1989. Print.

Newson, Adele. "The Fiction of Zee Edgell" in *Caribbean Women Writers: Fiction in English* eds. Mary Conde and Thourin Lonsdale. London: Macmillan, 1999. Print.

Ogwude, Sophia. Bessie Head: *An Exile Writing on Home*. Zaria: ABU P, 1998. Print.

Ojo-Ade, Femi. "Bessie Head's Alienated Heroine: Victim or Villain?" *Ba Shiru*. 2 (1977): 13–21. Print.

Olney, James. *Metaphors of Self: The Meaning of Autobiography*. Princeton: Princeton UP, 1972. Print.

Oriaku, Remy. *Autobiography as Literature*. Ibadan, Nigeria: Humanities Research Centre, 1998. Print.

Porter, Abioseh M. "*Second Class Citizen*: The Point of Departure for Understanding Buchi Emecheta's Major Fiction." In *The International Fiction Review*, 15.2 (1988): 123–129. Print.

Shea Hausmann, Renee. "Zee Edgell's Home Within: An Interview." *Callaloo*, 20:3 (1997): 574–583. Print.

Stratton, Florence. *Contemporary African Literature and the Politics of Gender*. London: Routledge, 1994. Print.

Wilentz, Gay. "Interview with Zee Edgell." Conde and Lonsdale, 185.

Maternity and Writing:
An Expedition into the Ojibwe Land of Letters with Louise Erdrich

Elisabeth Bouzonviller

Contemporary American novelist Louise Erdrich is an enrolled member of the Turtle Mountain Band of Ojibwe. *Books and Islands in Ojibwe Country* from 2003 is one of her rare autobiographical works, the other one being the earlier *Blue Jay's Dance: A Birth Year* from 1995.[1] Both memoirs tackle the subject of maternity and writing, the latter being a maternal adventure at home from pregnancy to birth and early motherhood whereas the former deals with a family journey through Ojibwe land with Tobasonakwut and their daughter, Nenaa'ikiizhikok.

Erdrich always defines herself first as a mother, then as a writer and a mixed-blood Indian. Interviewed by Bill Moyers, she said: "I'm always a mother. That's my first identity, but I'm always a writer too. I have to write. I have to be an artist." In both autobiographies, telling the reader about herself and her family, which is often a synecdoche for her tribe, seems to be a way of reflecting about literature and the act of writing. We shall see therefore how motherhood involves narratives of the self which rely on intergenerational transmission but also on a universal female heritage that transcends place and time. We shall then ponder the way these autobiographical works can be viewed as a quest for personal identity which turns out to be a quest for tribal identity. Eventually, this maternal and tribal experience will be apprehended in its links with writing, which emerges, in the end, as an essential issue at the heart of those autobiographies.

---

[1] Throughout this article, we will adopt the abbreviations BJ for *Blue Jay's Dance: A Birth Year* and BI for *Books and Islands in Ojibwe Country*.

Motherhood

Both texts immediately acknowledge the importance of family links as *The Blue Jay's Dance* is dedicated to Erdrich's husband, Michael Dorris, and their daughters (X), while *Books and Islands in Ojibwe Country*, written after the couple's separation and Dorris's suicide, is said to be for her youngest daughter, Nenaa'ikiizhikok, and "her brothers and sisters." *The Blue Jay's Dance* establishes from the start what Philippe Lejeune calls an "autobiographical pact," actually suggesting autofiction as defined by Serge Doubrovsky,[2] since Erdrich explains in a preamble that this is an evocation aimed at their daughters of "what it is to be a parent" and that "[t]he baby described is a combination of [their] three babies" (IX). *Books and Islands in Ojibwe Country* is far less explicit, at first, in terms of autobiography as it opens only on a map of "Ojibwe Country," thus insisting both on the trip and Erdrich's tribal origins; but after having mentioned the goal of her journey in the first page, the narrator refers to her traveling companion, her "eighteen-month-old and still nursing daughter" (4) and introduces herself openly by using the first person pronoun and adding her age (4). This mother–daughter adventure is therefore claimed as a real one recollected after their return home. In both works, despite the fictional arrangement of the former, what is at stake is the narrator-author's maternal link with a daughter. Both texts are meditations on this link before and after birth and are rooted in two different territories: a family home in New Hampshire for the former and Northern Minnesota and Ontario, that is "Ojibwe Country," for the other. In both texts, although fathers are mentioned and present at times, what the narratives focus on is clearly a female experience which involves alternately excitement, joy, fulfillment, fear, pain and frustration.

Writing about her maternal experience, Erdrich adopts a feminist stand in keeping with many tribes' original attitude before colonial times, as claimed by Paula Gunn Allen:

> [p]re-contact American Indian women valued their role as vitalizers because they understood that bearing, like bleeding, was a transform-

---

[2] "Autofiction is the fiction I have decided, as a writer, to give myself of myself, including, in the full meaning of the term, the analysis experience, not only as regards the subject but also the production of the text." My translation from the original French: "L'autofiction, c'est la fiction que j'ai décidé en tant qu'écrivain de me donner de moi-même, y incorporant, au sens plein du terme, l'expérience de l'analyse, non point seulement dans la thématique mais dans la production du texte" (1980: 87).

ative ritual act.[...] They were mothers, and that word implied the highest degree of status in ritual cultures. (28)

In *The Blue Jay's Dance*, the narrator insists on a lack of interest granted to mothers' heroic labors that goes back to biblical times:

> Over all of the millennia that women have endured and suffered and died during childbirth, we have no one story that comes down to us with attendant reverence, or that exists in pictures (...) In our western and westernized culture, women's labor is devalorized beginning with Genesis. (35)

In a way, this autobiography devoted to pregnancy and early motherhood may be perceived as filling this narrative gap, although, paradoxically, the narrator has to admit the limits writing encounters when dealing with such topic: "Even though I am a writer and have practiced my craft for years, and have experienced two natural childbirths and an epidural-assisted childbirth, I find women's labor extremely difficult to describe" (42).

In both texts, Erdrich enlarges her individual experience to a universal, timeless female one: "[...] this sense of my sex, an overwhelming consciousness of the simple fact of my femaleness, assails me" (BJ 189). She definitely acknowledges her belonging to a gender group that shapes her and defines her, thus being not so far from Beauvoir's feminist idea of a femininity born out of education and environment[3] although she also insists on a physical femaleness that cannot be ignored: "In talking to other women over years, I begin to absorb them somehow [...] Mothering is a subtle art whose rhythm we collect and learn, as much from one another as by instinct" (161). She also declares: "[...] when it comes to pregnancy I am my physical self first, as we are all of us women." (9) The personal experience quickly becomes a celebration of female strength—"Women are strong, terribly strong. We don't know how strong we are until we're pushing out our babies" (12)—and her writing even turns into a sort of feminist manifesto:

> To teach the *no* to our daughters. To value their *no* more than their compliant *yes*. To celebrate *no*. To grasp the word *no* in your fist and refuse to give it up. To support the boy who says *no* to violence, the girl who will not be violated, the woman who says *no, no, no*, I will not. To love the *no*, to cherish the *no*, which is so often our first word. *No*–the

---

[3] *Cf.* "One is not born, but rather becomes, a woman" (translation from the original French: "On ne naît pas femme: on le devient" [Beauvoir 13]).

means of transformation. We are born in cauls and veils, and our lives as women are fierce and individual dances of shedding them. (140)

As a writer, Erdrich thus offers her female version of life, her female narrative, as requested in the following lines: "A woman needs to tell her own story, to tell the bloody version of the fairy tale. A woman has to be her own hero" (104).

As announced in the preamble of *The Blue Jay's Dance*, she does not name her baby and daughters but the names of relatives, friends, acquaintances and even pets abound. In *Books and Islands in Ojibwe Country*, she mentions the numerous names of family members, including her youngest daughter this time, friends, acquaintances and writers. All these proper nouns designating people, but also animals and places, anchor the texts in Erdrich's reality, they also weave links between the past and the present. For example, the youngest daughter's name is explained as referring to a character in Ojibwe mythology but also to "[t]he original Nenaa'ikiizhikok," "[h]er grandmother on her father's side" (BI 12).

A section of *The Blue Jay's Dance* is entitled "*Three Photographs*" (138-140). It describes family photographs which draw a family tree over three generations and compose a kind of family narrative that echoes the visual narrative of much older roots to be found in the description of the petroglyphs in *Books and Islands in Ojibwe Country*. In a kind of reverie process, the narrator imagines how the "original Nenaa'ikiizhikok" may have met her own relatives while visiting the Turtle Mountain reservation (BI 12–13), but also how her ancestors may have painted the petroglyphs before moving to the Great Plains (BI 80–81). In both cases, the use of the verb "imagine" qualifies her family evocations based on spiritual wandering and the desire for a deeply-rooted Native lineage:

> I like to imagine Nenaa'ikiizhikokiban dancing with one of my mother's aunts, maybe Jane or Shyoosh. (13)

> I can't help but imagine that these two women, whose names my mother and sister have searched out of old tribal histories, walked where I've walked, saw what I've seen, perhaps traced these rock paintings. (80–81)

Thus, her two autobiographies become tools of exploration focusing on the recollection of family history, but also on the reconstruction of a desired past in a typical autofictional process.

From Personal to Tribal Quest

Even if *The Blue Jay's Dance* extends over a year, with four parts corresponding to the four successive seasons, and *Books and Islands in Ojibwe Country* follows the chronology of the trip North, there are many diversions in time and space as the narrator takes the opportunity to wander here and there depending on her imagination, desire, anger, fears, memories and future projections. The narratives often seem to correspond to the free evolution of her thoughts, almost as in a process of stream of consciousness, while she constantly departs from what is directly observable at the time of her writing or from the linear chronology of events. She often moves from her individual case to larger concerns and conclusions while her narratives definitely evolve from an individual to a tribal quest. Thus, family and roots remain at the heart of her writing and this recalls Barthes asking: "Isn't telling stories always a matter of looking for one's origins, telling about one's problem with the law, getting into the dialectic of love and hate?"[4]

In *The Blue Jay's Dance*, pregnancy seems to induce many wonderings, which eventually depart from the mere maternal situation to reach more fundamental questionings and reflections about the self, just as the trip to Ojibwe land leads the narrator to reflect about herself as a mother and a mixed-blood Ojibwe. Lejeune defines autobiography as "the retrospective prose narrative that someone makes about his own life, when he emphasizes mainly his individual life, in particular the story of his personality," which is clearly what Erdrich offers with these two books. At the beginning of *The Blue Jay's Dance*, she explains that "[f]or a writer, work is also emotional and intellectual survival: it is who I am" and she announces that "[t]hese pages are a personal search and an extended wondering at life's complexity" (5). She wonders about her identity and imagines areas beyond her control, as during sleep, for example, thus suggesting poet Arthur Rimbaud's famous 1871 phrase "I is another.": "I wonder (…) if my sleeping self understood what it read, and indeed, if I will ever know who I am during these dark hours? Asleep, we are strangers to ourselves." (BI 97) Referring to the overwhelming presence of her baby at the expense of her sleep, independence and free time, she concludes "I lose track of what I've been doing, where I've been, who I am" (57), which is not simply the result of her

---

[4] My translation from the original French: "Raconter, n'est-ce pas toujours chercher son origine, dire ses démêlés avec la Loi, entrer dans la dialectique de l'attendrissement et de la haine." (75)

busy days but also an aspect of her human condition leading her to writing as an investigating process about the self.

Kenneth Lincoln notices that "[t]o Indians tribe means family, not just bloodlines but extended family, clan, community, ceremonial exchanges with nature, and an animate regard for all creation as sensible and powerful" (8). In Erdrich's autofictions, writing about herself, writing about motherhood, becomes a search for her Native roots, whether they are realistic or more desired ones. By writing about herself, she remembers, but also creates herself, just as when she imagines her ancestors beyond what is established as certain, "If I try to remember, I invent myself [...] I am a fictitious being," says Doubrovsky.

At the beginning of *Books and Islands in Ojibwe Country*, the narrator mentions a route, which clearly places the trip within the frame of a return to origins, in quest of tribal identity:

> we travel along a highway that was expanded from a road that was once a trail, an old Ojibwe trade route, heading north.
>
> Songs traveled this route, and ceremonies, as well as pelts and guns. Medicines, knowledge, sacred shells, and secular ideas traveled this road, but never at sixty-five miles per hour. (14)

During this founding trip in Ojibwe land, intergenerational fears reappear when she reaches the Canadian border (100–101), which clearly stands for an arbitrary sign imposed by colonizers who did not care if this administrative line separated people who had formed one tribe in the past. Then, the narrative turns into a postcolonial palimpsest erasing the official American narrative. Quoting Kimberly Blaeser, David Stirrup concludes:

> The passage northward essentially retraces-and replaces-those colonial routes Erdrich follows, going back *beyond* the colonial moment. This retracing does not simply offer another American palimpsest, but partially erases the imposed surface narrative, rearticulating territory in a modern 'pilgrimage' of sorts, where 'stories of pilgrimage ... are seldom the account of individual movement ... they are braided accounts that entwine themselves with the destinies of communities, generations, tribal nations, the ecosystems of a region, the spiritual inheritance of a people'. (177–78)

Like some other critics, William Bevis defines Native American literature as centripetal because its characters have a tendency to try to go back home since this is the place of identity for them, and he opposes it to Euro-American literature, which is said to be centrifugal. In both her autobiographies, Erdrich seems to hesitate about the precise location of this home and tends to equate it with the place where her daughters are, yet Ojibwe land is also a strong magnetizing place for her.

Given this uncertainty about home, which echoes centuries of voluntary and forced movements, it is not surprising that food, animals and plants should acquire such importance in both texts because they stand for roots despite distance and displacements. Exiled in New Hampshire, the narrator plans and observes her garden while referring to her parents and grandparents: "It is hereditary. My family has always planted in the wrong season" (BJ 27) *The Blue Jay's Dance* also includes several recipes and what is at stake with these food references becomes clear when she declares: "This fabulous menu includes my favorite Ojibwa traditional food—wild rice" (125). In the narrator's mind, food is definitely cultural and related to family and tribal roots. This becomes obvious in *Books and Islands in Ojibwe Country*, where the mentioning of wild rice recurs in a whole section entitled "*The Wild Rice Spirit*" (51–54). The narrator mentions the Ojibwe term for the wild rice spirit, "*Manoominikeshii*" (51), and the text includes the reproduction of an anthropomorphic petroglyph picturing the plant (53). There, the reference is not only a matter of Ojibwe traditional food and ancestral agricultural practices, but it is also a sign of the postcolonial ecological degradation of the landscape since Tobasonakwut points out the poor state of the rice fields which is the result of provincial decisions on lake levels (51–52). Eventually, confirming the previous idea of food implying a cultural and tribal signified, the narrator concludes on a more general tribal mythical reference: "The great teacher of the Anishinaabeg, whose intellectual prints are also on this rock, was a being called Nanabozho, or Winebojo" (53).

Beyond the displacements, exile, natural destruction, land and family losses evoked in these autobiographical texts, which turn out to be a personal but also a tribal quest, the narrator manages to focus on the inescapable weight of the past and the intergenerational transmission at stake. Having detailed her family origins, she goes back to the history of the Ojibwe. The idea of a genocide is then looming through a mise en abyme process when she mentions her reading of W. G. Sebald's *Austerlitz*, the protagonist of which is a surviving Jew from Prague, and its final pages a reference to a book by Dan Jacobson, another survivor from the Holocaust. The narrator of *Books and Islands in Ojibwe Country* describes *Austerlitz* as "the reconstruction of [Jacques Austerlitz's] memory" and shows him digging for "the truth of his origins," through photographs in particular (95), which is obviously what Erdrich does herself in her autobiographies (BJ 138–140, BI 12–13).

Sebald's narrative necessarily echoes Erdrich's family and tribal quest, but the American writer refuses the idea of a vanished past, just as Natives have proved the theory of the "vanishing race" a mistake since the mid-twentieth century in terms of population statistics (Zimmerman 168–169). In *Books and Islands in Ojibwe Country*, while in a boat on Lake of the Woods, she sees a living sturgeon in the wild for the first time (75). This animal, which used to be common in that Ojibwe area, may be perceived as a metaphor for resilient indigenous people, despite the extended time reference, when she says: "The sturgeon is a living relic of life before the age of dinosaurs, and to see one is to obtain a glimpse of life 200 million years ago" (75). She clearly links the species with Ojibwe people and their diminishing numbers through the reference to the colonial extinction of their natural resources when she adds: "The sturgeon up here on Lake of the Woods were the buffalo of the Ojibwe. Greed and overfishing by non-Indians caused their population to crash around the turn of the nineteenth century" (75). Eventually, at International Falls, she even sees "some sort of museum" with an aquarium "filled with live sturgeon" (98), yet even if Natives, like sturgeon, may be the object of intellectual interest and museums, they are still alive and part of contemporary America.

If both autobiographies are filled with references to the past, they are also literary proofs that Natives are not extinct like certain villages or species. The numerous references to the narrator's children in both works is an obvious denial of the vanishing state of the Ojibwe people. Moreover, both autobiographies insist on a survival linked to culture. The myths, petroglyphs and traditional stories mentioned in the autobiographies and, eventually, Erdrich's books themselves are signs of the lively state of the Ojibwe. Above all, the narrator of *Books and Islands in Ojibwe Country* emphasizes the power of a Native language that has resisted the colonial conquest of English. This resistance is of course encapsulated in her daughter's Ojibwe name, Nenaa'ikiizhikok, the child being a living proof of "survivance" herself, to use Vizenor's term (69), but Ojibwemowin also insistently invades the text with multiple references, which are not always translated, as Erdrich creates a new literary language corresponding to her mixed-blood origins, a "third space of enunciation," as Bhabha puts it (157). A whole section of *Books and Islands in Ojibwe Country* is entitled

"*Ojibwemowin*," i. e. the Ojibwe language (81–89), and recalls the characteristics of "one of the few surviving languages that evolved to the present (…) in North America" (85). The narrator evokes her slow learning of it after it disappeared as a first language in her family and Tobasonakwut's struggle to preserve it when sent to residential school, but the living state of the Native language is also displayed in the baby books belonging to her daughter, "[…] many of which [she has] laboriously blotted with Wite-Out, removing the English, and replaced with Ojibwe words written in Magic Marker" (10). Eventually, the liveliness of the language is to be found in her daughter herself to whom she speaks "part Ojibwe, part English, and part mother-baby nonsense" (118). Thus, the child displays the promise of Ojibwemowin survival and even rebirth through an adaptation to modernity, as suggested by the narrator with the examples of the contemporary Ojibwe words for "movie" or "television set" (5).

"Books Why?"

If *Books and Islands in Ojibwe Country* opens on a map defining the destination of the two travelers, the text also focuses immediately on literature, as a chiasmus mentions the narrator's double obsession, thus replicating the title itself: "Books, islands. Islands, books" (3). She then explains the purpose of her trip, which seems to set the tribal quest aside for a while:

> I can't travel aimlessly. I always seem to have a question that I would like to answer. Increasingly, too, it is the same question. It is the question that has defined my life, the question that has saved my life, and the question that most recently has resulted in the questionable enterprise of starting a bookstore. The question is: Books. Why? The islands are only incidental. (4)

This question—"Books. Why?"—recurs then like a chorus throughout the text, and several answers are provided which all point out the human desire for contact, transmission and survival in life and beyond (6, 55, 95, 99, 141).

In both autobiographies, the narrator is surrounded by books whether at home or during her trip. Eventually, both texts themselves are filled with references to the books she is reading or has read, thus establishing a mise en abyme of the reading act. This could be a sign of the narrator's western education but she also relates this activity to her Ojibwe origins when she claims that "[t]he Ojibwe had been using the word *mazinibaganjigan* for years to describe dental pictographs made on birchbark, perhaps the first books made in North America" (BI 5).

In *Books and Islands in Ojibwe Country*, despite the natural environment, one of her goals is Ernst Oberholtzer's library located on Mallard Island. This ecologist was deeply interested in Ojibwe culture and he gathered rare and valuable books in an amazing place isolated in Ojibwe country; thus the trip becomes an intricate quest for both origins and literature. In another mise en abyme process, one of the books she intends to see there is a first edition of *Tristam Shandy*, the eponymous character's pretended autobiography and what she claims to be "the first novel in the English language" (120). As if to balance this English literary reference, she also recalls her fascinated youthful reading of John Tanner's 1830 captivity narrative, *The Falcon, a Narrative of the Captivity and Adventures of John Tanner during Thirty Years Residence among Indians in the Interior of North America* (42). Once again, literature and Ojibwe origins intertwine, as the narrator recalls that she and her sisters enjoyed this autobiography thoroughly which mentions briefly one of their ancestors (43) and can be considered as "the first narrative of native life from an Ojibwe point of view" (46). Thus, reading is constantly referred to and even the landscape is deciphered like a book: "So these islands, which I'm longing to read, are books in themselves" (3).

For the narrator of both autobiographies, if reading is omnipresent and possible whatever the situation, writing is another obsession that involves far more difficulties. Like reading, writing is traced back to her tribal roots when, recalling the origin of the term "Ojibwe," she offers her favorite analysis: "The meaning that I like best of course is Ojibwe from the verb Ozhibii'ige, which is 'to write.'" (BI 10–11) But if the young mother can read while nursing her baby, as in one of the drawings inserted in the text of *Books and Islands in Ojibwe Country* (17), writing requires a state of solitude and independence that motherhood does not allow, as *The Blue Jay's Dance* insistently demonstrates. It seems that, like canonical American novelist F. Scott Fitzgerald, who, in his three essays from 1936 later collected under the title *The Crack-Up*, kept writing about his inability to write, in *The Blue Jay's Dance*, Erdrich keeps mentioning how hard it is for her, as a young mother, to find time and space to be able to write, while, at the same time, offering her version of a mother's autobiography. In both these very different autobiographical attempts, writing is, therefore, not the natural task of inspired artists mastering their craft but the result of painful obsession and the source of a continuous sense of frustration.

At the same time, Erdrich details the intricate links between writing and motherhood and values their imprint on the future: "The need to write and to reproduce are both all absorbing tasks that attempt to partake of the future" (BJ 79). She exposes the difficulties of mother-writers in general and goes on with a long list of female writers and paratactic biographical details (BJ 144), the humorous conclusion being: "Reliable birth control is one of the best things that's happened to contemporary literature" (145). However, experiencing the particular fusion of a nursing mother, she concludes that literature is a substitute for the kind of perfect wholeness and plenitude that nursing mothers experience:

> the mystery of an epiphany, the sense of oceanic oneness, the great *yes*, the wholeness. There is also the sense of a self-merged and at least temporarily erased—it is death-like. (…) Perhaps we owe some of our most moving literature to men who didn't understand that they wanted to be women nursing babies. (148)

French psychoanalyst Joël Clerget defines the act of writing as the consequence of a rupture followed by a quest for origins:

> Writing from a rupture point. "The writing urge finds its strength in the depths of exile. Writing points to the desire to find one's origins—the primeval place and the time before history" writes Claude Louis-Combet.[5]

This is precisely what happens in *Books and Islands in Ojibwe Country*, which turns out to be a metaphor for the process of writing as the two travelers leave home and move North looking for signs of their ancestors whose life was disrupted by colonization. This family trip becomes an experience of limits and echoes the writing adventure as described by Clerget when he asserts that "[w]riting is a matter of crossing borders, of pushing through bodies, inscribing in lands and letters."[6]

Discovering the rock paintings she has been longing for, the narrator tries to decipher them like a text and wonders about writing as a linking trace:

---

[5] My translation from the original French: "Écrire à partir d'un point de rupture. La nécessité d'écrire 'puise sa vigueur dans la profondeur de l'exil. Elle témoigne du désir de retrouver les origines—l'enclos du lieu primordial et le temps d'avant l'histoire' écrit Claude Louis-Combet" (23).

[6] My translation from the original French: "L'écriture tient à des passages de frontières, à des traversées de corps, à des inscriptions de terres et de lettres" (100).

I am standing before the rock wall of Painted Rock Island and trying to read it like a book. (BI 51)

The line is a sign of power and communication. It is sound, speech, song. The lines drawn between things in Ojibwe pictographs are extremely important, for they express relationships, usually between a human and a supernatural being. (56)

Psychoanalyst Jacques Lacan has noticed that, in French, "to link and to read are the same letters"[7] and Clerget insists on writing as a consequence of lineage when he declares:

Writing weaves a network of passages.

It speaks of birth. It is nothing like a return to the womb. On the contrary, it is only possible and effective when birth is over (...)

He who is born can write, he who comes from those who have given birth, life to him ... that is to say, he who is not self-made but generated by, he who is part of a lineage.[8]

In front of the rock paintings, the traveler may lack archeological and ethnological knowledge but she immediately relates them to family, tribe, tradition and transmission, the same way she perceives writing in its polysemy and didactic links with origins:

One thing certain is that the paintings were made by the ancestors of the present-day Anishinaabeg, for the ancient symbols on the rocks are as familiar and recognizable to Tobasonakwut as are, say, highway and airport and deer crossing signs to contemporary Americans. Of course, the rock paintings are not just pointer signs. They hold far more significance. They refer to a spiritual geography, and are meant to provide teaching, and dream guides to generations of Anishinaabeg. (49–50)

Within "the autobiographical pact" frame, both her texts adopt a form of direct address to the reader and a rather intimate tone which are reminis-

---

[7] My translation from the original French: "[L]ier et lire, c'est les mêmes lettres" (109).
[8] My translation from the original French: "L'écriture tisse un réseau de passages. Elle témoigne de la naissance. Elle n'est nullement un retour au sein maternel. Tout au contraire, elle n'est possible et effective que lorsque la naissance est consommée ... Écrit celui qui est né, issu de ceux qui lui donne le jour, né de ... c'est-à-dire pas fait tout seul, mais généré et filié" (43).

cent of the tribal tradition of oral storytelling. Moreover, they can also recall the oral autobiographical tradition of the Great Plains warriors and their "coup stories."[9] Both Erdrich's narratives eventually emerge as a combination of the European and Native autobiographical traditions, as already suggested by her literary references in *Books and Islands in Ojibwe Country*. They are the result of her own family's mixed-blood heritage and education, but they are also a reflection about writing that transcends cultural references and is intimately linked to the human experience of maternity and lineage. Thus, *The Blue Jay's Dance* ends on the evocation of a child's evolution, which echoes the one of a literary work. The insistent anaphora "She will walk" (222–223), referring to the newly-born daughter, forecasts the long way toward independence to be followed by the child but also the fate of any accomplished book to be published and abandoned to the imagination of readers, the mother-writer's conclusion being: "She will walk until her sense of balance is the one thing left and the rest of the world is balanced, too, and eventually, if we do the growing up right, she will walk away from us" (223).

In *Books and Islands in Ojibwe Country*, the narrator's daughter owns a Chinese-made toy called Alpha-Bug which can produce sounds and even combine letters into words but her older children have noticed its limited capacity at producing these combinations, especially if they are "suggestive or swear words" (129). Unlike this industrialized and limited language producer, in her autobiographies, as in all of her texts, Erdrich explores the endless possibilities of language and writing. A tool to embark on a personal and tribal quest, her autobiographies celebrate the fruitful combination of cultures and words through the writing experience. The texts seem then to offer a remapping of America as Indian country where the narrator evolves beyond the usual limits of Ojibwe land but she also embeds the writing act within the female and especially maternal experience, thus offering a writing metaphor beyond culture. Apart from her tribal attachment and her perpetual genealogical and ethnic quest, in *The Blue Jay's Dance*, Erdrich also insists on a writing experience defying limits as she perceives it rooted

---

[9] "One type of autobiographical narrative is the coup stories of the Plains Indians, an example of communo-bio-oratory.... On returning from battle with fellow warrior-witnesses to vouch for his words, the warrior would narrate his martial accomplishments to his community" (Wong 26).

in feelings beyond will, in the same way she insists on the idea that a writer does not control his/her story when it is good:[10]

> We cannot choose who our children are, or what they will be—by nature they inspire a helpless love, wholly delicious, also capable of delivering startling pain. [...]
>
> Love is an infinite feeling in a finite container, and so upsets the intellect, frustrates the will? An anarchic emotion that transcends rules of age, race, blood, passionate love has a wild philosophy at base. Because we can't control the fixation of love and desire, we experience emotional mayhem—stories, fiction, works of art results. (105-106)

Works Cited

Allen, Paula Gunn. *The Sacred Hoop: Recovering the Feminine in American Indian Traditions*. Boston: Beacon, 1986. Print.

Barthes, Roland. *Le Plaisir du texte*. Paris: Éditions du Seuil, 1973. Print.

Beauvoir, Simone de. *Le Deuxième sexe. II L'Expérience vécue* (1949). Paris: Gallimard, 1976. Print.

Bevis, William. "Native American Novels: Homing In." *Native American Writing*. Ed. A. Robert Lee. London and New York: Routledge, 2011. 103-135. Print.

Bhabha, Homi K. "Cultural Diversity and Cultural Differences." *The Post-Colonial Studies Reader* (1995). Ed. Bill Ashcroft, Gareth Griffiths and Helen Tiffin. Oxford: Routledge, 2006. 154-157. Print.

Bruchac, Joseph. "Whatever Is Really Yours: An Interview with Louise Erdrich." *Conversations with Louise Erdrich and Michael Dorris*. Ed. Allan Chavkin and Nancy Feyl Chavkin. Jackson: UP of Mississippi, 1994. 94-104. Print.

Clerget, Joël. *L'Enfant et l'écriture*. Ramonville: érès, 2002. Print.

Doubrovsky, Serge. "Autobiographie/Vérité/Psychanalyse." *L'Esprit Créateur*, 3 (1980): 87-97. Print.

—. *Le Livre brisé*. Paris: Grasset, 1989. Print.

---

[10] "The story starts to take over if it is good. You begin telling, you get a bunch of situation characters, everything together, but if it's good, you let the story tell itself. You don't control the story" (Bruchac 104).

Erdrich, Louise. *The Blue Jay's Dance: A Birth Year* (1996). New York: Harper Perennial, 2002. Print.

—. *Books and Islands in Ojibwe Country*. Washington: National Geographic Society, 2003. Print.

—. Interview with Bill Moyers. *Bill Moyers Journal*. 9 April 2010. http://www.pbs.org/moyers/journal/04092010/profile.html. 5 March 2012. Web.

Fitzgerald, F. Scott. "The Crack-Up," "Handle with Care," "Pasting It Together" (1936). *The Crack-Up with Other Pieces and Stories*. Harmondsworth: Penguin, 1965. Print.

Lacan, Jacques. *Livre XX Encore*. Paris: Éditions du Seuil, 1975. Print.

Lejeune, Philippe. *Le Pacte autobiographique*. Paris: Éditions du Seuil, 1975. Print.

—. *L'Autobiographie en France*. Paris: Armand Colin, 1971. Print.

Lincoln, Kenneth. *Native American Renaissance*. Berkeley: U of California P, 1983. Print.

Stirrup, David. *Louise Erdrich*. Manchester and New York: Manchester UP. 2010. Print.

Vizenor, Gerald. "Native American Indian Literature: Critical Metaphors of the Ghost Dance." *Native American Writing*. Ed. A. Robert Lee. London and New York: Routledge, 2011. 61–69. Print.

Wong, Hertha D. *Sending my Heart Back Across the Years: Tradition and Innovation in Native American Autobiography*. New York: Oxford UP, 1992. Print.

Zimmerman, Larry J. *Les Indiens d'Amérique du Nord*. Cologne: Taschen, 2002. Print.

"My Mother Composed Me as I Now Compose Her": Catharsis and Cathexis in Alison Bechdel's *Are You My Mother?*

Eva-Sabine Zehelein

With her 2012 sequel to her "strangely successful"[1] *Fun Home: A Family Tragicomic* (2006) Alison Bechdel returns to the intricate art form of the graphic narrative in order to 'talk' about herself, her family her-story and to 'draw' an intimate double-portrait of herself and her mother. In this "memoir" (6) subtitled *Comic Drama*, the illustrious circle of Virginia Woolf, Donald Winnicott, Sigmund Freud, Alice Miller, Dr. Seuss, P.D. Eastman, Adrienne Rich and C.G. Jung serves to support the autographic narrator's endeavor to re-approach and understand her mother Helen Bechdel, to verbalize/pictorialize and analyze the painful gulf between mother and daughter and to find "meaningful patterns" (31) in the artifacts of memory which serve not only to heal her mother (82–83), but to bridge the divide and find and accept her own self. Applying Smith/Watson's definition of memoir it becomes clear that the book's scope is by no means limited to historically situating the subject in a social environment (Smith/Watson 198), but includes at least as much autobiographical material. The book is just as much a "memoir about my mother" (6) as a confessional, an autopsychoanalysis, and an auto(bio)graphy of its narrator/author. It conflates what Lee Quinby has painstakingly tried to keep distinct: "[W]hereas autobiography promotes an 'I' that shares with confessional discourse an assumed interiority and an ethical mandate to examine that interiority, memoirs promote an 'I' that is explicitly constituted in the reports of the utterances and proceedings of others" (as quoted in Smith/Watson, 198).

---

[1] Bechdel quoted in Medley.

Nancy K. Miller has observed: "Autobiography's story is about the web of entanglements in which we find ourselves, one that we sometimes choose" (544). And Alison Bechdel[2] attempts to "figure out what the story is" (28, 29), and to untangle the web of interpersonal relationships and psychological predicaments in order to crystallize her own identity through a process of self-assertion. The book is about patterns and structures, the representation and interpretation of (bodily) experiences, the search for hidden meaning(s) in existence. In a solipsistic a-chronological spatio-topical system, through an idiosyncratic interaction of the triad words-images-sequentiality, Bechdel writes associatively about her troubled quest for her self via an investigation of the severed bond to her mother by interweaving her narrated present with depictions of memory. She represents the therapy sessions she attended over decades, the attempt to see meaning in everyday events, to understand her fixation(s). By doing so, she tells us at least as much about herself ('autobiography') as about her mother ('memoir').

For Bechdel, writing and graphic art are forms of Obsessive Compulsive Disorder (OCD)—from which she and her mother, she says, have occasionally suffered. Bechdel's creative process is determined by the challenge to be 'truthful to the material'. She takes photographs of herself or others and of objects from which she then draws her panels. She reproduces—in an idiosyncratic digital 'handwriting'—pieces of text, she attempts to copy 'truthfully' her mother's and father's handwriting, their conversations, the stories. Thus she creates what in the context of *Fun Home* (which is just as applicable here) has been labeled an "archive of feelings" (Cvetkovich 119) or a form of scrapbook: "She re-created absolutely everything in the book, re-inhabiting the elements of her past to re-present them—and to preserve them, to publically re-archive them" (Chute 183).[3] Ever since childhood, Bechdel has attempted to write a diary and 'record the truth'. In *Fun Home*, this theme had figured prominently and some iconic panels are referenced in *Are You My Mother?* —for instance a redrawn page from her childhood diary dominated by a curved circumflex as shorthand signifier for "I think" (49). At the moment when she had reached this impasse, this inability to write because of doubtfulness of the veracity of the written word, her

---

[2] Autobiographical storytelling tempts the reader to blend the narrating self/author with the narrated self/character. In order to demarcate this difference, "Bechdel" shall be used in the following for the extradiegetic author, "Alison" for the intradiegetic character; "Alison Bechdel" shall be used in cases where both merge.

[3] Cf. also Alison Bechdel at Institut Charles V, Université de Paris VII.

mother had temporarily stepped in and written her diary for her. Now, in *Are You My Mother?* it is Alison who (secretly) records/transcribes the phone conversations with Helen. Thus, "my mother composed me as I compose her" (14). Whereas in *Fun Home* Bechdel illustrated that both image and word can fail and the only 'better way' was to blend both, here language is granted a core function. For instance, Alison undergoes a form of 'talking cure' with her therapists, numerous of phone conversations are represented, and various psychoanalytical texts and excerpts from Virginia Woolf's novels as well as autobiographical writings are interlaced.

Reality is, of course, filtered through Bechdel—her perception, her memory, her body, her art of drawing and writing, her talent at organizing material into a narrative (always a-chronological, elliptical), her mind and heart. Yet she struggles with objectivity, with the attempt not only to fulfill Lejeune's "autobiographical pact" between writers and readers, but to approximate ultimate truth and insight in/with/through her panels. Her therapist suggests drawing more spontaneously, "without so many preparatory sketches" (251) and Alison responds firmly: "That's impossible. The kind of drawing I do has to be meticulously planned, every line has to convey specific information" (252). Bechdel hence creates a metafictional discourse on the complexities of the graphic memoir, the "fidelity constraint" on the one hand and the idea and illustration/visualization of the constructedness of the self on the other hand.[4] In graphic memoir, "the power of memory must always share the act of self-representation with the devices of fiction" (Gardner 2008, 6).

The book is thus, as Helen so succinctly remarked, a metabook (285) in which the processes of autobiographical as well as biographical storytelling are pondered and performed. And auto(bio)graphy, then, suggests not only the writing and drawing of and about the self, but also a certain signature or autograph which provides the work with an imprint of self-assertion and identification.

The following brief analysis focusses only on the role of two inter- and intratextual references, P.D. Eastman's *Are You My Mother?* and Dr. Seuss' *Sleep Book* to analyze some key panels in order to illustrate how much this "memoir about my mother" (6) is in fact an auto(bio)graphy, illustrates Freud's concept of cathexis and is the artifact of a cathartic process. Alison Bechdel's mother is her other, her critic and her support, her nemesis and her muse: "For nothing was simply one thing" (V. Woolf, epigraph).

---

[4] Cf. Williams and Gardner (2008) for a similar argument for *Fun Home*.

"I did have a mother. I know I did. I have to find her. I will!" The search for the mother leads Alison, just as the baby bird in P.D. Eastman's classic 1960 children's book, to various individuals and "No"s. The baby bird finally learns to tell the difference and name the Other; it tells the earth mover: "You are not my mother! You are a snort!" And in the moment of ultimate distress, when it cries out: "I want my mother!" the snort flings it back into the nest and mommy returns. "You are a bird and you are my mother." By identifying the 'You,' the 'I' is secure(d).

Alison Bechdel, too, has been searching for comfort, security and sustenance, a nest and someone who is just like her; a loving mother, a mothering lover. James Strachey used the term "cathexis" as a translation for Freud's *Besetzung*, meaning a process in which mental or emotional energy is invested in a person, an object or an idea. Bechdel combines this notion with Winncott's object relations theory where the "transitional object" employed by infants helps them "learn that they're separate from their mother;" "it's not 'me', but not 'not-me', either" (56). Alison Bechdel's transitional object is a teddy bear—linked to "Winnie-the-Pooh" who features on the only page with a red background (56)!

Alison Bechdel, suffering from the loss of connection to her mother, from a "lack, a gap, a void" (288), has sought emotional surrogates, cathectic objects: the analyst Jocelyn (280), Winnicott (21), some partners (e.g. Eloise, 221)—she had them, she was torn between them, she lost them, and never did she find what she was looking for. In Chapter 5 ("Hate") the depiction of sexual/erotic play with Eloise is subverted or complicated by the caption placed midpoint: "I liked the built-in distance of this arrangement" (184). Intimacy and distance, togetherness and separation characterize her relationships, observes the extradiegetic narrator. Where she craves mutuality with her mother, she resists it with her partners. In Chapter 6 her constant search for patterns is also turned on her liaisons. "But the only constant I can find is that as soon as I'm sure the other person has cathected me, too, I want to flee" (220). Torn between Eloise and Donna Alison is again in an "in-between" state—as her new lover Donna titles a photo she has taken of Alison in Karate gear (226).[5] This sequence is followed by the depiction of a phone conversation between Alison and her mother in which Alison is brave enough to mention her recent commercial successes as a cartoonist. But Helen is uncomfortable with her new role as

---

[5] Ironically, the fourth precept in Karate is "First know yourself before attempting to know others."

the mother of a lesbian writer and also with the exposure of her family through her daughter's (auto)biographical work.[6] "Whatever it was I wanted from my mother was simply not there to be had. It was not her fault" (228), but Alison breaks down in tears after hanging up. This panel, covering two thirds of a page, shows her crying, bent over, holding her belly with her left and the telephone with her right hand. Her bodily representation is framed with captions. Two read: "Mom had supported me for nine months." "The significance of this particular length of time does not escape me" (229). The author is well aware that the financial support was a surrogate for the sustenance provided by the mother to her embryo, and this conversation between them has proved yet again that the umbilical cord is severed. This panel is repeated in slight variation and with a black background shortly after. Here, the posture is identical, yet the clothes Alison wears are clearly different. Also there are books underneath the telephone and a photo camera is visible which takes a picture of this—(re)staged—scene. On the next page we see Alison scrutinizing the photograph she has just taken with the selftimer; "It's just that instead of playing a character, I'm playing myself" (234).[7] The traumatic experience is re-performed and metafictionally 'worked through'.

This scene connects to the book's two central panels, two two-page spreads. The first in Chapter 1 ("The Ordinary Devoted Mother") is highly multimedial. It shows an assemblage of a series of redrawn photographs. The originals were taken in short succession by her father on Christmas 1960 (developed in January 1961); they show three-month old Alison in her mother's arms. The baby imitates the mother's facial expressions suggesting an intimate connection between the two which is disrupted when the baby discovers the father as photographer. Bechdel as extradiegetic narrator and analyst claims in the first caption upper left that she is not sure about the actual chronology of the photos, but has "arranged them according to my own narrative" (32)—just as the entire book is an arrangement of images and text according to the author's own compositional decisions. Bechdel also integrates a rewritten excerpt from Winnicott's essay on the ordinary devoted mother in which he claims that for a brief period of time the

---

[6] In her review of *Are You My Mother?* Shauna Miller provocatively remarks: "It can't be easy to read that your best attempt at mothering landed your kid in therapy. (But really, why else is anyone in therapy?)."

[7] And we may wonder in how far the diagnosis "narcissistic cathexis" (149) which Alison Bechdel and her therapist identify as the appropriate label for her mother does not also apply to Alison Bechdel herself: the cathectic other exists only so that it can be used as investment of emotional energy.

mother is the child and *vice versa*. Text and image thus reinforce each other in the depiction of an *unio mystica*. The splash page also integrates writing and drawing tools—Faber Castell artist pen, brush, calligraphy pen, rubber (made in Germany), triangular plastic ruler (ironically enough labeled "Helix") and Gerber ink—as well as Bechdel's glasses. The creative process, the constructedness of narrative (images), as well as of chronology plus the subjectivity of perception are thus underscored. With the red-colored onomatopoetic "Drrinng!" in the lower left, sound enters the panel, and the only speech bubble indicating a Bechdelian intradiegetic speech act is positioned right underneath: programmatically: "Mom!" Her mom is on the phone as an off voice and the zigzagged speech bubbles lower left and spread over the right page provide the reader with Helen's chatter about Lady Gaga at the Grammys the night before, her dreams of the dead husband and about Sylvia Plath, the "spoiled brat" (33). Despite the connection via the telephone line, the distance between Alison and her mother is not only spatial, but also mental-emotional. The intimacy of the images, of the redrawn photographs, clashes with the oddly dysfunctional day-to-day small talk as intradiegetic monologue.

The image of the embryo in the maternal womb might well be the central image of the book. The second two-page spread (Chapter 4, "Mind") might be the book's center-fold with another intricate *mise en abyme*. It features to the left reproductions of letters and at the center the large-scale reproduction of a double page from Dr. Seuss's *Sleep Book* superimposed partly by a rewritten excerpt from Winnicott's article on the "good-enough-mother" (lower right). Upper left Bechdel has redrawn a part of a handwritten letter from her father to her mother, in which the words "I love you" can be deciphered twice. However, some panels later, a larger and more extensive excerpt from the same letter is redrawn presenting "a more complicated picture" of dad's reaction to Helen's pregnancy with Alison: "I refused to treat your condition lovingly. My soul should rot in hell! It doesn't seem possible that I could stoop to such crassness. Well I love you—and our baby" (139). It seems as if he was at first not happy about the pregnancy and might even have proposed an abortion (140). However, this detail or context is not visible on the spread page where the words "I love you" come to the fore.

Love and pregnancy are connected to the image of the womb. The background story of the Bechdel's struggle with Helen's pregnancy is a subtext which might be mirrored in Seuss's plexiglass dome. Alison Bechdel uses this image already shortly before the splash page to explain "how my mom would go off duty at night." "You could see her right there in her chair, reading and smoking. But you couldn't talk to her. She was clocked out." "It was like she had this invisible dome over her." "This plexiglass dome" (129). And young Alison in reaction would fashion her own "enclosed, impregnable spaces" (131) and call them her "office"—just as Seuss's chap sits in his plexiglass dome with a "keep out" sign, "physically cut off from the outside world," "but taking detailed mental note of it" (133).

Where Seuss's little man wears a hat connected to the machinery which helps him count and jot down the number of Biggel-Balls as they "plup in a cup. And that's how we know who is down and who's up," the therapist tells Alison: "The thing is you relate to your own mind like it's an object" (152). Helen "failed" to breast feed Alison and stopped kissing her good night when Alison was seven years old. According to Bechdel's Winnicott, "erratic mothering" can lead to "an opposition between the mind and the psyche-soma," and the second picture of Seuss's chap is captioned with: "This mind-psyche that takes over and replaces the mother is a version of the compliant false self" (141). Young Alison discovered that "I am in my brain" (141) and has suffered ever since from the lost bond with her mother and the inability to permit being loved by others.

The story which "has no beginning" (6) and no end, but a manufactured one (284) closes with yet another programmatic double page: from bird's eye perspective we look down into the family kitchen, Helen standing with hands in hips, little Alison crouching on the floor. Despite the single image, the reader's gaze is guided via the captions from top left to lower left to upper right and lower right. They are interjected by two speech bubbles situated rather in the middle of the right and left page. Helen says "How's that?" (left) and Alison answers "I think I can get up now" (right)—now that her mother has given Alison imaginary leg braces and special shoes. Bechdel explains: "There was a certain thing I did not get from my mother." "There is a lack, a gap, a void." "But in its place, she has given me something else." "Something, I would argue, that is far more valuable." "She has given me the way out" (288–289).

On the previous page, Bechdel had depicted how her mother had equipped her with the braces and shoes and added in the captions closing the page: "I can only speculate that there was a charge, an exchange, a mutual cathexis going on...." "She could see my invisible wounds because they were hers, too" (287). "I have always thought of the 'crippled child' game as the moment my mother taught me to write" (287, upper right). The way out, then, is writing, the creative process, at the end of which she, her mother and we, the readers, now find ourselves. Bechdel has been searching for the connection, the umbilical cord, the mutual understanding. She discovers that it is in language, in the creative process. The book has rejoined them, maybe healed her mother, her self.

This ending closes the narrative bracket by connecting back to the first scene, the depiction of a dream in which Alison finds herself trapped in a dank basement while engaged "in some sort of home-improvement project" (2). Initially, the only way out seems to be "to squeeze through the small spidery window" (2)–and the panel shows three spiders in their webs! In the final chapter we had learned about her mother's arachnophobia which Alison had reported to her analyst and read up on in Winnicott's work (275-277). In the first dream scene Alison however detects to her surprise an unlocked door and can leave the house without further ado only to be faced with a brook she surrenders to by jumping in the water. Is this the way out? She does not squeeze through the spidery small window but simply steps out the door, immerses herself in the "sublime feeling of surrender" (3) to her creativity (10). The page bleeds out lower right, and, like a page turner, leads us and her thus straight into the plot. Chapter 2 begins with a dream in which a spider web is crucial, too. It prompts Alison's insight that "it's our very capacity for self-consciousness that makes us self-destructive" (41[8]). Is that her mother's ultimate message? Maybe the "search for meaningful patterns" such as the spider web, has come to an end.[9] Alison has carried on "her mother's mission" (31) by creating this love letter to her mother, which for her is also a cathartic process of renewal and regeneration through the act of experiencing deep emotions connected to past traumatic experiences. The *Comic Drama* with the performers of a cathartic process constitutes an artifact of autopsychoanalysis leading the way out, to a separate piece/peace and Bechdel realizes that "love" is a verb as well as a noun (cf. 150: "love"). *Are You My Mother?* verifies that the self has a place in good writing after all (cf. 200).

Works Cited

Bechdel, Alison. *Fun Home: A Family Tragicomic*. Boston, Mass.: Houghton Mifflin Harcourt, 2006. Print.

---

[8] See also page 65 where the blanket with the spider web reappears.
[9] Alison shares with her mother, a devotee to *The New York Times* crossword puzzle, the urge to find patterns; Helen once wrote to her that "patterns are my existence. Everything has significance. Everything must fit" (31).

—. At Institut Charles V, Université de Paris VII, January 25, 2007 on *Fun Home: A Family Tragicomic. GRAAT* issue #1, March 2007. Web.

—. *Are You My Mother?* New York, NY: Houghton Mifflin Harcourt, 2012. Print.

Chaney, Michael A., ed. *Graphic Subjects: Critical Essays on Autobiography and Graphic Novels.* Madison, Wisconsin: U of Wisconsin P, 2011. Print.

Chute, Hillary. *Graphic Women: Life Narrative and Contemporary Comics.* New York, NY: Columbia University P, 2010. Print.

Cvetkovich, Ann. "Drawing the Archive in Alison Bechdel's *Fun Home.*" *WSQ: Women's Studies Quarterly* 36.1&2 (Spring/Summer 2008): 111–128. Print.

Dr. Seuss [Theodor Seuss Geisel]. *Dr. Seuss' Sleep Book.* New York, NY: Random House, 1962 (1990). Print.

Eastman, P.D. *Are You My Mother?* New York, NY: Random House, 1960 (1988). Print.

Gardner, Jared. "Archives, Collectors, and the New Media Work of Comics." Hillary Chute and Marianne DeKoven. Eds. *Graphic Narrative.* Special Issue of *Modern Fiction Studies* 52.4 (Winter 2006): 787–806. Print.

—. "Autography's Biography, 1972–2007." *Biography* 31.1 (Winter 2008): 1–26. Print.

Lejeune, Philippe. *On Autobiography.* Ed. Paul John Eakin. Trans. Katherine Leary. Minneapolis, Minnesota: U of Minnesota P, 1989. Print.

McCloud, Scott. *Understanding Comics. The Invisible Art.* NY, New York: HarperCollins, 1993. Print.

Medley, Mark. "The mother of all memoirs: Alison Bechdel's touching letter to a parent" *National Post* May 4, 2012. Web.

Miller, Nancy K. "The Entangled Self: Genre Bondage in the Age of the Memoir." *PMLA* 122.2 (March 2007): 537–48. Print.

Miller, Shauna. "Alison Bechdel's Sad, Funny, Sprawling Graphic Memoir." *The Atlantic* (May 2012). Web.

Pedri, Nancy. "Graphic Memoir: Neither Fact Nor Fiction." in: Daniel Stein, Jan-Noel Thon, eds., *From Comic Strips to Graphic Novels. Contributions to the Theory and History of Graphic Narrative.* Berlin: De Gruyter, 2013; 127–153. Print.

Smith, Sidonie, Julia Watson. *Reading Autobiography. A Guide for Interpreting Life Narratives.* Minneapolis, Minnesota: U of Minneapolis P, 2001. Print.

Spurgeon, Tom. "CR Holiday Interview #1 -- Alison Bechdel." *ComicsReporter* December 18, 2012. Web.

Watson, Julia. "Autographic Disclosures and Genealogies of Desire in Alison Bechdel's *Fun Home*." *Biography* 31.1 (Winter 2008): 27–58. Print.

Whitlock, Gillian. "Autographics: The Seeing 'I' of the Comics." Hillary Chute and Marianne DeKoven. Eds. *Graphic Narrative*. Special Issue of *Modern Fiction Studies* 52.4 (Winter 2006): 965–79. Print.

Williams, Ian. "Autography as Auto-Therapy: Psychic Pain and the Graphic Memoir." *Journal of Medical Humanities* 32.4 (2011): 353–66. Print.

Like Father Like Daughter?
Autobiography as Defacement in Leslie Stephen's *Mausoleum Book* and Virginia Woolf's *Memoirs*

Floriane Reviron-Piégay

Leslie Stephen wrote his only autobiographical text (named the *Mausoleum Book* by his children) barely a fortnight after his second wife, Julia Prinsep Stephen, died on the 5th of May 1895. His intention was clearly to alleviate his grief but also to let his children know about their mother's beauty, dedication and loving personality. He meant simply to "talk to them about their mother" (Stephen, *The Mausoleum Book* 3). The text was meant as a private commentary on a photograph album he had compiled for his children and on a series of letters he had collected as a means to pay tribute to his wife. *The Mausoleum Book* proves to be an emotional evocation of a deceased and beloved wife and mother and would thus seem typically Victorian if its genre was not so problematic.

Not originally intended for publication, Virginia Woolf's autobiographical texts were published under the title *Moments of Being* by Jeanne Schulkind in 1976. Chronologically, "Reminiscences" was written first, in 1907, during Virginia Woolf's period of apprenticeship: it was addressed to Julian Bell, the first child of Vanessa (Virginia's sister) and Clive Bell and meant to tell him about his mother. "A Sketch of the Past," written in 1939, because Vanessa had urged Virginia to write her memoirs before she became too old, is the longest and perhaps the most complex autobiographical enterprise launched by Virginia Woolf, at a time when her literary reputation was well established.

So the texts I am bringing together here in a somewhat artificial way were written by two different people, at different moments of their lives and under different circumstances. In this respect, the comment Jeanne Schulkind makes upon Virginia Woolf's memoirs, also applies to the group of autobiographical writings under scrutiny here: studying the memoirs of father and daughter together, instead of resulting in an absence of coherence or in a "random heaping together of fragments of life" means that the fragments in question "arrange themselves into a meaningful order; a pattern emerges which expresses [both] Virginia Woolf's [and Leslie Stephen's] view of the self generally and of themselves in particular, in ways that a conventional autobiography could not have done" (Schulkind 12).

I shall look into the way both writers considered the genre of autobiography which seems to have been considered as a family tradition, the image of the father looming large in Virginia Woolf's texts. Then I shall ponder over the hybridism of these texts as a symbol of ambivalence, letters, photographs, autobiography and biography battling for prominence: different images and portraits emerge from this confrontation between genres and generations, attesting to the cross-fertilization between the masculine and patriarchal Victorian voice and the feminine modernist one. Finally, both texts pay homage to Julia Stephen's haunting presence,[1] they are very different attempts at making her voice heard beyond the grave; auto/-biography can therefore be construed as "restoration in the face of death" (De Man 74), hovering between disfiguration and transfiguration.

Leslie Stephen is well-known for his innumerable contributions to the development of biography, whether thanks to his monumental work as an editor of the *Dictionary of National Biography* or because of the numerous biographies he wrote for the English Men of Letters Series. He also wrote his friend Henry Fawcett's biography (*Life of Henry Fawcett*, 1885) and that of his brother (*The Life of Sir James Fitzjames Stephen*, 1895); his *Studies of a Biographer* (1898–1907) reached four volumes. So one cannot help but remark that his autobiographical production was rather scant compared to this biographical profusion. Yet he professed a real admiration for the autobiographer and vowed that

> autobiography (…) should be considered as a duty by all eminent men, and indeed by men not eminent. As every sensible man is exhorted to make his will, he should also be bound to leave to his descendants some account of his experience of life." ("Autobiography," *Hours in a Library*, vol III, 223)

But both in theory and in practice, Stephen rather shunned autobiography, so much so that he seemed to have resolved to write his memoirs only

---

[1] Julia Prinsep Stephen was Leslie Stephen's second wife and Virginia Woolf's mother.

reluctantly or incidentally as he said himself: "I have no intention of writing autobiography except in this incidental way" *(Mausoleum Book* 4). Both Virginia and her father were accidental autobiographers, moved by circumstances rather than by an internal need and they shared the ambivalence of their feelings regarding the disclosure of intimate thoughts to the public eye. Even if Stephen did not forbid his children to publish the memoir after his death he nevertheless insisted upon its confidentiality:

> I intend however that this document shall remain absolutely private among us eight as long as I live. I mean further to write in such a way as to put out of the question any larger use of it than I have indicated, even after my death. Having said so much, I leave the whole matter to you. (*Mausoleum Book* 4)

It would be convenient to label this reticence "Victorian" but Woolf herself was quite ambiguous as to the future of her papers: her very last words in the letter she left Leonard just before her suicide were: "will you destroy all my papers."[2] Woolf expressed her distaste of autobiographical outpouring under many different circumstances, either confiding it to her diary or to friends.[3]

The fact that she agreed to write a memoir and her letter to Ethel Smyth on the 9th of July 1940 seem to hint that her fear had abated a little by the time she launched into "A Sketch of the Past."[4] She may also have felt the need to add to the family tradition of memoir writing: Leslie Stephen's own father, James Stephen, had written his memoirs for the use of his children. Besides she had been the direct repository of her father's last memories as

---

[2] Letter to Leonard Woolf, 28th of March 1941, (Letters VI, 487). I have elsewhere commented on the ambiguity of the phrase with its interrogative style and final dot which transforms the question into an order or at least a strong suggestion. See Floriane Reviron-Piégay "Les dernières lettres de Virginia Woolf: hantise et obsession de la fin," in *Dernières Lettres*, Ed. Sylvie Crinquand. Dijon: Editions universitaires de Dijon, 2008, 193.

[3] The entry of her diary on the 20th of May 1938 runs as follows: Time & again I have meant to write down my expectations, dreads, & so on, (…) but haven't, because what with living in the solid world of Roger, & then (…) in the airy world of Poyntz Hall I feel extremely little (…). Also I'm uneasy at taking this role in the public eye, afraid of autobiography. (Diary, Vol. V, 141).

[4] "Its [sic] a curious light on your psychology; that you can confess so openly, what I should have hidden so carefully. And of course as I see, youre [sic] absolutely right" (*Letters*, Vol.VI, 404). Just before her death on the 8th of March 1941, she was to avow that she detested introspection: "No, I intend no introspection. I mark Henry James's sentence: Observe perpetually. Observe the oncome of age. Observe greed. Observe my own despondency. By that means it becomes serviceable. Or so I hope" (*Diary*, Vol. V, 357-358).

Leslie Stephen dictated his autobiographical notes to her shortly before he died. Writing her own autobiographical fragments might therefore have been a means for her to come to terms with the anxiety of influence she might have felt as a young woman. Leslie Stephen gave voice to the Victorian masculinity Virginia Woolf defined herself against all her life, and she was well aware that his influence upon the course of her destiny was prominent. Memoir writing might have been a double-bind, both a means of breaking away from a tradition (by changing the rules of the genre) while at the same time acknowledging its necessity and perpetuating it:

> Who was I then? Adeline Virginia Stephen, the second daughter of Leslie and Julia Prinsep Stephen, born on the 25th January 1882, descended from a great many people, (…) born into a large connection. (…) I do not know how far I differ from other people. That is another memoir writer's difficulty. Yet to describe oneself truly one must have some standard of comparison (…). ("A Sketch of the Past" 65)

> This influence, by which I mean the consciousness of other groups impinging upon ourselves; public opinion; what other people say and think; all those magnets which attract us this way to be like that, or repel us the other and make us different from that; has never been analysed in any of those Lives which I so much enjoy reading, or very superficially. Yet it is by such invisible presences that the "subject of this memoir" is tugged this way and that every day of his life; it is they that keep him in position (…) if we cannot analyse these invisible presences, we know very little of the subject of the memoir; and again how futile life-writing becomes. I see myself as a fish in a stream; deflected; held in place; but cannot describe the stream. ("A Sketch of the Past" 80)

Both Virginia and her father seemed to share a dread of what they might find if they looked too closely inside. Or conversely, one might say that their reluctance at complying with the demands of autobiography was characteristic of a lack of confidence which led them to consider that their inner lives were unremarkable and could interest no one. Although Leslie Stephen thought that in the lives of most great men the history of a conversion was one of the most important aspects of their inner lives, he passed his own conversion under silence:

> My mental and moral development followed a quiet and commonplace course enough. (…) There was nothing unusual or remarkable about my inner life; although I may say also that without a knowledge of the facts

to which I have referred, nobody could write an adequate history of my life. As the knowledge is confined to me and will never be imparted by me to others, it follows that no adequate history of my life can ever be written. The world will lose little by that. (*The Mausoleum Book* 4)

It is therefore impossible to read these Memoirs as pure autobiography (if any such thing exists), both Leslie Stephen's text and Virginia Woolf's are hybrid forms, testimony-cum memoir, cum letter, cum biography, cum obituary. Fairly emblematic of this tendency to blur the boundaries between biography and autobiography, memoir and testimony is Leslie Stephen's propensity to refer the reader to other genres better suited to render character: biographies are mentioned,[5] and letters play a prominent part, either those written by Julia Stephen herself or by other people about Julia. In fact, the *Mausoleum Book* itself was meant as a running commentary on the letters exchanged between Julia and her different correspondents, preciously kept in a box for the children. Leslie Stephen deemed these letters to be "an authentic record of the most interesting part of [his] life" (*Mausoleum* 50). This epistolary memoir was also meant as a commentary on a photograph album and Leslie Stephen insisted that photographs were an excellent means to convey personality. The numerous photographs of Julia Stephen recalled her "like nothing else "according to him" (32). Virginia was to agree with this idea that the photograph could convey a person's character more than a portrait at least. She also thought that the best way for Julian to know what Vanessa was like when she was a child would be to look at photographs: "A photograph is the best token there is of her appearance, and the face in this instance shows also much of the character" ("Reminiscences" 28).

Thus, generically both texts seem to flaunt their interest in several genres and techniques to render personality, Stephen's text in this regard is surprisingly modern yet remains Victorian in its search for *mimesis* and likeness and in its endeavour to transform grief into art. There are echoes and repetitions from one text to the other, but there are also gaps, incon-

---

[5] Stephen refers us to the biography he wrote of his brother Sir J. F. Stephen for information about his childhood:"It gives the best picture that I could draw of the household in which I spent my days till I went to College" (*Mausoleum Book* 5). He also mentions his friend Henry Fawcett's biography for information about his adolescence: "I have given some account of the following period in my life of Henry Fawcett, my closest friend during the greater part of the 14 years which I spent at Cambridge" (*Mausoleum Book* 5). In this respect at least, Virginia Woolf's autobiographical fragments differ greatly from her father's in that they concentrate upon her childhood and adolescence.

sistencies, and contradictions: and it is precisely the interest of bringing these texts together. They offer a kaleidoscopic vision of Julia Stephen, her portrait in Leslie Stephen's account being completed and modified by Virginia Woolf's memoirs.

Both texts may be read as portraits of Julia Stephen more than as autobiographies. If the initial purpose of "Reminiscences" was to speak about Vanessa, it ends up being an account of her mother and of the effect of her premature and sudden death on all the Stephen children. In "A Sketch of the Past" the autobiographical pretence lasts only for one paragraph: Woolf's first memory is of her mother and her mother becomes central in the narrative, just as she was central to her childhood (83). Leslie Stephen's hagiography turns his wife into the "Angel in the House" (Coventry Patmore was a friend of Julia's mother); she is alternately the Sistine Madonna (*Mausoleum* 31), "to see her as she was is to me to feel all that is holy and all that is endearing in human affection" (33), "she was for very sound reasons, a better saint for me than the Blessed Virgin (…) and I can say now more than ever, that my love was blended with reverence. She is still my saint" (54–55). Leslie Stephen's portrait is akin to the pre-Raphaelite paintings he mentions (for which Julia Stephen was truly a model), teaming with details, symbols, full of chivalry, exalting the nobility of feelings and the moral values and virtues of their model. But visibly it failed to give a likeness. Virginia Woolf's fragments are more akin to the post-impressionist paintings she admired:

> If I were a painter, I would paint these first impressions [those of her mother] in pale yellow, silver and green. (…) I should make a picture that was globular, semi-transparent (…) I should make curved shapes, showing the light through, not giving a clear outline. ("A Sketch of the Past" 66)

And further down:

> Yet if one could give a sense of my mother's personality, one would have to be an artist. It would be as difficult to do that, as it should be done, as to paint a Cézanne. (85)

The reference to Cézanne whose portraits were rather studies in composition than conventional portraits shows that, by the end of her life, Woolf had understood that biography was less a matter of likeness than of impressions.

Both Leslie Stephen's text and Virginia Woolf's memoirs attempt to translate Julia Stephen's personality but whereas Stephen's text does so by concentric circles, Woolf's text heads straight at her. Indeed Stephen first tells us how he met his first wife, then how he met Julia, then how Julia met her first husband Herbert Duckworth. All this is interspersed with his own feelings during these different events so much that by the middle of the text we have only got a glimpse of Julia's personality. No wonder Virginia thought Julian would not be able to recognize his grand mother from the portrait drawn in the *Mausoleum Book*:

> Written words of a person who is dead or still alive tend most unfortunately to drape themselves in smooth folds annulling all evidence of life. You will not find in what I say, or again in those sincere but conventional phrases in the life of your grandfather, or in the noble lamentations with which he fills the pages of his autobiography, any semblance of a woman whom you can love." ("Reminiscences" 36)

The main difference between Leslie Stephen's text and the fragments written by Virginia Woolf is perhaps the fact that Woolf was aware that words would in no way make her mother alive to her reader's imagination. The self-reflexive aspect of her texts contrasts with the earnest but inefficient didacticism of Stephen's tribute to his wife.

If both Leslie Stephen's text and Virginia Woolf's memoirs are torn between the autobiographical and the biographical, the tension is perhaps more blatant in Leslie Stephen's text which ends up disclosing his own personality more than his wife's: his remorse and fear of being likened to Carlysle for his ill-treatment of his wife were such that the *Mausoleum Book* reads more and more as a series of lamentations over his own loss. Just as the *DNB* was a monument to the Victorian Age (Annan 85), the *Mausoleum Book* was probably intended by Leslie Stephen as a monument to Julia Stephen: it is not a coincidence if the Stephen children called it that way. They must have perceived all the weight of the artificial structure their father had built to pay homage to the spirit of his wife, stifling it in the process. William Epstein reminds us that considering the biographical narrative as a monument to the biographical subject's memory is a familiar image that Walton's *Life of Donne* helped to incorporate into English Biography. And indeed the various intertwined senses of the terms "monument" and "memory" suggest how appropriate the image is to memoir writing:

> The biographical narrative as monument/memory/memorial is a written document which records, identifies, enshrines and entombs—a textualized token of fact which functions as the sacred, monumentalized structure of perpetuated memory. (28–29)

Leslie Stephen's text is a magnificent tomb and the term itself seems to toll the knell of biography as prosopopeia, the attempt to make us hear his beloved wife's voice. Indeed Virginia Woolf herself was obsessed by this idea that autobiography should try to restore the voice of the departed: "What would one not give to recapture a single phrase even! or the tone of the clear round voice, or the sight of the beautiful figure" ("Reminiscences" 36). As Paul De Man said about Wordsworth's *Essays upon Epitaphs*, "our topic deals with the giving and taking away of faces, with face and deface, *figure*, figuration and disfiguration" ("Autobiography as Defacement" 70). Manifestly Leslie Stephen failed to revive their mother in the children's imagination, perhaps because grief stricken as he was, he was unable to take the necessary distance with the events and was too preoccupied with the image of himself his descendants would get. His discourse was not read as one of restoration in the face of death but rather as a discourse transforming their mother into a hideous phantom, disfiguring her:

> All these tears and groans, reproaches and protestations of affection, high talk of duty and work and living for others (…) unfortunately did not quicken our feeling for the living, but hideous as it was, obscured both living and dead, and for long did unpardonable mischief by substituting for the shape of a true and most vivid mother, nothing better than an unlovable phantom. ("Reminiscences" 45)

This is perhaps the origin of Virginia Woolf's mistrust of memoir writing: she knew too well how a well-meaning homage could turn into the pathetic exposition of an unreasonable personal grief. Family autobiography may not be the best means to do away with haunting figures, Virginia Woolf got rid of the ghosts of her parents only by writing fiction (*To the Lighthouse*). Reading *The Mausoleum Book* together with Virginia Woolf's own reminiscences brought me closer to the truth, allowing me to discover different facets of the same personality. These texts are about self-exploration but while Leslie Stephen memoir tells us that to speak well of the other one must speak first about oneself, Virginia Woolf's fragments teach us that to speak well of oneself, one must get to know the other. In the process we have gained a multifaceted portrait of Julia Stephen worthy of any modernist painting drawing our attention to the fictional dimension at the heart of any auto/biographical attempt.

Works Cited

Annan, Noel. *Leslie Stephen, the Godless Victorian.* London: Weidenfeld & Nicolson, 1984. Print.

Bell, Alan, Ed. *Sir Leslie Stephen's Mausoleum Book.* Oxford: Clarendon P, 1977. Print.

Bell, Anne Oliver. Ed. *The Diary of Virginia Woolf.* Vol. V (1936–1941). London: Hogarth P, 1984. Print.

Bevington, Merle, M. Ed. *The Memoirs of James Stephen. Written by Himself for the Use of his Children.* London: Hogarth P, 1954. Print.

De Man, Paul. "Autobiography as De-Facement." *The Rhetoric of Romanticism.* New York: Columbia UP, 1984. 67–81. Print.

Epstein, William H. *Recognizing Biography.* Philadelphia: U. of Pennsylvania P, 1987. Print.

Fleishman, Avrom. *Figures of Autobiography, the Language of Self-Writing in Victorian and Modern England.* Berkeley: U. of California P, 1983. Print.

Reviron-Piégay, Floriane. "Les dernières lettres de Virginia Woolf: hantise et obsession de la fin." In *Dernières Lettres.* Ed. S. Crinquand. Dijon: EUD, 2008. 187–201. Print.

Schulkind, Jeanne. Ed. *Moments of Being: Unpublished Autobiographical Writings of Virginia Woolf.* Sussex: UP, 1976. Print.

Stephen, Leslie. "Autobiography" in *Hours in a Library.* Vol. III. [1879] London: Folio Society, 1991. Print.

—. Ed. *The Dictionary of National Biography.* London: Smith, Elder & Co, 1885. Print.

—. *Life of Henry Fawcett.* London: Smith, Elder & Co., 1895. Print.

—. *The Life of Sir James Fitzjames Stephen by his Brother.* London: Smith, Elder & Co., 1895. Print.

—. *Studies of a Biographer.* London: Duckworth & Co. 1902. Print.

Woolf, Virginia. "Reminiscences." [1907] In *Moments of Being: Unpublished Autobiographical Writings of Virginia Woolf.* Ed. J. Schulkind. Sussex: UP, 1976. (28–59). Print.

—. "A Sketch of the Past." [1939] In *Moments of Being: Unpublished Autobiographical Writings of Virginia Woolf.* Ed. J. Schulkind. Sussex: UP, 1976. (64–137). Print.

—. *Between the Acts.* London: Hogarth P, 1941. Print.

What's Wrong with Me?
A Cautionary Tale of Using Contemporary 'Damage Narratives' in Autobiographical Life Writing

Jo Woodiwiss

Introduction: Narrating the Self

As the sociologist Ken Plummer has argued in his influential work *Telling Sexual Stories*, "everywhere we go, we are charged with telling stories and making meaning—giving sense to ourselves and the world around us" (20). We must constantly interpret and reinterpret our lives and the world we live in, and we do this with the help of stories and narrative frameworks. They help us narrate (or construct) our biographies and our sense of self, and they help us plan for the future, but the stories and autobiographies we can tell in the 21st century are not the same as those we could tell in the past. This is not to suggest that past stories were untrue or less true and contemporary stories (more) true, but to argue that all stories, including our own autobiographies, are informed and limited by the circumstances or contexts of their telling. In telling our life stories or biographies we do not simply slot ourselves into readymade narratives but draw on those stories that are currently in circulation. However, not only are these stories both culturally and historically specific (Woodiwiss, *Contesting* 11), they are also differentially available, both in their telling and their hearing, to those positioned differently within society.

In telling our (and others') life stories we are not free to tell any story but, Bauman argues, we must confine ourselves *"to toing and froing among the options on offer"* (7). However, as the novelist Chimamanda Adichie warns in her talk entitled *The Danger of a Single Story*, if we hear only a single story about another person or country, we risk a critical misunderstanding. This is also true when we draw on one story to help us make sense of our own, or indeed others' lives. In this paper I explore narrative constructions of self and identity and argue that a single story or narrative framework has come to dominate our contemporary story telling. This is a story informed by therapeutic culture, pop-psychology and self-help literature which, I argue, encourages us to focus on the inner world of our psychologies and construct ourselves as damaged and in need of healing. It is also a story that, in looking to the inner world of damaged psychologies, ultimately renders our personal experiences irrelevant.

Self-help Texts as Narrative Frameworks

We live in a society that is increasingly informed by a therapeutic culture (Furedi) and this culture, reinforced through a variety of cultural texts, including self-help and self-improvement literature, also informs the stories we can and do tell. The dominant stories or narrative frameworks currently in circulation provide "*a script through which individuals develop a distinct understanding of their selves and of their relationship with others*" (Furedi 23). The late twentieth and early twenty-first centuries have seen an explosion of self-help/self-improvement literature, where an ever greater emphasis is placed on looking inward for possible causes of and solutions to difficulties we are encouraged to identify, but which we might not have been aware of, or indeed seen as problematic. Whilst this might have an authoritarian and coercive dimension (Furedi, Lasch, Sennett), it is also one, as Rose argues in *Governing the soul*, in which we are "*educated in a therapeutic discourse of the emotions*" which we can use "to turn our own 'cases' into stories, and become the authors of our own plot" (257), albeit one constructed within cultural and historically specific parameters.

Walk into any bookshop in Britain or visit on-line bookstores such as Amazon and you will find a vast selection of self-help, self-development and pop-psychology literature. These "inspirational" and "life changing" texts promise particularly (but not only) women a brighter, happier, healthier, more successful life if only they are willing to identify their failings and look to themselves for the cause of and solution to any unhappiness or dissatisfaction in their lives. Whilst not necessarily written by survivors (although some are), these texts often contain vignettes of survivor stories which both reinforce and give authority to the messages they promote. We do not need to read beyond the titles to know what these messages are likely to be. With titles like: *You can heal your life*; *Lost and found The adoption experience*; *Coming Home to Self: Healing the Primal Wound*; *Self Esteem for Women: A Practical Guide to Love, Intimacy and Success*; *The courage to heal*; *The Sexual Healing Journey: A Guide for Survivors of Sexual Abuse*—these texts encourage readers to focus on healing and recovery, whilst also identifying aspects of their lives that they should be good at or which they need to improve. It is often this "need for improvement" which ultimately leads readers to identify themselves as "damaged," as this perceived damage is said to prevent the reader from achieving the aims identified in the literature. We can also see from the titles that healing or recovery is often based on finding an authentic or "true self," a pre-damaged self that can be returned to.

This dominant storyline of damage and recovery is not limited to self-help literature but can be seen in a vast array of other contemporary cultural texts. One example is the many survivor auto/ biographies such as *The Lost Boy* by Dave Pelzer and *Out of the Dark* by Linda Caine and Robin Royston. Like these two texts this genre is often written either by "survivors" whose survivor status gives them authority, or jointly with therapists or counsellors, often conveying additional authority, and can themselves be seen as part of a broader body of self-help/ therapeutic literature. This literature has a tendency to locate all difficulties within a liberal discourse of "choices"—making it easier to identify difficulties experienced by readers as individual (internal) problems, and render invisible or irrelevant the wider power dynamics and imbalances that inform these "choices."

Whilst not suggesting that the readers of the various manifestations of self-help literature, in writing their own life stories, take readymade narratives or off-the-peg scripts, I would like to argue that they are confronted with a narrative framework within which to construct their own autobiographies. This framework not only encourages them to construct themselves as damaged and in need of healing, but makes it difficult to construct biographies that are not centred on damage. These texts provide a narrative framework within which the reader can make sense of their life but they do so in part by promoting particular ways of being that the reader is expected or encouraged to conform to and identify deviation from those norms as evidence of damage. This encourages particular biographies that, irrespective of the experience, are remarkably similar, as it is the identification of damage and the journey to healing and recovery that becomes the central narrative. Whether or not one is a "victim" of childhood sexual abuse, adoption, alcoholic or toxic parents, or some other childhood trauma, the cause itself is rendered irrelevant. Increasingly, anyone who is unhappy or dissatisfied can construct their own damage narrative, as they have 'evidence' of damage even if they do not have "knowledge" of its cause. This is particularly clear in narratives based on recovered memories of childhood sexual abuse where readers identify themselves as victims through the correlation of symptoms rather than the memory of sexual abuse (Woodiwiss, "Bridging the Gap").

Although the focus is on damage, there is also a relentless optimism in much of this literature which has as its selling point the promise of a new and better self. However, the watchword of therapy is 'recover or repeat' (Giddens 79), and this optimism is accompanied by an imperative that suggests that a failure to embark on this *project of the self* will lead to a catalogue of ills—from unhappiness and dissatisfaction to victimisation and self-sabotage. This literature promotes itself as a means of 'self creation,' 'damage control' and 'revival' whilst at the same time promising to reveal the 'true' self (Simonds 16), and readers are directed to return to this 'real,' 'authentic,' or un-damaged self. This contradictory formulation of the self, as both core and in the making, enables the reader to identify all kinds and degrees of damage at the same time as promising a way to remove that damage and 'start again' (Woodiwiss, *Bridging* 138), thereby enabling the reader to construct themselves as damaged, without that construction being permanently damaging.

Narrative Frameworks for Stories of Childhood Sexual Abuse

The thinking behind this chapter comes out of my research looking at adult women's engagement with the childhood sexual abuse (CSA) recovery literature, often by women who had no concrete memories of having been abused, but who believed that their lives showed evidence of such abuse. This research has since been extended to other self-help literature, including that aimed at "victims" of adoption. Whilst the CSA recovery literature might seem somewhat removed from that aimed at adoption or other perceived traumatic experiences, they share a number of similarities. In focusing on (perceived) psychological damage, this literature encourages the construction of narratives that identify an inner world of damage at the expense of the external world, and in doing so ultimately render events or experiences irrelevant to the construction of one's autobiography. In the remainder of this chapter I will use the examples of CSA and adoption to show how the damage narratives promoted in much self-help literature increasingly inform and delimit the autobiographies that we can tell, or not tell, in the twenty-first century.

We can get a sense of the messages promoted in much of the CSA self-help literature, together with an understanding of what the writers identify as problematic and in need of healing or improvement in the lives of their potential readers by looking at the titles of these texts. Some of the more popular texts aimed at adult victims of CSA have titles like: *The courage to heal: A Guide for Women Survivors of Child Sexual Abuse; Rescuing the Inner Child: Therapy for Adults Sexually Abused as Children; The Path to Wholeness: A Guide to Spiritual Healing & Empowerment for Survivors of Child Sexual & Spiritual Abuse*, and *From Child Sexual Abuse to Adult Sexual Risk: Trauma, Revictimization, and Intervention*.

As these titles suggest, the contemporary story of CSA, which emerged in the late 1980s and 1990s, portrays CSA as a "profoundly deforming experience" (Contratto 1) whose victims are "not well adapted to adult life" (Herman 110). This is a singular story of psychological damage in which child sexual abuse is said to be so inevitably and overwhelmingly damaging that the effects, or 'symptoms,' could be identified in the lives of adult women. These 'symptoms' are often presented in the form of checklists which readers are encouraged to tick. Those aimed at women include questions such as the following taken from *The Courage to Heal* (Bass 35): Are you able to enjoy feeling good? Do you feel unable to protect yourself in dangerous situations? Have you ever experienced repeated victimization as an adult? Do you have trouble feeling motivated? Can you accomplish things you set out to achieve? Do you feel you have to be perfect? These 'symptoms' can also be found in other CSA recovery texts. In *Rescuing the Inner Child*, Parks, for example, suggests that victims of CSA are "guilt ridden, self-sabotaging, sexually dysfunctioning on-going victims" (Parks 13), whilst Herman argues in *Trauma and recovery* that they are at "great risk of repeated victimization" and find it "difficult to form conscious and accurate assessments of danger" (Herman 111). These checklists are "general enough to include everybody" (Tavris 323) and, as Haaken (*Heretical texts*), Showalter (*Hystories*), Tavris, and Woodiwiss (*Alternative memories, Beyond a single story*) argue, can apply to most women at some point in their lives whether or not they were abused in childhood.

Often, these symptoms or difficulties are said to be caused by a damaged psychology or damaged inner child. This identification of symptoms is particularly significant because it locates the cause of a variety of, often unrelated, problems within the damaged psychologies of victims and it enables those with no memories or knowledge of sexual abuse in childhood to recognize themselves in the CSA narrative, and rewrite their own biographies to include such a history. So firmly established has this damage narrative become that it is increasingly difficult for those who identify themselves as victims of CSA to tell different stories, or construct different identities. Importantly, it is also increasingly easy for those with no concrete memories to construct such an autobiography for themselves, particularly where such stories focus on damage and recovery. Indeed, it is increasingly difficult to construct an autobiography that does not contain an element of damage to be recovered from—whether or not one has memories of having been sexually abused.

Narrative Frameworks for Stories of Adoption

It is not only the singular story of CSA that constrains our possibilities but, as the novelist Jeanette Winterson argues, "*We need better stories for the stories around adoption*" (Winterson 226). Whilst they might seem to be very different experiences, we can see a similarity between the narrative frameworks available for 'victims' of CSA and those available for 'victims' of adoption, not least because of the promotion of a victim identity. The identity of those who are adopted, along with the families created through adoption, are constructed as lacking authenticity, separated from their true selves. The dominant narrative frameworks available for adult adoptees are often centred on missing histories and abandonment within which adoption is often seen in terms of trauma, stigma and loss both for birth mothers and those they give up for adoption.

Within contemporary narratives, adoption is often seen as "more risky (because less real)" (Herman, Child 11) and "likely to produce deeply troubled children" (Fisher 344). It is also thought to result in a form of kinship widely understood as "artificial and second rate" (Herman 11), viewed as both "a last resort" (Herman, Child 12) and "not quite as good as the real thing" (Fisher 344). It is a narrative framework that constructs adult adoptees as likely to experience: higher rates of psychological and interpersonal problems than non adopted adults; to suffer the "crippling effect" (Soll, *Adoption* xvii) of trauma and abandonment (Verrier, *Coming* 6); to have difficulties with trust and intimacy, and to experience a fractured sense of self and lack of wholeness (Lifton *Journey* 48). This is a story told in the adoption self-help literature but also retold in the popular media and public imagination. Underlying these stories are assumptions that human qualities are innate and intrinsic, and therefore a return to the pre-adopted self (like the return to the pre-abused self) will enable the adoptee to 'know' who they really are. A return to this authentic, pre-adopted self will also, like the return to a pre-abused self, enable the 'victim' to start again and in doing so remove the effects or damage of their traumatic pasts.

Whatever relationship they have to their own adopted families, this narrative also informs the background against which adoptees make sense of and live with their own adoption, and construct their own life stories or autobiographies. We can see these storylines in the titles of self-help texts aimed at adult adoptees, with their focus on damage, recovery, and the search for a true self (untouched by traumatic experiences). Some of the popular texts sold on Amazon books include: *Journey of the Adopted Self: A Search for Wholeness*; *Lost and found: The adoption experience*; *Adoption Healing... a path to recovery*; *Coming Home to Self: Healing the Primal Wound*. Nancy Verrier, the author of this last text (published by the British association for adoption and fostering, BAAF, in 2010), says on her website that adoptees have suffered "a loss that you can't consciously remember and which no one else is acknowledging, but which has a tremendous impact on your sense of Self and others, your emotional responses, your behavior, and your world view" (Verrier website).

Tensions within the Self: Autobiographical Limbo and Narrative Uncertainty

Like the CSA recovery literature, adoption self-help texts identify similar difficulties in the lives of adult victims which they also correlate with past (traumatic) experiences. They also place significance on the damaged and 'authentic' self, the search for which, both sets of readers are promised, will lead to healing and wholeness. As Homans argues, adoption is lived and represented through an irresolvable tension between belief in the innate nature of human traits and belief in their contractedness, contingency, and changeability. There is a similarity here to the tension in CSA narratives between the self damaged by sexual abuse and the undamaged core self who can be returned to and healed. This contradictory self is also a feature of contemporary autobiographies which are informed by these 'damage narratives.'

Contemporary self-help literature does not simply encourage a rewriting of the self but it provides a narrative framework for the construction of a new self, only connected to its past, and indeed future, self through the identification of damage and the need to heal. Whilst there is a degree of optimism in these texts there also lurks a warning and an element of blame for those who fail to exercise their inner power and claim their right to happiness. Increasingly the biographies or stories we are encouraged to tell, direct us to recognise, or even search for, an authentic self—a pre traumatised, pre-damaged (or pre-adopted) self that can be returned to and, through healing, can 'grow-up' to be the person she would or should have been—a person who is happy and satisfied with their lives, but who knows deep down that if she isn't, it's her own fault. In a new version of victim blaming she is not to blame for the damage caused to her but for her failure to heal. But, in an ironic twist, this search for an authentic 'pre-damaged' self, 'the self you really are,' can lead to ontological insecurity through the removal or dismissal of the life experiences that contribute to the self you are (becoming) (Woodiwiss, *Bridging* 136). With the omission of experiences contemporary auto-biographers risk *"autobiographical limbo"* (Tietjens-Meyers 246) and narrative uncertainty—certain only in the knowledge that they have been damaged and only connected to their biographical past through their damaged selves.

Works Cited

Chimamanda, Adichie. *The Danger of a Single Story.* TEDGlobal http://www.ted.com/talks/chimamanda_adichie_the_danger_of_a_single_story/transcript?language=en 2009 Film.

Bass, Elizabeth and Davis, Laura. *The courage to heal: A Guide for Women Survivors of Child Sexual Abuse* 20th Anniversary Edition. New York: Harper Collins, 2008. Print.

Bauman, Zygmunt. *The Individualized Society.* Cambridge: Polity, 2001. Print.

Caine, Linda and Royston, Robin. *Out of the Dark.* London: Corgi, 2004. Print.

Contratto, Susan and Gutfreund, M, Janice. "Introduction' in Contratto Susan, and Gutfreund M, Janice Eds *A Feminist Clinician's Guide to the Memory Debate.* New York: Harrington P, 1996. Print.

Field, Linda. *Self Esteem for Women: A Practical Guide to Love, Intimacy and Success.* London: Vermilion, 2001. Print.

Fisher, Allen "Still 'Not Quite as Good as Having Your Own'? Toward a Sociology of Adoption."*Annual Review of Sociology,*29 (2003): 335–61. Print.

Furedi, Frank. *Therapy Culture.* London: Routledge, 2004. Print.

Giddens, Antony. *Modernity and Self-identity: Self and Society in the Late Modern Age.* Cambridge: Polity, 1991. Print.

Grodin, Debra, and Lindlof, Thomas. Eds. *Constructing the Self in a Mediated World.* London: Sage, 1996. Print.

Haaken, Janice. "Heretical Texts: the Courage to Heal and the Incest Survivor Movemen." In Lamb, Sharon Ed *New Versions of Victims: Feminists Struggle with the Concept*. New York: New York UP, 1999. Print.

—, and Paula Reavey. Eds. *Memory Matters: Contexts for Understanding Sexual Abuse Recollections*. London: Routledge, 2010. Print.

Hay, Louise *You Can Heal your Life*. London: Hay House, 1984. Print.

Herman, Judith. *Trauma and Recovery: from Domestic Abuse to Political Terror*. New York: Basis, 1992. Print.

Herman, Ellen. "Child Adoption in a Therapeutic Culture." In *Society* 39 (2002): 11–18. Print.

—. "The Paradoxical Rationalization of Modern Adoption." *Journal of Social History*. 2002. Print.

Homans, Margaret. *The Imprint of Another Life: Adoption Narratives and Human Possibility*. Ann Arbor: U of Michigan P, 2013. Print.

Koenig, Linda, Lynda Doll, Ann O'Leary, Ann, and Willo Pequegnat,. Eds. *From Child Sexual Abuse to Adult Sexual Risk: Trauma, Revictimization, and Intervention*. Washington DC: American Psychological Association, 2004. Print.

Lasch, Christopher. *The Culture of Narcissism*. New York: Norton, 1979. Print.

Lawler, Stephanie. "Narrative in Social Research." May 242–58

Lifton, Betty Jean. *Journey of the Adopted Self: A Search for Wholeness*. New York: Basic Books, 1995. Print.

—. *Lost and Found: The Adoption Experience*. Ann Arbor: U of Michigan P, 2009. Print.

Maltz, Wendy. *The Sexual Healing Journey: A Guide for Survivors of Sexual Abuse* (3rd edition). New York: William Morrow, 2012. Print.

May, Tim. Ed. *Qualitative Research in Action*. London: Sage, 2002. Print.

Nelson, Hilde Lindemann. Ed. *Feminism and Families*. London: Routledge, 1997. Print.

Parks, Penny. Rescuing the Inner Child: Therapy for Adults Sexually Abused as Children. London: Souvenir P, 1994. Print.

Pelzer Dave. *The Lost Boy* (3rd impression). London: Orion, 2000. Print.

Plummer, Ken. *Telling sexual stories*. London: Routledge, 1995. Print.

Rose, Nicholas. (2nd edition) *Governing the Soul*. London: Free Association Books, 1989. Print.

Sennett, Richard. *The Fall of Public Man* (New edition). London: Faber and Faber, 1993. Print.

Showalter, Elaine. *Hystories: Hysterical Epidemics and Modern Culture.* London: Picador, 1997. Print.

Simonds, Wendy. "All Consuming Selves: Self-help Literature and Women's Identities." Grodin and Lindlof 15–29

Soll, Joseph. *Adoption Healing... ...a Path to Recovery.* Baltimore: Adoption Crossroads, 2000. Print.

—. *Healing... a Path to Recovery... — Supplement.* College Station, Texas: Virtualbookworm.com Publishing, 2012. Print.

Tavris, Carol. *Mismeasure of woman: Why Women are not the Better Sex, the Inferior Sex, or the Opposite Sex.* New York: Touchstone, 1991

Tietjens-Meyers, Diana. "The Family Romance: A Fin-de-Siecle Tragedy." Nelson 235–54

Tuttle, Carol. *The Path to Wholeness: A Guide to Spiritual Healing & Empowerment for Survivors of Child Sexual & Spiritual Abuse.* Utah: Covenant Communications, 1993. Print.

Verrier, Nancy. *Coming Home to Self: Healing the Primal Wound.* London: British Association for Adoption and Fostering, 2010. Print.

—. Website http://nancyverrier.com/ Accessed 5th March 2014. Website.

Winterson, Jeanette. *Why Be Happy When You Could Be Normal?* London: Vintage, 2012. Print.

Woodiwiss, Jo. *Contesting Stories of Childhood Sexual Abuse.* Basingstoke: Palgrave Macmillan, 2009. Print.

—. "Alternative Memories of Childhood Sexual Abuse." Haaken and Reavey 105–27

—. "Bridging the Gap between Past and Present: Childhood Sexual Abuse, Recovery and the Contradictory Self." *Women's Studies International Forum* 38 (2013): 135–46. Print.

—. "Beyond a Single Story: the Importance of Separating 'Harm' from 'Wrongfulness' and 'Sexual Innocence' from 'Childhood' in Contemporary Narratives of Childhood Sexual Abuse." *Sexualities* 17 (2014): 139–58. Print.

Trans-Autobiographies as Sites for Decolonization

John C. Hawley

I do not have the duty to be this or that [....] I am not a prisoner of history. I should not seek there for the meaning of my destiny [....] In the world through which I travel, I am endlessly creating myself [....] The Negro is not. Any more than the white man [....] Before it can adopt a positive voice, freedom requires an effort at dis-alienation [....] O my body, make of me a man who questions! (Fanon, *Black* 229, 231–232)

[...] we recognize companion souls as we make our way through the world in awkward bodies that betray us at every turn. This is not the special dilemma of the transgendered person; it's all of us. (Boylan, *She* 299)

Despite Frantz Fanon's notorious view that homosexuality is a Western disorder arising from negrophobia, a disorder from which African and other colonized peoples are free (cf. "Homophobia and Postcolonialism"), the above quotation can be easily read metaphorically as a theoretical underpinning for notions of the queer. As I have discussed elsewhere (2001), both postcolonial and queer theorists for many years viewed the other with suspicion and some hostility, or as simply living in rather hermetically-sealed academic confines that had nothing to do with each other. Views like Fanon's provided license for some postcolonialists to ignore the comparability of LGBT legal rights to those of the colonized world. That has undergone significant changes in the last several decades, but Fanon is a forefather of postcolonial theory and must be dealt with when one enters that temple. As noted, his proclamation beginning this essay could as easily have been made by a transgender advocate as by a Marxist politician. As we will note in what follows, though, transgender autobiographies are anomalies not only for some postcolonialists: they also stand koan-like in the midst of lesbian and gay political rallies.

The second quotation, on the other hand, drawn from Jennifer Finney Boylan's fictionalized account of a true story of "a life in two genders," seeks to universalize the transgender experience, or at least to render it less "othered." Its presumption is that all readers will have felt "betrayed" by their bodies, and thus that all can share a common humanity still generally denied to transgender individuals. Much of society professes bewilderment at this perverse other breed of human. In fact, as with the history of colonized peoples, the very question of the transgender individual's categorization *as* human—at least in the sense of a stable category that can be recognized and named—becomes a powerfully emotional barrier to full visibility. In what follows I hope to suggest the results of this social rejection as it has played out in individual lives, and to describe it as an unacknowledged colonization. Once it is named, this colonization seems rather obvious. Helped along by autobiographies that have been appearing in recent years, a welcome decolonization is under way.

In *The Wretched of the Earth*, Fanon writes that "because it is a systematic negation of the other person and a furious determination to deny the other person all attributes of humanity, colonialism forces the people it dominates to ask themselves the question constantly: 'in reality who am I?'" (250). Reading transgender autobiographies, one is confronted on almost every page with a similar phenomenon. Naomi Scheman, writing about transgender individuals, notes that "Those who cannot readily be classified by everyone they encounter are not only subject to physically violent assaults, but, perhaps even more wounding, are taken to be impossible to relate to humanly" (132).

Sadly, one effect of this regimented contextualization of experience for transgender people can have results in their ego development similar to the experience described by Fanon from his psychiatric work. "The imperialist cultural tradition in its colonial form," he writes "... was meant to undermine [subjugated peoples'] belief in their capacity to struggle successfully for control of their whole social and natural environment" (wa Thiong'o 44). Subjugated peoples are taught helplessness, as their centers of meaning are ridiculed and stripped away. Even those with special intellectual talents, identified by their masters and sent off to schools in metropolitan capitals, come back as fully converted mini-colonizers, in Ngũgĩ's view. His signature issue, of course, is the choice of language in which the colonized write their novels, etc. "Unfortunately" he suggests, writers who should have been mapping paths out of [European] linguistic encirclement of their continent also came to be defined and to define themselves in terms of the languages of imperialist imposition. Even at their most radical and pro-African position in their sentiments and articulation of problems they still took it as axiomatic that the renaissance of African cultures lay in the languages of Europe. (wa Thiong'o 5)

In the lives of perhaps all transgender people much time is lost to the "language" of the binary gendered world. Beyond this ocean in which transgender people are willy-nilly compelled to swim, the language of day-to-day coping no doubt teaches an ability to hide behind language, rather than to use it for honest self-expression. "Bambi" instantiates the personal damage that is done by families in their attempt to squeeze children in a procrustean binary mode, in which her beloved mother withheld affection until her son gave up his preferred name ("Marie") in favor of the one given him at birth: Jean-Pierre. "What was the use of her love to me," she writes, "if it caused me so much pain? She had won the battle against me, but she had not changed anything of my essence or my very being [....] I was only 6-and-a-half years old, but I knew with certainty that my life was at stake" (Pruvot 34, 41).

Cressida Heyes demonstrates the frequency with which the manipulation of language might be observed in transgender autobiographical accounts. She records that others have observed "a set of tropes that define the genre of autobiography, and particularly the autobiographies of transsexuals" (Martin 1988, Phelan 1993, Mason-Shrock 1996, Prosser 1998) and concludes that "these tropes in both cases may well inspire post hoc interpretations of a life that fit a recognizable template" (Heyes 209), in effect a kind of reclamation of one's life, but according to a by-now expected schema.

Why such a template might be seen as necessary is described in more detail by Dan Irving, who analyzes the transgender individual's compelling reasons to conform to society's desire that s/he demonstrate that the medical intervention desired by the individual will transform him/her into a normalized and productive member of society. "The emergence of transsexual voices in and beyond academe," in Irving's view, "echoes hegemonic socioeconomic and political discourses grounded in conceptualizations of citizenship defined through laboring bodies" (22). Much like any other subjugated people, many transgender people will conform, whether sincerely or not, to the expectations of those in power over them. Transsexual autobiographies, in fact,

> are often written by transsexual participants in gender-identity programs to gain a 'favorable' diagnosis necessary to undergo transition. The underlying logic of economic productivity presented in these autobiographies makes Gramscian 'common sense' to both expert and patient. Whether transsexuals individually subscribe to this particular notion of productive citizenship is not at issue here. It was common knowledge among patients at GICs [gender identity clinics] that only a particular transsexual narrative—one that subscribes to hegemonic and heteronormative categories of sex/gender—will be accepted as a reflection of genuine transsexualism. (Irving 23)

Unconsciously echoing the concerns expressed by Fanon about the cultural consequences of this understandable submission to authority, Irving laments that "even if some individuals produce these rigid narratives only for functional purposes, the rearticulation and circulation of these narratives serves to embed trans-sexuality within a discourse of productive citizenship" (Irving 23). Any "otherness" is surrendered as the necessary price to be paid for the procedures felt by the autobiographer to be absolutely essential. One must read these autobiographies (as one might read fiction written during a period of colonization) with a double consciousness, reading through the printed word to discern the psychic dilemmas that produced such works. As Scheman describes the crimped options for such individuals: "The apparently conservative gender-boundary-preserving choices (surgical, hormonal, and behavioral) of many transsexuals have to be read in full appreciation of what the real options are" (Scheman 133).

Building her argument on her analysis of the autobiographies of transsexuals, Bernice Hausman isolates the detailed description of the operations in several of the personal accounts and finds them graphic but glossed over in the various authors' unconvincing conclusion that it was all worth it. This, she surmises, is explained by the "transsexuals' investment in the idea that identity resides in the body's tissues, regardless of the fact that the official medical story of transsexualism treats the body as contingent to the mind's identifications" (341). In Hausman's view, Christine Jorgensen "defin[es] herself against transvestites and homosexuals, the two categories of sexual aberration most closely associated with transsexualism" (341), whereas "more recent transsexual autobiographies continue to make gestures toward intersexuality as a rationale for cross-sex behavior, but few rely as heavily on this reasoning as did Jorgensen and [Roberta] Cowell" (344). Ludwig Trovato suggests the reverse image that an FTM like himself can pose for society: "Upon reading my book," he writes, "a friend, the painter Vincent Corpet, made the following observation: Other people, not I, find themselves forced, compelled to define themselves in relation to me, in a word, to find their own positioning. In a sense, they have to justify themselves for being only what they are" (Trovato 46). This formulation of the transsexual challenge makes a nice parallel to that posed, in postcolonial theory, by the "savage": the conqueror must see the Other as what he is not, and which therefore, by God's will, must be tamed.

More recent autobiographies are "more sporadic representations of intersexuality in conjunction with a developing discourse about gender identity" (344). One of these is *Emergence*, in which Mario Martino, "like most transsexual autobiographers ... denies any identification as a homosexual" (Hausman, 344). Having read so many of these accounts, Hausman broadly concludes that

> in the context of these autobiographies, gendered meanings are unilinear and very clear. The possibility that gender might pose a problem itself does not occur to the authors, who believe that all nontranssexual people experience gender as they do, only in the 'right' bodies.... [And] significantly, the 'right bodies' are always considered to be heterosexual ones, in these autobiographies and in the medical literature. (346)

She finds this to be especially true of Jan Morris's autobiography, *Conundrum*. With a vague sense of *Frankenstein* as backdrop she concludes that "once we turn away from 'gender' as the causal mechanism of transsexualism, we can recognize it as an authorizing narrative that works to ward off the disruptive antihumanism of technological self-construction" (358).[1]

---

[1] The wording is reminiscent of Raymond's observation that "now, patriarchy is molding and mutilating *male* flesh, but for the purpose of *constructing women*" (xvi)—coupled to an equally ominous allusion, whereby "female-to-constructed-male transsexuals are the 'final solution' of women perpetrated by the transsexual empire" (xxiv). It is against the backdrop of Hausman's arguments, which echo those of Janice Raymond (1979), that one should analyze studies by Aaron H. Devor and Jay Prosser, being mindful that Hausman is seeking to invalidate the legitimacy and agency of transsexual autobiographies. Devor and Prosser do not share this goal. Indeed, both Devor and Prosser assign the etiology of transsexual identity to biological causes, but Devor emphasizes the

Representing themselves has not been an easy task, since so many others appear to have a stake in defining them. Activists in the feminist movement joined gays and lesbians in looking with suspicion at transgender individuals (see Gayle Rubin, 2011; Stryker, 2008, 2011). With the rise of the queer movement, other rifts appear in the communities that might be expected to find support in each other's cause, and for these theorists the question comes down to: "Should trans identities be legitimized or is it better that transpersons remain, as [Judith/Jack] Halberstam proposes, 'unintelligible,' as a way to resist incorporation?" (Elliot, 2). But trans authors themselves continue to define themselves, gradually building up a library that confounds most categorization.

Roughly analogous to the charge brought against some African Americans by other African Americans that they are not "black" enough, "other transsexual individuals viewed the genderqueer respondents in the Beemyn/Rankin study as not 'transgender enough' because they had often not transitioned completely (or not at all)" (153). Genderqueer identities are apparently the least acceptable category in many LGBT communities where "the intolerance ranged from genderqueer identities being dismissed as a joke at an LGBT gathering to threats of violence for not conforming to gender and sexual expectations" (153).

As in the cases of Bambi and Ludwig Trovato, fluidity in these matters, as in so many others, has generational markers (Pruvot; Trovato). Max Wolf Valerio, who got his first shot of testosterone in 1989, records that "I probably cried more as Anita in six months than I have as Max in four years" (304), implying a rather permanent sense of transition. Similarly, Mario Martino writes in 1978 that "I am no longer a man searching for himself. My search ended in finding that man I always knew myself to be" (Ames, 116). An anthropologist would not be surprised by the individual nature of these autobiographies (Hawley 2014), nor by the complex dance that individuals perform with their societies. "As Durkheim pointed out," writes Jack Goody,

> The social factor is internalized. But internalization is not a matter of imprinting on a tabula rasa, a wax impression; it is part of an internal dialogue, of which "the nature of the human mind" (the initial structure in Chomsky's Descartian usage, the programmed, developmental structure in the Piagettian sense) and the continued reaction with what is

---

similarities between transsexual and non-trans individuals, and Prosser emphasizes the differences (85).

outside (the environment in the sense of books as well as deserts), all play their part. (160-161)

Finding a voice in such singular circumstances must be a tentative and frightening process. Like so many postcolonial novelists, trans autobiographers continue to reflect the evolution in self-understanding that would not surprise Frantz Fanon.

Works Cited

Ames, Jonathan, Ed. *Sexual Metamorphosis: An Anthology of Transsexual Memoirs*. New York: Vintage/Random House, 2005. Print.

Bahri, Deepika. "Homophobia and Postcolonialism." http://postcolonialstudies.emory.edu/homophobia-and-postcolonialism/. 31 July 2014. Web.

Beemyn, Genny and Susan Rankin. *The Lives of Transgender People*. New York: Columbia UP, 2011. Print.

Boylan, Jennifer Finney. *She's Not There: A Life in Two Genders*. New York: Broadway Books, 2003. Print.

Brodzki, Bella and Celeste Schenck, Eds. *Life/ Lines: Theorizing Women's Autobiography*. Ithaca, N.Y.: Cornell UP, 1988. Print.

Devor, Aaron H. and Nicholas Matte. "ONE Inc. and Reed Erickson: The Uneasy Collaboration of Gay and Trans Activism, 1964–2003." Stryker and Whittle 387–406

Elliot, Patricia. *Debates in Transgender, Queer, and Feminist Theory*. Farnham, UK and Burlington, VT: Ashgate, 2010. Print.

Fanon, Frantz. *Black Skin, White Masks*, tr. Charles Lam Markmann. New York: Grove, 1967. Print.

—. *The Wretched of the Earth*, tr. Constance Farrington. New York: Grove, 1963. Print.

Goody, Jack. *The Domestication of the Savage Mind*. Cambridge: Cambridge UP, 1977 [1990]. Print.

Hausman, Bernice L. "Body, Technology, and Gender in Transsexual Autobiographies." Stryker and Whittle 335–61.

—. *Changing Sex: Transsexuality, Technology and the Idea of Gender*. Durham: Duke UP, 1995. Print.

Hawley, John C. "Trans Autobiographies as Performative Utterances." Zabus and Coad 137–152. Print.

—, Ed. *Postcolonial and Queer Theories: Intersections and Essays*. Westport, CT: Greenwood P, 2001. Print.

—, Ed. *Postcolonial, Queer: Theoretical Intersections*. Albany, NY: SUNY P, 2001. Print.

Heyes, Cressida. "Feminist Solidarity after Queer Theory: The Case of Transgender." Stryker and Aizura 201–12.

Irving, Dan. "Normalized Transgressions: Legitimizing the Transsexual Body as Productive." Stryker and Aizura 15–29

Jorgensen, Christine. *A Personal Autobiography*. San Francisco: Cleis, 2000 [1967]. Print.

Martin, Biddy. "Lesbian Identity and Autobiographical Difference[s]." Brodski and Schenck 77–103

Mason Schrock, Douglas. "Transsexuals' Narrative Construction of the 'True Self.'" *Social Psychology Quarterly* (1996) 59.3. 176–92

Meyers, Diana, Ed. *Feminists Rethink the Self*. Boulder, Colo.: Westview, 1997. Print.

Phelan, Shane. "(Be)Coming Out: Lesbian Identity and Politics." *Signs: Journal of Women in Culture and Society* (1993): 18.4. 765–90

Prosser, Jay. *Second Skins: The Body Narratives of Transsexuality*. New York: Columbia UP, 1998. Print.

Pruvot, Marie-Pierre (Bambi). "Marie, Because it is Beautiful." Zabus and Coad 31–42

Rubin, Gayle. "Blood under the Bridge: Reflections on 'Thinking Sex.'" *GLQ: A Journal of Lesbian and Gay Studies* 17.1 (2011): 15–48

Scheman, Naomi. 1997. "Queering the Center by Centering the Queer: Reflections on Transsexuals and Secular Jews." Meyers 124–62

Stryker, Susan. *Transgender History*. Berkeley, CA: Seal P, 2008. Print.

—. "The Time Has Come to Think about Gayle Rubin." *GLQ: A Journal of Lesbian and Gay Studies* 17.1 (2011): 79–83. Print.

—. Introduction. Jorgensen v–xiii.— and Stephen Whittle, eds. *The Transgender Studies Reader*. New York and London: Routledge, 2006. Print.

—, and Aren Z. Aizura, eds. *The Transgender Studies Reader 2*. New York and London: Routledge, 2013. Print.

Trovato, Ludwig. "My Sex is in My Head." Zabus and Coad 42–48

Valerio, Max Wolf. *The Testosterone Files: My Hormonal and Social Transformation from Female to Male*. Emeryville, CA: Seal Press, 2006. Print.

wa Thiong'o, Ngũgĩ. *Moving the Centre: The Struggle for Cultural Freedoms*. London: James Currey, 1993. Print.

—. *Decolonising the Mind: The Politics of Language in African Literature.* London: James Currey, 1986. Print.

Zabus, Chantal and David Coad, Eds. *Transgender Experience: Place, Ethnicity, and Visibility.* New York and London: Routledge, 2014. Print.

Autobiography and Autofiction: No Need to Fight for a Place in the Limelight, There is Space Enough for Both of these Concepts

Karen Ferreira-Meyers

Traditional literary categories such as fiction and autobiography tend to become increasingly blurred. In contemporary literature autofiction is constantly growing in popularity. However, this leads to questions of classification. One of the emerging trends is to define autofiction as a literary genre, recognizing its hybrid nature. The neologism autofiction is well represented in reading habits and meta–literary speech. However, its meaning is neither stable nor unequivocal. In this paper, I will use both the existing variations of definitions and the historical evolution of the concept of autofiction (in comparison or opposition to the concept of autobiography) to arrive at the essential questioning of the need and usefulness of such a concept and answer the question posed by Philippe Gasparini in 2008: "Is autofiction the real name of a genre or the name of a contemporary genre?"

The word autofiction refers, according to various authors and critics, to very different realities. Everyone seems to use the term in his/her own way. Colonna summarizes this phenomenon as follows: "Since there is neither a codified genre, nor a simple form, but a sheaf of joined and joining practices, a complex shape, nobody is altogether wrong: each grabbed a "piece" of autofiction, a blow of the great whirlwind that inspires him or her" (2004, 15). Each stakeholder of contemporary literature having thus seized a piece of autofiction, the notion is found in several reviews, analyses and reflections on contemporary literature and, in this way, has become an important concept. One of these definitions, probably the most common is that autofiction is a genre that is defined by an oxymoronic pact or contradictory contract involving two opposite types of narratives: it is a narrative based, as autobiography, on the principle of the three identities (the author is also the narrator and main character), which however claims to be fiction in its narrative and in terms of its peritextual allegations (title, back cover).

The birth and evolution theory (Philippe Vilain speaks of an "overtheorisation" which "does not seem to work in its favour," 463) and practice of the concept will introduce the key issues for which my paper aims to find a proposal of a solution, in particular the issue of a genre close to autobiography, and yet quite distinct from it, and the difficulties a reader may have to distinguish between autobiography and autofiction.

The Word Autofiction: Definitions in Different Areas and Subsequent Extension

Most researchers assign the creation of the term autofiction to French author and literary critic Serge Doubrovsky. I include the full quote here in order to show the double play on words and the apparent 'innocence' of the concept's invention. The narrator, Serge Doubrovsky, is in his car after a session with his psychoanalyst named Akeret in the novel; he imagines that the dreams he notes in his notebook may become the subject of a fictional book, a fiction he would write at the wheel of his car. Here is my translation of the manuscript:

> I write a TEXT AS A MIRROR a TEXT IN REFLECTIONS
> if I write the scene I live I see it is there it is strong
> sitting there on literally it is true it is literally true it is copied
> live I write recta it falls straight
> the scene seems to be repeating the same scene directly
> experienced as REAL not a doubt it is certain I sit
> there on the seat back of the hand on the wheel enough that I put
> the beige notebook between my fingers book of dreams built in dreams
> I volatilize I am there it is real if I write in my car
> my autobiography
> will my AUTO-FICTION

The shift from autobiography to autofiction was done without the narrator Doubrovsky realizing its implications.[1] From 1977 onwards, the term was

---

[1] In addition, Doubrovsky deletes the passage in the edition of *Fils* which was published in 1977. However, the reader finds the word autofiction (one word, no hyphen, italics) on the back cover of *Fils*. Doubrovksy will remember the word later, when trying, as author and literary critic, to fill the box left empty by Philippe Lejeune in 1975.

picked up by different artistic fields. It became overused, both in literature and even outside the literary field, and eventually came to apply to all kinds of confessions, of autobiographical stories—though it initially designated, according to Serge Doubrovsky, texts whose material falls within the experience of the author, more or less transposed, but whose form and function are specifically romantic. In fact, if you look at the evolution of the term, it appears as if the word autofiction appeared in time to translate and crystallize the many doubts raised since the beginning of the twentieth century, with regard to concepts of subject, identity, truth, sincerity and self-writing.

In his 1975 overview of the structure of the novel and autobiography, Philippe Lejeune talked about the famous "empty box" and indicated that he had not identified any occurrence in which the hero of the novel had the same name as the author, but he immediately went on to say that nothing would prevent this from existing, especially since there was, according to him, an internal contradiction which could yield interesting effects (31). It is since then that literary critics have tried to find examples that could fill this blank identified by Lejeune. Serge Doubrovsky focuses on autofiction in particular because his autobiographical project fails: for him autofiction "authorizes the construction of personal myths: to exist as several entities at various levels in dream and reality, whatever it may be" (cited by Grell, 45). It was later that Doubrovsky defined 'his' newly coined term, for him autofiction is "a dream instead I put WHAT a book of course substitute it's not the original product is not real is ersatz [...] but a book that's never REAL it's like a dream to inscribe myself in a book is to inscribe myself FALSELY even if it's true life that one related it is a mere fiction [...] YOU BELIEVE IN IT it says TRUE but as in a TALE" (Doubrovsky 1977, folio 1645).

Whereas traditional autobiography tries to describe a character which really existed in the most realistic and effective way possible, autofiction fictionalizes a character which really lived. That is the pragmatic point of view regarding autofiction raised by Doubrovsky in 1977.

Recognition of autofiction by critics and literary theorists began a few years later. The inclusion of the concept of autofiction in *La littérature en France depuis 1968* (1982) will be followed by a slow process of recognition of the genre, often misunderstood and badly accepted. Jacques Lecarme was one of the earliest and staunchest defenders. The concept as originally conceived by Doubrovsky, will be included in the *Encyclopedia Universalis* in 1984. At a later stage, several deviations from the Doubrovskyan interpretation come about (Colonna, Genette, Darrieussecq, Gasparini, Michineau, etc.). For Jacques Lecarme and Eliane Lecarme-Tabone, autofictions were born of a desire of the modern writer: first there was a generalized drift to the first person and to autobiography and, secondly, a theoretical questioning of the relationship between two previously distinct areas, those of fiction and autobiography.

The effort of notional disambiguation made by Gasparini in 2004 resulted in nothing tangible since he saw autofiction as contiguous to the autobiographical novel category, but with a more limited extension. Jean-Louis Jeannelle, Catherine Violet and Isabelle Grell draw the following conclusion: "Therefore, the only difference between the two competing models [autobiography and autofiction] is that, in the case of autofiction, the subject's identity is clearly fictional while it remains ambiguous in the case of the autobiographical novel" (26). In sum, three main approaches can be distinguished today. First, the approach advocated by Doubrovsky for which a text is autofictional when it answers to the three basic criteria set by him: onomastic correspondence, literary form and the focus on the (psycho-analytical process. This is to say that, for Doubrovsky, autofiction is the answer to classic autobiography by a literary world trying to solve the ontological instability of the postmodern era. Secondly, there is Gasparini's hybrid approach, also adopted by Madeleine Ouellette-Michalska (she speaks an autofiction flow) and Régine Robin, according to whom autofiction is "a border area, where fantasies, illusions, aspirations, cultural imagery rooted in the writer takes form and content" (47). Under this approach, it is impossible to say whether autofiction is more fiction than autobiography or vice versa. To avoid having to decide on this generic question, in order to cover the majority of the production of contemporary texts that are difficult to classify, and to reflect the dynamism of this literary category, Gasparini offers hybridity as a common denominator. The third, and last to date, approach tips the balance in favor of autobiography. In this context, which involves an openly referential reading pact, is what Arnaud Schmitt calls "autonarration" (430).

From my point of view, autofiction can only exist as an independent literary category if it exemplifies hybridity. If I analyze it according to the first or the third approach, it has no reason to survive. In the first case, the text is a novel, an autobiographical novel. In the latter case, we can speak of autobiography or fictional autobiography. What then of all these texts within which the authors seem to demonstrate the hybrid, unstable, unpredictable, fragmented, and scattered aspects of life, memory and textual reconstruction of the everyday? Vilain notes that the basis of this 'mid-referential' position is an author in a degrading position since, on the one hand, he is forced to prove his sources, to fill the referential gaps of his text by peritextual statements and, on the other, he must constantly defend and justify him/herself, editing misinterpretations, adjusting the text to life. I hypothesize that, although some authors of autofiction see this position as 'humiliating', most of them love it and benefit from it.

Autofiction and the Notion of "Genre"

According to Forest (137), autofiction arose in response to two symmetrical forms of literary orthodoxy: the first being "the imperative to represent reality" and the second the inability to do so because "all fiction must, in one way or another, be an answer to reality."

Blurred and porous, the notion of genre raises many practical and theoretical controversies all the way to its perceived uselessness according to Ernstpeter Ruhe (1992, cited by Garcia, 151) because it leads to "nullity, as it is neither this nor that." According to Colonna, "virtually all good genre names are imprecise, ambiguous or polysemic, even malformed, yet effective and popular generic tools." (2010, 399) In general, the reader makes an assumption about the type of text while reading. This hypothesis guides the reading; the reader will correct it if the text contradicts the assumption; in the reader's mind the following thoughts might be: no, this is not a non-fiction text, no, it is not an autobiography, etc. To classify a work, it must be read by making assumptions about its generic affiliation and then revising these assumptions as it is read. These assumptions can only be verified and then accepted or rejected when the reader knows the intra-, extra- and paratextual clues of a particular genre and is, as a detective or hunter on the lookout for these indices. Reading therefore resembles puzzle solving, in accordance with what Barthes called the 'hermeneutic code'. The genre assists in interpreting the code, since it is an instance ensuring the comprehensibility of the text in terms of its composition and its content. The importance of the concepts of reception, interpretation, and readers should be noted when talking about 'genre', which cannot be seen as a fixed essence, but rather, as indicated by Lejeune (2005, 116) as a "precarious combination."

Many theorists agree that autofiction is not, and cannot be, a genre. They often base their opinion on the theoretical difficulties that the concept raises rather than the very coherence of the literary model it offers. Thus, Garcia (157) states that it is impossible to make an empirical genre of autofiction as defined by Genette, that is to say, "evidenced by a historical tradition and more or less conscious of itself" (2002, 40–41). However, according to him, critics and readers today might call autofiction an analogous genre, "that is to say, built by theoretical means and able to designate in a timeless manner a thematic entity just like 'epic literature in general'" (Garcia, 57). Lecarme concludes that, besides the four major novel genres—autobiography, its subcategory heterodiegetic autobiography, historical narrative and homodiegetic fiction—the notion of autofiction has an important advantage, that of questioning the relationship of identity or otherness between the author and the narrator especially when written under the same name.

Which definition should we retain, then? There is a danger in appropriating the term—not very accurate—of Genette who defines autofiction as a "narrative in which the author puts himself on the stage, more or less clearly and more or less by name in situations that present themselves, at the same time, more or less firmly as imaginary or fictitious" (Genette, 1987, 32). If you release, as does Gasparini (26), the requirement of the strict identity assumption and at the same time you admit the equivalence of evidence indices, it is unclear what distinguishes autofiction from the autobiographical novel, something that has led critics such as Lejeune to say that the autobiographical novel is part of autofiction, but its share of invention is smaller than in pure autofictions. Then it is better not to let this distinction go, to keep it, and analyze autobiography as autobiography and autofiction as autofiction, even though the distinction is not as easy as one might think, although several attempts have already been made. However, autofiction is not without some signs of singularity in that it combines, through the prism of a single narrative voice, two *a priori* antagonistic vectors—the referential and the fictional—and in that it develops an original autobiographico-fictional device which is relegated to the margins of established genres, but by which, via a whole set of referential reversibility, fiction becomes referential and reality is fictionalised. No doubt the ambiguity of autofiction's dual generic status promotes misunderstandings and the possibility of a boring synonymy with autobiography for the reason that, generalizing the 'autobiographical' field, it deprives autofiction of its fictionalising properties (if you classify autofiction within autobiography the reader will take the text literally and only see true facts, no part of fiction will be acceptable in his/her eyes) and its theoretical autonomy; or, conversely, the reader will interpret an autobiographical text as fiction, a real text would be falsified by becoming a so-called novel solely because autobiography and autofiction would be accepted as synonymous.

For me, autofiction seems to have a clear advantage over autobiography: the fictional part of autofiction can 'protect' (Ernaux 219) the author in that it allows him/her to ramble on about the self and especially to confess without exposing others. This is an advantage which benefits many autofictional authors. By inserting autobiography in another generic structure—autofiction—the writers affirm the writing of the mix "where the rights to imagination are at least as strong as those of testimony, where the poetic function overwhelms, works, transforms and reveals the testimonial function" (Chaulet-Achour 116).

Autofictional Characteristics

Everything said above about genre seems irrelevant if you cannot identify a specific genre from typical signs of this genre. Genette (2004) analyses several textual clues—order, speed, frequency, mode, voice and intertextual borrowings and exchanges—to see if there are significant differences between the factual and fictional narratives, evidence which, if significant, could enlighten readers. In my doctoral thesis, entitled *Functional definition of 'autofiction' and comparative analysis of representative European (Amélie Nothomb), North African (Nina Bouraoui) and Central African (Calixthe Beyala) autofictional feminine literary works* (Ferreira-Meyers 2012),[2] I compiled a list of intra-, extra- and paratextual clues that help the reader to distinguish between autobiography and autofiction. There exist different autofictional formal indices/textual clues/stylistic and thematic indices. The paratext seems extremely important in the case of autofiction as it can in some cases allow the reader to differentiate between the novel (whether autobiographical or not), autobiography and autofiction. Lecarme (1993, 227) argues that the main feature of autofiction is that "author, narrator and protagonist share the same nominal identity and the generic title indicates that the narrative is a novel." But he also suggests that there might be versions of autofictions in which the proper name is masked by the use of a pseudonym.[3]

---

[2] It was published in 2012: Ferreira-Meyers, Karen. *L'autofiction d'Amélie Nothomb, Calixthe Beyala and Nina Bouraoui*, Sarrebruck: Editions universitaires européennes, ISBN 978-3-8381-8120-2, 536 pages.

[3] Colonna speaks of a *"disambiguation by substitution"* (2004, 56) where the writer uses a third term that will establish an equivalence between the two. This equivalence will be indirect and requires greater decoding from the reader. But it will not be less effective since it will be far from being a mere resemblance, but rather a *"structural correspondence"* (56). According to Lejeune (1984), the autofictional pact would be "a pact that is used to break the pact. The substance of the book would be fatally like that of a novel. But if this book was truly fictional, would it really have been necessary to specify this?" (30)

The Autofictional Pact

Motivated by the desire to immerse themselves within themselves in order to become better acquainted to themselves and to events of which they were privileged spectators to educate their readers, authors have rushed en masse to the autofictional genre; they made a solemn commitment to faithfully transcribe their lives and have provided acclaim to the autobiographical act because, according to Lejeune, it gives them many important advantages. The benefits of autobiographical and autofictional texts are nonetheless offset by certain constraints, such as the requirement not to aim at anything but the truth and get away from all that is fantasy and fiction. Sometimes readership goes as far as to compare the writer to what he writes. So the writer must accept confrontations with documents and testimony on the past that the autobiographical text proposes to describe.

These limits have of course contributed to the definition of the concept of autofiction, where mixing of reality/fiction allows much more. Therefore, critics began to talk about an autofictional pact, which would seal "an intimate narrative whose author, narrator and protagonist share the same nominal identity and whose text and/or peritext indicate it is a fiction," (Sicart 2005) a pact of imagination where the actual dimension of an action may be seen as incredible because it is invented. Jacques Lecarme talks about an autofictional pact that has to be contradictory. Sébastien Hubier agrees with this and speaks of the "contradictions of autofiction which, as a sly variant of autobiography, would never be anything also but an undecided, hybrid,[4] simultaneously self-referential and fictional genre." (100) According to Chloé Delaume, the traditional autobiographical pact involves the author's sincerity and the audience's sympathy, while the autofictional pact is different in that the author no longer proclaims his truthfulness; therefore an author of autofiction may not be as sincere as an autobiographer, because

> autofiction involves an extremely special pact between author and reader. The author is committed to one thing: to lie to the reader. Actually transmitting, through feeling, his own experience, "outside of wisdom and outside of the novel's syntax, traditional or new." Truth, falsehood, discourse. His and that of the world. The latter by nature unfolds in a cacophonous manner. (67)

---

[4] Garcia (149) quotes an article on the boom of autofiction published in *Clubcultura* (FNAC, 1, 82) where one is happy to merely qualify the genre of 'mixed race' to turn it into literary prêt-à-porter.

In 2007, Darrieussecq thus speaks of a pact of "assured no confidence": "reader, do not believe me. Do not be naive enough to adhere to the narrative, do not be fooled. Writing is not real life." (8)

One feature of the autofictional pact mainly concerns its relationship with truth "is always an intention, never a reality" (i121) because of all these hoaxes that dot the autofictional story. The only truth that it can claim is the discourse in which it occurs. Linked to this subjectivity is a desire for freedom from the author. Delaume puts it this way: "The autobiographer writes *about* his own life. The autofictional author writes *on* his own life. The use of fiction gives the author total freedom" (20). We should nevertheless apply a *proviso* on that use of total freedom, since, while the autofictional author can probably escape the generic expectations, it becomes almost impossible to ignore the linguistic rules: he must use the words of the language in which he writes or invented words that are still transparent enough so that the reader understands them. Another feature is that autofiction is mainly meta-discursive, which refers to the comments on the way of literarily telling these events that provide the framework for the literary work's organisation and inducing the most significant narrative reversals (128).[5]

Each reader of autofictions is invited "to position a cursor on a line of modality." Colonna (2010,437) puts it like this:

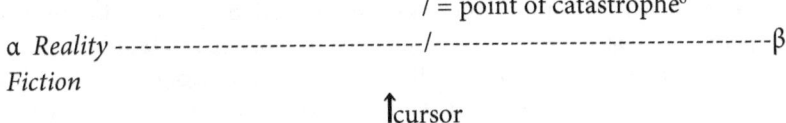

---

[5] It is important to strongly link the notion of autofictional pact to the concepts of reader and readership. This cannot be done in detail within the scope of this article though. In 2001, during an interview with Michel Contat, Doubrovsky clarified his approach: "This is fiction not in the sense that false events would be recounted, because I believe that in my books I really told my life as truthful as if I had written my autobiography—and also as false ... But it becomes fiction from the moment it reads like fiction. For me, it is a fiction when I put it into words" (120). For him, fiction is fiction only "from the moment it reads like fiction." Although it seems that for him fictionalisation happens only by the act of 'putting it into words,' a heavy responsibility is still given to readers: fiction is only fiction that when it is read as fiction.

[6] Colonna (2010, 437) explains that, in *Kant et l'ornithorynque*, Umberto Eco presents a similar structure similaire with an axis going from realistic *mimésis* to abstraction. The midpoint is called point of catastrophe by Kant.

Because of the hybrid nature of autofiction, the reader will change the cursor's position during his reading, he constructs, deconstructs, and reconstructs his own point of catastrophe according to his reading.

Fiction, Fictionality and Literature: How to Distinguish Autofiction and Autobiography

In fact, it is only the pragmatic framework which gives a fictional or referential status to a text. Hence, the ambiguity of autofiction, since it combines a referential nominal protocol and a fictional modal protocol. The dividing line between fiction and non-fiction is surely one of autofiction's distinctive properties. Most attempts (see Hamburger (1977) seeking to find a logical-syntactic definition of fiction, for example) to find universals of fictional discourse seem to have failed. Is it then no longer possible to distinguish autobiography and autofiction? Should we be making a difference? What does the difference serve? The answer to these questions is at the same time the answer to the question of autofiction's legitimacy. The definition Darrieussecq gives of autofiction seems based on an *a priori*. She confines it to the analysis of works that meet pre-established criteria:

> To transcribe the meaning that is most commonly accepted today for the phenomenon at hand, I would say an autofiction is a story in the first person, it makes itself appear as fictional (often, one can find "novel" on the cover), but in which the author appears homodiegetically under his own name, and where likelihood is a stake held by multiple 'effects of life' (1996, 369–370).

The conclusion she reaches is then that a specific element separates autofiction and autobiography:

> The fundamental difference between autobiography and autofiction is just that the latter will *voluntarily* assume that the reduction of autobiography to a statement of fact, to a biographical statement, a scientific, historical, clinical, in short, 'objective' statement, is impossible; autofiction will voluntarily—hence structurally—assume this impossible *sincerity* and objectivity, and integrate blurring and fiction in particular due to unconsciousness. (377)

This finding of Darrieussecq is legitimate. Autobiography, which seeks to tell the truth, is in any case destined to fail because of memory's fallibility.

We know we cannot rely on memory to provide an accurate representation of the past, even if identity is constructed largely based on our mnemonic capacity. In an autobiography, we do not reveal these "deficiencies arising out of oblivion" (Ricoeur 26), and it would be fair to say that the autobiographer often looks to even do the opposite by saying that s/he tells the truth without recognising the gaps that always exist in memory. In addition, it is certain that the writer of autofiction does not purport, nor necessarily want, to be telling a life's story through precise and perfectly true facts of the past s/he remembers.[7]

Without going into the details of what an autobiography is and the long history that the genre has experienced, some remarks are necessary as a common starting point. By 1975, theorist Philippe Lejeune gives a generic definition of autobiography: "Retrospective narrative in prose that a real person makes of his own life when putting emphasis on his/her personal life, especially on the history of his/her personality." The word "retrospective" is important because autobiography is usually written at an advanced stage of life, to the extent that there is a desire to recall and justify certain events and facts. This is why the relationship is in the past because it is of facts in the past which the author attempts to relate with precision to give them an overall meaning.

Annie Ernaux seems to be the first to outline the benefits of autofiction in the sense that fiction protects the writer from committing the indiscretions about others 'characters' (that is to say, real people, who lived in the same society and at the same time as the central character) of an autobiographical text: she believes the autofictional pact of the peritext (the appearance of the word 'novel' on the cover, for example) lifts 'interior censorship' and allows the author to "go as far as possible in the exposure of familial, sexual and school-related unspoken" (220). In recent years, the ethics of the novel and the status of truth in fiction are topics of discussion in the literary world. Several authors have used autofiction to talk about life around them

---

[7] According to Pierre-Alexandre Sicart, the difference between an autobiographical novel and an autofiction is that the author 'assumes' and 'claims' that which is only 'hidden' and only felt by the reader in an autobiography: "The autofictional author a big kid, with sophisticated pleasures. It's also a big kid who affirms her/himself, who puts her/himself forward into a character on the front of the scene of the self, unlike the author of autobiographical novels who "hides" behind the text." Sicart takes the example of Alain Robbe-Grillet and notes that the early novels of Alain Robbe-Grillet were not autofictions, even if the system was already in place, as the autobiographical aspects remained unacknowledged. If they are tinted by autofiction, this is only *a posteriori* because of confidences about them in *Le Miroir qui revient* ("I never talk about anything else but me"), first real autofiction by this author.

by legally protecting themselves behind the fictionality of the text. Beyond all these ethical debates, there is also one on the rights of the author to fictionalize his ego. To fictionalize one's self is essentially an autofictional enterprise. If we are to believe Freud's theory on screen memories, according to which the memories we have of our childhood are only screens that hide repressed contents, autofiction would in Laouyen's terms be a more authentic way.[8] Authenticity is always related to subjectivity, and "lies and fiction author can give a truer picture that autobiography" (Hubier 46).

Serge Doubrovsky explained his views on the difference between autofiction and autobiography on the back cover of his novel *Fils*:

> Autobiography? No, that is a privilege reserved for the important people of this world, at the end of their lives, in a refined style. Fiction, of strictly real events and facts; autofiction, if you will, for having entrusted the language of an adventure to the adventure of language in liberty, outside of the wisdom and the syntax of the novel, traditional or new. Interactions, threads of words, alliterations, assonances, dissonances, writing before or after literature, concrete, as we say music. (Doubrovsky, 1977) (my translation)

Doubrovsky's description, according a large part to stylistic strategies, of the differences between autobiography and autofiction has inspired debate among literary critics, journalists, and authors in France over the past three decades.

Autofiction is distinguished from autobiography mainly by the fact that it is not written at the end of life by someone good or great and known or shown, but can be written at any time in the life of anyone. It is different also because it does not intend to write life as a whole, in one go, it rather gives fragments of life, not necessarily in a chronological order. Autofictional authors also 'allow' themselves to reverse dates, to 'forget' 'true' items, to interfere with the objective truth and to describe a subjective Self, without 'feeling guilty' about doing so because they are not 'bound' by the autobiographical pact.

---

[8] Thus, notes Laouyen: "According to Barthes — but also to Foucault, Derrida and Lacan — the Self is nothing other than the product of language, a being exists only through discourse" (344).

Conclusion

Darrieussecq explains clearly that autofiction is situated between two opposing literary practices: in a single text, a writer states that what he says is true (criterion of autobiography), but s/he immediately cautions the readers against this assertion (back to the criterion of fiction). The elements of the story then become ambiguous and are divided between a factual and a fictional value, without the reader being able to really decide in favor of one of both.

Autofiction which, as the autobiographical novel, starts by an 'I' narrator who carries the same name as the writer, is almost never linear. Its shape is much more random, which does not mean it is a product of chance. Instead, leaps in time, strata of temporality, of history, are arranged in order so that the reader does not necessarily identify with the narrator. Autofiction moves within reality. The facts are real, but the writer starts from these facts to weave threads which, while preserving the pact with the reader, state that what is told has also been lived in reality. Autofictional authors allow themselves to reverse dates, to 'forget' 'true' elements, to interfere with the truth. One thread is pulled from the wool ball of life. And this thread is woven into others, who come from elsewhere and, tapering, take more space, like a cobweb in which the reader can get caught and which, in the case of a good autofiction, s/he will not escape unscathed.

Even without a coherent literary theory of autofiction, readers will read and interpret certain texts as autofictional and will have fun reading them. The public, as an interpretive community, according to Colonna, is the only source of literary vitality since it is the only one capable of using "new reading strategies, new hermeneutic postures" (402) and authors must be able to tap into these new orders to sell and be read.

Works Cited

Chaulet-Achour, Christiane. *Noûn. Algériennes dans l'écriture*. Biarritz: Atlantica, 1998. Print.

Colonna, Vincent. *L'autofiction. Essai sur la fictionnalisation de soi en littérature*, PhD dissertation, Paris: EHESS, 1989. Print.

—. Commentaire de l'article de M. Laouyen "L'autofiction: une réception problématique." Colloque en ligne *Les frontières de la fiction*, http://www.fabula.org/forum/colloque99/208.php.

—. *Autofiction & autres mythomanies littéraires*, Auch: Editions Tristam, 2004. Print.

Darrieussecq, Marie. "L'Autofiction, un genre pas sérieux." *Poétique* (1996): 107 Print.

—. *Moments critiques dans l'autobiographie contemporaine: l'ironie tragique and l'autofiction chez Serge Doubrovsky, Hervé Guibert, Michel Leiris and Georges Perec*, 1997. Print.

—. "De l'autobiographie à l'autofiction, *Mes Parents*, roman ?" *Le Corps textuel d'Hervé Guibert*, La Revue des Lettres modernes, Minard, 1997. 115–130.

—. Lettre à Jacques Lecarme, 4 février 2005 (citée par Lecarme-Tabone, 5).

—. "Je est un autre." Annie Oliver, ed. *Ecrire l'histoire d'une vie*. Rome: Spartaco, 2007. Print.

—. "La fiction à la première personne ou l'écriture immorale." In Burgelin, Claude, Grell, Isabelle and Roche, Roger-Yves (dir.), *Autofiction(s). Colloque de Cerisy*. Lyon: Presses universitaires de Lyon, "Autofictions, etc.." 2010. 507–25.

Delaume, Chloé. *La règle du je. Autofiction: un essai*. Paris: PUF, 2010. Print.

—. "S'écrire mode d'emploi." In Burgelin, Claude, Grell, Isabelle and Roche, Roger-Yves (dir.), *Autofiction(s). Colloque de Cerisy*, Lyon: Presses universitaires de Lyon, "Autofictions, etc.," 2010. 109–126.

Doubrovsky, Serge. *Fils*. Paris: Galilée, 1977; Paris: Gallimard, Collect. Folio, 2001. Print.

—. *La vie l'instant*. Paris: Balland, "L'instant Romanesque." 1985. Lyon: Presses universitaires de Lyon, 2011. Print.

—. *Le livre brisé*. Paris: Grasset, 1989. Print.

—. *Laissé pour conte*. Paris: Grasset, 1999. Print.

—. "Le dernier moi." In Burgelin, Claude, Grell, Isabelle and Roche, Roger-Yves (dir.), *Autofiction(s). Colloque de Cerisy*. Lyon: Presses universitaires de Lyon, "Autofictions, etc." 2010. 383–93. Print.

—. "Quand je n'écris pas, je ne suis pas écrivain." Entretien entre Serge Doubrovsky and Michel Contat. In *Autobiographies*. Genesis, collec. Jean-Michel Place, 2001. Ernaux, Annie. "Avant propos", Journal du dehors, Paris: Gallimard, 1993. Print.

—. Ferreira-Meyers, Karen. *Functional Definition of 'Autofiction' and Comparative Analysis of Representative European (Amélie Nothomb), North African (Nina Bouraoui) and Central African (Calixthe Beyala)*

Autofictional Feminine Literary Works. PhD Dissertation, University of KwaZulu-Natal, April 2012.

—. *L'autofiction d'Amélie Nothomb, Calixthe Beyala and Nina Bouraoui*. Sarrebruck: Editions universitaires européennes. Print.

Forest, Philippe. Propos recueillis par Audrey Cluzel in March 2001, online on http://www.manuscrit.com.

—. "La vie est un roman." In *Genèse et Autofiction*, 2007. Print.

—. "Post-scriptum: 'Il faut continuer, je ne peux pas continuer, je vais continuer.'" In Burgelin, Claude, Grell, Isabelle and Roche, Roger-Yves (dir.). *Autofiction(s). Colloque de Cerisy*. Lyon: Presses universitaires de Lyon. "Autofictions, etc.," 2010. 127–44. Print.

Garcia, Mar. "L'étiquette générique *autofiction:* us and coutumes." *Cédille, Revista de Estudios franceses*, 5 (2009): 146–63. Print.

Gasparini, Philippe. *Est-il je? Roman autobiographique and autofiction*. Paris: Seuil, 2004. Print.

—. *Autofiction. Une aventure du langage*. Paris: Seuil, 2008. Print.

—. "De quoi l'autofiction est-elle le nom?" http://www.autofiction.org/index.php?post/2010/01/02/De-quoi-l-autofiction-est-elle-le-nom-Par-Philippe-Gasparini. 24 April 2015.

—. "Le lieu de l'amour." In Burgelin, Claude, Grell, Isabelle and Roche, Roger-Yves, eds. *Autofiction(s). Colloque de Cerisy*, Lyon: Presses universitaires de Lyon. 2010. 281–304. Print.

Genette, Gérard. *Figures III*. Paris: Seuil, 1972. *Palimpsestes, La littérature au second degré*. Paris: Seuil, Paris, 1982. Print.

—. *Fiction and diction (Introduction à l'architexte)*. Paris: Seuil, "Points – Essais", 2004 [1991]. Print.

—. *Seuils*. Paris: Seuil, 2002 [1987]. Print.

Grell, Isabelle. "Pourquoi Serge Doubrovsky n'a pu éviter le terme d'autofiction?" In *Genèse et Autofiction*. J.-L. Jeannelle and C. Violet (Dir.), Academia Bruylant, 2007. Print.

Jeannelle, Jean-Louis, Catherine Viollet and Isabelle Grell. Eds. *Genèse et autofiction*. Louvain-la-Neuve: Bruylant-Academia, 2007. Print.

Hubier, Sébastien. *Littératures intimes. Les expressions du moi, de l'autobiographie à l'autofiction*. Paris: Armand Colin, 2003. Print.

Lecarme, Jacques. "Indécidables ou autofictions." In *La Littérature en France depuis 1968*. Jacques Bersani, Jacques Lecarme and Bruno Vercier, Paris: Bordas, 1982. 150–55. Print.

—. "L'Autofiction: un mauvais genre." In *Autofictions & Cie*. Doubrovsky, Lecarme and Lejeune, 1993. Print.

"Paysages de l'autofiction," In *Le Monde des livres*, Paris, 24 janvier 1997. Print.

—, and Eliane Lecarme-Tabone. *L'Autobiographie*. Paris: Armand Colin, 1999, edition 2004. Print.

Lejeune, Philippe. *L'autobiographie en France*. Paris: Colin, 1971. Print.

—. *Le Pacte autobiographique*. 1975. Paris: Seuil, 1996. Print.

—. *Moi aussi*. Paris: Seuil, Collect. Poétique, 1986. Print.

—. "Le Journal comme 'antifiction.'" In *Poétique*, no. 149.

—. *Signes de vie. Le pacte autobiographique 2*. Paris: Seuil, 2005. Print.

Michineaux, Stéphanie. "Autofiction: entre transgression and innovation." In *Ecritures Evolutives*, éd. Presses universitaires de Toulouse Le Mirail, 2010. 17–23. Print.

Ouellette-Michalska, Madeleine. *Autofiction and dévoilement de soi: essai*. Montréal: XYZ, 2007. Print.

Robin, Régine. *Le Golem de l'Ecriture. De l'Autofiction au Cybersoi*. Montréal: XYZ, 1997. Print.

Schmitt, Arnaud. "De l'autonarration à la fiction du réel: les mobilités subjectives." In Burgelin, Claude, Grell, Isabelle and Roche, Roger-Yves (dir.), *Autofiction(s). Colloque de Cerisy*. Lyon: Presses universitaires de Lyon. 2010. 417–440. Print.

—. *Je réel / Je fictif. Au-delà d'une confusion postmoderne*. Toulouse: Presses universitaire du Mirail, coll. Cribles, 2010. Print.

Sicart, Pierre-Alexandre. *Autobiographie, Roman, Autofiction*. PhD dissertation, 2005, online at www.fr.wikipedia.org/wiki/Autofiction.

Vilain, Philippe. "Démon de la definition." In Burgelin, Claude, Grell, Isabelle and Roche, Roger-Yves, eds. *Autofiction(s). Colloque de Cerisy*. Lyon: Presses universitaires de Lyon. 2010. 461–82. Print.

The Ordeal of the Soul:
Ordinary People's Autobiographies of Mental Illness in Finland 1870–1935

Kirsi Tuohela

The history of madness and the history of the care of mentally disturbed people follow the same kind of pattern in the case of Finland as elsewhere in Northern Europe. From medieval times following the Reformation and the Enlightenment at the end of the eighteenth century, only slight changes took place in the care of mentally ill people. Even though medical thinking varied, changed and created new combinations of humoral theory, Christian thought and pagan rites in order to cure continued. The treatment focused on driving away evil spirits from the minds of the disturbed, and the main form of "care" for these unfortunate people was chains and boxes. Mad people were kept in prison-like conditions in order to prevent them from violating or doing any harm to the rest of society (Sarvilinna 12–13, Porter 14–17).

Even though progress in mental care was slow, some changes took place. In 1699, the King of Sweden (Finland was part of Sweden until 1809) gave S.A. Sparre, a governor, permission to start to cure "raving mads" with a new method that was a combination of feeding and prayer. A patient was asked to say the Lord's Prayer and a psalm in order to get food. If he/she prayed, he was fed, but if he refused, and if he, after a serious warning, continued to be disobedient, he was punished, usually whipped with a crop. He was warned to seriously fear God (Sarvilinna 12–13). In this curing method serious prayer and a sincere try to feel the right kind of fear of God were new types of efforts and they were required of the insane, the patient himself, who needed to actively take part in the process of getting better.

The autobiographies studied here are from a later time period but reveal a continuation in the tradition of using religious tools like prayer in care.

They continue the habit of seeing a balanced and sane mind through a harmonious relationship to God. To be abandoned by God, alienated from him or tricked into sinful distance from the Christian life path, these were misfortunes that even these later writers of the late nineteenth and early twentieth century thought could deprive a person of his reason and lead to madness.

If madness as a form of abandonment of God was not new, ordinary people writing testimonies of experiences of madness was. Autobiography is arguably a genre of the "enlightened individual" (Smith and Watson 2) that covers two centuries of European literature from 1770 onwards (Lejeune 4). As self-referential literature this has been part of Western culture from ancient times, but it is only after the Enlightenment's keen interest in the self that personal life narratives started to flourish. This meant not only the rise of biographies and family stories but also of autobiographies. These activities of different sorts of life writing spread from the bourgeoisie to the working class during the nineteenth century in the Nordic context (Kuismin 103–105). Personal confessional writings on episodes of mental breakdown are, however, a phenomenon of the late nineteenth century (Tuohela 16–18, 24). The focus of this paper is on three Finnish autobiographies that are the first ones in the subgenre of memoirs and autobiographies of mental breakdown in Finland.

At a very personal level, the three autobiographers dealt with here write about feeling inner chaos, imbalance, and horror. Their close ones saw in them the signs of madness, of mental illness, and took them to doctors. Between the years 1874 and 1934 they visited mental institutions more or less according to their own will and wrote about these visits and about the care of patients in mental asylums and hospitals of their time. They depict the experience of losing their reason, feeling fear, anxiety and horror in the process of getting mentally ill, and they try to gauge and judge the meaning of these experiences as well. As the first published memoirs or autobiographies of mental illness in Finland they are a group but hardly a genre for they clearly differ from each other. However, they share some elements as well. They all try to make sense of the mad lives or the episodes of mental disorder in their lives. To make meaning they seem to seek support in moral and everyday thinking, but also in science and religion. The concept of the soul and the relationship to a transcendental power, a Christian God, plays a crucial role in the autobiographies, in their reasoning and telling about inner lives in chaos and recovering. In this paper I focus on the religious discourse and the concept of the soul.

Counsellors' Notes

Karl Johan Lind (1832–1917) published his *Notes* (*Ur en själasörjares anteckningar I. Angående sinnesjuka och deras vård*) in 1911, but they refer to the years 1873 and 1874 when the then 41 year-old Lind fell ill and was hospitalized in a mental institution. In 1866 Lind had started as a minister in a women's prison in the city of Lappeenranta in Eastern Finland ('spinnhuspredikant'), and he kept this position until 1880 (Mattila 4–5). So his period of illness, his experiences of mental disorder and writing his notes about all of this, fall within the time span of working with the "miserable souls" of female prisoners. He found time to publish the notes in 1911 only after retiring.

It was not a publishing house or a professional printing house that brought out the text but Karl Lind himself. He was a religious man, an ordained minister since 1854, who wanted to speak for mentally ill people and reform their care. It was customary to publish religious literature at one's own cost during the nineteenth century and when Lind started his task the whole professional publishing sector was still just beginning in Finland. As a writer, Lind was an amateur. He had studied theology in the Imperial Alexander University in Helsinki, Finland, and he had written different kinds of religious material to serve the salvation of sinners. He was, however, a modest person, and despite his academic education he preferred to live among ordinary countryside people even seeking the company of the weak, poor, and criminal people in a state of distress. That is also why he chose to take a job as a counsellor for women prisoners in 1866.

Lind starts his *Notes* by writing that it is his duty to take care of people's souls. According to the *Notes* he encountered many mad and melancholy persons because of his profession, and that during his administration of an office in a women's prison some ardent religious awakenings had led to mental disorders—with the result that as a care taker of these disordered women he himself had fallen ill (Lind 3).

The autobiography consists of two parts: "In home" and "In mad house." Lind starts the story by telling how he fell ill at home in July 1873. He continues by describing the first five months at home when he was taken care of by his wife who got assistance from the doctor and the guards of the prison. The second part tells about his visit to the "mad house." When Lind was already recovering, he wanted to travel to Helsinki, to the Lapinlahti mental hospital that was the main mental institution in Finland at that time. He wanted to be healed properly but in the hospital he also insisted that he was needed there as a counsellor, and he demanded a permit to help in the care of other patients. The doctor of the hospital did not welcome the idea but neither did he truly forbid it and Lind started to tend to his friends there.

From the very beginning, Lind writes that the problem, the illness of a mentally disturbed person, lies in the soul. Traditional medicine, treatment that he knew, received and observed himself, too, was not the right way to deal with the mentally ill. He writes:

> That one with the chloroform and other narcotics makes the ill person dull, it seems only to prolong the healing, and it makes the nervous system only weaker and limper. Physical troubles are usually only symptoms of illness that like in the case in question [Lind] is located in the soul. That's why the battle against the illness needs to take place in the soul and the means need to be spiritual: word, sacrament and pray. (14, my trans.)

According to Lind mental disorders were caused by passions and demons. When he himself had fallen ill he wrote that he had encountered a demon that was stronger than he. He links perfectly to the Christian tradition of autobiographies; like Päivi Kosonen has stated, the essential themes of life narrative in this tradition include battles against demons and other enemies of the soul (Kosonen 126–127). Originally, the demons had come to Lind's world when he by profession was chasing them off from the women prisoners. But the meaning of the demons, the phase of his life in which he was fighting his own demons, was in the nature of that experience: it was an ordeal. It was chaos, a painful mental torture happening in the mind but simultaneously it was an ordeal allowed by God, even set by him as a rough task to go through. Similarly, it was a test of faith in which the one who truly feared God, loved and trusted him enough regained his reason. The soul that won the fight was rerouted to reason, became ennobled, more favourable to God, and was even a step closer to his personal salvation.

Lind can be said to have lived through Hell. His experience of the first months of illness included straitjacket, forced baths, and a totally dark room. He was restless with hallucinations, and even though he was taken care of at his own home by his own wife, force was used. He describes his inner mental pain as being in flames when a horrible despair seized him. He remembers how an evil seducer tried to convince him to commit suicide, to crash his head, and eventually hang himself (20). His wife and the guards were watching him carefully and his deed did not succeed, but the episode is told in the autobiography to portray the deep, horrible despair Lind suffered from. In his narrative, this can be regarded as a visit to Hell.

This visit is an important point making Lind a person that has been there, in the Hell of madness, but who has come back. As an autobiographer he writes about an abyss, a darkness and an inner, spiritual torture that is original and rare—only a few people can really witness it. Rachel Falconer, who analyses Hell in contemporary literature, calls these stories descent narratives and katabatic memoirs. She writes that autobiographical accounts of mental disorder, about addiction, neurosis and psychotic breakdown, are narrated as journeys of descent into the underworld and return from it (Falconer 113). Lind's narrative is no exception. However, in contrast to memoirs of today that use Hell as an allusion, Lind's Hell has a theological ground and a status of firm truth. It is a dreadful place of afterlife for lost souls, minds that have lost their connection to God. The shipwreck that has occurred is mental in its symptoms and has social consequences, but for Lind the true meaning of mental illness lies in the broken relationship to God.

Becoming a Sleep-preacher

A twenty-year-old young woman called Maria Åkerblom who published her autobiography in 1920 had been close to death. She was about to die of tuberculosis when her life changed dramatically: lying on her death bed suffering from high fever, she suddenly started to preach, see visions and prophecies lasting up to three hours. She was in dormancy, a sleep-like condition, and when she woke up she was weak but fully recovered from her disease. The phthisis was gone but the ability to fall in dormancy and preach in that condition remained. Maria and her mother saw it as God's work, God's mercy and a precious gift meaning that Maria was a prophet, God's instrument on earth with a special task to fulfil.

Maria Åkerblom's autobiography is a life narrative depicting her childhood and youth. The message mediated through it, however, concerns legitimation: the purpose is to tell and reveal how she became the chosen one, the prophet and religious leader of a movement that had just been formed and that had just started to carry her name, the Åkerblomians. The autobiography narrates how the process of becoming a prophet had had its costs: a materially miserable childhood, severe illness, near death situation and a doubt of being mad instead of a prophet. As a counter-image there is however a deep spiritual upbringing thanks to Åkerblom's iconic, saint-like pietistic mother. Thus besides the battle there is a sense of continuation, a straight line from Jesus, the apostles, prophets and saints to mother Johanna and Maria Åkerblom.

The battle depicted in the autobiography is a battle against different kinds of obstacles, natural and social, that need to be overcome. One of the battles takes place in a mental institution and the fight goes between the secular diagnoses on mental illness versus the mysterious workings of God. Maria Åkerblom's brother Albin and the doctor of their home village had been worried and wanted a psychiatric evaluation on Maria's condition to be made. They refer to a mental illness of the nineteenth century, the preaching disease ('predikosjukan'), suspecting that Maria is mentally disturbed rather than heavenly blessed. In the spring of 1917 Maria Åkerblom is taken to Kammio private mental hospital in Helsinki for observation, and she narrates this visit with a photograph in her autobiography (57–67).

From the very start, the concepts of mental illness and psychiatric diagnoses used in institutions are rejected by Maria Åkerblom. She reports the discussion with doctors and their advice on how to get cured from her sick behaviour. She writes trying to follow the orders and fight back the fits, not letting herself fall to dormancy and preach, but serious paroxysms and cramps follow. Åkerblom's conclusion is that it is not she who has power over what happens, but God. Finally, her opinion is that it would be against God's will to try to be "cured." Thus she aims to leave the hospital as soon as possible and start her work as God's hand on earth.

Åkerblom's autobiography reveals a world that is divided in two: good and bad, true and false, godly and worldly. Accordingly the mission of the autobiographer is to lead people from the bad and false to the right, from sin to truth, by making as many people as possible true believers. The activities that are said to have happened are aimed at that goal and the autobiography as a published piece of writing has the same target. The texts of autobiography preach about the same necessity of all people to abandon worldly ideas in order to avoid the burning flames of Hell. The autobiography preaches about these options bringing a binary language to the description of real situation:

> On the Senate Square Once, during the summer 1917, while I was talking on the afternoon at 5 o'clock it was said through me that I would talk at eight o'clock in the same evening at the Senate Square against the ones that hated the Truth, the wild masses, and show to all that were

present a way to the brighter future that most of them could imagine to long for. (89 my trans.)

The soul that is in need of care and salvation is in Åkerblom's autobiography a synonym for the person rather than a concept of mind. In line with the long Christian tradition it is immaterial and immortal and it does not die, but after the death of the body it has an afterlife in Heaven or in Hell.

Maria Åkerblom's style as a writer was vernacular. She was educated by a deeply pietistic mother whose literature was the Bible and the psalms. The family was a poor working family with many children so Maria Åkerblom really came from common people. As a prophet, however, she wanted to narrate herself as a special one, not like an ordinary sinner. She aimed to be a leader of a religious movement and constructed herself as an ideal but also as an exception, chosen by God. The meaning of the hardness of life and obstacles she wrote about was in the idea that she was tested harder than others by God. Even though humility was a key virtue and Maria Åkerblom stressed that it was not she herself that acted but God that worked through her, by claiming to be a special chosen one she could raise herself above her weaker, lesser brothers and sisters. Compared to Karl Lind's autobiography the difference is clear. Lind, too, is an example to follow and learn from, but he is a man who confesses a failure, a man who became raving mad, a consequence threatening anyone losing his true faith. When regaining his reason with the help of praying, singing psalms and believing in the mercy of God, Lind could see his story as an example for others, but he dared not raise himself to the category of prophet, above ordinary Christians. If Lind's autobiography is testimony and confession, Åkerblom's is closer to apology, a mixture of realistic life narrative and idealized, conventional apology, a song of praise (on apology see Kosonen 34–41).

Autobiography might seem to be easy to define: it is a life narrative of a person dealing with his/her own life and composed by him/her. However, as soon as we relate the text to life lived and ask for the identity constructed in the text, the definition becomes more complicated. Like Marja Rytkönen states, in an autobiography the relation to life lived is shifty and the identity constructed is manifold. Subjects of an autobiography are narrated as relating to each other, and the text is produced in context, in a dialogue with the social, cultural and textual environment (Rytkönen 140–145). Sidonie Smith and Julie Watson likewise remind us that autobiographies of mental breakdown are filled with uncertainties and, especially in this subgenre, the boundary between the fabled and the documented is unstable (Smith and Watson 145–146). A narrated subject is thus always trumped-up, a kind of fiction. Merete Mazzarella puts this in words by writing that "all autobiographies are lies and more damn lies" (Mazzarella 10, my transl.). Åkerblom's autobiography is no exception; it is a mixture of facts and made up elements. It has features of biography and saint legend, realistic lines on the poverty of the childhood but also imagined strength and idealized goodness of Maria Åkerblom, the true believer and born again prophet that goes against evils and oppressors.

Broken Souls of the 1930s

The first asylum narrative, a published memoir of madness and hospitalization in the Finnish language seems to be a book named *Viesti yöstä*, a message from the night (1935) written by an amateur writer, Aino Manner, and published by the major publishing house of the day in Finland, Werner Söderström company. The book reports a very different context of mental care compared to Lind's Lapinlahti in the 1870s or Åkerblom's Kammio hospital in 1917. Aino Manner fell ill for the first time in 1924 and the last, the sixth visit to a mental institution took place before the writing and publication of the book in 1934 and 1935. From Lind's time to Manners the number of psychiatric hospitals had increased from two to more than twenty, and Aino Manner had been taken care of in one of the brand new district hospitals that municipalities organized in the 1920s as a part of the modernization of the mental care system in Finland.

Aino Manner starts her story by telling about her grandparents, her parents, and the possibility of heredity behind her disorder. She writes about the first signs of illness, its breakthrough and the events taking her to hospital. The experience of being imprisoned in a mental institution is horrible at first, but she calms down, becomes more balanced and after being diagnosed with manic-depressive psychosis she is dismissed from the institution as "better." After the first episode of illness, followed by a nearly full recovery, she gets support and even finds a new job as an accountant. She had worked throughout her life doing long hours as a shop assistant and then as a bookkeeper for the local magazine *Ilkka*. Beside her work she had been an enthusiastic amateur actress performing on local stages and in 1916 and 1917 Aino Manner even acted in some Finnish films. Exhaustion because of too much work was, according to herself, the major cause behind her broken health.

Towards the end of the autobiography that reports five more breakdowns and hospitalizations with sometimes detailed descriptions of other patients, nurses and care, Manner takes up the issue of religion. During her illness episodes Manner has sights of a fearful Hell, and she describes the department of unruly patients as limbo, a forecourt of Hell (182-183). She writes how she sees the hospital community as an eternal damnation and compares herself to Dante writing that "[t]hese people, that I see around me—nurses and patients alike—are all lost souls. I myself am like Dante in his "divine play" [Divine Comedy] seeing them but not belonging to them" (183). Manner continues: "these lost ones were not damned to stay there in the old world. They had stayed voluntarily because they did not want to come to Heaven" (184 my trans.). For Manner, the mental institution and its unruly departments represented a Hell on Earth, a form of ultimate misery, suffering, and pain. But it was not only allusion: it was an eternal damnation because, according to Manner, people there had lost the immaterial essence of their souls, and were only material beings. To medical psychiatry of the 1930s and the secular, scientific world they more or less were that, physical bodies. For Manner, a human being without a Soul, without connection to eternity and God, was impossible. It was the same thing as damnation, Hell, and mental illness.

Manner's autobiography is messy and bouncing. The narrator is unreliable and slippery in a way that Smith and Watson remind us is often the case in narratives of mental breakdown. The confusion arises from the fact that she is in the "crazy" institutionalized and the "sane" recovered worlds simultaneously (Smith and Watson 146). Despite the volatility of the text the role of religion is stressed towards the end. Before the last chapter, "The End," there is a chapter titled "Jesus opens the gate!," and Manner clearly wants to compose a positive end suggesting that madness is bearable, even possible to beat with the help of Jesus. The story tells us that Manner's aunt, with whom she has shared an apartment, has moved, and her belongings have been sold. Manner has recovered and the doctor suggests she leave the hospital, but she has no place to go. She has no job, no money, no family, and a dark shadow spreads over her otherwise joyful recovery. Finally, she ends up in a municipal home, the last haven for the outcasts of society. There the world turns upside down once again. Manner is not taken to hospital this time but moved to a guarded and locked room in the municipal home. Her breakdown consists of fears and hallucinations this time, too, for example sights in which a car will come and take her to an unknown place, as happened to haunted communists in Finland in the

1930s. But she experiences pleasant things as well. A prince comes to invite her to dance, which feels nice. The most wonderful sights, however, are about Jesus. She writes of seeing him as a child saint and then later as an adult master in blue silk robes. She writes how this figure walking ahead of her making her being easy, her path safe and trouble-free (208–216). In "The End" she writes that the vision of Jesus has miraculously calmed her down and opened the gate to recovery, gratification, and happiness.

Lost and Found Souls

In the frame of discussion and negotiations on mental illness, being diagnosed with mental disorders, these early Finnish autobiographers coming from the common people took up pen and made sense of their experiences. They obviously had some audiences in mind when they started to write and they deliberately chose to write about themselves; they wanted to share their stories. They asked what went wrong, what broke their minds, and it is clear that the hardships of life, including diseases and heavy workload, played a role. They discuss the role of biology, Aino Manner living in the culture of psychiatric practices of the 1920s more than others, but they were not convinced by the scientific, medical ideas of their time. They dug deeper and found their faith, their perhaps previously unreflected ideas about the "I," self and its nature as an immortal, immaterial soul. Even though the autobiographies of these three writers differ in many ways, they all in their distinct ways tell that in mental collapse the soul, the spiritual aspect connected to God, has been shipwrecked, and it was this relation they needed to reconstruct in order to get better and move forward.

Works Cited

Åkerblom, Maria. *Maria Åkerbloms autobiografi och första delen av hennes verksamhet*. Utgiven av Eino Vartiovaara. Kokkola: Kokkolan kirjapaino, 1920. Print.

Falconer, Rachel. *Hell in Contemporary Literature. Western Narratives since 1945*. Edinburgh: Edinburgh UP, 2005, 2007. Print.

Kosonen, Päivi. *Isokrateesta Augustinukseen. Johdatus antiikin omaelämäkerralliseen kirjallisuuteen*. Jyväskylä: Atena, 2007. Print.

Kuismin, Anna. "From Family Inscriptions to Autobiographical Novels. Motives for Writing in Grassroots Life Stories in 19th-Century Finland." *White field, black seeds. Nordic literacy practices in the long nineteenth* century. Ed. Anna, Kuismin and M. J. Driscoll, M.J. Helsinki: Finnish Literature Society, 2013. Print.

Lejeune, Philippe. *On Autobiography*. Trans. Katherine Leary. Ed. Minneapolis: U of Minnesota P, 1989. Print.

Lind, Karl Johan. *Ur en själasörjares anteckningar I. Angående sinnesjuka och deras vård*. Mikkeli: Suur-Savon kirjapaino, 1911. Print.

Manner, Aino. *Viesti yöstä. Mielisairaalakokemuksia*. Helsinki: WSOY, 1935. Print.

Mazzarella, Merete. *Att skriva sin värld. Den finlandssvenska memoartraditionen*. Helsinki: Söderström, 1993. Print.

Porter, Roy. *A Social History of Madness. The World through the Eyes of the Insane*. New York: Weidenfeld & Nicolson, 1987. Print.

Rytkönen, Marja. "Omaelämäkerta, fakta ja fiktio. Feministisiä tulkintoja." *Erot ja etiikka feministisessä tutkimuksessa*. Ed. Kirsti Lempiäinen, Taru Leppänen and Susanna Paasonen. Turku: Utukirjat, 2012. 140–160. Print.

Sarvilinna, A. *Mielisairairaanhoidon kehitys Suomessa vuoteen 1919. Lääketieteellis-historiallinen tutkielma*. Uusikaupunki: Vakka-Suomen kirjapaino, 1938. Print.

Smith, Sidonie, and Julia Watson. *Reading Autobiography. A Guide for Interpreting Life Narratives*. Minneapolis: U of Minnesota P, 2010. Print.

Motions and Emotions
in Jamaica Kincaid's *The Autobiography of My Mother*

Lamia Mokrane

The Autobiography of my Mother, published in 1995, is a novel written by Jamaica Kincaid that has received much praise. Indeed, it has been nominated for The PEN/Faulkner Award in 1997 and The International IMPAC Dublin Literary award in 1998. It also won The Anis field-Wolf Book Award in 1977 and The National Book Critics Circle Award in 1996. What is most striking to the reader before opening the book is the title and the question that immediately comes to your mind is: Is it really possible to write an autobiography about somebody else? Actually, the prefix auto means self or same; so, why didn't Kincaid write a novel entitled the biography of my mother? Could it be an error? No, such a brilliant and poetic writer could not have misused language. It is only while reading the novel that we understand this paradoxical title.

    Like most of Kincaid's novels, this one is simple and complex at the same time. The use of the language seems plain at first sight but it is full of poetic significance. In Jamaica Kincaid's Prismatic Subjects, Giovanna Covi argues: "her use of language is deceptively (sic). The transparency of the elaborate political message betrays a faked primitive, child-like voice" (32). In reality, it is a very complex novel since it is paradoxical and has a lot of hidden significances and messages. In addition to the illogicality of writing an autobiography of somebody else, the title suggests that it is a memoir rather than a fictional work, characterized by contradictory feelings such as love and hatred. Moreover, it is the autobiography of an inexistent person whom the narrator has never known or met. Another interesting paradox is the book's cover, a sepia image that is repeated in order to mark the unnumbered chapters. This image is like a puzzle since there is a new part of it for each chapter. At the end of the book, we have the full image of a woman. At first, the reader can interpret it as being the picture of the protagonist's mother, because of the title, but when reading the story he realizes that Xuela, who is the narrator and the heroine of the book, doesn't know what her mother looked like.

Divided into two parts, this chapter aims to analyze Xuela's character and memories to show to what extent the latter could be compared to the Cyborg as it is presented in Donna Harraway's A Manifesto for Cyborgs. On the one hand, we will study the life and behavior of Xuela and see how she struggles to build an armor that would protect her from love taking and giving and thus from suffering. On the other hand, I will compare her to the Cyborg and see if she shares its characteristics and dualities.

The Autobiography of my Mother recounts the story of Xuela Claudette Richardson, a seventy-year-old woman, whose identity is revolving around her motherlessness. The story takes place in Dominica, an island colonized by Britain. The title indicates that the narrator will speak about her mother; however, Xuela does not know anything about the latter. She tells her own story which has been marked by her mother's absence. In this context, Xuela says: "This account of my life has been an account of my mother's life as much as it has been an account of mine…. In me is the voice I never heard, the face I never saw, the being I came from" (Kincaid, *The Autobiography of my Mother* 227). Xuela's story is marked by a feeling of loss and futility and this is what shapes her identity and personality.

The opening statement "My mother died at the moment I was born, and so for my whole life there was nothing standing between myself and eternity; at my back was always a bleak, black wind" (3), gives the tone to the novel and sums up the life of the protagonist. In fact, the sentence above may refer to Xuela's rootlessness and lack of knowledge of her own history. It also indicates that Xuela's life has been a very difficult and loveless one.

Xuela was born to an African-Scottish father and a Caribbean mother. This latter died while delivering her and her father abandoned her after a short period. Indeed, he left her along with his dirty clothes in the care of his laundress, Ma Eunice. Xuela spent the first nine years of her life with this woman and her children. Yet, she could not feel any love for her and the feeling was mutual. This may be for two reasons: on the one hand, Ma Eunice has so many children and is so poor that she does not have enough time and love for the little girl. On the other hand, it may be the result of Xuela's behavior towards her. In fact, even when Xuela is only a baby she displays a lot of stubbornness and does not want anybody to replace her mother. She longs for her mother's care and affection and does not want anybody to replace her. In this regard, Xuela refuses to drink Ma Eunice's milk when she is a baby. In Family Matters in Jamaica Kincaid's *The Autobiography of My Mother*, Alexandra Schulteis writes that the protagonist rejects Ma Eunice's milk because she identifies it with the maternal role. She thinks that Xuela desires compensation for the loss of her mother as a newborn; however, when she becomes a bit older, she refuses to satisfy this desire with substitutes or symbolic objects (4).

Constantly haunted by her mother's phantom, Xuela has a very sad childhood and lives with the hope of seeing her mother's face at least once in her life. She dreams of her but can only see her heels and she has a permanent feeling that her mother will appear as it is expressed in this passage:

> I missed the face I had never seen; I looked over my shoulder to see if someone was coming, as if I were expecting someone to come, and Ma Eunice would ask me what I was looking for at first as a joke, but when, after a time, I did not stop doing it, she thought it meant I could see spirits. I could not see spirits at all, I was just looking for that face, the face I would never see, even if I lived forever. (5)

When Xuela attends school she is mistreated by her classmates who consider her inferior because her mother was Caribbean. But, there, she discovers the power of words and writes letters which are meant for her mother. However, as the latter is dead, Xuela chooses to address the letters to her father. In these letters, she implores him to save from the life she leads and the injustices she experiences. When Xuela's teacher finds the correspondence she sends it to her father, Mr. Richardson, who comes to take his daughter home.

Once with her father, Xuela experiences the jealousy of her step-mother who views her as a threat and who even tries to kill her with a poisoned gift. Xuela lives there for five years, but at the age of fifteen her father sends her to live the house of a friend who becomes her lover for a period. This relationship results in a pregnancy that Xuela decides to interrupt. This act is very significant and changes her life. Feeling that she is reborn, she decides that she will never give birth. However, she chooses to get pregnant and to have abortions instead of not getting pregnant at all. She says "I had never had a mother, I had just recently refused to become one, and I knew then that this refusal would be complete" (96). This act makes her feel powerful and permits her to take control of her body and her life.

Since the only person she loves is dead, Xuela's life is empty of love. She does not look for a man to love. Instead, she prefers to have affairs which do not last long. However, she feels passion and affection for one of her lovers, Roland. The reason for that fondness may be their similar backgrounds. Like her, Roland comes from a small island and has no history. After a while, Roland tells her that he wants to have children. Afraid of being trapped in that love, Xuela decides to end the affair and to marry Philip, an English doctor, whom she does not love. Once again, she leaves a person she cherishes because she thinks that "love might give someone else the advantage" (48). She believes that love is a threat of losing control of her life and depending on somebody else. Xuela is lucky to have a loving husband who tries to make her happy. Nevertheless, the feelings are not reciprocal and she does not make any effort to get closer to Philip with whom she spends the rest of her life. Throughout her existence, she gets pregnant several times but she prefers to abort and persists in her decision not to give birth.

Furthermore, in the second part of this chapter, I compare Xuela's personality and characteristics to the Cyborg as defined by Donna Harraway. Interestingly, Xuela shares some features with the Cyborg which is like a hybrid, composed of two parts. In this section, I will attempt to demonstrate the complexity of the protagonist's personality and analyze it in order to determine if this character inspires sympathy or hatred.

Donna Harraway argues that the figure of the Cyborg is at once a product of, and a response to, new structures of power. We can say that the Cyborg is a chimera, a creature made of machine and organism. It is both a mythic creature that looks to the future and a representation of present human reality. Essentially, the Cyborg is a conglomeration of parts that work together through a networked communication system. Harraway also argues that the tradition of socialist-feminism fails to address the new power structures and reconfigured social relations in new technology-driven realities. She advocates new theoretical and political strategies, which must grow from within the structures of science and technology.

Like the Cyborg, Xuela seems to have two sides, a human, emotional side and an unemotional one. On the one hand, we experience sympathy for her as she is an orphan who feels lost and abandoned. The little girl who feels lonely in the world and who longs for her mother's affection and the poetic language she uses, make the reader sensible to her suffering. At the beginning of the story, she seems like a fragile child who lacks love and who does not know what love is. She says about Ma Eunice "I never grew to like this woman.... I did not know how" (5). For Shannon E. Seanor, this statement implies that love is something that you "learn" as if it is taught by someone else, perhaps a parent (21). So, we can think that it is not Xuela's fault and that she feels all that hatred because she has never learned how to love. Besides, the only person she loves and to whom she wants to belong is dead and thus she builds an armor to protect herself from all the suffering she could undergo if she opens her heart. Moreover, the protagonist may see her abortion as being the best thing to do for the children as well. In other words, Xuela has never received any love; so, she does not feel capable of giving any. She states "I felt I did not want to belong to anyone, that since the one person I would have consented to own me had never lived to do so, I did not want anyone to belong to me" (112). Thus, she thinks that she takes the right decision for herself and for the babies she aborts.

Furthermore, she is rejected by her family and by society. An illustration of the former is her father who leaves her in the care of his laundress along with his dirty clothes, which he paid more attention to. Xuela says "He would have handled one more gently than the other, he would have given more careful instructions for the care of one over the other, he would have expected better care for one than the other, but which one I do not know, because he was a very vain man, his appearance was very important to him" (4). An instance of the latter is when she goes to school and is mocked and teased by her mates because her mother was from the Carib people, who had been exterminated by the colonizer. Another reason why Xuela does not trust people and does not want to open her heart is that, the rare times she does so, she is betrayed and abandoned. In fact, one of the few women she likes is Madame Labatte whom she feels to be honest and caring; however, all that care turns out to be part of the latter's plan to make Xuela bear her child. Knowing that, the reader has no problem empathizing with a character who is so disappointed with life and who lacks affection so much that she decides to live without taking or giving love.

At the same time, the protagonist, like the Cyborg, has another mechanical, stony side. One instance is her arrogance and insensitivity in living her first abortion as a rebirth. She does not have any regrets or pain for the baby she killed. She takes the major decision of aborting the babies she would bear without hesitation:

> I would never become a mother, but that would not be the same as never bearing children. I would bear children, but I would never be a mother to them. I would bear them in abundance; they would emerge from my head, from my armpits, from between my legs; I would bear children, they would hang from me like fruit from a vine, but I would destroy them with the carelessness of a god. I would bear children in the morning, I would

bathe them at noon in a water that came from myself, and I would eat them at night, swallowing them whole, all at once. (96–97)

This passage shows Xuela's insensibility in the act she performed and her willingness to do it again. It is very significant that she compares herself to God because her decision of bearing and aborting children may come from the fact that she feels powerful while doing so. In other words, it may make her feel that she controls her life and that even though she comes from a defeated people, she is independent and is free to choose her destiny. Another example of Xuela acting like a machine without feelings, is when she turns her back to the only man she loves, Roland, without any hesitation, because he wants her to bear his children. She has multiple affairs and uses men as objects. Besides, she chooses to marry a man she does not love, Philip. Yet, he loves her so much that he does not care if it is not reciprocal. She states "He grew to live for the sound of my footsteps, so often I would walk without making a sound; he loved the sound of my voice, so for days I would not utter a word; I allowed him to touch me long after I could be moved by the touch of anyone" (217). She does not only deny him her affection but she also does not accept his love. Even if the reader tries to empathize with Xuela's character when considering her misfortunes, he might feel irritated and annoyed by her lack of feelings and her haughtiness.

The Autobiography of my Mother is a book in which the protagonist does not only speak about her mother; it is the autobiography of the narrator and the biography of Dominica's people. In fact, the inhabitants of the island could be compared to motherless children. The story reflects the suffering of and the effects of colonization on those people, whom Xuela calls the defeated. Like her, they have been separated from their 'motherland' England, after their independence. The story also demonstrates the effects of being rootless and ignoring one's history. Indeed, Xuela does not know her history and where she comes from. Similarly, the colonized country has lost its history and culture and thus its people were neither fully Dominicans nor English. In addition, the story, like Kincaid's other novels, is semi-autobiographical. Indeed, it also reflects the complex relation that Jamaica Kincaid had with her own mother.

This paper has analyzed Xuela's personality with regard to whether or not it matches the characteristics of the Cyborg. Xuela is a complex character with whom the reader can either empathize or hate. At first sight, she is an anti-heroine as she rejects life, she is insensitive and unlovable, but if we look at the deep messages hidden in the novel, we understand that she is a victim because she does not know how to love. She lost the person she loved the most, her mother, and therefore has created a carapace to avoid feeling so much pain again. For her, love is a sign a fragility and "romance is the refuge of the defeated" (216).

To conclude, Xuela's situation and life can be summarized through the proverb "An empty hand has nothing to give." In other words, she has nothing from the beginning of her life, not even the love of her mother. Consequently, she cannot offer much. She does not know what a mother's warmth and love is like and thus decides to abort her babies. For her, death is less painful than growing up without affection. She has experienced that situation and does not wish her babies to suffer as she did.

Works Cited

Covi, Giovanna. *Jamaica Kincaid's Prismatic Subjects*. London: Mango, 2003. Print.

Haraway, Donna. *A Manifesto for Cyborgs*. London: Cambridge UP, 1994. Print.

Kincaid, Jamaica. *The Autobiography of my Mother*. New York: Straus and Giroux, 1996. Print.

Schulteis, Alexandra. *Family Matters in Jamaica Kincaid's The Autobiography of My Mother*. George Washington University, Washington D.C. Winter 2001. Web. 14 March 2011. Print.

Seanor, Shannon E. *From Longing to Loss: Mother-Daughter relationships in the novels of Jamaica Kincaid*. Florida State U. Fall 2008. Web. 6 February 2011. Print.

"No Shadows Under Us:"
Fictional Freedoms and Real Violations in Louise Erdrich's *Shadow Tag*

Laura Castor

The various representations of self in Louise Erdrich's *Shadow Tag* (2010) suggest that any move toward self-understanding and liberation demands a deliberate subversion of violating power structures. This includes resisting conventional assumptions about who the readers of autobiographical fiction are, and how we position ourselves critically, psychologically, and ethically. Autobiography theorist Leigh Gilmore notes that this resistance includes the ability to question the assumption that is central to Philippe Lejeune's influential "autobiographical pact." Lejeune defines autobiography as "Retrospective prose narrative written by a real person concerning his own existence, where the focus is his individual life, in particular the story of his personality." According to Lejeune's criteria in "The Autobiographical Pact," "the narrator and the principal character are identical" (*On Autobiography* 4).

Lejeune asserted in *On Autobiography* (1989) that the writer makes a "pact" with the intended reader promising that the protagonist and narrator speak for him or her as author. What distinguishes autobiography from biography or the novel is the underlying agreement with the reader that the writer tells the truth, at least is trying to do so. In Lejeune's framework, it is the writer who is ethically accountable to the reader, while the reader is imagined as a curious or discerning recipient, not one whose own ethical accountability is considered. The issue for Lejeune is that within a general "autobiographical space," a writer might choose to write in the genre of autobiography and thus to establish a direct pact with the reader, or he or she might establish what Lejeune calls an "indirect pact" though fiction. But whatever the chosen form, it is expected that the writer of the text expresses truths about the self through the autobiographical protagonist.¹ Leigh Gilmore notes that

> To admit the difference between the writer of the text and the autobiographical protagonist threatens the truthfulness of the scene for some readers and critics. Such an admission reveals too clearly the constructedness of autobiography, both its inevitable affiliation with fiction and its recalcitrant realism. (98)

For her, "the two locations of representation and identity (...) emerge in relation to each other" (98). Given his extensive consideration of the autobiographical pact in its various expressions, I do not consider Lejeune to be among these skeptical readers and critics. But a number of feminist critics since the early 1980s, including Gilmore, have pointed to the reality that, in many cases, the reader might not wish the writer well.² Gilmore suggests that the prototypical reader/writer relationship in autobiography (as defined by Lejeune) is similar to nationalism, in that autobiography "never quite fulfills its promise in local terms. It is considerably more partial and exclusive as a practice, though as a fantasy it seems 'free' and available to all" (Gilmore 13).

Erdrich develops various connections between the autobiographical mode and fiction in ways that I will argue are both valid and valuable. She does so in terms of the kind of empathetic reader she encourages in a world where self-representation is not necessarily freely available to all. In *Shadow Tag* multiple narrative perspectives are interwoven in a larger six-part structure that consists of five parts of increasingly shorter length, and a final chapter entitled "Riel." Riel is the daughter of Irene America and her husband Gil, an acclaimed painter of iconic Native American images that feature his wife as representative of the suffering and victimization of indigenous Americans. The novel begins with a passage from Irene's secret "Blue Notebook." Excerpts from the notebook appear at intervals throughout the novel, as do passages from Irene's fictional "Red Diary." In both journals, Irene attempts to subvert Gil's control over her and their family as he becomes increasingly depressed and withdrawn. Riel's last chapter also

---

[1] See Lejeune (22–30) for a nuanced discussion of this space, and how it is expressed differently in the genres of biography, the novel, and autobiography.
[2] See Smith and Watson on the "History of Autobiography Criticism" in *Reading Autobiography: A Guide to Interpreting Life Narratives* (2010) for an overview of feminist approaches since the 1980s.

takes a first person perspective, and it, too, focuses on the need to take away Gil's power.

The name "Riel" alludes to multiple layers of self-representation: Riel tells the reader that she is the real, apparently "omniscient" narrator in earlier sections of the book between Irene's journal entries. In a narration that resembles a confessional autobiographical account, she explains how she constructed the earlier chapters by integrating her mother's two types of journal excerpts; historical context from Irene's doctoral thesis on the 19th century painter of Indians, George Caitlin; passages about her own historical namesake, the Canadian Metis warrior and poet Louis Riel[3]; and her own "memory charts." These charts include memories of the past and possible scenarios for the future about various ways that Riel imagined her family could survive a disaster (Erdrich, *Shadow Tag* 116); In short, *Shadow Tag* threads multiple life narratives along with Irene's two diary versions of her life with her husband Gil and her children. It is also a biography of Irene from Riel's perspective, Riel's representation of her family history, and it is her own emerging story within Native North American history that places Louis Riel's identity as poet and warrior at the center. All of these perspectives, including the omniscient voice she uses to connect the first person passages, are, to use philosopher Donna Haraway's term, true but only partially (Haraway).

Characterized by several reviewers as an autobiographical "roman à clef,"[4] the novel has been a *New York Times* bestseller. However, the small body of scholarship on the text has avoided dealing directly with the parallels between the characters in the novel and Erdrich's marriage to the Native writer Michael Dorris.

Several critical studies (Peterson, Roemer, Hudson, Friedman, Hudson, Morrison) address the serial characterization in Erdrich's writing as a whole. Peterson (2012) discusses Erdrich's interest in continuing characters and stories across novels, comparing her larger concerns with personal and collective memory and histories of place to Faulkner. Peterson states that Erdrich's work as a whole is a serial narrative that has autobiographical

---

[3] See Reid for a compelling intellectual history of Louis Riel's power in the Canadian historical imagination. Reed notes that there have been more biographies written on Riel than on any single other Canadian figure.
[4] See, for example, Cohen (2010). She notes, "The novel's final chapters contain a series of shocks that resound both thematically within the context of the narrative and—for the considerable number of readers who will come to this book well versed in the publicized details of Erdrich's own life—beyond the page."

elements: "Through her interlinked novels, Erdrich is writing her own epic, her own tale of the tribe" (107).

Peterson notes that Erdrich's most compelling characters, such as Nanapush, Fleur Pillager, Lulu Lamartine, Gerry Nanapush, and Lipsha Morrissey, use old stories and traditions to resist oppression and seek justice for their communities. These characters function as tricksters, defined in indigenous contexts as figures whose intentions are to restore balance to an imbalanced world. Although it is not the purpose of this paper to discuss the trickster in *Shadow Tag*, Riel and Irene both try to devise trickster methods of subverting Gil's power over them.

In a related emphasis on Riel's role, Morrison (2014) explores the ways in which the main characters in *Shadow Tag* exemplify Frantz Fanon's stages of colonization. He argues that Riel exemplifies Fanon's notion of the "hybrid" who finds a way to transform the earlier stage of colonization represented by Gil as "colonizer" and Irene as "colonized" subject. Peterson's commentary provides an apt summary of the larger issues that link all of these studies: "Erdrich's fiction as a whole emphasizes that the struggle to survive in the world reveals that wisdom and compassion may result from the struggle" (107).

This observation includes the ways in which Erdrich constructs an intended reader who does not easily fit into categories of the product of historical colonizer or colonized subjects. For Roemer, Erdrich's approach to narration encourages new ways of listening that move beyond this opposition (Roemer 2).

Taking relationship conflicts between men and women in clinical experience as a starting point, Friedman (2012), in "Destructive Women and the Men Who Can't Leave Them" sees Gil's attitudes and behavior toward Irene as similar to that of his clients. While Friedman acknowledges that both Gil and Irene contribute to the dysfunction in their relationship, he observes that Gil's own self-destructive patterns of thinking of himself as Irene's victim make it impossible for him to know whether or not he even wants to remain in the relationship: "Irene might hate Gil, while he had no idea how much he hated Irene because he was so focused on winning back her love." (Friedman 149). Hudson (2013) uses Family Systems Theory to explore Erdrich's characters, especially the psychological ways in which they create images of the "self" through narrative. In contrast to Friedman's emphasis on harmful relationship patterns, he considers the novel as exemplary of "the ways in which individuals can use narrative to escape destructive cycles of family dysfunction" (Hudson 2).

The issue of why may have more to do with the assumptions that the claim of autobiographical fiction tends to generate, than with a lack of interest in the obvious connections.

Gilmore notes that one of the recurring questions that critics and theorists of autobiography have asked has been about the relationship between the fictional and the real: "Invoking the 'autobiographical' as a dimension of writing raises or ought to raise, as many questions as it seems to answer. Unfortunately, its invocation seems to settle things down rather than open them up" (Gilmore 100). Too often, when the label "autobiographical" is applied, the approach to reading the text stops with questions about how "real to life" the text is. This includes not only autobiographical novels, but also first person accounts that claim connections with lived experience, such as memoirs, testimonials, and confessions.

My first question, then, is "On what basis is it valid to read *Shadow Tag* as autobiographical?" Second, "For what purpose, and for whose benefit is it valuable to read the text as autobiographical?" In addressing the first issue, I intend to trouble the waters of autobiographical interpretation rather than settle things down. As for the second question, I consider "trouble" in terms of the politics of belonging implied in autobiographical reading. These dynamics include not only an imagined Indian or non-Indian audience for Erdrich's fiction, but also her wide readership transcending these categories.[5]

One important reason for these limited kinds of readings has been that autobiographical interpretations have more often than not looked for representations of the "real" through metaphor rather than metonymy (Olney, Eakin, Smith and Watson *Reading Autobiography*). Gilmore observes that

> The autobiographical subject represents the real person not only or even primarily as a metaphor of self, wherein the self in the text transcends its materiality and becomes an emblem for a person's striving. But by emphasizing metaphor, autobiography seems to represent or be represented by the metaphor for truth beyond argument, or identity beyond proof, of what simply is. (Gilmore 101)

A more productive way of reading this relationship is in terms of contiguity, where the writer "extends the self in the writing, and puts her in another place" (101).

---

[5] See Roemer's discussion of the ways in which Erdrich's narration across novels encourages ways of listening that move beyond the dualistic expectation that her ideal readers identify as either historically colonized Indians or descendants of non-Indian colonizers.

Reading Shadow Tag as Autobiographical: How is it Valid?

One means by which Erdrich extends herself comes midway through the novel, when a character by the name of "Louise" appears and then disappears. The reference is so fleeting that it could be missed by a casual reader, or assumed to be an editing glitch. Yet it seems to beg the question: Is Erdrich giving us a hint that she means to do some autobiographical work here? Irene is at a restaurant with the half-sister, May, whom she has recently met, when the narrator writes:

> I'm going to tell her, [Irene] thought. I'm going to tell her that I am leaving Gil. If I tell just one person, I can do it. She will be that person.
>
> May, she said.
>
> Wait! More bread, please?
>
> Louise made an elaborate show of getting more bread. Now that Irene was here, she was uncomfortable, embarrassed. It had not upset her when Gil had called her up and asked for her help in creating a party for Irene. (134)

There are only two characters in this scene, Irene and May. Gil had called May, not a character named Louise, for help in arranging a party for Irene. Erdrich is a trickster here in using the name of her character "May" to introduce a kind of indeterminacy: When "May" becomes "Louise" for a single line, the reader "may" see that the author's presence in this narration as passing "shadow" that reinforces the book's title at the level of authorship and character. Louise as the author does not place her own life narrative as an overt subject of the novel. Rather, she puts herself in "another place" covertly not only in the passage above, but in other ways as well.

In 1997, Erdrich's husband, the writer Michael Dorris, from whom she was separated at the time, took his own life after years of struggling with depression. Erdrich could have chosen to write a memoir or a more obviously autobiographical text, as she had done for her early experience of motherhood in *Blue Jay's Dance* (1996) and in *Islands and Books in Ojibwe Country* (2003), where she combines a travel narrative with another story of motherhood and the opening of her independent bookstore in Minneapolis. Erdrich talks about the difficulty of speaking and writing directly about her relationship with Dorris in a 2010 interview for the *Paris Review*:

> I've not spoken much about what it was like to work with Michael, partly because I feel that there's something unfair about it. He can't tell his side of the story. I have everything that we once had together. It touches me that he left me as his literary executor. I think he trusted that I would be good to his words, and I have tried to do that. So it's difficult to set the record straight because it would be my view, the way I see it. Still, he controlled our narrative when he was living. I am weary of all of the old leftover assumptions, and what else, really, do people have to go on?
>
> I would have loved for Michael to have had his own life as a writer and not covet my life as a writer. But he couldn't help himself.

The characterization of Dorris in the lines above has some parallels with the character of Gil, an acclaimed visual artist in the novel. Gil, like Dorris, controlled the narrative of his marriage as long as he and Irene lived. Both Gil as an artist who made his living through painting, and Dorris who made his living through writing, were creative people whose work depended largely on their relationships with their wives. In addition, the novel is situated in Minneapolis, and the subject of Irene's doctoral dissertation, George Caitlin was also one of the subjects of Louise's sister, Heid Erdrich's doctoral dissertation, and the focus of a play she performed in Minneapolis in 2010 (Erdrich, H., Conversation with Castor, Regan). The issue, however, is not how factually accurate in Erdrich's actual experience the novel is. Rather, how might she use memories and material from her experience as a way of getting her readers to do their own cultural work of questioning violence in relationships between men and women? This includes the psychological and ethical dimensions of looking at the ways in which gendered and racial violence, including historical trauma, may be internalized through suicide.[6]

Erdrich's personal process of healing the trauma in her marriage to Michael Dorris and of his suicide may be just as important as her cultural work on behalf of America's trauma as a nation from the time of contact between European immigrants and Native peoples. However, in terms of reader responses, there is an important difference between individual and collective psychological healing encouraged through a particular use of the autobiographical mode, and the revelation of intimate details that feeds into tabloid sensationalism. The reality is that Erdrich chose to publish this particular novel with all of its autobiographical subtexts, and therefore

---

[6] See Denham for a discussion of historical trauma in Native American experience.

intends the text to serve the needs of a broad audience aside from her own therapeutic needs. How, then, does she encourage a reader who is less voyeuristic, and more reflective? Erdrich's ideal reader respects the problematic nature of self-representation and the individual author's right to privacy. At the same time, she or he is empathetic with the author, narrators, and with certain characters more than others.[7]

In the novel, this question is posed during a conversation about a person's right to privacy. Irene asks,

> Gil, do you ever think about privacy, I mean, as a notion, how much people are entitled to it? How much people give up when they're together, say, how much privacy is important or right? Gil?
>
> He was still staring at her, his eyes moving in tiny, sharp jabs.

At this point in their conversation, Gil starts talking about how American citizens are spied upon illegally and wiretapped, and how nobody seems to care that we are giving up one civil right after another in the name of national security. Irene tells him to please "stop talking political shit," that she didn't mean privacy as in civil rights, but "between humans in an emotional sense (Erdrich L. *Shadow Tag* 33).

Irene's question relates to Erdrich's concern that as literary executer of Dorris's work, he had trusted her to "be good with his words" in the sense of maintaining a certain degree of respect for the difference between his literary production and his personal struggles. The question is also relevant to the legacy of the confession for the genre of autobiography. As Gilmore states, "Any self-representational act is fully burdened by its public charge to disclose a private truth" (Gilmore 14). For Gilmore, and, I would argue, for Erdrich, "there are other ways to bear this burden" (14). *Shadow Tag*, like the texts in Gilmore's study, "confronts how the confessional limits of autobiography might prevent" certain stories from being told. One such story is Erdrich's version of "what it was like to work with Michael" (Erdrich, *Paris Review*), and her subsequent recognition that unlike Irene in the novel, she is determined to stay alive. When asked by an interviewer about her remark in *Blue Jay's Dance* that there were "moments in which suicide was appealing," Erdrich responded,

---

[7] See Lyman.

Postpartum depression, but I beat that thought down. Certainly after Michael's death it became clear that I wouldn't kill myself to save my life. At that point I realized that the main thing a parent has to do is stay alive. It doesn't matter how rotten you are, or if you fail. A failed parent is better than a dead parent. A failed parent at least gives you someone to rail against. A former army psychiatrist said something that struck me. He said that there are people who will kill themselves no matter what, and there are people who won't do it no matter what. There are people who can go through an endless level of psychological pain, and still they will not kill themselves. I want to be that last person. (Erdrich *Paris Review*)

In the novel, Riel's admission at the end of the book that "I am still mad at you, Mom" reinforces the conviction behind Erdrich's statement above that "a failed parent is better than a dead parent." Riel also has the deluded idea that she has the gift of omniscience, which she claims "is something—I don't know if it's generally known—that children develop once they lose their parents" (Erdrich, *Shadow Tag* 251). This notion might have been corrected if she still had a living parent to give her more perspective. Whatever Riel's connections with Erdrich's own imagined or actual life experience, the question remains as to how *Shadow Tag* can be read as autobiographical in more than occasional examples.

Reading Shadow Tag *as Autobiographical: How is it Valuable?*

To approach the novel autobiographically requires an attention to the ways in which Erdrich uses the "shadow" of her title. The shadow can have a literal meaning as when Irene, Gil, and their children play a game called shadow tag in the snow (143). It can have an uncanny symbolic meaning when, during the game, "Gil found a place just under the light where he could hide his shadow tightly" and later, spring across the field (143). It can have a metonymic relationship in history and conflicting European and Native tradition, as in the narrator's observation that the tribes Caitlin visited produced visual art that was "one dimensional and contained no shadows" (140). Caitlin, says the narrator, "brought shadows" into his paintings of Indians, and "because of the shadows, his paintings had the direct force and power of the supernatural" (141). These references are reinforced implicitly in the shadow psychological sides of her main characters. For example, Riel consciously and unconsciously develops her own identity in relation to her father's power. Just as Gil becomes increasingly determined to control his family's actions and thinking, Riel learns over time how to subvert his consuming power: "(…) she decided that she would not be just a Native person, an American Indian, an Ojibwe or a Dakota or a Cree, but a person of example. She would become a girl of depth, strength, cunning, and truth. Over time, she was sure, if she observed her father closely enough, she would figure out how to get the better of him. Her basic decision was this: she would take away his power" (62).

Taking away his power might not be possible in her life time, and Riel is still angry at the end. She does succeed, though, in becoming a "person of example" through her narration, perhaps in ways that are more apparent to the reader than to her. What matters to us is not that we are duped into taking her word that she can see into the minds of her dead parents. Rather, she shows readers that she may be fallible in some of her representations, but that at the same time she listens to the various contexts and discourses that have shaped her parents' and siblings' lives. In effect, if not in intention, Riel avoids the kind of consuming "god trick" objectivity that Gil wanted when he began his "heart's desire project" (Haraway). Instead, the various historical accounts, journal excerpts, and shifts in narrative voice, all contribute to encouraging the reader to see how the knowledge produced in this text is situated and true from its limited perspective.

At the same time, the power of the Gils in the world still kills the spirits of many people. Taking away their power, for Erdrich, is more about using the imagination to diffuse it, rather than exposing it directly—either in a court of law or in a confessional autobiography. This approach develops for Riel over time. As a young girl, when she had started her memory charts, she had assumed she could fight him directly and physically: "She would be what she was—and Indian, only a *real* one. Stoic, with killer instincts" (114). Ironically, as a girl, her ideas about what it meant to be a "real" Indian were just as much a fantasy as were Gil's ideas about the iconic Indian woman that Irene represented in his paintings.

At the time of her narration of her master's thesis, she has come to see herself as the windigo-killer[8] of a story her grandmother had told: "[Irene's mother] Winnie Jane had once shown Irene a photograph of children attempting to extinguish a shadow by covering it with pebbles. She had told Irene of a medicine person who healed the sick with his shadow. An evil

---

[8] A windigo is a cannibalistic figure whose consuming hunger for food or sex has made him or her devoid of humanity. In Ojibwe mythology, the only way to defeat the windigo is by killing it, and this act must be carried out by a member of the windigo's family. Erdrich develops this motif more fully in *The Round House* (2012) through the character of the rapist and murderer, Linden Lark. See also Johnston, Borrows.

windigo warrior whose strength was in his shadow but whom a little girl was able to kill exactly at noon (40).

The image in this passage returns in the closing lines where Riel remembers the day her parents died: "And now as I remember it, I see it was midday, the sun right over us that day, and the pavement was hot on our feet, stinging hot, and it felt good, and it was noon and there were no shadows under us, or anywhere around us, it was all bright, flat, dazzling, and then the sirens began to rise and fall and grow louder in their rising and falling until they were here" (Erdrich, *Shadow* 253). Whether or not we believe that Riel is telling the literal truth here is less important than our awareness that she has drawn imaginative connections between several layers of memory: her own remembrance of the day her parents died, her grandmother's story, and the mythical story of the windigo. As such she finds a way to narrate the memory of her father's suicide and mother's sacrifice of her own life on his behalf, and thereby to reclaim a sense of her own agency. The knowledge that we are reading a work of autobiographical fiction and not a straight autobiography, leads us to expect and delight in these layers of meaning. We are fully aware that the pact the author had made with us is indirect rather than direct, to use Lejeune's terminology.

What the details of this passage mean in terms of Louise's autobiography is less apparent, but just as real if we consider the connections in terms of what Gilmore terms "limit-case autobiographies." She argues that it is often the case that the emotional and moral desire for self-representation comes to a halt because of the expectations for full and transparent disclosure in the Lejeune tradition.[9] As Gilmore states, using religious language, this approach "institutionalizes penance and penalty as self-expression" (Gilmore 14). Although the issue of how to define and verify what "truth-telling" means has been highly contested, the assumption about what constitutes the "truth" of an autobiographer's personal narrative is interpreted with more leeway for the writer of autobiographical fiction, where what matters are developing perspectives more than the factuality of experience. What matters more for the reader of autobiographical fiction is whether or not the events in the text *could* have happened. The critical distance Erdrich creates between herself as author and Riel as narrator therefore frees Louise from the confessional double bind of having to face an audience poised to presume they are in a position to judge her choices. It also frees her from

---

[9] Emily Dickinson spoke of this conundrum and a way out of it in her line, "Tell the truth but tell it slant" (Poetry Foundation).

the moral dilemma of which she speaks in the *Paris Review* interview. She doesn't need to tell her side of the story when Dorris cannot tell his.

Gilmore takes issue with the confessional autobiographical mode's legal and moral implications for numerous trauma survivors in the past half-century, and the need of many people to use self-representational narration as a means of working through it. This process poses a problem for both readers and the writer operating in the mode of Lejeune's "pact." As trauma theorist and literary critic Cathy Caruth and others have noted, trauma is experienced as an inability to find a way to narrate the intense, painful event or events. Nonetheless, these must be expressed in order for the person to heal and transform their pain (Caruth).[10] Since the events do not fit into the rubric of shared cultural narratives, the question for the reader is: on what basis can they be believed? A second problem is that for the traumatized person, a sense of safety has been violated. This means that there is a real issue of what to represent, and how to represent it in such a way that the telling does not provoke further danger and at worst, retraumatization.

According to Gilmore, the conventional autobiographical genre can be harmful at worst and uninteresting at best to many in the past half century who have chosen to publish accounts of their traumatic experiences.

> The Western mode of self-production, a description that is both a corollary to the Enlightenment and its legacy, and which features a rational and representative 'I' at its center, doesn't (sic) serve the needs of many people who are nonetheless finding rich and compelling ways of representing their own, and larger historical memories. (Gilmore 2)

In contrast, the ways in which Riel, in the last chapter of the novel, describes the methods she used to construct her family's history provides Erdrich's reader with a metanarrative about self-representation through narrative. Riel tells us that the forms she has integrated are all part of her Master's thesis, and that the last chapter is a kind of "Acknowledgements" section where she thanks her mentors. The reader, then, does a double reading of this part of the text. It is a first person, fictional narration, but also a commentary by Erdrich on the various other forms through which a personal history may need to be narrated.

---

[10] An extensive body of scholarly work in the Humanities has developed around trauma theory since the early 1990s. Caruth was one of the early influential theorists to consider the role of narrative in the process of healing. Others include Shoshona Felman and Dori Laub, Judith Herman, and Dominick LaCapra.

What we observe is that there "may" be a number of autobiographical connections, and that the kinds of relationships we see include a particular use of power. For Erdrich, self-representation (through Irene in her Blue Notebook and Red Diary, Riel's "omniscient" narration about her family, and the last, first-person chapter of the novel) has everything to do with belonging and the politics of belonging. Once this paradox is recognized, readers are freer to "trouble the waters" of interpretation rather than assume that making the claim (that the novel is autobiographical) settles things down.

There are a variety of ways in which the text motivates readers to question the authority of any one autobiographical representation, whether because the writer is lying to us, lying to herself, or invents detail where her memory fails her. For example, Irene says in the Red Diary that she stopped loving Gil the day their youngest child, Stoney, was born on 9/11. In her Blue Notebook she writes back to herself that there was no single moment, that "there are always many moments, there is never just one" (48).

Perhaps a more striking hint that readers should be skeptical of any clear parallels between Louise the author and Irene the character, is where Erdrich introduces May. Gil has hired her because she is an artist who he thinks can contribute to his "heart's desire" project to figure out what his children want more than anything, and grant them their wishes. This is an apparently benign project, although to the reader it might seem like an obvious effort to demonstrate his power. While this might at first glance make Gil a sympathetic character, it also is about his need to control the minds of his wife and children. In fact, any sympathy the reader has for him quickly disappears when we read that he not only hires May to paint Stoney's ceiling with stars, but also to follow Irene around with the intention of learning who her secret lover is (as Irene hinted about in the fabricated experiences of her Red Diary).

What happens is not what Gil intends, and also not what Irene expects. Irene discovers through talking with May that she has a half-sister she has not met before. As an Indian, she doesn't know any of her relatives because her own mother had left: (Irene to May): "I do have lots of cousins but I don't get together with them. My mother broke away. Things were bad for her back home. So there are pieces of family, half brothers, and half sisters. I don't know them. I can't absorb this. You're my half sister" (71).

She imagines in May a kind of rescue figure, not only a companion and confidant, but also someone who can relieve her from her isolation within her family, and especially with Gil: "She is almost like another me, a twin" (72).

Irene's overwhelm also reflects the magnitude of her own confusion and sense of victimization, turned inside out in all she hopes May can be for her.

May, in short, represents a shadow side of Irene, and May and Irene both express parts of Louise, the author and passing shadow character in the novel. What all of these connections suggest is that self-representation is never just about an individual who chooses freely to express a central metaphor of her life (Olney). The connection between the marriage of Irene and Gil is complicated by the presence of this character May, whom Erdrich, as a passing shadow image, calls by her own name just once in the novel. May also complicates the relationship between Erdrich and the characters Irene and Riel.

In particular, her self-representation of the trauma in her marriage to Michael Dorris might provide material for her readers to see the ways in which conscious choices about belonging can make an "ethics of care" possible—but only if there is power to back up these practices (Yuval Davis).

In Erdrich's process of self-representation, philosopher Nira Yuval-Davis's insights on the "politics of belonging" offer some valuable perspectives. She unpacks three kinds of belonging which are relevant to the novel: The first kind concerns social location. It is expressed through Irene's relationship to the institutions of marriage and family, to motherhood, to the professional art world (as subject of her husband's painting and as object of iconic representation). It also relates to the world of Indian relatives, most notably in Irene and Riel's sense that they are missing something by hardly knowing their relatives. Finally, social belonging relates to the narrator Riel's connection to the academic world in her final chapter (251).

The second kind of belonging is about people's identification and emotional attachments to various collectivities and groupings. Following this approach is a third belonging that relates to the ethical and political alliances that people build, sometimes across social locations and emotional attachments. In the novel, Irene remains trapped in her alliance to Gil: "By remaining still, in one position or another, for her husband, [Irene] had released a double into the world. It was impossible, now, to withdraw that reflection. Gil owned it. He had stepped on her shadow" (Erdrich, *Shadow Tag* 39).

But Riel as narrator and Louise as author have chosen *not* to remain silent. Louise, unlike her fictional protagonist Irene, has chosen not to let her shadow to be stepped on. Writing in the autobiographical mode through a novel, Erdrich finds a valid and valuable mode in which to express what it was like to work with Michael Dorris. As such, her novel contributes to displacing the violating discursive structures that assume that autobiography as a genre is free and available to all in American culture. Erdrich instead creates imaginative spaces in her novel, a text that can also be read as a limit-case autobiography where a range of power inequalities are scrutinized. These include the public arenas for writing and art, the emotional dynamics between marriage partners, and especially dynamics between parents and children. In short, through her narrator's voice and her underlying authorial consciousness, Erdrich allows room for empathy by her readers along with their possible judgments. In *Shadow Tag*, she chooses imagination over the presumption of ownership of a personal identity, and encourages her readers to do the same.

Works Cited

Balaev, Michelle. *The Nature of Trauma in American Novels*. Chicago, IL: Northwestern U P, 2012. Print.

Borrows, John (Kegedonce). *Drawing Out Law: A Spirit's Guide*. Toronto: U of Toronto P 2010. Print.

Caruth, Cathy. *Unclaimed Experience*. Baltimore: Johns Hopkins U, 1996. Print.

Paul John Eakin, Ed. *American Autobiography*. Madison: U of Wisconsin P, 1991. Print.

Cohen, Leah Hager. "Cruel Love." *New York Times*. 5 February 2010. http://www.nytimes.com/2010/02/07/books/review/Cohen-t.html?page wanted=all&_r=0. 11 August 2014. Web.

Denham, Aaron R. "Rethinking Historical Trauma: Narratives of Resilience." *Transcultural Psychiatry* 45:391, 2008. http://tps.sagepub.com/. 16 September 2013. Web.

Dickinson, Emily. "Tell the truth but tell it slant." http://www.poetry foundation.org/poem/247292. 11 August 2014. Web.

Erdrich, Heid. Conversation with Laura Castor. July 2005. Unpublished.

Erdrich, Louise. *Blue Jay's Dance: A Birth Year*. New York: Harper Perennial, 1996. Print.

—. *Islands and Books in Ojibwe Country*. Washington, D.C.: National Geographic Directions. 2003. Print.

—. *Shadow Tag*. New York: Harper Perennial, 2010. Print.

—. "The Art of Fiction." *The Paris Review*.

http://www.theparisreview.org/interviews/6055/the-art-of-fiction-no-208-louise-erdrich. 11 August 2014. Web.

—. *The Round House*. New York: Harper Collins, 2012. Print.

Felman, Shoshana and Dori Laub. *Testimony: Crises of Witnessing in Literature. Psychoanalysis, and History*. New York: Routledge, 1992. Print.

Friedman, Henry J. "Destructive Women and the Men Who Can't Leave Them: Pathological Dependence or Pathological Omnipotence?' *The American Journal of Psychoanalysis*. 72, 139-151. 2012. www.palgrave-journals.com/ajp/. 11 August 2014. Web.

Haraway, Donna. "Situated Knowledges: The Science Question in Feminism and the Privilege of Partial Perspective." *Feminist Studies*. 14:3, 575-599. Print.

Herman, Judith. *Trauma and Recovery*. New York: Basic Books, 1992. Print.

Hudson, Brian Jason. *Family Narratives and Self Creation in Louise Erdrich's* The Plague of Doves *and* Shadow Tag." Master's Thesis, May 2013. Univeristy of Texas San Marcos. https://digital.library.txstate.edu/bitstream/handle/10877/4534/HUDSON-THESIS-2013.pdf?sequence=1. 11 August 2014. Web.

Gilmore, Leigh. *The Limits of Autobiography: Trauma and Testimony*. Ithaca: Cornell UP, 2001. Print.

LaCapra, Dominick. *Writing History, Writing Trauma*. Baltimore: Johns Hopkins U P, 2001. Print.

Johnston, Basil. "Weendigo" in *Ojibway Heritage*. Lincoln: U of Nebraska P 1976, 165–167. Print.

Lejeune, Philippe. *On Autobiography*. Minneapolis: U of Minnesota P, 1989. Print.

Lyman, Rick. "Writer's Death Brings Plea for Respect, not Sensation." *New York Times,* April 18, 1997. http://www.nytimes.com/1997/04/18/us/writer-s-death-brings-plea-for-respect-not-sensation.html. 11 August 2014. Web.

Morrison, Scott. "Defining Hybridity: Frantz Fanon and Post-Colonialism in Louis Erdrich's *Shadow Tag*." *Univeristy of Central Florida Undergraduate Research Journal*. 7:1. https://urj.ucf.edu/vol7issue1/morrison/. 47–52. Published May 14, 2014. Accessed 11 August 2014.Web.

Olney, James. *Metaphors of Self: The Meaning of Autobiography*. Princeton: Princeton UP, 1981. Print.

Peterson, Nancy J. "American Indian Fiction." *The Cambridge Companion to American Fiction After 1945.* Ed. John N. Duvall (106, 107). Cambridge Companions Online. http://universitypublishingonline.org/cambridge/companions/author.jsf;jsesionid=0AD7DADB8C16F293ADC8DB821F51300D?name=Nancy+J.+Peterson. 11 August 2014. Web.

Reid, Jennifer. *Louis Riel and the Creation of Modern Canada: Mythic Discourse and the Postcolonial State.* Albuquerque: U of New Mexico P, 2008 (Second Edition 2011). Print.

Regan, Sheila. "Theater: Reversing the Gaze: Heid Erdrich's "Curiosities." *Twin Cities Daily Planet: Local News for Global Citizens.* 23 November 2010. 11 August 2014. http://www.tcdailyplanet.net/arts/2010/11/21/reversing-gaze-heid-erdrichs-curiosities. Web.

Roemer, Kenneth. "They Talk, Who Listens." *Reception Studies Journal: Texts, Readers, Audiences, History.* 3 (Summer 2011). http://receptionstudy.org/journal-volume-3. 11 August 2014. Web.

Smith, Sidonie and Julia Watson. *Reading Autobiography: A Guide for Interpreting Life Narratives.* 2010. Second Edition. Minneapolis: U of Minnesota P, 2010. Print.

—. *Subjectivity, Identity, and the Body: Women's Autobiographical Practices in the Twentieth Century.* Umi Books on Demand, 2001. Print.

Yuval-Davis, Nira. "Power, Intersectionality and the Politics of Belonging." *The Feminist Research Centre in Aalborg (FREIA) Working Paper Series,* 75. http://vbn.aau.dk/files/58024503/FREIA_wp_75.pdf. 11 August 2014. Web.

"My Own Face as Personal Vanishing Point": Writing the Body in Lucy Grealy's *Autobiography of a Face*

Laure de Nervaux-Gavoty

Autobiography has often been analyzed as an attempt to build a coherent self through language. Georges Gusdorf's seminal essay "Conditions and Limits of Autobiography" is emblematic in that respect: "The author of an autobiography ... sets out to ... reassemble the scattered elements of his individual life and to regroup them in a comprehensive sketch.... [He] strains toward a complete and coherent expression of his entire destiny" (35); "autobiography assumes the task of reconstructing the unity of a life across time" (37). It is through this act of recomposition and interpretation that the autobiographer can reach a form of self-knowledge according to Gusdorf (38).

While it is clear that this ideal can only be achieved by smoothing over inner contradictions, it has nonetheless retained its appeal to autobiographers as a structuring pattern. Shari Benstock, in "Authorizing the Autobiographical," has shown how women autobiographers, because they are "more aware of their 'otherness'" (16), have consistently called into question this illusory dimension of the autobiographical project. This fiction of unity and accessibility of the self to itself becomes even more problematic, however, when illness is at the heart of the autobiographical project. Lucy Grealy's account of her painful efforts to come to terms with facial disfigurement highlights both the appeal and the limits of this interpretive paradigm.

Diagnosed with Ewing's sarcoma, a rare form of jaw cancer, at the age of nine, Grealy underwent heavy surgery. The removal of two thirds of her right jaw was followed by chemotherapy t didreatment for two and a half years. She then engaged as a young adult in a long series of reconstructive procedures. While *Autobiography of a Face* devotes a significant number of pages to the narrator's cancer and its treatment, the memoir is mostly concerned with the aftermath of her disease, the construction of her identity through painful interactions with an often hostile environment.

Grealy's "pathography"—"a form of autobiography or biography that describes personal experience of illness, treatment, and sometimes death" (Hawkins 1)—invites us to look at the genre of autobiography from a different standpoint. What happens to self-representation when autobiography is premised on loss, the absence of a body part? How can the individual negotiate the ideal and fiction of a unified self with a damaged face, the part of the body most closely identified with personal identity?

The intriguing title of Grealy's text encapsulates two key features of its poetics which suggest how much it departs from the autobiographical tradition. First of all, it points to the complex interplay of corporeality and textuality involved in the construction of self. *Autobiography of a Face* offers itself as a prosopopeia; giving voice to a face, it goes against the grain of most autobiographical texts, which tend to reassert the primacy of the mind at the expense of the body and to show the former in control of the latter. As Thomas Couser points out, "[u]ntil quite recently, life writing has participated in the general evasion or effacement of the body" (10); what emerges from Grealy's narrative instead is the power of the body, the way it shapes identity. But the title also hints at the way this body keeps turning itself into text. Writing about her reconstructive procedures in a book of essays, the author said that she tried to "revise" her face (*As Seen on TV* 38). The metaphor is highly significant as it suggests that her quest for integrity, while apparently surgical, is also textual. The narratives she constructs about herself as a child and an adult as well as the more ambitious text of the autobiography itself are integral to it.

Secondly, the title can be read as a synecdoche in which the face substitutes itself for the whole self of the narrator. This movement of displacement reverberates throughout the text; just as the face displaces body and self in the title, the hole in her face comes to stand for many other forms of emptiness and blanks, calling into question the possibility for the self to decipher itself:

> This singularity of meaning—I *was* my face, I *was* ugliness—though sometimes unbearable, also offered a possible point of escape. It became ... the one immediately recognizable place to point to when asked what

was wrong with my life. Everything led to it, everything receded from it—my own face as personal vanishing point. (7)[1]

Grealy's autobiography is haunted by the idea of wholeness; it reveals how much she craved for it in her life and at the same time distrusted it as a textual device. The two directions she followed in her life to achieve it—revising her face through operations and the script of her life by performing a range of identities—expose the inadequacy of the concept in her case; her autobiography therefore enacts a displacement from a search for wholeness and an illusory coherence to a quest for self-recognition.

Fixing the Body: Gothic Subjectivity

The unity most autobiographers strain toward bears strong similarities, Shari Benstock has shown, commenting on Gusdorf's above-mentioned essay, to Lacan's analysis of the mirror stage. Lacan explains that the coherence experienced by the child suddenly seeing his image as a whole is an illusory one which inhibits whatever disorderly movement may animate him; similarly the ideally unified self of the autobiographer is a fiction which represses certain aspects of his identity (Benstock 11–12). Grealy's self-representation challenges this fiction of unity through autobiography with a vengeance: not only is the ideal coherence produced by the mirror image impossible to achieve, but the subject fails to acknowledge the image she sees as her own. The body asserts itself as an autonomous entity, endowed with a will of its own and reluctant to be reformed through surgery. This resistance to society's normalizing injunctions acts out a return of the bodily repressed which is figured in gothic tropes.

Grealy's identity crisis is largely told through the story of her relationship with mirrors. The removal of part of the child's jaw opens up a gap between the self and its reflection, setting off a gradual process of estrangement from her body. She starts avoiding her own reflection and bewilderment prevails on the rare occasions when she catches sight of herself: "I knew to expect a scar but how had my face sunk in like that? I didn't understand" (112). Her attempts at facial reconstruction, far from reconciling her with her image, make her even more aware of the very otherness of her own body, as suggested by the following description of her face after one of her surgeries:

---

[1] The edition used in the article is the 1994 edition (Oxford: Isis, 1995).

"This new thing on my face was huge, almost touching my collar bone. What repulsed me most of all was a large strip of foreign skin, much paler than my facial skin, running along the lower half of the graft" (174). The same idea is taken up a few lines later: "I had not anticipated how *foreign* it would look" (175).

In *L'Intrus* [*The Intruder*], a meditation on his heart transplant, Jean-Luc Nancy, a French philosopher, explains how such operations call into question the very notion of identity:

> And so *I* become an intruder to myself...
>
> ...never has the strangeness of my own identity, of which I have always been acutely aware, struck me with such intensity ... Between me and myself, there has always been time and space: but now there is the opening caused by an incision and a foiled immunity... (my trans. 36)[2]

Although it is taken from her own hip, the skin graft produces a comparable effect of estrangement in Lucy Grealy's case. The deep unease brought by the body's disruptive presence is made worse by the unconscious associations it seems to conjure up in her mind. The word "foreign" actually resonates strangely with echoes of the narrator's family history. Her swollen face comes to concentrate all that is different about her and her family; it acts as a kind of symptom, drawing attention to the narrator's earlier allusions to her immigrated family's outsider status as well as the myth of lost grandeur spun by her Irish parents. In a displacement typical of Grealy's autobiography, the suffering caused by her damaged face turns out to be actually related to something that has nothing to do with it, thus compromising any reconciliation with her appearance.

This experience of otherness characterized by excess finds its symmetrical opposite in the ghostly disappearance of her grafts, which are in most cases gradually reabsorbed by her body (191). The latter asserts itself as an independent force, a character in its own right, capable of preying on itself as on an enemy. More than her body's responses to surgery, however, it is the physical norms internalized by the narrator which deepen the gap with her reflection. The face she dreams of solidifies into an idealized

---

[2] "C'est donc ainsi moi-même qui deviens mon intrus, ... jamais l'étrangeté de ma propre identité, qui me fut pourtant toujours si vive, ne m'a touché avec cette acuité... Entre moi et moi, il y eut toujours de l'espace-temps: mais à présent il y a l'ouverture d'une incision et l'irréconciliable d'une immunité contrariée...." (36)

double forever out of reach; she becomes haunted by a ghostly image, an elusive, fantasized face which superimposes itself upon her features: "Looking in the mirror, I would pull and push the various parts of my face I thought were ugly until I arrived at a facsimile of what I was meant to look like" (187). This fantasy of an original face which her operations are meant to recover translates into self-division and a negation of her body, cast away as a doppelgänger trying to substitute itself for the "real" self:

> Maybe life was going to be alright, after all. Maybe there was a chance that this wasn't my actual face at all but the face of some interloper, some ugly intruder, and in reality my "real" face, the one I was meant to have all along was within reach. I began to imagine my "original face," the one free from all deviation, from all error. (159–160)

Wholeness seems to recede forever in the distance as the narrator enters an endless cycle of surgeries. The thirty reconstructive procedures she goes through testify to an obsession with closure at the same time as they keep postponing it. Illness, far from being a temporary stage in her life, comes to define it: the narrator becomes a permanent patient, always at some stage of a reconstructive process. The wound which was originally located in her face proliferates as skin comes to be taken from the rest of her body, leaving it in a permanent state of incompletion and transformation.

Disturbingly, even successful operations seem unable to reconcile her with her reflection: "I had to admit I looked better. But I didn't look like me. ... I simply could not conceive the image as belonging to me" (226). Grealy's case sheds light on the nature of identity. The latter, far from being static, is above all relational, Jean-Luc Nancy explains in a conversation with Professor Lantieri about face transplants[3]: "we think that there is such a thing as identity, that someone is identical to himself; to be yourself, however, you must identify with yourself. So the self is just a reflexive turn of the subject upon himself; it is a movement and it is not there once and for all" (65, my transl.)[4]. In Grealy's case, it is as if the reflection in the mirror, no matter how flattering, had become autonomous, something purely external, an image to which she cannot relate, let alone claim as her

---

[3] Laurent Lantieri is a professor of medicine famous for performing the first full face transplant in France in 2010.
[4] "Nous sommes persuadés qu'il y a une identité, que quelqu'un est identique à lui-même. Alors que, ce qui fait l'identité, c'est que, pour être soi-même, il faut s'identifier à soi-même. Donc, le soi n'est qu'un retour à soi, c'est un mouvement, ce n'est pas posé une fois pour toutes" (65).

own. Liberation comes with what she describes as the "shedding" (229) of her image, her decision to stop defining herself primarily in visual terms and equating face and self. It is this "shedding," not the surgery meant to make her whole again, which makes the narrator's confrontation with a mirror possible again at the end.

Performing Identity: The Seduction of Narratives

Grealy's second strategy to achieve a sense of wholeness involves building a series of narratives meant to help her make sense of her condition. As a number of autobiography scholars have shown, narratives do not simply reflect lives; they play a central role in the construction of subjectivity: "When it comes to autobiography," notes Eakin, "narrative and identity are so intimately linked that each constantly and properly gravitates into the conceptual field of the other. Thus, narrative is not merely a literary form but a mode of phenomenological and cognitive self-experience, while self— the self of autobiographical discourse—does not necessarily precede its constitution in narrative" (100). Developing the same idea in "Life as Narrative" Jerome Bruner underscores the importance of culturally dominant narratives in this constitution of the self, noting that we become "variants of the culture's canonical forms" (694). These remarks do not apply merely to autobiographical writing but also to the narratives we produce about ourselves in our daily lives. We understand who we are by reconstructing a narrative about ourselves. As Oliver Sacks writes, "It might be said that each of us constructs and lives a 'narrative,' and that this narrative *is* us, our identities" (110).

In Grealy's case, however, the identity crisis triggered by the child's status as a patient and then by her appearance translates into not one but a dizzying proliferation of narratives. TV, its ready-made scenarios and its heroes loom large as role prescribers in the first chapters of the novel, later superseded by other publically approved cultural figures. Starting with her stay in hospital, the child evolves a series of narratives in which vulnerability and power, difference and exception are inextricably bound up: "I wanted nothing more than to be special, and so far the role of patient had delivered" (26). "As horrified as I was by the idea that people might view me as someone to feel sorry for, I also knew that I possessed a certain power. After all people noticed me.... I was never overlooked" (102). Allowing disease to become the basis of her identity, her self-definition, the child and then the young woman weave a succession of narratives in which pain and difference turn into a paradoxical form of election: she successively takes on the role of the heroic patient who never complains (30), the abandoned orphan (39), the saint (155), the bohemian poet (199), or the expatriate artist (219).

The narrativization of her life thus veers toward the theatrical as narratives multiply and turn into a series of roles performed for an audience: "I slipped in and out of my various personae with great ease, even flair" (39). The plotlines she embraces underscore her imperious need to define herself through culturally determined narratives and socially approved outsider roles. Narrative, far from becoming the empowering structure through which the subject can build a self or achieve self-representation, stiffens into a figure of fate (83), an alienating "script" performed for an unfriendly house: "I was, however, dependent upon my audience. It was their approval or disapproval which defined everything, and, unfortunately, I believed with every cell in my body that approval wasn't written into my particular script" (3–4).

Instead of helping her reach a sense of wholeness, the plotlines which the narrator forces upon her life deepen her feelings of inadequacy, turning the tenuous feeling of election through pain into its very opposite. Her incapacity to live up to her mother's repeated injunction to be brave and not to complain thus results in a deep sense of failure and a feeling of guilt. The child's failed heroic plot enacts the kind of displacement announced by the title; occurring within the context of difficult family relationships, her disease becomes the cipher for all that goes wrong at home, saddling her with the responsibility of rescuing everyone: "all I had to do was perform heroically and I could personally save my entire family" (30).

The various personae she assumes also deepen the rift between body and self. Only aware of the potential of her scar to reinforce the heroic persona she is building, she retreats from a confrontation with her own image: "it hadn't occurred to me to scrutinize how I *looked* ... I felt only proud of my new, dramatic scar and was eager to show it off .... I was a hero" (62–63). The changes brought about by puberty are also censored by her ascetic version of self: "I looked at my child's body, utterly unlike a woman's. I considered the desire to have it develop into a woman's body a weakness, a straying from my chosen path of truth" (153). Her shift to "slinkiness" (214) to quote her own words, signals no improvement in her self-image: utterly divorced, disconnected from her own body, she can only envision gender as a theatrical performance, switching from an androgynous, sexless style (208) to an extremely provocative one (213) without actually becoming aware of herself as a woman.

Writing as Self-Recognition

Pathographies are usually underlain by a need for meaning and closure, Hawkins explains in *Reconstructing Illness*: "the 'pathographical act' is one that constructs meaning by subjecting raw experience to the powerful impulse to make sense of it all, to bind together the events, feelings, thoughts, and sensations that occur during an illness into an integrated whole" (18). It is therefore very tempting to read Grealy's autobiography as an attempt to create through language the wholeness she failed to reach in her life. The formal perfection of the book lends support to this interpretation: Grealy's memoir is an extremely well-crafted book, elegantly written and neatly structured into twelve chapters of almost equal length.

Grealy's ambivalence about the idea of wholeness complicates this pattern, however. Asked in an interview if she thought writing her autobiography had a "cathartic effect," she said "no," adding "I hate the words healing and closure." In her study of myth in pathographies, Hawkins identifies several structuring patterns which often shape narratives of illness: the myth of rebirth, illness as a battle or as a journey into a distant country. Grealy's narrative does not subscribe to any of them. Any form of triumph or redemption though illness is exposed as illusory. The book closes on a hopeful note but remains open-ended, as several critics have noted (Mintz 182; Brown 314): "I looked with curiosity to the window behind him, its night-silvered glass reflecting the entire café, to see if I could, now, recognize myself" (229). Denying the reader a description of what she sees, the last words show how careful she is to avoid artificial closure.

Rather than a deceptive form of wholeness or closure, Grealy is looking for self-recognition, the previous quotation suggests—not self-analysis or introspection, but something more radical and basic, the turn of self upon self analyzed by Nancy which allows us to say "I am I." That process, in Grealy's case, implies understanding the real meaning that the hole in her face took on over the years. Her autobiography can thus be read as a remedy to the unsaid, a way of making sense of a life dominated by false narratives, semantic displacements leading to misinterpretations, but also silence. The hole she is trying to mend through her autobiography is perhaps not so much the one in her face as the hole in language that she experienced during her illness.

The destructive power of silence comes to the fore in the second chapter, when the narrator explains that it was only many years later that she realized that she had cancer as a child: "In all that time, not one person had ever said the word cancer to me, at least not in a way that registered as pertaining to me" (43-44). The difference between her mother's and her version of facts—her mother claims Lucy *was* told she had cancer (43)—reveals how this failure to name things stems from tense family relationships. The child's lack of awareness about her situation before her operation—"I hadn't a clue about how sick I was or what was going to happen" (54)—and during her chemotherapy—"Despite the fact I knew that I'd lost weight and was a bit pale, I never actually did consider myself all that sick" (102)—shows silence settling in. Inadequate communication also contaminates her relationships with the rest of her family: the narrator mentions the "chasm" (58) which opens between her and her siblings after her operation, the empty, polite conversations they have in hospital.

Silence repeats itself uncannily, resurfacing without being cleared, a later episode suggests: researching her disease in a library as a teenager, the narrator finds out that her chances of survival did not exceed 5%. She is suddenly overwhelmed by an emotion which she cannot articulate, however:

> Placing my hand on my neck, feeling my pulse there, I stood for some minutes on the verge of either moving or speaking or sitting or something. But I couldn't think of what it was, and then it passed over, I was on the other side of it, feeling that there was something I'd forgotten, some name or object or emotion I'd meant to take note of but had carelessly allowed to slip by. (68)

The brutal revelation goes unacknowledged, and the trip to the library, far from bringing any relief, only deepens the weight of the silence.

The hole in her face thus comes to stand for many other forms of emptiness over the course of her life. It is only through her autobiography that she can start coming to grips with silence by naming facts and arranging events in a meaningful sequence that traces the development of her disease and clarifies her relationships with her family.

Grealy's attempt to give voice to her body, to write the story of her face significantly changes the rules of autobiography. The light her memoir sheds on corporeality as a prime definer of identity—the responses of her body to surgery in particular—expose the ideal of the transcendent, autonomous autobiographical self as illusory while the multiple narratives she weaves about herself undermine any notion of a unified self. *Autobiography of a Face* does not mend the hole in Grealy's face and the wound in her ego but replaces it within the realm of language, stopping its endless proliferation and the semantic displacements and misinterpretations it gives rise to.

In "Autobiography as De-facement," with which the title of Grealy's memoir resonates strangely, Paul de Man argues that the gap between the self and its textualized double turns every autobiography into a fiction: "autobiography veils a defacement of the mind of which it is itself the cause" (81). It is difficult to take issue with de Man's analyses for they encapsulate all the ambiguities inherent in any attempt at self-representation. Grealy herself insisted on the creative dimension of her work; asked at a reading how she managed to remember all the details, she replied, "I didn't remember it. I wrote it. I'm a writer" (Patchett 231). While Grealy's text certainly gives room to fictional amplification or recreation, thus enacting, to a certain extent, the "de-facement" de Man sees as inherent in autobiography, the narrative's emphasis on the body's disruptive presence and its resistance to the scripts forced on it may call for a more nuanced analysis of the slippage of meaning inherent in autobiography. Because it refuses to take the self as a purely textual entity and tries to get to grips with the displacements inherent in language itself, *Autobiography of a Face* becomes a place of self-recognition rather than defacement.

Works Cited

Benstock, Shari. "Authorizing the Autobiographical," in Benstock, Shari, Ed. *The Private Self. Theory and Practice of Women's Autobiographical Writings*. Chapel Hill and London: U of North Caroline P, 1988. 10–33. Print.

Brown, Sylvia A. "Scripting Wholeness in Lucy Grealy's Autobiography of a Face." *Criticism* 48.3 (Summer 2006): 297–322. Web.

Bruner, Jerome. "Life as Narrative." *Social Research* 71.3 (2004): 691–710. Web.

Couser, Thomas G. *Signifying Bodies. Disability in Contemporary Life Writing.* Ann Arbor: U. of Michigan P., 2009. Print.

De Man, Paul. "Autobiography as De-facement." In *The Rhetoric of Romanticism*. New York: Columbia UP, 1984. 67–81. Print.

Eakins, Paul John. *How Our Lives Become Stories: Making Selves*. Ithaca: Cornell UP 1999. Print.

Grealy, Lucy. *In the Mind's Eye. An Autobiography of a Face*. 1994. Oxford: Isis, 1995. Print.

—. *As Seen on TV. Provocations*. New York and London: Bloomsbury, 2000. Print.

—. Interview with John Ritter (2000). http://www.youtube.com/watch?v=1RFVS-jT4MA. Accessed 30 June 2014. Web.

—. *An Autobiography of a Face*. New York: Harper, 2003. Print.

Gusdorf, George. "Conditions and Limits of Autobiography," in Olney, James, ed. *Autobiography: Essays Theoretical and Critical*. Princeton, NJ: Princeton UP, 1980. 28–48. Print.

Hawkins, Anne Hunsaker. *Reconstructing Illness. Studies in Pathography*. West Lafayette IN: Purdue UP 1999. Print.

Lacan, Jacques. "Le stade du miroir comme formateur de la fonction du Je." *Ecrits I*. Paris: Seuil, 1966. Print.

Lantieri, Laurent and Nancy, Jean-Luc. "Volte face" (interview with Catherine Poitevin) *Philosophie Magazine* 64 (2012): 63–65. Print.

Mintz, Susannah B. "Writing as Refiguration: Lucy Grealy's Autobiography of a Face." *Biography* 24.1 (2001): 172–184. Web.

Nancy, Jean-Luc. *L'Intrus*. 2000. Paris: Galilée, 2010. Print.

Patchett, Ann. "Afterword." Grealy *Autobiography* (2003) 227–236. Print.

Sacks, Oliver. *The Man Who Mistook his Wife for a Hat and other Clinical Tales*. 1985. New York: Harper, 1987. Print.

Female Autobiography and Otherness in The Grand Piano: An Experiment in Collective Autobiography

Manuel Brito

Rae Armantrout, Carla Harryman, and Lyn Hejinian were among the ten authors engaged in publishing a collective autobiography of ten volumes entitled, *The Grand Piano: An Experiment in Collective Autobiography. San Francisco, 1975-1980*. Their intention was to show what lay behind the sense of community of these Language poets combined with an avant-garde poetics that revolves around the other: "as Heidegger claims, our being is *with* others, not with *knowing* others. And it is in the context of being with others—to include reading and writing with others, which we do, even when ostensibly alone—that questions of address and reception arise" (Pearson, "Etude III" 107). Armantrout, Harryman, and Hejinian filled this generalized vision of the Language group with a comprehensive approach to experience as a totality.

The postface repeated in each volume of this autobiography clarifies its goals: 1) to re-explore the unique events in the literary life of the protagonists during the period 1975-1980 in San Francisco, with added documentary materials, 2) the use of non-linearity and non-prescribed themes to dramatize the multi-faceted memory and autonomy of the authors, and 3) the authors appearing in a different sequence for each volume. When in 1956 Georges Gusdorf referred to autobiography as a "conscious awareness of the singularity of each individual life" (29), he was describing it as a genre focused on the presentation of personal identity. However, this model was clearly rejected by these female language-centered authors, who aimed to disrupt identity in their own writing. Moreover, they continually sought to establish a community of writers engaged in hybridizing this literary genre. Many of these women's chapters—or entries and essays as sometimes they call them—reinforce this view. For instance, Harryman acknowledged "the difficulty of saying something meaningful about hybrid literary forms while attempting to be true to the psychological adventure of writing in our genre of collective memoir" ("Love" 37). Hejinian proposed a radical practice for understanding the present beyond the normative account of the immovable past, "A semantics of the present could be constructed from past materials, freed of their original syntax. History was to enter here" ("Femme" 27). Armantrout reaffirmed her alternative emphasis on the other by looking at autobiography as a product of the social and political process:

> What interests me is the way it gets more complicated still. People not only objectify the other; they objectify themselves for the other—or for what they imagine the other to be. The way we want to see ourselves is hopelessly conjoined with the way we want to show ourselves. This gets pretty disturbing, especially as the capitalist media participates by producing the Personality as a commodity. ("Untitled" Part 1, 61)

Therefore, this collective autobiography is best understood in terms of an avant-garde project with a backdrop of alterations and dispersal of authority. These women authors were more clearly committed to Sidonie Smith and Julia Watson's framework for women's autobiography as "contextually marked, collaboratively mediated, provisional" ("Introduction" 9)—and particularly focused on the continued action of writing, traversing both space and time as a modification of the author's identity. Smith and Watson recognize that working within the old claims for women's autobiography makes the writer vulnerable to some kind of neurotic rigidity: "nonlinear narrative, fragmented textuality, relationality, the authority of experience" ("Introduction: Situating" 40). The trait of women capable of moving toward a more flexible terrain—such as Jeanne Perreault's concept of "autography"—"may be desirable to designate a kind of life writing practised by women that continually calls its own boundaries and activity into question" (Smith and Watson, "Introduction: Situating" 40). Precisely, Harryman recalled how some concepts deployed in her previous works—such as *La Quotidienne: An Atmospheric Play* and *The Middle*—would remain in her mostly textual frame of autobiography: "[These works] reflect a preoccupation with the concept "everyday life" that includes a reading of the world as a text layered into the reading and writings of "works" ("Drift" 9). These two quotations from her entry in volume 7 of *The Grand Piano* stress the articulation she was interested in using in her texts for the Poets

Theater: an "emphasis on process, on idea as theory no to be proved, mental process of the work, emphasis on the mentality of the viewer, the challenge to audience/viewer conditioning" ("Reflections" 30), and "calling attention to materials (...) the performer would be conceived as an instrument of the writing; the writing performed would in a sense become a character" ("Reflections" 35). This way of seeing writing has been projected in her entries for this autobiography. On reflecting upon the possibilities of writing rather than its consideration as mere representation, Harryman placed herself far from Luce Irigaray's "logic of the Same" (133), that is, repeating the masculine pattern of submission to external authority.

These potentialities of autobiography particularly focused on the challenges of writing also appear in Lyn Hejinian and Rae Armantrout. Hejinian's account of her return to the Bay Area in 1977 does not narrate her life in this period. Instead, she associates it with how her books, *Writing Is an Aid to Memory* and *Gesualdo*, opened analogies to her life experience:

> I had to denaturalize my world view and to de-aestheticize my approach to writing, so that it could never reach (and refused to seek) a sublime point of completion. Its unfolding, simultaneous with that of my thinking, was to be dialectical and willful (...) I had to volunteer the irrational—or at least the incomprehensible. I had to commit myself to not understanding what I'd previously thought I'd understood. ("Untitled" Part 1, 58)

Her behavior was not subjected to tranquility but aligned with a subject in process that continually individuated herself as a distinct writer. Furthermore, her brief aphorisms dispersed throughout her memoirs can be reconstructed to adumbrate a theory of poetry: "Writing itself provides a perfectly viable site for sequential (and, more rarely, simultaneous) alterities" ("Terra" 103).

Perhaps more definitely, Armantrout evokes what is ostensibly a poststructuralist view of the Language poets' activities in the 1970s: "What cultural work were we doing? Learning to say 'Not me' and 'Not so.' To disassemble the apparatus (Deconstruction begins at home)" ("Untitled Part 7, 177). Dwelling on language and calling attention to its power, her lyricism "gestures towards what's left out: it participates in a dialogue with the unspoken. It emphasizes the boundary, the mysterious, arbitrary division between outside and in (or now and later)" ("Lyric" 36). From this perspective, this autobiography is not alienated with therapy, ethics or the usual connection of "woman" and "difference." Instead, women cohered around incomplete narration, semantic permeability, and continual aggregation to their identity.

Of course, the three women authors of *The Grand Piano* did not refuse to present their private experiences. For instance, Harryman dissected her childhood and youth in just three short paragraphs: that is, her birth in the town of Nemole, her teenage years spent wanting to be a surf jock, and her friendship with war protesters, communalists, and footballers in the late 1960s. Hejinian's retrospection redeemed her domestic family life and maternal pride. And Armantrout accentuated the role of her husband, son and the county of San Diego, paradoxically all remaining between the speakable and the unspeakable. However, rather than offering a therapy of recovery and growth, they are conscious that their references are an act of writing involved in re-circulating doubts. In Hejinian's words, this resonates with George Oppen and Louis Zukfosky's sincerity:

> as it's bound to thinking that is self-reflective, self-critical, but that radiates outward too, away from the proprietary, the assimilable, or the confessional (…) polyvocal, fraught, dense with interference, dialogic, symphonic, overbearing, funny; its temporality is fragmented, multifarious, and both expansive and condensed, bearing pasts through the durée of long and multilayered thinking. ("Unlikelihood" 140)

As Sidonie Smith argues, this kind of autobiographical text "becomes a narrative artifice, privileging a presence, or identity, that does not exist outside language. Given the very nature of language, embedded in the text lie alternative or deferred identities that constantly subvert any pretentions of truthfulness (*Poetics* 5). Therefore, following Philip Lejeune here, she concludes that autobiography becomes a "mode of reading" as well as a "mode of writing" (*Poetics* 6). In fact, female identity appears eroded in these three poets' autobiographical entries. This is illustrated in Harryman's approach to Creeley's poem "The Door." Rather than being assimilated into the femaleness of the Lady in this poem, she adopts a position of "non-Lady" ("Love" 31) and prefers the writing experience, "the shadows of language" ("Love" 32). This resistance to absorption of conventional meanings brings into being a subject open to the multiplicity of linguistic substance.

In Hejinian's case, her discourse turns out to be political and clearly separated from her feminine condition: "Is this the place in which to invoke the feminist credo, 'the personal is the political'? No. The asymptotic rather than overlapping relation between the poetry world and my family life was not, as it turned out, personal but, as it came to a crisis in 1980, it was political" ("Discomfort" 73). Hejinian's political crisis was mainly associated with Ronald Reagan's presidency but her crisis was especially motivated by the incapacity of writing to change society: "why write poems?" ("Discomfort" 74). If the burden of limitation was gender-constructed, she went beyond to empower language for a more political intervention. Coincidentally, Armantrout described Harryman and Hejinian as women poets transcending the reification of feminism. The example she provides about the gender issue is her poem "Necromance" in which the female speaker could be a Siren or a victim of her own song. Armantrout recognizes that this is unclear ("Untitled" Part 6, 130-131). Given this incapacity of the text to produce gender accuracy, she ends up: "In either case the poem implies the search is doomed from the start" ("Untitled" Part 6, 131).

Therefore, instead of female identity what we have is a sense of commonality through this non-linear memory, which coincides with Smith and Watson's defense of memory as "a means of 'passing on', of sharing a social past that may have been obscured, in order to activate its potential for reshaping a future of and for other subjects" (*Reading* 20-21). It is true that Smith and Watson add that the speaker or "producer of the story" is essentially an autobiographical 'I' "comprised of multiple 'I's" (*Reading* 58): 1) the real or historical 'I'—her signature appears authoring the text, and located in space and time; 2) the narrating 'I'—the speaker directly addressing the reader and exerting agency of discourse; 3) the narrated 'I'—the story is focused on her; and 4) the ideological 'I'—the cultural construction of personhood (cf. *Reading* 58-63). But the multiplicity of 'I's as sketched here might be said to involve different responses from the reader as facing the various sides of the self: "The routing of a self known through its relational others undermines the understanding of life narrative as a bounded story of the unique, individual narrating subject" (Smith and Watson, *Reading* 67). For sure, the collective memory of these Language poets aligns with the fact that this group has not collapsed over the years, instead it is alive and involved in the avant-garde practice of still being fascinated with the possibilities of language.

Hejinian was driven by precisely the need for focusing on writing beyond any genre's rules and expectations, "I had a point but it had to do not with lists but with the active phenomenological capacity of writing. I wanted to test it as a medium for thinking, that is, for putting things together, in acts of productive invention and heuristic synthesis" ("Untitled" Part 3, 56). Hejinian's deep analysis of this topic signals a disjunction between writing as an aid to memory and as a vehicle, form, and content in itself. This latter would favour meanings and connections illuminating the hermeneutic force of writing and reading: "I was aiming for something encyclopaedic; I was interested in epistemology: in consciousness, in knowledge, in the ways that knowledge is organized and structured" ("Untitled" Part 3, 57). To exemplify her formal technique, Hejinian broadened her consideration on this book in this same entry and showed the interplay of a textual landscape that "emerges out of a dense syntactic field (...) full of gaps" ("Untitled" Part 3, 65) and the formal strategy she followed to provoke a potent response in the reader: "One of the structuring principles governing *Writing Is an Aid to Memory* is alphabetical (...) all lines beginning with *a* are placed flush against the left hand margin, lines beginning with *b* start one space in (...) etc." ("Untitled" Part 3, 62-63). Hejinian's intellectual integrity is not attached to the claimed truth of history or literary genre, but rather is preoccupied with "writing as aid to chance" ("Untitled" Part 3, 63). For this, the techniques she most used were "sentence-memories" and not the naming of particular public events or larger historical conditions, leaving the reader with the pressure either to fill in or ignore the gap.

Armantrout inserted a poem in her last entry to this collective autobiography, in which she attempted to show "the oddities of memory, identity, autobiography" ("So Far" 154). Her recognition of a flexible selfhood was mediated by incompleteness and depending upon the fallible faculty of memory, "but the past is tricky" ("So Far" 154). The point of such an exercise is to see that both the poem and her life yield a continual remapping, "So are we really moving?" ("So Far" 154). To answer this question, the final lines of this entry challenge the reader to consider the coexistence of past, present and future in her poetry:

> If you watch me
> From increasing distance
> I am writing this
> always. ("So Far" 157)

From this perspective, these women Language poets' autobiographical texts were not necessarily limited to intentions toward a particular identity within the group but become many, revealing the complexity of personality. Although they share the label "Language poet" and *The Grand Piano* is a collective memoir of some members of this larger group, we can also think of Armantrout, Harryman, and Hejinian's sense of membership to reinforce commonality. However, identities are not only provisional but also "They are constructed. They are in language. They are discursive" (Smith and Watson, *Reading* 33). Against the authority of the universal subject offering an enduring source of coherence, the new identity resists linear development and favours a love relationship within the group and the capacity to join others in search of an emancipatory politics.

Works Cited

Armantrout, Rae. "The Lyric." *The Grand Piano: An Experiment in Collective Autobiography. San Francisco, 1975-1980*. Part 8. Lyn Hejinian et al. Detroit: Mode A, 2009. 35-41. Print.

—. "So Far." *The Grand Piano: An Experiment in Collective Autobiography. San Francisco, 1975-1980*. Part 10. Ted Pearson et al. Detroit: Mode A, 2010. 151-57. Print.

—. "Untitled." *The Grand Piano: An Experiment in Collective Autobiography. San Francisco, 1975-1980*. Part 1. Bob Perelman et al. Detroit: Mode A, 2006. 61-62. Print.

—. "Untitled." *The Grand Piano: An Experiment in Collective Autobiography. San Francisco, 1975-1980*. Part 6. Ron Silliman et al. Detroit: Mode A, 2008. 127-31. Print.

—. "Untitled." *The Grand Piano: An Experiment in Collective Autobiography. San Francisco, 1975-1980*. Part 7. Lyn Hejinian et al. Detroit: Mode A, 2008. 176-77. Print.

Gusdorf, Georges. "Conditions and Limits of Autobiography." *Autobiography: Essays Theoretical and Critical*. Ed. James Olney. Princeton: Princeton UP, 1980. 28-48. Print.

Harryman, Carla. "Drift á Deux." *The Grand Piano: An Experiment in Collective Autobiography. San Francisco, 1975-1980*. Part 4. Carla Harryman et al. Detroit: Mode A, 2006. 9-32. Print.

—. "Love, Discord, Asymmetry." *The Grand Piano: An Experiment in Collective Autobiography. San Francisco, 1975-1980*. Part 1. Bob Perelman et al. Detroit: Mode A, 2006. 28-38. Print.

—. "Reflections on the Incomplete Project of Poets Theater." *The Grand Piano: An Experiment in Collective Autobiography. San Francisco, 1975-1980*. Part 7. Lyn Hejinian et al. Detroit: Mode A, 2008. 28-50. Print.

Hejinian, Lyn. "'Discomfort Marks the Boundary." *The Grand Piano: An Experiment in Collective Autobiography. San Francisco, 1975–1980*. Part 2. Barrett Watten et al. Detroit: Mode A, 2007. 69–76. Print.

—. "The Femme Fatale and the Schoolyard." *The Grand Piano: An Experiment in Collective Autobiography. San Francisco, 1975–1980*. Part 8. Lyn Hejinian et al. Detroit: Mode A, 2009. 11–34. Print.

—. "Terra Firma and the Desk." *The Grand Piano: An Experiment in Collective Autobiography. San Francisco, 1975–1980*. Part 6. Ron Silliman et al. Detroit: Mode A, 2009. 84–103. Print.

—. "An Unlikelihood." *The Grand Piano: An Experiment in Collective Autobiography. San Francisco, 1975–1980*. Part 5. Tom Mandel et al. Detroit: Mode A, 2009. 128–41. Print.

—. "Untitled." *The Grand Piano: An Experiment in Collective Autobiography. San Francisco, 1975–1980*. Part 1. Bob Perelman et al. Detroit: Mode A, 2006. 56–60. Print.

—. "Untitled." *The Grand Piano: An Experiment in Collective Autobiography. San Francisco, 1975–1980*. Part 3. Steve Benson et al. Detroit: Mode A, 2006. 55–68. Print.

—. "Untitled." *The Grand Piano: An Experiment in Collective Autobiography. San Francisco, 1975–1980*. Part 4. Carla Harryman et al. Detroit: Mode A, 2007. 99–116. Print.

—. "What's Missing from *My Life*." *The Grand Piano: An Experiment in Collective Autobiography. San Francisco, 1975–1980*. Part 9. Rae Armantrout et al. Detroit: Mode A, 2007. 16–47. Print.

Irigaray, Luce, *Speculum of the Other Woman*. Trans. Gillian C. Gill. Ithaca: Cornell UP, 1985. Print.

Pearson, Ted. "Etude III: Angles of Incidence." *The Grand Piano: An Experiment in Collective Autobiography. San Francisco, 1975–1980*. Part 3. Steve Benson et al. Detroit: Mode A, 2007. 103–112. Print.

Smith, Sidonie. *A Poetics of Women's Autobiography: Marginality and the Fictions of Self-Representation*. Bloomington: Indiana UP, 1987. Print.

Smith, Sidonie, and Julia Watson. "Introduction." *Getting a Life: Everyday Uses of Autobiography*. Ed. Sidonie Smith and Julia Watson. Minneapolis: U of Minnesota P, 1996. 1–24. Print.

—. "Introduction: Situating Subjectivity in Women's Autobiographical Practices." *Women, Autobiography, Theory: A Reader*. Ed. Sidonie Smith and Julia Watson. 3–52. Print.

—. *Reading Autobiography: A Guide for Interpreting Life Narratives*. Ed. Sidonie Smith and Julia Watson Minneapolis: U of Minnesota P, 2001. 433–440. Print.

"Memoir as Well as Biography":
Generic Indeterminacy in Vikram Seth's *Two Lives*

Mélanie Heydari

Vikram Seth's work has a staggering versatility. It is characterized by movement and metamorphosis, displaying a firm rejection of any definitive anchor in a place, theme or genre. Skipping from economist to poet, to travel writer, to novelist-in-verse, to translator and to children's writer, Seth even tried his hand at writing libretti in *The Rivered Earth* (2011), his most recent collection of poems, which partakes of a musical collaboration with the composer Alec Roth and the violinist Philippe Honoré. Seth's treatment of genre crystallizes both his affinities with his contemporaries and his irreducible originality. On the one hand, he radicalizes the pursuit of formal plurality that distinguishes other Indo-Anglian authors such as Amitav Ghosh; on the other, each of his works complies strictly with the distinct constraints and conventions of a specific literary genre. In contrast to the postmodern blurring of generic categories exemplified by Ghosh or Salman Rushdie, Seth's works usually exhibit an ostensibly unfashionable sense of form—a willfully "anachronistic" (Parker 673) reverence for generic classifications. That Seth should strive to maintain boundaries not only between the genres, but also the various cultures he explores, is one of the central paradoxes of this profoundly heterogeneous work, which highlights the futility of closed taxonomies.

Seth's œuvre thus appears as a postcolonial enigma. As exemplified by Mala Pandurang's book *Vikram Seth: Multiple Locations, Multiple Affiliations* (2011), the problem of location is the one insistent question that runs throughout current critical appraisals of Seth's centrifugal work: where does one place Vikram Seth? Where does he belong and whom does he address? No explicit anti-colonial discourse surfaces in *A Suitable Boy* (1993), the only work by Seth that deals with the aftermath of colonialism in India; his other works seemingly ignore the colonial process, as is epitomized by *Two Lives* (2005), his most recent prose text, which deals primarily with the pre-postcolonial genocide of the Shoah, offering a reflection on the part that Germany and the German-speaking people played in the culture and history of the twentieth century. Seth's writing does not evince any creolisation or "chutneyfication." The final English text displays a deceptive homogeneity on its surface, for in reality it alternates translated material from German with original commentary in English. So infused is the narrative with references to German/Austrian culture—both verbal (Heine, Trakl, Goethe, Hölderlin) and aural (Bach, Schubert)—that it has been described as downright Eurocentric.[1] While *Two Lives* has generated some uneasiness among critics, it has received little in-depth scholarly attention. In particular, there has been a lack of rigorous critical perspective on the formal aspect of the text, which explores the border area between biography and autobiography, offering a subtle, illuminative counterpoint to the rest of Seth's work.

A highly complex textual phenomenon, *Two Lives* chronicles the lives of two exiles of the twentieth century: Seth's Indian great-uncle Shanti Behari Seth, an immigrant from India who settled in Berlin to study dentistry in the 1930s, and Helga Gerda Caro, the German Jewish woman he befriended before the war and later married in England, where they retreated in 1937 and 1939 respectively. Using interviews with his great-uncle as well as letters, photographs, and official documents retrieved in a forgotten trunk, the author portrays the lives, variously separate and intertwined, of these two relatives he held dear. A hybrid couple, Shanti and Henny bridge different cultures. The image of the bridge is particularly fertile in *Two Lives*, a book about borders, boundaries, the closing of borders, and the crossing into new ones. The text is marked by porous geographical, lin-

---

[1] Rashmee Roshan Lall, for instance, has expressed her profound discomfort with the book, which looks suspect, as it were, in terms of its postcolonial credentials; she accuses Seth of effacing his Indian identity: "Seth, who is at ease in Austrian villages, enamoured of obscure German poets and comfortable with Europe's bloodied past, just happens to be Indian by birth and breeding; his literary sensibilities are European. This book could easily have been written by a European." The charge of Eurocentricism underlies many critiques of Seth's writing, which berate Seth for evading the politics of his own cultural, historical and political location: *The Golden Gate* (1986) and *An Equal Music* (1999) have also raised eyebrows owing to their lack of "Indianness." All too often, critics tend to focus on digging up a buried motif or symbol that might reveal the cultural "origin" (a term that betrays a fantasy of purity, of authenticity) of the author, disregarding the fact that the affiliations of a writer like Seth are too complex to be summed up in rigid dichotomies.

guistic, and even generic frontiers, as Seth questions the formal rigor that governs the rest of his literary production. The biographical screen thus discloses a fragmented self-portrait, as if the author sought out his own identity in the crucible of the biographical enterprise: "(…) seeing through a glass, however darkly, is to be less blind" (Seth 498). Through this Biblical reference to 1 Corinthians 13:12, the mirror emerges a central motif. Like a pilgrim, Seth retraces his relatives' peregrinations through Biswan, Monte Cassino, Berlin and London, searching for his own truth as a postcolonial writer in this geography of pain.

Divided into five parts, *Two Lives* throws into sharp relief Seth's interest in formal issues: Seth seems to view everything he writes as deliberate experiment, embodying all the characteristics of which a given form is capable. As the book draws to an end, he indulges in a methodological reflection on the innovative structure of his work:

> In a double biography, an intertwined meditation, where the author is an anomalous third braid, sometimes visible, sometimes not, there are intriguing possibilities of structure. For one thing, in what order should one recount events? The sequence of a biography with a single subject can be directly chronological. But it would have made little sense to ricochet from one protagonist to the other through their first two decades, before they had even met. Though I know where to end this book, I did not at first know where to begin it. There was too large a choice of starting-points […]. In the event, I chose to start the book with a moment involving all three of us: when, as a boy of seventeen, I went to live with them. It was not dramatic in the grand scheme of things, even if fraught with tension for my more nervous younger self. (491-492)

This crucial metatextual passage stresses that the biographical enterprise does not reduce to a simple historiographical project but is also a literary creation in its own right.[2] That Seth problematizes the question of the incipit and selects a starting-point of relevance to himself highlights the focal

---

[2] A hybrid, impure genre, biography straddles two different disciplines: literature and history. In Biography: Fiction, Fact and Form, a book that delineates a poetics of biography, Ira Bruce Nadel underlines the literary proprieties of biographical writing, which are often underestimated: "The excitement and interest in composing (and reading, I would argue) a biography derives not so much from the fact themselves but from the form of their presentation. For the biographer, the issue is not what are the facts but, as White explains, 'how are the facts to be described in order to sanction one mode of explaining them rather than another?' Readers, however, prefer the reverse, believing that what they read is the only way to present the facts" (Nadel 156).

point of the text—a question often overlooked in biographies, as Martine Boyer-Weinmann stresses in *La relation biographique* (2005).[3] Thus, the relationship between Seth and his relatives immediately moves to the foreground. In fact, this relationship is such an important component of *Two Lives* that it blurs the boundaries between biography and autobiography. Seth's work lies somewhere on the fault line between these two referential genres, which both claim to provide information about a reality exterior to the text while exhibiting striking points of difference on the formal level. In autobiography, the narrating and narrated 'I' are one and the same, whereas biography draws a clear line between narrating 'I' and narrated "he" or "she;" to borrow Philippe Lejeune's words, "[i]dentity is the real starting point of autobiography; resemblance the impossible horizon of biography" (Lejeune 24). In the last pages of *Two Lives*, another metatextual comment underlines the generic indeterminacy which characterizes the text, setting it apart from the other works by Seth, which are distinguished by a strong penchant for generic conformity: "Indeed, the lens has also turned around upon its wielder, for this book is memoir as well as biography" (491). This phrase functions retrospectively as a reading contract. Though the paratextual thresholds of the text anchor Seth's work into the biographical genre,[4] an autobiographical impulse surfaces from the outset. Indeed most of the sections of Part One begin with the pronoun 'I'—"the great refrain of the autobiographers" (Lejeune 8)—or the possessive adjective "my" (followed by a noun). A fragmented self-portrait thus emerges in *Two Lives*, as is epitomized by section 5.14, in which Seth encloses a copy of a wedding anniversary card to his parents on the grounds that Shanti added a few

---

[3] Martine Boyer-Weinmann deplores the theoretical indigence characteristic of most biographies. Boyer-Weinmann uses the phrase "white biographies" to refer to those biographies that rely on implicit epistemological, methodological and aesthetic assumptions and do not offer any conceptual framework.

[4] The title and the dedicatory poem function as generic promises, determining a specific horizon of expectation. The poem to Shanti and Henny clearly draws on the rhetoric of biography, as Seth stages his own insufficiency as a biographer: "To trace this pulse through its confusions,/Illusions, allusions, elusions/And limn its complex graph of love,/No skein of words is fine enough." A persuasive appeal follows: "Does this half-filial endeavour/Hold half a chance of half-success—/Even to track your lives, much less/Not to let these recede for ever?/No, if I'd hoped to grasp the whole;/Yes, if some shard may touch the soul" (1). Legitimizing discourse plays an important role in the biographical genre. The repetition of the adjective "half"—which suggests from the outset partial or fractured belonging, a permanent negotiation of languages, cultures and histories—thus enhances the author's posture of humility; together with the antithesis "No"/"Yes" and the rhyme "whole"/"soul," it offers a typical example of captatio benevolentiae.

straggling words. The letter is presented as "Shanti's last lines to my parents" (471): Seth elaborates upon his uncle's cryptic handwriting but does not offer any comment on his own lines, though they take up most of the letter. Since Seth's handwriting is quite legible—in contrast to Shanti's—the reader has no difficulty deciphering these lines. They offer personal information that Seth fails to mention in the body of the text—comments on his admiration for his parents, his relationship with a certain Philippe (Honoré), and the unnamed novel he is in the process of completing (*An Equal Music*, judging from the date). The letter, however, does not appear in full: the last sentence comes to an abrupt halt. Significantly, it stops with the first person singular, "I," thus bringing to light Seth's oblique quest for identity in *Two Lives*.

As if the autobiography of the biographer were inseparable from the biographical enterprise, Seth puts forth a reflection on his work as a writer. He provides a considerable amount of information about himself, the discovery of his true vocation, and the background to his writing process for *From Heaven Lake*, *The Golden Gate*, *A Suitable Boy*, *Arion and the Dolphin*, *An Equal Music*—and *Two Lives* itself. As Part One draws to an end, Seth ascribes the idea of the book to his mother: "We talked about [Shanti Uncle] in the car, and Mama said, turning to me, 'You don't know what exactly to write about next. Why don't you write about him?'/My first reaction was not eager. 'I don't know if I want to write about someone so close to me,' I said" (50). By stressing his initial reluctance to write *Two Lives*, Seth leads the reader to question his reliability as a biographer. His account of his final interview with Shanti achieves precisely the same effect. By transcribing his rough notes (composed of substantives, adjectives, imperatives, past participles, aphorisms, etc.) the author forces the reader to adhere to a tedious writing process:

- ice
- so weak – chair
- Nikera – Kenya
- money stolen
- marriage: George
- sexy novel?
- swollen feet (raise them)
- you can be heavy when you want to be (471–472)

Seth attempts to fathom these inscrutable annotations: "What could those notes mean? 'Ice' might represent his demand for what he loved to suck and crunch, perhaps because his mouth was so dry. [...] 'Nikera' might be my attempt to remember 'Nakuru'—possibly the town in Kenya where one of his nurses came from" (472). Whether Seth transcribes his notes *verbatim*—as he claims to—is beside the point. What matters is that he casts doubt on his dependability through the adverbs, modals and question marks that proliferate in the above-quoted passage.

In contrast to *A Suitable Boy* or *The Golden Gate*, which exude a strong sense of mastery, *Two Lives* ends in chaos. While the beginning of the narrative is limpid, the utmost confusion reigns in Part Five, as is typified by the numerous "illegible" annotations that punctuate Shanti's testament: "At the beginning of the fifth clause, above Colin's name, were seven words, again not countersigned or witnessed, which I later pored over but was unable to make sense of, so illegible was Uncle's handwriting at this stage. They read as follows: [illegible] [illegible] Arun Seth Vikram Seth [illegible]" (486). It is by no means coincidental that this document is riddled with black holes. On the question of Shanti's testament Seth hits an interpretative deadlock: in Part Five he harks back to the feeling of utter dismay that his great-uncle's testament instilled in him, dooming his first attempts at writing *Two Lives*. The curt sentences reflect his rancor:

> I felt sick to my stomach. [...] I cannot describe the deep revulsion of feeling that overcame me after this conversation. It changed my view of—indeed, my faith in—Uncle. I had loved him and greatly respected him. This love was now tinged with anger and this respect with something corrosive. All Uncle's talk about the family and what it meant to him came back to me. The sense of his rejection of the family—and that the remark he had made about my mother was made in this context: it was all too much to take. (480–81)

The bitterness that such passages convey is troubling. Why did Seth choose to keep the last part on his deeply ambivalent feelings for his uncle? What is one to make of the character of Colin, the man who looked after Shanti in the twilight of his life and whose motivations Seth leads us to suspect? This chaotic ending is a reflection of the generic indeterminacy of Seth's project in *Two Lives*. This indeterminacy poses a taxonomic problem which is quite apparent in an interview Nermeen Shaikh conducted with Seth: "(...) there were two completely different textures involved in the book: the interviews with my uncle, and the letters that my aunt sent, together with the responses that came. So those added two quite different textures to the general narration, or memoir, or biography that I was trying to write" (Shaikh). The repetition of the conjunction "or" stresses how arduous it is to define *Two Lives* generically. The uneasiness the reader feels as *Two Lives* draws to a close is not psychological; it stems from the sense that the author has lost control.

Two Lives offers an invaluable key to construe Seth's literary production as a whole. While Seth's neatly compartmentalized texts usually rely on "passion and anxiety bridled by classical forms" (Woodward), displaying a rare confidence in the possibility of an orderly representation of the world, doubt dissolves generic categories in *Two Lives*. The troubling grey areas surrounding genre in this text reveal that Seth's œuvre oscillates between unity and plurality, totality and fragmentation, purity and ambiguity, in a constant attempt to negotiate between the modern and the postmodern. Owing to this constant oscillation, Seth occupies a highly original place on the postcolonial literary scene.

Works Cited

Boyer-Weinmann, Martine. *La relation biographique: Enjeux contemporains*. Seyssel: Champ Vallon, 2005. Print.

Lejeune, Philippe. *The Autobiographical Pact*. Accessed on 5 December 2013. URL: https://edocs.uis.edu/Departments/LIS/Course_Pages/LNT501/RN/Rosina's_on-ground_course_storage/Rosina's_LNT_501_Readings/On%20Autobiography%20pp3-30%20%20by%20Philippe%20Lejeune.pdf

Nadel, Bruce Ira. *Biography: Fiction, Fact and Form*. London, Macmillan and New York: St. Martin's, 1984. Print.

Pandurang, Mala. *Vikram Seth: Multiple Locations, Multiple Affiliations*. Jaipur & Delhi: Rawat, 2001. Print.

Parker, Pete, Ed. *The Reader's Companion to the Twentieth-Century Novel*. Oxford: Helicon, 1994. Print.

Roshan Lall, Rashmee. "An Indian dentist and his frau." *The Times of India*. October 08, 2005. Accessed on 19 August 2012. URL: http://articles.timesofindia.indiatimes.com/2005-10-08/bookmark/27839021_1_vikram-seth-dentist-biography.

Seth, Vikram. *Two Lives*. 2005. London: Abacus, 2006. Print.

Shaikh, Nermeen. "Vikram Seth: *Two Lives and One Century*." Accessed on 9 January 2012. URL: http://asiasociety.org/arts/literature/vikram-seth-two-lives-and-one-century.

Woodward, Richard B. *"Vikram Seth's Big Book," The New York Times.* May 02, 1993. Accessed on 18 August 2012. URL: http://www.nytimes.com/1993/05/02/magazine/vikram-seth-s-big-book.html?pagewanted=all&src=pm.

The (Un)making of a Novelist's Self: 'Late Style' in Günter Grass' and J. M. Coetzee's Autobiographical Writing

Melissa Schuh

Ob heute oder vor Jahren, lockend bleibt die Versuchung, sich in dritter Person zu verkappen: Als er annähernd zwölf zählte, doch immer noch liebend gern auf Mutters Schoß saß, begann und endete etwas. Aber läßt sich, was anfing, was auslief, so genau auf den Punkt bringen? (Grass 7)

[Whether today or years ago, the temptation to disguise oneself in the third person continues to beckon: When he was close to twelve years old, yet still liking to sit on his mother's lap, something began and something ended. But is it possible to exactly pinpoint in this manner what began and what ended?][1]

This opening statement from Günter Grass's autobiography *Beim Häuten der Zwiebel* [Peeling the Onion] poses a question which underpins any reading of autobiographical material: which style and narrative strategy may be best suited for writing a life? By alluding to the "temptation to disguise oneself in the third person" (7) in spite of traditional first-person autobiographies, Grass draws attention to the challenge of representing a life and finding a suitable autobiographical voice to narrate one's life-story.

Indeed, Grass's rendering of autobiographical perspective through first-person as well as third-person narrative, that he already alludes to in this quotation provides a point of departure from which one can analyse the significant shift from fictional to explicitly autobiographical writing in the late phase work by prominent contemporary novelists, such as Grass and

---

[1] For the purposes of this paper own translations from the original German text into English are provided in square brackets.

Coetzee, on whom this paper focuses. Both Grass and Coetzee are acclaimed writers. Amongst several prizes and achievements, both received the Nobel Prize for Literature, Grass in 1999 and Coetzee in 2003. Although both authors are known to draw on what Joe Moran calls a "hall of mirrors effect" (104) in their fiction—which invites readers and critics to engage with allusions to autobiographical content—I want to argue that a shift towards autobiographical writing which explicitly enters into "the autobiographical pact" (Leujeune 5), by assuming the author's name on the cover of the book to be synonymous for the protagonist and narrator of the life-story. This marks a significant turn in their oeuvre which provokes innovations on the level of style.

This paper will be divided into three sections: To begin, I will outline the use of lateness as a factor of style in autobiographical life-writing, drawing on Edward Said's theory of late style. Then I will focus on those narrative strategies, which I consider as representative in conveying lateness and late style in the autobiographical context: first in Grass' *Beim Häuten der Zwiebel*, then in Coetzee's *Summertime*. Finally I will conclude by assessing Grass and Coetzee's autobiographical portrayal of the novelist's writing life as a source of stylistic innovation.

In his posthumously published book *On Late Style*, Edward W. Said explores the idea of "late style" (7) in artists' works which he develops from Theodor W. Adorno's concept of "Spätstil" (translated from German as "late style") in Beethoven.[2] According to Said, the work and intellectual thought of artists can "acquir[e] a new idiom" as they are nearing the end of their lives, "a new idiom" which he chooses to call "late style" (Said 6). Drawing on his reading of Adorno, Said combines ideas about notions of "lateness" on the one hand and "style" on the other hand in the term "late style."

> [There is an] accepted notion of age and wisdom in some last works that reflect a special maturity, a new spirit of reconciliation and serenity often expressed in terms of miraculous transfiguration of common reality ... [This is expressed in a] renewed, almost youthful energy that attests to an apotheosis of artistic creativity and power ... Each of us can readily supply evidence of how it is that late works crown a lifetime of aesthetic endeavour ... But what of artistic lateness not as harmony and resolution but as intransigence, difficulty, and unresolved contradiction? ... I'd like to explore the experience of late style that involves a nonhar-

---

[2] See Adorno, Theodor W. "Spätstil Beethovens"/ "Late Style in Beethoven." *Essays on Music*. Ed. Richard Leppert. Berkeley, Los Angeles, London: U of California P, 2002. Print.

monious, nonserene tension, and above all, a sort of deliberately unproductive productiveness going *against*... (Said 6–7)

Edwards Said conceptualises late style as an aesthetic quality in an artist's late work, which can convey either of two notions: reconciliation or contradiction. Reconciliation encompasses a sense of "harmony and resolution" which completes and crowns an artist's oeuvre with a unifying creative burst. Lateness as an expression of contradiction, on the other hand, exhibits the tensions, struggles and difficulties which may undercut an artist's late work as juggling unresolved issues. As the quotation suggests, Said is more interested in the latter form of late style, in contradiction rather than reconciliation. Nevertheless he sets out this distinct categorisation quite definitely, which begs the question where the possibility of a work of late style would fall which may itself present contradictory notions hereby, however, presenting a unifying experience of the artist's work as a whole. This paper will return to this question when it discusses Grass and Coetzee's use of late style in detail, but it is worth bearing in mind that Said's categories of reconciliation and contradiction could simultaneously apply to different levels in a single work as well as in an artist's oeuvre as a whole.

Said's conceptualisation of late style can very fruitfully be applied to lifewriting, in particular the instances of life-writing shown by prominent authors of fiction which Grass and Coetzee certainly are. The imminent link between late style and autobiographical writing can best be illustrated by the idea that lateness entails self-conscious and timely reflection in artistic creation: "Lateness is being at the end, fully conscious, full of memory, and also very (even preternaturally) aware of the present." (14) The autobiographical act shares a prominent affinity with lateness as a factor of style. The retrospective nature of life-writing provides the most obvious connection to lateness, but the particular circumstance of consciously looking back and remembering one's life in light of the present is the very condition which defines the autobiographical impulse. Lateness arises from the deliberate process of remembering and presenting as well as structuring memories of the past due to an impetus whose motivation clearly lies in the present. The autobiographer's position is therefore at once rooted in the present time and circumstance, while drawing a chronological trajectory from the past to this current moment of recollection. As Said notes, this must have consequences for the aesthetic form and style of writing lateness:

> Any style involves first of all the artist's connection to his or her own time, or historical period, society, and antecedents; the aesthetic work, for all its irreducible individuality, is nevertheless a part—or, paradoxically, not a part—of the era in which it was produced and appeared. This is not simply a matter of sociological or political synchrony but more interestingly has to do with rhetorical or formal style. (134)

Although Said rightfully asserts that any style responds to and is therefore rooted in the writer's socio-historical context and tradition, narrative strategy and formal style in autobiographical writing seems to encompass the very nature of late style due to the genre's unique condition of a narrative perspective, which recollects the past due to a motive that lies in the present.

I will now return to my initial remarks about Grass's use of first- and third-person narration in conveying his autobiographical voice and perspective. Despite having pointed out the danger of distorting truth by using the disguise of impersonally writing in the third person, Grass proceeds to describe his younger twelve year old self in precisely that mode:

> Also schreibe ich über die Schande und die ihr nachhinkende Scham. Selten genutzte Wörter, gesetzt im Nachholverfahren, derweil mein mal nachsichtiger, dann wieder strenger Blick auf einen Jungen gerichtet bleibt, der kniefreie Hosen trägt, allem, was sich verborgen hält, hinterdreinschnüffelt und dennoch versäumt hat, " warum" zu sagen. (17)

> [So I write about the disgrace and the shame, which lags behind it. Rarely used words, set in a process of catching up; meanwhile my sometimes forgiving, then again strict gaze is directed at a boy, who wears knee-length trousers, snooping for everything which is hidden and yet he failed to say 'why'.]

Through this occasional use of third-person narration Grass' younger self oscillates between being referred to as 'I' and being perceived separately, much like a character who is judged "sometimes forgiving, then again strict[ly]" (17) by the author himself. Accordingly the reader is invited to share the opportunity of judging Grass and his younger self separately or combined in the unifying 'I'. Furthermore this narrative strategy alludes to Grass' first novel, *Die Blechtrommel* (The Tin Drum), in which the protagonist Oskar Matzerath tells his story in a similar fashion by including third-person narration in a first-person narrative. Consequently Grass' combination of first- and third-person narrative undercuts the notion of a straightforward relationship between the self, the novelist and his works. This shows how the very "temptation to disguise oneself in the third person" (7) which marks the beginning of the autobiography permeates the work, as if the novelist's characteristic trait of fictionalising could not be completely abandoned. I want to suggest that Grass uses autobiography's affinity to lateness as a springboard from which to launch a unique narrative investigation into his late self as also inevitably shaped by his work as a novelist, thus pointing towards a concept of writerly identity which encompasses the multifaceted self.

However, Grass's choice of narrative form for *Beim Häuten der Zwiebel* has implications beyond advocating for the multifacetedness of a novelist's identity. It shows the constant struggle between a straightforward confessional first-person account and a more distanced but intensely self-scrutinising third-person perspective. The artifice of his past self as a character in this life story is foregrounded through third-person narrative. The voices of possible past selves, "als Entwurf meiner selbst [as a draft of myself]" (43), are included in the formation of his present authorial voice, represented in the first person.

> Schicht auf Schicht lagert die Zeit. Was sie bedeckt, ist allenfalls durch Ritzen zu erkennen. Und durch solch einen Zeitspalt, der mit Anstrengung zu erweitern ist, sehe ich mich und ihn zugleich. (51)
>
> [Layer upon layer time is stocked. What it shrouds can be identified through cracks at best. And through such a crack in time, which is to be widened with effort, I see myself and him at the same time.]

By narrating "myself and him at the same time" (51)—that is to say the present self of his narration as well as a past version of himself—varying derivations of Grass' current self in the third-person, a self-contradicting, at times even self-denying picture of the novelist's struggling self emerges. This is a site of self-scrutinising judgment of the past and its memories, which can only exist within the textual encounter of Grass' presently writing authorial voice with the deriving characters of himself that occupy the biographical—yet also fictional—narrative space of autobiography. Late style as a reflection of difficulty and contradiction is therefore explicitly expressed in Grass' form of narration to account for the ethical dilemma which ensues from his voluntary enlistment with the "Waffen-SS," but also from the belatedness of this confession. Nevertheless, by adopting a distantly self-scrutinising third-person perspective alongside a self-emulating first-person account, the novelist's self emerges as a figure which can unify aesthetic and ethical expression in autobiographical life-writing.

The narrative structure of Coetzee's *Summertime* is no less ambiguous and complex:

> But what if we are all fictioneers, as you call Coetzee? What if we all continually make up the stories of our lives? Why should what I tell you about Coetzee be any worthier of credence than what he tells you himself? (226) [Sophie Denoël]

> Of course we are all fictioneers. I do not deny that. But which would you rather have: a set of independent reports from a range of independent perspectives, from which you can then try to synthesize a whole; or the massive unitary self-projection comprised by his oeuvre. I know which I would prefer. (226) [Mr Vincent]

With this statement from *Summertime* Sophie Denoël challenges J.M. Coetzee's biographer, Mr Vincent, to question his own assumptions about the value of accounts by contemporary witnesses in relation to biographical information drawn from the published as well as private writings by the biographical subject Coetzee himself. However, Sophie's critical question of how her own opinion about Coetzee should be "any worthier of credence" than his own voice (which could be extrapolated from his writing) gains further significance when the entire narrative structure of *Summertime* is considered: the author Coetzee, while alive and still actively writing, composes a collection of fragmented notes as well as interviews with five people who supposedly know him, as if they had been compiled, conducted and written up by a biographer who aimed to publish a book about him after his supposed death. Sophie, as well as Julia, Margot, Adriana, Martin and Mr Vincent, can then be seen as characters whose voices and opinions are composed and phrased by the supposedly biographical subject Coetzee, who nevertheless features prominently as *Summertime*'s author on the cover of the book. Due to this specific layout of the text's narration, Sophie's argument which places Coetzee's authorial voice, as it is contained in his writing, next to "independent reports" (226) by contemporaries gains a further dimension. After all, what Mr Vincent calls "a set of independent reports from a range of independent perspectives, from which you can try to synthesize a whole" (226) then turns out to be a significant part of Coetzee's "massive unitary self-projection comprised by his oeuvre" (226)— of which *Summertime* is a considerable fragment.

Therefore, although *Summertime* adopts the narrative appearance of a collection of biographical material about the subject of Coetzee, the fragmented compilation of different, supposedly "independent" voices can be unified in its origin and destination. We are invited to trace the provenance of these voices back to the novelist Coetzee, who simultaneously occupies the roles of author and mutual character within the fictional autobiographical accounts of his contemporaries. The question of autobiographical and biographical form as well as value, which is most explicitly expressed in Sophie's and Mr Vincent's earlier quoted remarks, continuously permeates *Summertime* as a whole and remains curiously suspended and unanswered within the narrative's structure, even though the entire book is dedicated to its exploration. Said, whose critical work has helped pave the way for postcolonial theory, and his ideas about late style are particularly relevant in the case of Coetzee's writings as a South African author. In fact, Said's observations about contradiction and reconciliation as factors of late style are uniquely inscribed in *Summertime*'s narrative premise as an autobiographically directed compilation of biographical materials and accounts. Opposing and possibly contradictory accounts of memories featuring the biographical subject of Coetzee—as a "minor character" (44) within Julia's marriage problems, as Margot's "favourite cousin" (136), as "nothing, just an irritation, an embarrassment" (193) to Adriana and "just a man" (242) to Sophie—trace a character who is scattered almost to the point of disappearance among the interviewees' personal histories. Nonetheless, the text as a whole is constantly underpinned by the authorial presence as well as the recurring character of the novelist Coetzee, who emerges as a unifying yet elusive figure.

Although the described stylistic choices by which Grass and Coetzee frame their autobiographical perspectives differ considerably, late style in the form of fragmentations, tensions and contradictions within the presented selves of the authors characterises the products of their autobiographical impulses. Grass's combination of a confessional first-person perspective with a self-scrutinising third-person view on his past selves creates an aesthetic expression of ongoing struggles within his writerly self. Coetzee, on the other hand, relinquishes his autobiographical control and perspective to a fictional biographer and a handful of contemporary witnesses, amongst whose reports his identity is dispersed such that it may almost disappear. However, both Grass and Coetzee's self-dissecting scrutiny of a stable autobiographical self is underpinned by the unifying and reconciling, yet elusive figure of the novelist. Paradoxically the novelist's presence becomes palpable through the very stylistic measures which fragment the novelist-self as suspended between fact and fiction, biography and autobiography, multiplicity and singularity.

I want to suggest that the significance of autobiographical writing which portrays the writing life in stylistically innovative ways goes beyond a postmodern experiment of questioning the boundaries between genres. Instead, I believe that contemporary novelists, such as Grass and Coetzee, transform their autobiographical impulse into a self-judging, self-scrutinising and self-emulating engagement with the writing life. The novelist's complex positioning as an authority in literary aesthetic as well as intellectual and ethical terms informs this complex engagement with the writer-self. As this paper has shown, narrative choices on the level of style create relating forms of autobiographical self-representation. Comparing these different stylistic strategies as they are employed by the authors in question uncovers the writing life of the novelist as a source of stylistic innovation which even bridges Said's opposition of contradiction and reconciliation. While the recurring themes of judgment, authorial voice and identity as well as memory are narratively rendered to reflect the writer's struggle with the autobiographical impulse, the novelist nevertheless emerges as a unifying figure which has the potential to reconcile the numerous and seemingly contradictory perspectives that represent the writing life. Therefore, the novelist's autobiographical text implicitly demands to be read to the full extent of how it makes and simultaneously unmakes the source of its own interpretation.

Works Cited

Coetzee, J.M. *Summertime*. London: Vintage, 2010. Print.

Grass, Günter. *Beim Häuten der Zwiebel*. Munich: Deutscher Taschenbuch Verlag, 2008. Print.

Lejeune, Philippe. *On Autobiography*. Ed. Paul Eakin. Minneapolis: University of Minnesota Press, 1989. Print.

Moran, Joe. *Star Authors: Literary Celebrity in America*. London/Sterling: Pluto Press, 2000. Print.

Said, Edward W. *On Late Style*. London: Bloomsbury, 2006. Print.

Eve Unchained:
Christina Stead's Recasting of the Christian Spiritual Autobiography

Michael Ackland

Christina Stead, who came of age as a writer in the 1930s, enjoyed trans-Atlantic fame before the outbreak of the Second World War, suffered ignominy and neglect during the Cold War, then rehabilitation as a precursor of Third Wave Feminism—a role which she flatly rejected (Wetherell, Whitehead). Readings of her oeuvre have similarly fluctuated, from early reviews that praised her imaginative exuberance or social insights (Rowley 156, 246), to more recent emphasis on her depiction of women's plight and the profound dependence of her fiction on lived experience.[1] For instance, according to Hazel Rowley's definitive, award-winning biography, Stead was far more interested in her characters, often based on friends, than ideas, and sought to write with "an intelligent ferocity" (316).[2] And creative ardour, fuelled by personal animus, is undeniably an aspect of her fiction, as when stark repulsion for fellow novelist and Communist, Ruth McKenney, resurges in long stretches of her last novel, *I'm Dying Laughing* (Rowley 361–64), or in the diverse ways her most famous book, *The Man Who Loved Children*, represents a delayed fictional reckoning with her overbearing father (Rowley 258–63). Indeed, if Rowley's account is to be believed, key Stead texts are strikingly auto-biographical, while vividly evoked scenes and occasional pieces are some-

---

[1] Monographs with a strong emphasis on her fictional treatment of womankind include those by Lidoff, Sheridan, Brydon and Gribble, while Stead's work was included in the feminist canon assembled in Gilbert and Gubar's *No Man's Land*.

[2] The phrase is Stead's, and in the same letter to Thistle Harris of 6 April, 1942 she states categorically: "The sensuality, delicacy of literature does not exist for me; only the passion, energy and struggle, the night of which no one speaks, the creative act" (qtd. Rowley 316).

times little more than autobiographical vignettes. The great marlin-boiling scene in *The Man Who Loved Children*, for example, can be traced back to her own family's boiling down of a captured shark in their backyard at Watson's Bay (Stead 1985 490), or the writer's final effort, "The Old School," is practically dismissed as easy material, ready to hand for an exhausted, largely disinterested author (Rowley 540). Yet the quest for alleged biographical parallels or sources can readily become reductive, especially when, as I hope to show, Stead's understanding and use of autobiographical material and tradition was complexly inflected by her role as both an engaged and a female author.

Like most writers Stead acknowledged that autobiographical material was a potentially rich fictional resource; what counted, however, were the uses to which it was put. In Stead's case these were dictated by a determinedly secular upbringing and education. Her father David, although an autodidact, became an eminent zoologist, government adviser and eclectic socialist. To his daughter Christina he imparted, as she boasted, the exacting habits of a naturalist. The world, according to David Stead, was rationally knowable, definable and best approached through careful observation and analysis. His models were the scientists and explorers whose portraits graced the family dining-room: "Cuvier, Buffon, Darwin, Huxley, and Captain Cook" (1985 488). This gallery was complemented by an awesome, at times glibly repeated life-motto: "Dare to be a Daniel, Dare to stand alone, Dare to have a purpose true and Dare to make it known" (1985 486). David's influence, however, proved problematical and was comprehensively eclipsed in the late 1920s by the American Communist William Blake, who completed Stead's induction into the Marxist-Leninist fold.[3] Theoretical schooling and unequivocal engagement were henceforth *de rigueur*. A writer's task was to dissect social conditions, to bring the insights of dialectical materialism to bear on historical problems, and to locate causality and potential solutions in material conditions. From the vantage point of her new secular faith Stead would later sweepingly arraign her father as "part of the Huxley-Darwin reasonable-rational nature-agnostic mother-of-all-things-fresh-air-panacea eclectic-socialist universal-peace-manhood-suffrage-and-vegetarianism of the English breed" (1992 89).

Her Marxist bona fides emerge clearly in writings from the early 1930s. Here, with the fervour of a recent convert, she rails against the bourgeois

---

[3] On first meeting her future paramour was formally known as Wilhelm Blech, but it was as William Blake that he later emerged as a public speaker in demand and, intermittently, as a bestselling novelist.

hegemony in France and denounces the country as a "Police State" (1992 23). Similarly, urban conditions now have clear ideological correlatives ("great London looked like a smoking garbage heap, so dark, smoky and unlighted it is: and so it is now in affairs, and socially" [1992 48]), while the absence of a revolutionary spark among the English proletariat, despite long-documented sufferings, leads Stead to describe "the working classes in England" as "amazingly and heartrendingly phlegmatic" (1992 47). Nevertheless, grounds for hope abound. 1931 is dubbed a "battle year fit to stand with 1517, 1848," ushered in by increasing signs of "financial trouble" and the 'marvellous [realization] that Soviet Russia has put itself into a position' not merely to "frighten" but to deal "the first serious blows" to world capitalism (1992 35-36). And her contemporaneous novel, *Seven Poor Men of Sydney*, which explores the struggle to kindle and act upon class consciousness, is similarly infused with Marxist-Leninist doctrine (Ackland, "Hedging on Destiny" 91-102).

Yet even in her first novel, *Seven Poor Men of Sydney*, as in mature later fiction, Stead is able to dramatise dogma and avoid unleavened didacticism—she was highly adept at creative assimilation. In fact, the book's one unambiguous advocate of Marxist-Leninism, Winter, is presented with ironic detachment as disturbing listeners with his bluntness rather than converting them. Instead, at her best, Stead is able to tease out and re-energize the implications of clichéd teachings, such as the adage of religion as the opium of the people. Most obviously, Joseph's mother is ensorcelled by the rites of the Catholic Church: "She saw the workaday world through a confessional grille, as a weevil through the hole he has gnawed in a nut" (66). Intent on spiritual panacea, she has overlooked the early aging of her hand, "withered with thousands of household and maternal labours" (66), as well as the possibility of terrestrial redress for an impoverished existence. She may think that faith sustains her; however, Stead locates her capacity for endurance in the genetic inheritance of "peasant ancestors bred to survive starvation, fireless winters and the scratching for crops in Irish tenant farms" (66), and derides the notion of an inalienable spiritual essence: "if she had a soul; but it was no soul, it was a dried leaf" (66). In brief, the Church and its practices are persistently branded as antithetical to emancipated thought, with the confessional absolving individuals not only of their sins but, more importantly, of responsibility for their own, and society's destiny. Henceforth religious insignia, traditions and practices could be informally deconsecrated and used to revolutionary ends.[4]

Also Stead from the outset was aware of the dilemmas faced by a radical female activist, as her fictional portrayal of youthful Catherine Baguenault diversely testifies. No one denies Catherine's fervour, or her insightfulness. She is praised as "a born soldier" (151), as a "firebell clanging" (132), or as able to perceive "reality [not] with studio-light and art effects" but "stark, harsh" (130). Also she has in large measure the imaginative empathy so crucial to a novelist: "My character is to undergo. Everyone and everything I meet is the further instrument" to enhanced understanding (149). Yet although she has acted on the belief that, "under many hoods and hats, we are all the same creature all the time trying to make its way out of a thicket" (50), grim experience has taught her that normative, supposedly non-gender-specific assumptions are actually weighted heavily in favour of men: "I've fought all my life for male objectives in men's terms ... [till] I am neither man nor woman ... That's why I fight so hard and suffer so much and get nowhere" (214). Hence this strong figure is constantly dissatisfied and on the verge of physical and mental breakdown. Elsewhere another outcast, the ambiguously-gendered Dacre Esme Eugene, underscores the impossible lot of women, gifted with "primeval force" and "unregimented talents," but obliged to remain "demurely nun-like in the background" and allow themselves to be imposed on (165).[5] To do otherwise would require nothing less than "a female Caesar," who "would positively cross the Rubicon twenty times a day" (165) in her bid to cut through patriarchal impediments. Stead was clearly aware of the opposition and risks she faced. Nevertheless, whereas Catherine eventually withdraws to an asylum, her author chose again and again to cross the Rubicon—but always with requisite caution.

With time Stead became a veritable "female Caesar," crafting open-ended, elusive novels and carefully recasting autobiographical material. At times this assumes the form of specifically autobiographical or biographical

---

[4] This point is explicitly underscored through Joseph too: "The confessional purified him and made it possible for him to live without thinking at all" (84), while the Church is repeatedly associated with obfuscating mystery and money, as when his mother's heart is likened to 'a stuffed chasuble continually repeating "Om, Om," with censers swinging and the tin cash-box clinking' (66).

[5] Apart from the exotic, androgynous ring of his name, Dacre is described as a little "fellow" or "little creature," and as a male who "chatters[s] in a strained feminine voice" (165).

sketches. Occasionally it provides a fictional plot-line and incidents; but rarely can her writing be mistaken for an unmediated record of lived experience. Crucially, too, Stead's unapologetically Marxist scorn of Christian rites and eschatology led to the selective deployment of Judeo-Christian motifs, rather than to their proscription. Marxism and the Bible share, for example, a vision of eventual apocalyptic collapse and rebirth that invites adaptation, as when Stead depicts an Ezekiel-like chariot, portending prophetic vision and epochal upheaval, manned by Marx and Engels, Lenin and Stalin (1938 26). More original is her re-envisaging of the received template of spiritual biography, genesis and the creation. The deity disappears from her narrative, other-worldly interventions are ruled out. Instead her focus falls on Adam, while Australia provides a primal landscape. The primacy of individual agency is asserted, and historical forces usurp godhead as the motor of social and individual becoming.

In Stead's biographical vignettes, her father David is cast as the Adam of a New World, as well as, in an early avatar, an all-encompassing nurturer and provider.

> David was an Adam; Australia was his prolific and innocent garden. This was his nature. He came to his young manhood and prime in the time of 'the optimists' ... he was a naturalist with its new (old) country and its wildlife to explore; his imagination and ardent love for his country called forth marvels. (1985 483)

David is an archetypal explorer/namer, with a partially unrecorded theatre of action available to him on land and sea. An exuberant imagination makes him receptive to the wonders of antipodean nature and of narrative (in both fiction and non-fiction), with which he nightly regales his first-born Christina. Yet even this local version on the "Arabian Nights" exhibits a distinctive ideological burden:

> I must leave out all the stories of those many nights, a thousand, between two and four and a half, which formed my views—an interest in men and nature, *a feeling that all were equal*, the extinct monster, the coral insect, the black man and us, the birds and the fish; and another curious feeling still with me, of *terrestrial eternity*, a sun that never set. (emphasis added, 1985 5)

Like a post-partum fluid, this veritable "ocean of story" in which the child drifts acts as a life-giver and stimulant. A bountiful surrogate for a lost mother, its tantalizing expanse kindles an urge to solo voyaging as well as the realization that the resources of imagination, like mankind and creation itself, are never-ending: "Some may and will die; but man's story never" (1985 11). There is little room for the sacred in these biographical accounts, except as another convenient and lulling fiction. The only eternity entertained is specifically "terrestrial" for Stead's concern is exclusively with the here-and-now and the joys or fulfillment that it can afford.

In a related move, large socio-historical forces, such as class interests, assume the former role of the Deity or Eve as a decisive catalyst and incontrovertible factor in the fashioning of events. Young Stead might intuit "that all were equal," but the mature author's sketch of her family lineage in "A Waker and Dreamer" unfolds against a backdrop of many-faceted social injustice. "In the nineteenth century," according to Stead, "little in England was Merrie" (1985 482), and she makes a point of finding each "bright picture ... fogged in one corner" (1985 484). The poor and less well-to-do are shown to be repeatedly imposed on by those-in-power, who fear in succession destabilising French influence, Chartism and Socialism ("all such meetings ... ILLEGAL" [1985 481]). Ever gullible, the downtrodden listen to the "engaging travel fiction" of emigration as a panacea for want, rather than to the unpalatable truths of the Communist Manifesto (1985 483). Similarly David, chock full of energy and self-belief, embodies self-deluding idealism: his "whiteness, fairness and all that goes with it, dazzled himself. He believed in himself so strongly that, sure of his innocence, pure intentions, he felt he was a favored son of Fate" (1985 486)—only to be publicly shamed and brought low by powerful vested interests. Clearly individual talent alone will not alter the status quo, while his sister's nonsensical belief in Kismit was a recipe for acquiescence and passivity. Also David was manifestly wrong to put his faith in "evolution not revolution," and in the collective efforts of "men of goodwill" (Ocean 491). The authorial message is muted but unmistakable. The manifestations of evil described here are of human and material origin. They are not part of an elaborate providential plan that surpasses mortal understanding, nor are they the work of the Devil. Hence their alteration through human agency remains both conceivable and necessary, and most assured through revolution rather than through the recurring patterns of co-opted radicalism, conciliation and disguised oppression that pass for progress in the West.

In addition, Stead produced fictional works that have been read as starkly autobiographical. Most notoriously *The Man Who Loved Children*, according to Rowley, revisits over hundreds of pages key events and formative circumstances of the author's childhood. Here actual letters, incidents and exchanges reappear virtually verbatim, but transposed from Watson's Bay to Washington, D.C. and Maryland in a bid both to attract an American readership and, presumably, to deflect attention from the work's autobiographical basis. Stead was avowedly "deep-bitten" by these years (1992 90), so that bringing them to book became allegedly a harrowing act of exorcism, therapy and revenge (Rowley 258–59). To intimates Stead acknowledged the novel's deeply personal nature: "It was a great weight off my mind, I ought really to say my soul, writing *The Man Who*—it was as if I escaped from jail, although it may seem savage and mean to others" (qtd. in Rowley 258). And its accuracy was confirmed by family members, such as her father's third wife, Thistle Harris, who found his depiction in the book to be "exact—my memory is faultless: and she has guessed most of it, she even believes it all ... So I hope you now believe your own woman and realize she is not crazy" (Harris 75). Similarly, but on a smaller scale, Stead's last completed work, "The Old School," has been treated (when not completely ignored) as a slight, perfunctory autobiographical performance. Supposedly "this poignant story, which describes the way under-privileged children were cruelly scapegoated by the others, reveals an older, mellow Stead reflecting on her past" (Rowley 540). According to these readings, then, the writer as "female Caesar" and autobiographer had, at most, to cross the Rubicon only once in composing her masterpiece, that is, in trampling on family sensitivities, while for her final piece she did not even need to get her toes wet—the material was low key and uncontroversial.

Stead as writer, however, was arguably far more ambitious and committed to the socialist cause than these generally accepted autobiographical readings allow. Although the subjects of these compositions were undoubtedly suggested by, and in the case of the novel broadly based on, her early life experiences, recent commentary has shown both works to be fully engaged with pressing political issues of the day: respectively the New Deal and the Cold War (Ackland "Socialists for a new socialism" and 2010). In each instance, tactical considerations urged extreme caution and the need for covert statement. At the time of writing *The Man Who Loved Children*, to have openly attacked the Roosevelt administration would have contravened the official line of the Communist Party of the United States—which under Earl Browder was making common cause with Washington (Ottanelli 135–37)—and potentially drawn unwelcome government attention to herself. Nevertheless, as diverse letters and miscellaneous notes attest, Stead entered fully into the febrile environment of Marxist analysis, in-fighting and expectation that prevailed in Manhattan during this period of immense social upheaval. The President, in her eyes, was a despicable opportunist and mountebank who had betrayed the once-lauded "forgotten man" (Harris 142); the American public morally and intellectually comatose: "Such a weak, soft middleclass has one foot in the grave and one on a banana-eel. They can't fight anything, so the first gangster who comes along will have them all on their knees" (Harris 308). But when Stead chose to tackle these issues publically, it was through the fictional microcosm of the Pollit family and their tumultuous, ill-fated actions. Behind and through this familial and autobiographical screen, she could revisit the crucial problem of America's flagging prospects, as well as evoke a "homespun brand of American socialism [that] threatened to render supererogatory the traditional parties of the Left, at a time when to criticize Roosevelt's policies was tantamount to attacking Browder" (Ackland "Socialists for a new socialism" 389–90)—yet hope to escape hostile repercussions. It is little wonder, then, that Stead confessed that writing the novel "had given her 'the gitters'" (Rowley 259), though not solely because of her unflattering depiction there of recognizable traits of her father.[6]

Far smaller in scale, but no less elaborate, is her creative assimilation and refocusing of supposed autobiographical matter in "The Old School." Pace Rowley, the sketch is not merely concerned with scapegoating, but with socialization and how a dominant system inculcates its values and harsh judgments. The identification of Stead with the narrator, and the assumption that she reproduces actual events from her girlhood, have been too readily made.[7] There is no evidence that these particular incidents occurred at a school in Lydham Hill, while the narrator, in contradistinction to Stead, is cast as largely unknowing and undecided: the vividness of these memories is attributed to him or her "never [being] able to make up my mind about" these events, so that "the burning question of good and bad" remains (1985 26). Stead felt no such uncertainty. Hypothetically her primary hesitation concerned how best to expose the dominant ideology and savage, discriminatory practices of her former host country (America) and of her homeland and final place of residence (Australia). The bulk of the pupils dressed in pink, blue and white, avidly internalise norms and ostracise offenders.

---

[6] On the debt of her fictional character, Sam Pollit, to her actual father, see her own accounts (Stead 1992 88–91, 93–94) and Rowley 1990.
[7] Stead's other major biographer, Chris Williams, provides a more lengthy account of this piece (33–35), emphasises its concern with "social morality" (33), and describes its narrator as an "autobiographical character" (35).

"Neighbours and busybodies (informants should I say)" (1985 22) abound; accusing eyes are likened to "little sparrows pecking at the odd-feathered one" (1985 23); and even a headmaster is punished "for his [socialist] opinions" (1985 18). Cruelty, administered by the conformist majority and ideologically aligned institutions, exacts submission, and "the legendary terrors of the system make even its enforcers quake" (Ackland 2010 138).[8] Pillorying the injustices inflicted by the supposedly liberal West (which Stead had amply tasted during decades of harsh post-war exile) required, in fact, a meticulously calculated, zigzagging course across the potentially fateful Rubicon, lest her bitter critique unleash official displeasure and diverse sanctions.

For a Marxist author, writing a traditional Christian spiritual autobiography was hardly an option, but as the example of Christina Stead demonstrates, it and the Judeo-Christian heritage could provide a considerable sampler of highly relevant imagery, archetypes and paradigms. Sacral motifs and practices were often transferable to strictly materialistic contexts. Communism, after all, was a rival world-faith, with its own dogmas, heresies, credo of infallibility and rites of passage, overseen by a disciplined, highly centralized, authoritarian order. It too could accommodate visions, prophecies and homilies. Moreover, according to Moscow's official line, to quote Stead's first novel: "There are no women ... There are only dependent and exploited classes, of which women make one. The peculiarities are imposed on them to keep them in order" (205). Stead knew otherwise. She may have paid lip-service to this reading of social history, but her early portrait of Catherine Baguenault provides a stark illustration of the potentially dire fate that awaited a left-wing, female radical. To unchain and completely liberate Eve was a utopian aspiration. Even to be a "female Caesar" was realizable only with guile and authorial cunning. In this venture the matter and accessories of autobiography provided an indispensable shield and mask. Potentially, in her hands they carried a dual burden of commentary on personal as well as broader, historical events. Thus an autobiographical veneer proved to be both enabling and protecting, as it became what story has been to the young Christina: "a grand cloak covering me, and allowing me to see unseen; 'the cloak of darkness'" (1985 5). Her *ultra ego* Catherine, left defenceless by her own uncalculating openness and naïve ardour, is depicted as "wavering in every breeze of masculine talent" (59)

---

[8] For a more detailed reading of these political analogies than is possible here see Ackland 2010, 136–140.

and eventually crushed. Stead used what incontrovertibly belonged to her, her own life-story recast, to achieve the liberating vistas promised by the original "ocean of story," and in the process displayed an intellectual freedom and boldness rarely enjoyed even by storied male Caesars. To borrow her father David's words, she "Dare[d] to be a Daniel, Dare[d] to stand alone, Dare[d] to have a purpose true and Dare[d, after a fashion] to make it known" (1985 486). To the end Stead placed her faith in individual agency, not Deity or Providence, and in the opportunities which fiction afforded to stand for many long years before the impartial, and hopefully insightful, bar of history.

Works Cited

Ackland, Michael. "'What a History is that? What an Enigma?': Imagination, Destiny and Socialist Imperatives in Christina Stead's *Seven Poor Men of Sydney*." *Southerly* 68 (2008): 189–212. Print.

—. "Christina Stead and the Politics of Covert Statement." *Mosaic* 43 (2010): 127–142. Print.

—. "'Hedging on Destiny': History and its Marxist Dimension in Christina Stead's Early Fiction." *Ariel* 41 (2011): 91–109. Print.

—. "'Socialists for a New Socialism?': Christina Stead's Critique of 1930s America in *The Man Who Loved Children*." *ELH* 78 (2011): 387–408. Print.

Brydon, Diana. *Christina Stead*. London: Macmillan, 1987. Print.

Gribble, Jennifer. *Christina Stead*. Melbourne: Oxford UP, 1994. Print.

Lidoff, Joan. *Christina Stead*. New York: Ungar, 1982. Print.

Stead, Christina. "Savage Aristocrat." Review of Vladimir Pozner, *Bloody Baron*. *New Masses*, 27 September 1938, 25–26. Print.

—. *Ocean of Story*. Ed. Ron Geering. New York: Viking, 1985. Print.

—. *I'm Dying Laughing*. Ed. Ron Geering. New York: Holt, 1986. Print.

—. *Seven Poor Men of Sydney*. 1934. Sydney: Angus & Roberston, 1987. Print.

—. *A Web of Friendship: Selected Letters (1928–1973)*. Ed. Ron Geering. Sydney: Angus & Robertson, 1992. Print.

Harris, Margaret. Ed. *Dearest Munx: The Letters of Christina Stead and William J. Blake*. Melbourne: Miegunyah, 2005. Print.

Ottanelli, Fraser M. *The Communist Party in the United States: From the Depression to World War Two*. New Brunswick: Rutgers UP, 1991.

Rowley, Hazel. "How Real is Sam Pollit? 'Dramatic Truth' and 'Procès-verbal' in *The Man Who Loved Children*'. *Contemporary Literature* 31 (1990): 499–511. Print.

—. *Christina Stead: A Biography*. Melbourne: Heinemann, 1993. Print.

Sheridan, Susan. *Christina Stead*. London: Harvester/Wheatsheaf, 1988. Print.

Wetherell, Rodney. "Interview with Christina Stead." *Australian Literary Studies* 9 (1980): 431–48. Print.

Whitehead, Ann. "Christina Stead: An Interview." *Australian Literary Studies* 6 (1974): 230–48. Print.

Williams, Chris. *Christina Stead: A Life of Letters*. London: Virago, 1989. Print.

Retouching the Past:
Vladimir Nabokov's *Speak, Memory*
as Fictive Autobiography

Mikołaj Wiśniewski

Autobiography and the problem of memory lie at the very heart of Vladimir Nabokov's work. When reading his novels, whether we are aware of it or not, we actually witness the author constantly rewriting himself, fashioning his characters out of certain aspects of himself, out of various incidents, details and crises of his own life. What is more, Nabokov sometimes seems to be envisioning alternative versions of his personal past, as for instance in *The Defense* or *Pnin*. The main protagonist of *Mary*, Nabokov's first novel, is an alter-ego of the young Russian aristocrat forced to leave behind his country and his first love in the wake of the Bolshevik revolution. In *The Real Life of Sebastian Knight*, the narrator's bizarre quest in search of his late half-brother's mistress can no doubt be seen as a dramatization both of Nabokov's decision to become an English writer, as well as of his own uneasy relationship with his brother Sergey. Finally, Nabokov's last published novel, *Look at the Harlequins!*, is a wonderfully distorted picture of the author's entire literary career, and at the same time a touching tribute to his wife, Vera. Nabokov also "distributed," as he himself puts it, many experiences and details remembered from his childhood to characters who, like Humbert in *Lolita*, cannot and should not be interpreted in a straightforwardly biographical way (although there is something tantalizing about the fact that the childish love-affair which determined Humbert's pathological inclinations seems to have been modelled after Nabokov's own early infatuations described in chapters seven and ten of *Speak, Memory*).

Nabokov's autobiography is also chronologically at the center of his work: for the most part, it was written in the late 1940s, soon after Nabokov had written his first two English novels. It was published in 1951 as

Conclusive Evidence and later renamed *Speak, Memory*. Together with his last Russian novel, *The Gift*, it might be seen as forming the bright center of Nabokov's oeuvre (the model of "good memory," redemptive and liberating) around which skulk shadowy figures of mnemonic deviants, as one might call them, trapped by the past, unable to distinguish reality from the phantasms of their own paranoid minds. I derive the opposition between "good" and "bad memory" from one of Nabokov's "strong opinions" in which he states that: "The bad memoirist re-touches his past, and the result is a blue-tinted or pink-shaded photograph taken by a stranger to console sentimental bereavement. The good memoirist (…) does his best to preserve the utmost truth of the detail" (*Strong Opinions* 158). In *Speak, Memory* this opposition is visualized in terms of two figures: the circle (the vicious circle of repetition) and the spiral, which represents development and elevation to ever higher planes of consciousness. All such efforts on Nabokov's part to strictly separate "good memory" from "bad" strike me as intentionally misleading and I believe that in the long run they are untenable. There is something suspicious in Nabokov's categorical tone, especially in view of the fact that in his novels, time and again, the line separating memory from consoling fiction, or outright delusion, artistic genius from madness, often turns out to be a very thin one. In fact, one might argue, it is precisely this ambiguity that makes Nabokovian characters so intriguing. I would therefore like to take a closer look at a few passages from *Speak, Memory*—which we may assume Nabokov considered the work of a "good memoirist"—to show that they bare traces of re-touching. Indeed, what makes *Speak, Memory* more than a sample of sentimental reminiscing is the irony with which Nabokov treats his own memories, casting a shadow of doubt on their accuracy and objectivity, their genuineness and veracity.

First, however, let us briefly say what Nabokov has in mind when he speaks of "good memoirists" and—by implication—of "good memory." Its *sine qua non* is sensitivity to "detail," because it allows the memoirist to discern a subtle pattern in past events, a "thematic design" thanks to which one's life turns out to be "Not flimsy nonsense, but a web of sense," to quote a line from John Shade's poem "Pale Fire" (*Pale* 63). Nabokov is quite explicit about this—at the beginning of *Speak, Memory* he states: "The following of such thematic designs through one's life should be, I think, the true purpose of autobiography" (12). On a higher level, this method is actually supposed to abolish time, it should culminate in an "enjoyment of timelessness" which allows us to glimpse some transcendent realm and reassures us that our fate is presided over by "tender ghosts" (101). These are the very terms which Nabokov uses at the end of chapter six of his autobiography where he describes how "around 1910" he hunted butterflies in "the marshland beyond the [river] Oredezh" (101). We find other, equally ecstatic and time-defying descriptions in *Speak, Memory*, among which one of the most striking is the recollection of Nabokov's schoolroom in the countryside estate of Vyra:

> I see again my schoolroom in Vyra, the blue roses of the wallpaper, the open window. Its reflection fills the oval mirror above the leathern couch where my uncle sits, gloating over a tattered book. A sense of security, of well-being, of summer warmth pervades my memory. That robust reality makes a ghost of the present. The mirror brims with brightness; a bumblebee has entered the room and bumps against the ceiling. Everything is as it should be, nothing will ever change, nobody will ever die. (52)

Let us now turn to the dark side of memory. As we have seen, Nabokov describes it in terms of photographical retouching, or, we could also say, of clichéd effects. Elsewhere, he compares the workings of "bad" or "corrupt memory" to cinematographic techniques and montage. In general, references to cinema throughout Nabokov's fiction are ominous: they are associated with self-destructive delusions which in many cases lead to murder. The obvious example is *Laughter in the Dark*, although cinematographic themes are consistently employed by Nabokov from *Mary* to *Lolita* and *Ada, or Ardor*. It is in the latter that personal memory is discussed by one of the characters in reference to cinematographic techniques:

> Someday (...) one's past must be put in order. Retouched, retaken. Certain "wipes" and "inserts" will have to be made in the picture; certain telltale abrasions in the emulsion will have to be corrected; "dissolves" in the sequence discreetly combined with the trimming out of unwanted, embarrassing "footage," and definite guarantees obtained; yes, someday—before death with its clapstick closes the scene. (253–54)

These are the words of Marina, an actress at whom the main protagonist of the novel, Van Veen, pokes fun, calling her a "dummy" with a "screen-corrupted mind" (253). However, what concerns me here is the fact that in *Speak, Memory* Nabokov seems unable to do without the strategies of montage described by Marina and that the tableaux which he paints of his childhood idyll in pre-revolutionary Russia are indeed quite heavily "tinted." In fact, one of the central images of his autobiography is that of a veranda, or "pavilion," with diamond-shaped "colored panes"—when peering through them, Nabokov says, the surrounding world acquired a "magic" and "strangely still and aloof" aspect (75). The memoirist here is quite aware that he is projecting, in his own words, "an exquisite simulacrum" (22) and indulging in a "stereoscopic dreamland" (70). But perhaps the most surprising thing, in view of Nabokov's denunciation of "screen-corrupted" memory, is the fact that *Speak, Memory* focuses so much on photographs, family albums, painting lessons, illustrations, slides, old newsreels, and pictures hanging on the walls of the various drawing rooms or classrooms mentioned in the book. And finally, the workings of memory are often described in terms which bring to mind cinematographic jargon: Nabokov speaks of "scenes" and often presents them in "frames" (usually frames of windows or mirrors) within which things and people are immobilized, as if captured in "stills." Nabokov's reminiscences progress in "a succession of fade-ins and fade outs" (129) and, most tellingly, the mention of "memory's luminous disc" and of its "magic-lantern projections" (114) suggests that the mechanism of memory is not unlike that of a movie projector. Incidentally, when Nabokov says that certain figures of the past are "projected, as it were, upon the inside of the eyelid" (17), this echoes Humbert Humbert's distinction between "two kinds of visual memory":

> one when you skillfully recreate an image in the laboratory of your mind, with your eyes open (…) the other when you instantly evoke, with shut eyes on the dark innerside of your eyelids, the objective, absolutely optical replica of a beloved face (…) (and this is how I see Lolita). (11)

Commenting on this passage in her book *Nabokov at the Movies* (2003), Barbara Wylie says that the "process of remembering is a process of visualization, activated and realized either as film or a photograph" (131). To a great extent something similar occurs in Nabokov's autobiography: access to the past is mediated—among other things[1]—by images construed along the lines of the aesthetics of photography and cinema.

---

[1] Another interesting theme throughout *Speak, Memory* is that of literature as a lens through which the past is perceived, or even—as a matrix which shapes recollection of past experience. This is especially evident in chapter twelve of the autobiography in which Nabokov describes his "first love," Tamara (whose real name was Lyussya Shulgin), and suggests that much of what he remembers might have been "induced" by

Let us take a closer look at the passage quoted earlier in which Nabokov describes his schoolroom in Vyra. With its arrangement of bright and dark geometrical figures (the oval mirror, the window frame, the dark bulk of the "leathern couch") it presents itself much like a photographic composition, and at that a "blue-tinted" one (due to the color of the wallpaper design), smacking of sentimentality which Nabokov denounced in his "strong opinion" about "bad memoirists." There is a pervading sense of stillness and immobility in the scene, with its lonely figure seated on the couch and immersed in reveries. The movement of the bumblebee does little to dispel this effect: it not only enhances the atmosphere of summer laziness, but might be interpreted in terms of entrapment and anxious repetition. This brings us to the astonishing final declaration of the passage in which time, change and death are refuted. Nabokov's tone here resembles that of Van Veen's who, when looking through Ada's eighty-year-old diary, states with nervous enthusiasm that "nothing, nothing, nothing has changed," (*Ada or Ardor* 49) and in an equally passionate but also palpably hysterical way denounces death: "I despise, I denounce death, dead bodies are burlesque, I refuse to stare at a stone under which a roly-poly old Pole is rotting, let him feed his maggots in peace, the entomologies of death leave me cold, I detest, I despise..." (297). Therefore, rather than "preserving the utmost truth of the detail," Nabokov seems to be "enchanting" the past in order to "console (...) bereavement" (*Strong* 158). The memory of trauma (in this case: uncle Ruka's untimely death of heart failure, mentioned earlier in the same chapter) is suppressed and substituted with "an exquisite simulacrum" (*Speak* 22).

This "simulacrum" of the past seems also to be constructed by employing the various techniques of montage described by Marina. I propose to look at one more episode from *Speak, Memory* which is crucial because Nabokov uses it to explain "the true purpose of autobiography," namely—"following thematic designs through one's life" (*Speak* 12). In section three of chapter one Nabokov talks about some of his first reminiscences of war: first of the Russo-Japanese war of 1904 and then of the Russian Civil War. The figure

---

his youthful readings in Russian poetry (particularly Pushkin and Alexander Blok's love lyrics). In fact, Nabokov states that the image of Tamara had been created by his literary infatuations even before he met the real girl: "I had daydreamed so ardently of meeting her, of creating her" (175). Similarly, the major theme of his adolescent poetry was „the loss of a beloved mistress—Delia, Tamara or Lenore—whom I had never lost, never loved, never met but was all set to meet, love, lose" (171). Another important literary matrix for Nabokov's recollections of childhood, acknowledged by the author in the "Appendix" to *Speak, Memory*, is Tolstoy's *Childhood*.

connecting both events is that of General Aleksey Kuropatkin, a friend of the Nabokov family. In 1904, when visiting the Nabokovs in Petersburg, Kuropatkin showed the five-year-old Volodya a trick using a box of matches. Fifteen years later, after the October Revolution, in Bolshevik-controlled Petersburg, Kuropatkin, fearing arrest, assumed the disguise of "a gray-bearded peasant in [a] sheepskin coat" (12). Chancing to meet Nabokov's father in the street, he asked him for a match to light a cigarette, and was instantly recognized by his old friend. With this incident Nabokov abruptly ends the story of the General and the matches by saying: "I hope old Kuropatkin, in his rustic disguise, managed to evade Soviet imprisonment, but that is not the point. What pleases me is the evolution of the match theme" (12), and then goes on to explicate his understanding of "the true purpose of autobiography" (12). It must be observed, however, that the similarity between the two incidents, which allows Nabokov to speak of a "match theme," is quite dubious or at least highly subjective. In fact, one might argue that the relationship between the scenes involving matches is established by means of a technique akin to that which in cinematography is called a "dissolve" (mentioned, among others, by Marina when she speaks about the necessity to put the past in order). Thus, one might get the impression that what we are dealing with here is not the discovery of any actual "thematic design," but the imposition of a very tentative order upon a past fraught with loss, confusion and disappointment. The trauma of war is somehow alleviated: the autobiographer's focus shifts away from disquieting events to magic tricks and—later in the same passage—to toy trains and armies, rather than the real ones.

But there seems to be something more at stake here. When Nabokov says that he hopes the General evaded imprisonment, he suggests that Kuropatkin's fate after the Revolution is unknown to him. This is surprising because Nabokov kept very good track of the post-war lives of his far less well-known acquaintances: servants, tutors, painting teachers, his late father's numerous friends. The facts concerning Kuropatkin are the following: he did indeed survive the civil war, but not in circumstances Nabokov would have found honorable. Although his son was executed during the "red terror" in 1919, the General endorsed the Bolshevik regime. He refused to join the White Army and persuaded the peasants in his estate not to support the "greens," to lay down their weapons and to enlist in the Red Army. Thanks to this the Bolsheviks spared him and he was allowed to lead a quiet life of a schoolteacher. It is, of course, impossible to ascertain whether Nabokov knew any of this, but it is likely (in view of other evasions in *Speak, Memory*, connected for example with Sergey Nabokov's homosexuality) that the autobiographer, in Marina's words again, is "trimming out unwanted [or] embarrassing 'footage'" (*Ada* 254).

Let me stress that I am not accusing Nabokov of prevarication here; if indeed he is turning away from certain unpalatable truths, this might as well be seen as simple tact on the part of the memoirist. He is bent on preserving a positive image of his father's old friend. But this also goes to show that for Nabokov memory cannot do without the distorting medium of art. Autobiography, if it is to be an expression of life and not a sterile accumulation of facts, needs to resort to such comforting, life-protecting tactics. It needs to put the past in order by retouching it, or, as Ada puts it, by adding to it a little "novelistic touch," by providing "a frame, (...) a form, something supporting and guarding life" (521). What makes *Speak, Memory* an unusual autobiography, and at the same time a great artistic achievement, is that it is both a personal narrative and a critique of the very process of representing the past. It cannot escape the attentive reader that the ambiguities of Nabokov's text (the tension between joyous affirmation and underlying anxiety, the clash between sentimentality and irony, or the uncertainty as to whether we are dealing with fact or fiction) are all carefully orchestrated by the author. As any Nabokov devotee knows, and as Nabokov himself admitted, "[d]eceit, to the point of diabolism" is one of his notions of literary strategy (Nabokov, *Speak* 220). I think therefore that the "strong opinion" about "good" and "bad memoirists," quoted at the beginning, should be treated with circumspection, or may even be seen as a "red herring," especially in the context of *Speak, Memory*, since what makes this work so engrossing is precisely the blurring of the distinctions Nabokov insists on.

How then should *Speak, Memory* be described as an autobiography? In a pseudo-review of his own book, Nabokov said that it was neither "true, more or less true, [nor] deliberately fictitious" (237). Perhaps the word "fictive" (as opposed to "fictitious" which suggests that something has simply been "made up") might better describe the way Nabokov combines recollection, imaginative creation and artistic manipulation. The best description of *Speak, Memory*, however, comes from Fyodor, the main protagonist of *The Gift*, who in planning an autobiographical work on a grand scale says that his intention is to "shuffle, twist, mix, rechew and rebelch everything, add such spices of my own and impregnate things so much with myself that nothing [will remain] of the autobiography but dust—the kind of dust, of course, which makes the most orange of skies" (362).

Works Cited

Nabokov, Vladimir. *Pale Fire*. New York: Vintage, 1989. Print.

—. *Ada or Ardor: A Family Chronicle*. New York: Vintage, 1990. Print.

—. *The Annotated Lolita*. London: Penguin, 2000. Print.

—. *Speak, Memory*. London: Penguin, 2000. Print.

—. *The Gift*. London: Penguin, 2001. Print.

—. *Strong Opinions*. London: Penguin, 2011. Print.

Wylie, Barbara. *Nabokov at the Movies*. Jefferson: McFarland, 2003. Print.

"Life Has Got Awfully Dramatic All of a Sudden, Hasn't It? Just Like a Fiction": The Art of Writing Life in Donna Tartt's novels

Pamela J. Rader

In her novels *The Secret History* (1992) and Pulitzer Prize winner *The Goldfinch* (2013), US writer Donna Tartt creates two works of fiction in the confessional vein.[1] Her narrators, respectively Richard Papen and Theo Decker, tell their life stories through a painterly lens and offer an homage to art: much of what they yearn to depict as real and truthful must be created and re-presented through their artistic sensibilities. The narrating protagonists use the tropes of beauty and immortality from classical literature and painting to color their "confessions;" both narratives employ innovations in ekphrasis, reminiscent of Homeric poetry and more modern poetry inspired by paintings. Unburdening themselves, they create narratives under the guise of truth, but the language and imagery of their narrations underscore a desire to create art (narrative) and to align oneself with beauty and its immortality. In creating a confession and a portrait of self, the narrators disclose acts of deceiving others and themselves. Tartt's novels are monologues narrated by the narrators, for themselves. Secret deeds, these monologues act as the raconteurs' artistic legacies, revealing what is both absent and present: a self-portrait. Tartt's characters' ekphrastic confessions testify to the power of art and beauty to sustain life, but also their power to sustain illusions about the paradoxical construction and loss of self through representational narratives.

Here, for the purpose of this paper, my use of the ekphrastic confession is not concerned with verifying or contesting Tartt's narrating protagonists'

---

[1] Unlike the first and third novels, Tartt's second novel, *The Little Friend* (2002), is narrated in the third person through the lens of several of the characters. I will parenthetically abbreviate *The Secret History as Secret* and *The Goldfinch* as *Goldfinch*.

confessions as true or false—because, as fiction, it *is* artifice—but these fictional confessions relate to the narrators' "underlying motive," in J.M. Coetzee's words, "to tell an essential truth about the self" (194). Francis Hart contends that "[t]ruth is a definitive but elusive autobiographical intention" (222). The truth they tell, in revealing their crimes and their questionable characters, may not be the truth they set out to outline in plot, but it is a truth about their own illusions whose end result is an ekphrastic self-portrait. Elke D'Hoker reminds us that, in a literary confession, the narrator "invite[s] the reader behind the façade to glimpse the real person crouching there" (32); readers are summoned to see what the fictional "public" does not or is not privileged to see.

While the confession reminds us of its performative religious origins with its motivation in guilt or shame, its literary and secular counterparts in the European and US traditions do not require an external authority to absolve the confessor. On the heels of Charlotte Brönte's eponymous heroine, Dostoyevsky's Underground Man, and Camus's Clamence, the literary confession is an established ruse in first-person fiction to reveal a truth, or truths, about the narrating self. As Derek Attridge contends, it is in the process of telling that the truth of self emerges, "if it emerges at all" (109). In the context of reading Tartt's novels as artifacts, their confessor-narrators appear at first to be motivated by guilt or shame.[2] However, upon closer examination of the narrative process, these two narrators are motivated by the ideals of love and beauty as well as the ache of loss and loneliness. For instance, Richard's and Theo's stories reveal the unrequited love of young women, Camilla and Pippa respectively, and underscore these narrators' orphan status; Richard feels emotionally abandoned by his working class parents, while Theo loses both parents prematurely. Encased in the larger narrative are the narrators' secrets (and lies), which include their crimes. To his unknown auditor, Richard discloses his role in conspiring to murder Bunny Corcoran, which "is the only story [he] will ever be able to tell" (*Secret* 2). Theo admits his theft and loss of the eponymous painting to the reader whom he imagines will and will not be Pippa: "I've written all this, oddly, with the idea that Pippa will see it someday—which of course she won't. No one will for obvious reasons" (*Goldfinch* 763). In

---

[2] I use confessor here in the more modern, secular sense as the one who confesses. Dennis Foster, in his seminal work *Confession and Complicity* in Narrative, makes a case for the confessional tradition where the narrating characters are "consumed with guilt and driven to talk about it" (18).

the narrators' ekphrastic prose, truths emerge to rupture the silence that comes with committing a crime and losing parents, friends, and love.

As their stories unfold, the confessional label is called in to question: are their stories confessions, or is the confession a ruse to paint a self-portrait through their medium of words and art? Clearly, a secular, literary confession is a contrivance—something between "reality" and fiction, truth and lies—where the confessor's act of telling and its resulting artifact are more important than what is told and whether he has an auditor. Tartt's two novels lend themselves to Derek Attridge's understanding of the confession as "autobiographies where one is led to feel that the truth has been hidden—for good reason—until the moment of articulation in language" (109). I would extend Attridge's definition to include a *visual* language and attainment of the picturesque for the fictional self-portrait. Both of Tartt's twenty-something male narrators are drawn to literature and art and to people who love the timeless, universal beauty of these artifacts, which are integral to their narrative self-portraits. I argue that Tartt's two novels *pose* as fictive literary confessions whose end results are ekphrastic self-portraits instead of confessions.[3] It is Theo and Richard's love for others and beauty in art and ideas that motivate them to tell their stories if only to themselves. They narrate for themselves to create something of beauty, namely a literary narrative, out of that solitary act of writing themselves onto the page. Theo and Richard create a new kind of literary self-portrait that celebrates art in their structural allusions to picaresque and tragic plotlines, characterization, and visual imagery borrowed from the masters of painting and the printed word. As a meta-commentary on the evolving, "tell-all" memoir, autobiography, and reality television genres, their narratives embrace artifice and illusion to make life more beautiful than reality's ugliness.

Tartt's subterfuge of the first-person confession appeals to human curiosity and interest in secrets, specifically a betrayal of those secrets.[4] The novels work with a ruse of complicity, or what Theo's fatherly friend Hobie calls the "secret whisper from an alley way. *Psst, you. Hey kid. Yes you*" that draws one to a particular work of art (*Goldfinch* 758). What appeals to one reader or onlooker, may not appeal to another; our attraction to a beautiful

---

[3] While James Wood of *The New Yorker* acknowledges the novel's passages centered on Fabritius's painting as the "eventless calm of ekphrasis," ekphrasis is at the very heart of the narrator's tale.

[4] In her 1992 *BOMB* interview with fellow Bennington College alumnus, Jill Eisenstadt, Tart comments on the act of narrating as a betrayal: "It's the narrator's business to betray, whether he's aware of it or if he wants it to be or not. That's his function in any novel."

object is not always rational. Just as the eponymous seventeenth century painting "speaks" to Theo and Greek drama appeals to Richard, readers are pulled in to discover what D'Hoker calls the "real person crouching" behind the masks. These young male narrators invite their readers to see their "true" selves behind their performed personas. In the prologue, Richard opens his narrative by admitting his collusion in the premeditated murder of a fellow student Edmund "Bunny" Corcoran. Like the audience of the Hellenic tragedians who knew the stories of Medea and Oedipus and their tragic outcomes, we are interested in, nay drawn to, the telling of these stories to discover *how* they unfold.

Richard seduces his readers with the implication that we are privileged to learn his secret, or even the "truth." Secrets hint at deception and lies whose motivations may be less clear in hindsight; when our secrets, or concealed narratives, are critical to our sense of self, it implies that the public self we present to the world is a fiction. Our self-image can be read as a more pleasing artifice than the horror and ordinariness we prefer to conceal. We learn in the first pages of the novel that *this story* is only one Richard will tell. But what he reveals is one story comprised of a chain of established fictions he creates about his life prior to the Elysian setting of Hampden College in rural Vermont. An only child raised in "a small silicon village" in northern California, Richard describes his childhood as "drab" and a period (7) where he recalls "little of interest, less of beauty" (*Secret* 8). His memory of his childhood has been replaced by his silences and occasional narrative creations for his Hampden peers. For instance, he testifies to a penchant for narrative and embellishments, "On leaving home I was able to *fabricate a new and far more satisfying history*, full of striking, simplistic environmental influences; a colorful past, easily accessible to strangers" (emphasis mine, *Secret* 7). This construction of a new-and-improved self points to the loss of its ordinary predecessor. Akin to literature's Jay Gatsby, Richard invents his past as he migrates east (as Gatsby does) to impress strangers who were then his fellow students and who are now his readers. In fabricating a sunnier, more picturesque, and trendier past, he re-invents himself in the narrating present; however, he retains and includes his falsified past as evidence of a perceived self-knowledge and of his pursuit of beauty. The greater truth revealed is Richard's continued desire to embellish and beautify his memories of his brief time at Hampden. His autobiography expresses a human desire to give his first year at Hampden meaning through revisiting and re-*presenting* it to the world by offering bucolic descriptions of the campus and its beloved personages to mask the horror and truth of murder.

Theo opens his narrative with the intimate disclosure that, while he is feverish, he "dreamed about [his] mother for the first time in years" (*Goldfinch* 5). Restless and cagey in an Amsterdam hotel room at Christmastime, his readers learn that he scans the international paper for "news of his predicament;" although his name is not in the papers, the story he is part of "was all over the Dutch papers" (6). Theo conveys here that he is part of a larger, external narrative outside his hotel room and a story that includes murder. However, these details are in Dutch and untranslated. Readers with a comprehension of Dutch language quickly understand that Theo links himself to an "Unsolved Murder" whose killer, corpse, and/or motives are "unknown" (6). Artfully created, Theo's *in medias res* narrative defines him as a motherless son who employs a conspiratorial tone without giving everything away. His "predicament" remains unknown, but his tactics of tone and plot tempt the reader to learn more.

Whether one writes fiction, autobiography, or a novel posing as a character's autobiography, one understand that the first person narrator selects these events and interprets them in the process of telling. The first person narrator not only selects which events he will tell, but the light in which he reveals himself. *The Secret History*'s narrator Richard calls attention to his lies and secrets and to those of the Classics clique that admits him. Lies, we learn, are a strategy for muting the burden of what terrifies us, such as death, truth, and the mundane. For instance, he hubristically declares, "If there's one thing I'm good at, it's lying on my feet. It's sort of a gift I have" (23). His avowal sheds light on his past and present utterances as fictions. Moreover, in a narrative where tense and mood are critical for its characters who execute English to Greek translations, Richard deliberately uses the present tense; he still claims this talent. Often recognized as the fatal flaw, hubris not only prevents one from seeing things as they are, but, in Richard's case, prevents him from representing things or people as they are. Here, I am not faulting him for this trait or for his unreliability as a narrator, but rather I wish to underscore the act of representation.[5] Comprised of a combination of lies and truth, representational art is never and can never be the thing it depicts; it is always artifice. While narrative and visual arts do employ conventions of verisimilitude and imitate life, they also

---

[5] Magritte's saucy image of a pipe verbally reminds its viewers, "Ceci n'est pas ue pipe" that the representation of the pipe is not the pipe itself.

reveal sleight of hand. Richard, therefore, in fashioning a new version of his Californian childhood and in retelling his pivotal year at Hampden, understands lies as representational and as the illusion he wishes to fabricate for and project to others. His lies, or, in other words, his fictions stand in for who he is; his fiction represents Richard Papen's idea of himself, blurring who he is and who he wants to be.

Theo Decker of *The Goldfinch* makes it clear to his audience that, had his mother lived, "things would have turned out better," which might be a way of saying his life would have turned out better (*Goldfinch* 7). That is to say he would have turned out better. He may not have walked out of the museum explosion with Carel Fabritius's seventeenth century painting, spent his adolescence self-medicating with drugs and alcohol, or met fellow picaroon, Boris. Mirroring his quest of self-knowledge, Theo reflects on Fabritius's painting and wonders what it reveals about the artist: "And if what they say is true—if every great painting is really a self-portrait—what, if anything, is Fabritius saying about himself?" (765). What do Theo's writings say, if anything, about himself? He claims his possession of the painting for his secret, which "raised [him] above the surface of life and enabled [him] to know who [he is]" (764). If Richard acknowledges and accepts his talent for lies as a truth about his character, Theo accepts that human beings cannot always choose who or what they love as a way to understand himself and what the painting means to him. Theo's narrative is a self-portrait of a young man who discloses that he *writes* to survive the trauma of the explosion that kills his mother and the ongoing suffering caused by her absence. His narrative self-portrait shows his capacity to love beautiful things, specifically the rescued painting and Hobie's restorations, and people: his mother, Pippa, Hobie, and Boris. The act of writing, as Theo's readers learn, is the very process by which he reveals his "self."

The reader learns the "truth" about Theo Decker's love for beautiful things: they connect him to and preserve the memory of his deceased mother. Recounting the day he lost his mother, Theo Decker relates the pair's Metropolitan Museum visit before a disciplinary appointment at school. Escaping the rain, they stop in to visit an exhibit of Dutch masters, where she shares her knowledge and reverence for the realism, beauty, and illusions of the Masters' still life paintings; the painter is "telling you that living things don't last—it's all temporary. Death in life. That's why they're called *natures mortes*. Maybe you don't see it at first with all the beauty and bloom, the little speck of rot. But if you look closer—there it is" (*Goldfinch* 24). Ironically, her implicit lesson before dying is life's defining trait:

ephemerality. Regardless of genre, art seeks to freeze, or immortalize, the beauty found in life even as it masks the decay, the harbinger of death. Although art captures both beauty and moments in time, it too can be lost or destroyed. "I guess anything we manage to save from history is a miracle," declares Theo's mother, moments before a bomb kills her and destroys art (28). In the age of reproductions and multiple editions, we are reminded that not just people, but things may perish. Advised by a dying art lover, Theo, in the post-explosion chaos, rescues the goldfinch painting from the rubble and looters; his adolescent quandary is not just how to get on with his life, but how and when to return the painting. The old man has passed on art's "*psst*" to Theo who cannot let the painting go. This object of beauty reminds us of the miracle of survival; it has survived the seventeenth century Delft explosion that killed its creator in 1654 and a second one centuries later. By rescuing the painting, Theo has joined his story with it and salvaged it for future generations. But the painting, like Theo, is a kind of picaroon in its own episodic story. The story of art lovers may account for the survival (and loss) of art and beauty.

Literature has ways of surviving history that art does not. As narratives are reformed and editions are reissued, new literature emerges, paying homage to the old. For instance, Richard beautifies his narrative with literary allusions to canonical Western literature, which underscores literature's immortality and its lasting influence. His references to the Classics and European tradition influence the confession of his "secret" in its Dantean dream-like quality. Unlike the Italian pilgrim, Richard does not acquire beatitude, but he dramatizes the events from this period in his life, and—like a good storyteller—creates suspense. Directly following his prologue, Richard poses a question: "Does such a thing as 'the fatal flaw,' that showy dark crack running down the middle of a life, exist outside literature? I used to think it didn't. Now I think it does. And I think that mine is this: a morbid longing for the picturesque at all costs" (*Secret* 5). Here, Richard performs a kind of self-knowledge: he longs for beauty to a fault. And he "now" believes that which exists in literature also exists outside of it: in life. The question he poses and answers illuminates how he has been formed by his study of literature under his professor Julian Morrow's tutelage. Instead of building on a Greek aphorism, he appropriates one of his professor's observations at the time of Bunny's disappearance, "Life has got awfully dramatic all of a sudden, hasn't it? Just like a fiction...." (*Secret* 350). Richard's narrative testifies to his desire to make life—his life—as interesting or dramatic as a novel. More importantly, he focuses on his brief time at Hampden, which points to his deliberate and profound omission of his life before and after Hampden. Life before and after are mundane and less like fiction—until he reinvents it. What he reveals to his audience is his epistemological perspective that life can be known through recognition of literary conventions such as hamartia, fate, and twin motifs of light and darkness. Aware of the power of literature on the imagination and the imagination's power to create literature, Richard uses literature as the lens for reading his life; he will strive to recreate beauty in his own narrative by retelling his story in a literary manner.

Literary but understated, Theo creates and appropriates literature differently from Richard. First, he adopts and internalizes *Fabelhaft*, a German word mentioned only twice throughout his narrative in association with the posh Mr. Barbour. While it translates as marvelous or fabulous, it does harken back to fables and myths; as a kind of fiction, it is at once unhistorical and legendary. His life after the explosion resembles that of a fable: an urban boy loses his beloved mother, steals a painting, and goes to live with his father and girlfriend in the desert, where he meets citizen of the world Boris. I read Theo's use of this word as a dismissive, yet ironic way of describing his own picaresque life. His life is the stuff of fiction to his readers, and he references the literature of Melville, Dostoyevsky, Dickens, and Thoreau, which documents life in ways that seem "unrealistic" to their readers. And it is Thoreau who introduces him to the larger-than-life "burnout boy" Boris in a high school honors English class (*Goldfinch* 235). Literature is a tool for Theo and Boris to understand the world and its people. Two thirteen year old boys make astute observations on the relevance of Thoreau to their lives in the subdivisions of Las Vegas, "'Now the desert is taking it back. And the banks.' [Boris] laughed. 'Fuck Thoreau, eh?' 'This whole town is like a Big Fuck You to Thoreau,'" concludes Theo (239). This first meeting leads to what will become a lifelong friendship between two boys whose alcoholic, mostly disinterested fathers leave them to their own devices, which include self-medicating and reading. The grown, entrepreneurial Boris claims a moral code to which he credits Myshkin of *The Idiot* and explains to Theo, "As long as I am acting out of love, I feel I am doing best I know how" (745). Boris's creed helps Theo articulate his love for Boris and for the painting. Literature and love—for others and art—anchors them in a world where adults have died and failed them. "Despite his faults, which were numerous and spectacular," Theo writes Boris into his narrative as a legendary figure of myths and fables who moves intrepidly and easily through the world (746).

While they are characters in *The Secret History*, Richard's fellow Classics students appear to him as elusive characters. Drawn to their physical presence, Richard finds these individuals attractive and mysterious (which he passes on to his readers), and he describes them in such a way that a reader might understand, even share, Richard's desire to belong to the group and align himself with their projected beauty and intellect. He compares these elite friends to figures in an allegory or dream that require interpretation. "In this swarm of cigarettes and dark sophistication they appeared here and there like figures from an allegory, or long-dead celebrants from some forgotten garden party" (*Secret* 16). The dream-like description echoes of a hero's encounter with shades in Hades; it also accentuates the universal-literary past as Richard's narrative inspiration, which he aligns with his own. His literary similes create vivid images akin to paintings and Homer's ekphrastic verse. Describing his library encounter with Professor Morrow's elite and aloof students, Richard recalls, and "it was as if the characters in a favorite painting, absorbed in their own concerns, had looked up out of the canvas and spoken to me" (*Secret* 19). Employing a painterly *trompe l'oeil* convention, Richard simulates the ambiguous boundary between painting and frame, between dream and reality, between the past as it happened and one's memory of it, and between art and life. From the position of hindsight, his visual analogies create a *mise-en-abîme* of illusions to represent life and history through a merging of the visual and verbal arts. However, only in hindsight, does he question their amorality and immorality, which foregrounds the narrative's larger revelation: Richard subtly interrogates his own moral code without drawing any definitive conclusions. His narrative superficially works with Aristotle's tragedian plot devices of recognition and reversal to show the power of fate, instead of choices, over our lives. More romantic than choice, fate maintains the illusion of external governing forces and does not require individual responsibility. As his life's story's narrating protagonist who leans on fate, he, unlike Theo, fails to contrive a literary epiphany for himself. His silent-reader confidants observe that the missing epiphany is a meta-realization: the narrator's audience witnesses his self-deception in his act of mimesis and ekphrasis. Dreams and memories, not truth, provide his narrative with its vivid descriptions.

The trope of the painting in Richard's narrative upholds his attraction to beauty and immortality and fails to accurately imitate the ugly and terrible. His beguiling narrative only briefly touches upon the two murders at the novel's core. In recreating classroom dialogue based upon a passage from

Klytemnestra's ekphrastic speech in the *Agamemnon* and the ideas in Aristotle's *Poetics*, Richard highlights the professor's conclusion that desire for the beautiful yields to an attraction to terror. Professor Morrow tells his class of six that "'[b]eauty is terror. Whatever we call beautiful, we quiver before it'" (*Secret* 38). Klytemnestra describes murdering her husband with such vividness that the language and imagery at once cloak and reveal the horror of her deed. The harsh truth of death and murder cause pain in life, but become things of beauty in Aristotelian terms. Understanding the nuances of still life paintings, Theo brings sensitivity to his interpretation of "...this staunch little portrait, [where] it's hard not to see the human in the finch. Dignified, vulnerable. One prisoner looking at another" (*Goldfinch* 766). Veiled by the bird's beauty and its technical rendering, the canvas reminds onlookers of their own mortality.

Humans create art to immortalize and further illusions of their perceived mortality. By joining our stories with art and literature human beings flirt with the idea of immortality. For writers like Richard and Theo, thoughtful allusions to canonical texts and visual arts align them with objects of beauty that continue to withstand the test of time; they stand on the shoulders of these giants of civilization, and, by honoring their predecessors, they take a chance on their own literary legacy. For Theo, the goldfinch painting is an object of beauty that sustains him through the traumatic event and throughout his life. While Theo believes he carries the canvas and his burdensome secret possession of it into the future, he is ensnared, like the feathered creature, until he returns the chained bird. Theo thinks of Fabritius's painting not only as an object of beauty but as his own. After the explosion, he reads about its disappearance in "the dense text [of the newspaper] for any further mention of my painting (already I'd begun to think of it as *mine*; the thought slid into my head as if I'd owned it all my life)" (*Goldfinch* 177). The story he tells himself as a traumatized, motherless survivor is that the painting is his. His younger self simultaneously knows and forgets that great art belongs to the museums, to the world, and "to the next generation of lovers, and the next" (771). Aware of his own sentimental illusions, Theo, through his deliberate act and diction, claims the painting and the bird of the painting as his; by saving it fourteen years earlier, he plays a minute yet critical role in its immortality. The cunning and sentimental Richard claims the group's secret murders for his own story, his only story. Seemingly less self-aware than Theo, Richard waxes nostalgic about his memories of Camilla's medieval beauty, Bunny's chumminess, Henry's valiant rescues, and his professor's affected interest and charisma. More interested in maintaining the illusions than dispelling them, he performs honesty, when he states, "But I am getting sentimental. Sometimes, when I think about these things, I do" (*Secret* 126). In affecting idealistic views of Henry and the others, Richard immortalizes their beauty, affluence, and charm in his narrative, which acts as a kind of eulogy for the clique and that turbulent year.

The eye of the narrating 'I' is and simultaneously is not the self, but the fiction it creates of the self. Moreover, literature might appear more exciting or "dramatic" than our lives to which Tartt's novels and first-person narrators attest. Spanning fourteen years, Theo's story resembles fiction more than the prosaic of life of one of his readers.[6] Pursuing a Ph.D. in literature, Richard Papen affirms his love for literature in his narrative's idealized characterizations, dream-like recollections, effective intrigue, and tidy epilogue, when he refashions a specific time in his life as a flawed quest for beauty. Inhabiting the nostalgic landscape of the campus's birch trees and the visual allusions to literature and film, he uses the conspiratorial, confidential first person monologue to hook his reader. However, he seeks to tell a compelling story while distancing himself from the terror lurking beneath its surface; Richard's extreme quest for and love of beauty supersedes any moral code. His quest also underscores his awareness of the irrational, which civilization suppresses through its privileging of art and art's order.[7] By contrast, Theo Decker, a survivor of trauma, wrestles with his possession of the painting, yet inhabits a limbo of inaction. Unlike Richard, Theo acknowledges and accepts his preference for living in that middle zone, where reality and illusion and good and bad are blurred. His self-acceptance comes through his profound understanding about the power of "his" painting. "Whatever teaches us to talk to ourselves is important: whatever teaches us to sing ourselves out of despair. But the painting has also taught me that we can speak to each other across time" (*Goldfinch* 771). Humans find ways of owning beauty in the literature and art they love; we buy

---

[6] The Dickensian debate will not be resolved here. The novel has stirred up the literary pot, and the allusions to Dickens abound. Theo's narrative—that is to say Tartt's novel—was first called Dickensian by *The New York Times* book reviewer Michiko Kakutani. *New Yorker's* James Wood observes that "Tartt's plot is unembarrassed by its loot of Dickensian accident." In a recent *Vanity Fair* piece, Evgenia Peretz recaps the literary debate around this novel, specifically Francine Prose's criticism, and concludes that we'll know in time whether Tartt's novel with pass its test: will it be read by future generations?

[7] In one of the only scholarly readings of *The Secret History*, Brian Arkins explores the novel's Greek themes, specifically what he calls "Dionysiac madness" and the loss of self (285).

reproductions of the art work, and we allude to them and their literary cousins in the narratives we create. Such is the power of art. Literature and art carry with them their secret histories and the secret, alternate histories of their lovers. Ever elusive, beauty is the ekphrasis for so many lives and how they are lived. Tartt's novels of Richard's and Theo's narratives successfully create a verbal *trompe l'oeil* of the ekphrastic self-portrait, blurring the boundary between life and the representational life writing.

Works Cited

Aristotle. *Poetics*. Trans. S. H. Butcher. *The Internet Classics Archive*. Web Atomic and Massachusetts Institute of Technology, 13 Sept. 2007. Web. 4 Nov. 2008. ⟨http://classics.mit.edu/⟩.

Arkins, Brian. "Greek Themes in Donna Tartt's *The Secret History*." *Classical and Modern Literature* 15.3(1995): 281–7. Print.

Attridge. Derek. "Deconstruction and Fiction." *Deconstructions: A User's Guide*. Ed. Nicholas Royle. Houndsmills, UK: Palgrave, 2000. 105–118. Print.

Coetzee, J. M. "Confession and Double Thoughts: Tolstoy, Rousseau, and Dostoyevsky." *Comparative Literature* 37.3 (1985): 193–232. Print

D'Hoker, Elke. "Confession and Atonement in Contemporary Fiction: J. M. Coetzee, John Banville, and Ian McEwan." *Critique* 48.1(2006): 31–43. Print.

Eisenstadt, Jill. "Donna Tartt." *BOMB* 41(1992): n.p. Web. 28 Jul. 2014.

Foster, Dennis. *Confession and Complicity in Narrative*. Cambridge: Cambridge UP, 1987. Print.

Hart, Francis R. "Notes for an Anatomy of Modern Autobiography." *New Directions in Literary History*. Ed. Ralph Cohen. London: Routledge & Keagan Paul, 1974. 221–247. Print.

Kakutani, Michiko. "A Painting as Talisman, as Enduring as Loved Ones are Not." *The New York Times*, 7 Oct. 2013. Web. 28 Jul. 2014.

Miller, Laura. "Donna Tartt: 'The Fun Thing about Writing a Book is that it Really is a Different Life.'" *Salon*, 22 Oct. 2013. Web. 28 Jul. 2014.

Peretz, Evgenia. "It's Tartt—But is it Art?" *Vanity Fair*, July 2014. Web. 21 July 2014.

Prose, Francine. "After Great Expectations." *The New York Review of Books*, 9 Jan. 2014. 61.1 Web. 27 Jul.2014.

Tartt, Donna. *The Goldfinch*. New York: Little, Brown and Co., 2013. Print.

—. *The Secret History*. 1992. New York: Vintage, 2004. Print.

Wood, James. "The New Curiosity Shop: Donna Tartt's *The Goldfinch*." *The New Yorker*, 21 Oct. 2013. Web. 29 Jul. 2014.^

Sexual Fingerprint:
Queer Diaries and Autobiography

Piotr Sobolczyk

Queer theory has attempted to challenge notions of sexual orientation based on gender-choice understood as genital difference. Returning to Magnus Hirschfeld's writings from the early twentieth century, some scholars have proposed that everyone has a different sexuality (Steakley 143). In 1918, James D. Steakley argued that there was "absolutely no such thing as two individuals identical in their sexuality" (145).

Later, Hirschfeld emphasized that to the average eye such subtle nuances and differences might not be fully detectable. Comparing sexual idiosyncrasy to fingerprints, he created the concept of "sexual fingerprints" that might seem very similar to an untrained eye but that could be seen in subtle examination. For contemporary queer theory this concept proved to be productive a metaphor because it questioned the idea of sexual orientation as a stable category and blurred the distinctions between the arbitrary object-choice as a primary sexual drive and various "perversions" such as fetishism, S/M, and other deeply personal practices or rituals as "secondary" (Sullivan 12).

However, for me and some other queer scholars (such as Donald E. Hall, who nonetheless understands it slightly differently than I do [20–30]), the consequence of this, the theoretical challenge, is not to acknowledge that people have different and original sexualities (and also personalities, and persona is also sexual), and to acknowledge furthermore that in folk situations some people reduce this variability to some landmark points of sexuality (i.e. homo-, hetero-, bi-, and bi-curious etc.) in order to simplify communication, but to get from this folk level to an expert level, where the fingerprints become visible and recognizable as wholly different between themselves, that is, the theoretical challenge is how to respond to this idiosyncrasy. My answer is: via idiography. This sexually inspired idiography is exactly what queer studies should do, and when it comes to literary studies that want to be queer, it involves reading as tracing those peculiarities and nuances that contribute to a generalized idiosyncratic sexual persona.

In such reading the scholar should not restrict himself to what is "sexual" in a common-sense meaning, i.e. expressed as an object-choice drive directly or via symbolisations or sublimations. These threads need to be identified, for sure, without being separated, while positioned in a weave of social, religious, political, personal threads, not to forget the style which ought not to be perceived as a transparent media.[1]

In this chapter, I want to turn to literature that calls itself autobiographic, i.e. the "secret diaries" of Polish queer writers which constitute a new genre in autobiographical writing, a novelty that comes not primarily from formal changes but rather from social changes and social histories of reading as well. In my firm belief they offer a splendid opportunity to read sexuality idiographically, that is, to trace the sexual fingerprint.

While homosexuality was not officially banned in Poland during the communist era, it was almost invisible. A significant number—not to say the majority—of Polish literary modernists and pre-postmodernists were queer, yet they functioned in their *glass closets,* which means that the public knew from gossip that they had nonconformist sexualities, yet in the public eye everyone, including themselves in most cases, behaved as if nobody knew.[2] On the whole, the cultural ideology of sexuality sent it away to the realm of secretive privacy, and in case of non-normative desires, this secret was even redoubled. This created a discrepancy between what was—and could have been—said in public and what was practiced privately, which influenced the communicative situation. Foucault's theory of the birth of confession under surveillance and prohibition is of use in this place (Gill 4, Radstone 172–173).[3]

---

[1] There are, therefore, similarities with the Clifford Geertz's idea of "thick description," or a postcolonial feminist idea of métissage in autobiography. See Lionnet. In the area of queer studies this idea seems close to Lee Edelman's concept of homographesis which foregrounds the textual and rhetorical aspect of queer sexuality, yet speaks less of idiographism (20).
[2] The construction of glass closets is brilliantly analysed by Eve Kosofsky Sedgwick.
[3] There is also the Polish connection to this. Between 1958 and 1960 Foucault worked in Warsaw at the Centre Français and maintained several relationships with men; one of them was an undercover agent of the communist security service which led to a diplomatic scandal and the expulsion of the philosopher from the country.

The second decade of the twenty-first century abounded in Poland in the posthumously published "secret diaries" written by authors who lived in glass closets, i.e. their nonconformist sexualities were known (or, better, "speculated," "rumoured") and even studied by scholars (from the 1990s on, with the emergence of gender, gay and lesbian and finally queer studies).

I will treat the term "secret diary" as a genre, but it was used as the title of a diary by Miron Białoszewski published in 2012 (the title was chosen by the editors, not suggested by the writer). I will pick four queer Polish modernists, all of them different artistically and sexually. All of them experienced international fame at some point in their career. What is surprising in all the four cases is that we find a similar scheme of communication levels: while all of them published "official diaries" or other "official" autobiographical writings with some queer hints, among which the most known worldwide is the *Diary* by Gombrowicz, all of them also published fictional literary works which dealt with queer issues—in Białoszewski's case this fictional literature would not be prose but poetry. All of them also run their diaries that were not meant for publication during their lifetimes, but in some (presumably 'better') future.

The reception of these diaries tells us quite a lot about Polish culture and its attitude towards homosexuality (I use the word "homosexuality" here, because these writers in the public eye were seen as "homosexuals" not as "queers" with distinctive sexual fingerprints). The reason why they left those diaries for posthumous publication was generally understood as a wish not to hurt living people by revealing their dark secrets, mostly of scandalous sexual nature; after the publication, however, there was a disappointment. This reception-reaction is rather contradictory, however. Expecing private confessions, the public complained that those private writings were not "elaborate enough" and proved that private lives and private styles might be the same as in the case of nonprofessional writers (i.e. "everybody"). In "straight" readings with regular, well-established codes, those diaries might in fact seem dull, offering nothing more than the accounts of "shopping and fucking," to use Mark Ravenhill's title. My answer is, however, that such specific texts require a queer eye, a shift in the gaze, whereby, first, the sexual component is not isolated, and secondly, it is not isolated to be downgraded as a secondary phenomenon compared with essayistic intelligent diagnoses or commentaries about literary works. On the whole, this receptive situation leads to the conclusion that Polish culture created a paranoid sexual politics and culture; and at the same time that in the Polish culture there is no actual understanding of a private writing mode, which is contradictory, because this very culture creates double standards for public and private spheres, and yet whenever faced with the private sphere it produced, it tries to read it in terms of the "public sphere." The phenomenon I am describing tells us less about the sexual narratives of the diaries than about the culture itself, even though it is obvious that culture influenced the writing styles of sexuality in the diaries.

I shall use Melanie Klein's concept of paranoid, depressive and reparative positions as well as the manic position or manic defense which Klein eventually rejected (271-283) and apply it to the three levels of writing sexuality as outlined above. In Kleinian thought, the paranoid position is the most dangerous for the psychic life, the depressive position is a step further on the way to reparation and helps the child gain a more "realistic" experience of the world. Most of the literary fictional works that deal with queerness place either their heroes or their whole construction (form) on the depressive or manic position. In this case it means that desire is impossible because unrealizable and/or threatened with the experience of loss, but at the same time it can be named and recognized. The desire has an object. The difference between the "official" autobiographical writings and "secret diaries" I see as two different reparative impulses answering the paranoid sexuality. However, the reparative impulse of the "official" diaries I see mostly as a failure—not an artistic failure, but a reparative failure. In order to understand this one needs to remember that the modernist construction of culture of that time exalted "the aesthetic," which in queer cases functioned as a "closet"; this very double bind of trying to remain a "high artist" and repairing the sexual paranoid created a space for a new gender of confessional writing, the "secret diaries," precisely because the "official" ones while not being an artistic failure, did not succeed as psychological reparations. Klein attributes to the manic defense the (unrealistic) feeling of total control which gives the illusion of controlling the objects. Gombrowicz's official *Diary* is the most exuberant example of this: the subject selects, adopts, elaborates, frames, builds his image and persona. In all the four cases of such autobiographical "official" writing the queer subjects do not fully "come out." For "paranoid readers"—until the publication of "secret diaries"—these tropes were understandable as queer, but those texts might have been read as "straight" or only "homophiliac" as well. It is with the publication of the "secret diaries" that we get the keys to decipher the allusions, the "lost and regained palimpsest" (which, it is important to remark, proved that queer scholars, formerly accused of delivering "paranoid readings," were not so paranoid, after all). The consequence of such manic defense—and the reason why it is a failure—is, as Klein describes it, the diminution of the objects's meaningfulness and even a kind of contempt for it. However, the ego might partially back out, something that, according to Klein, represents another step when compared to the depressive position. I am not trying to suggest that the "secret diaries" constitute a complete reparative success because everything was said in a safe and sound manner. I regard them as ambiguous: they attest to a world of sexual paranoia that they try to "repair." Melanie Klein says that the paranoid position means an anxiety of the ego's survival, while the depressive position, where the object can be recognized and even classified as good or bad, is the anxiety of the survival of the good object. The sexual paranoia I am referring to—in communist and post- communist Poland as well as in many Western and non-Western cultures—is a fear that the subject exists partially (only as long as it is not queer) and if it is invaded by the (queer) object it might be destroyed; or a fear that one is the only queer subject in the world and others might find out or already know something dreadful and plot the destruction of the outcast; or a fear that there are no queer subjects at all. Queer desire is not recognizable as an object that can be incorporated or projected; it is a floating paranoid message.

Therefore I would here like to introduce another aspect of psychoanalytic theory which I believe explains at least partially the idea of sexual paranoia and offers a way to connect it to the "sexual fingerprint" and idiographic readings of it. I refer to Jean Laplanche's theory of the "enigmatic signifier" and primary seduction (169-171) which was succesfully adopted by Leo Bersani and Ulysse Dutoit for a reading of paintings by Caravaggio, and also by me in an attempt to redefine camp and/as "gaydar" (Bersani, Dutoit 39-42; Sobolczyk *Interpellated on Camp?*). The biggest difference between the theories of Klein and Laplanche is that according to Laplanche read by Bersani the sexual paranoia is not a position, it is the very characteristic of our culture(s) and hardly escapable. As I argue, we have only begun to reformulate our understandings of culture with the "discovery" of the "enigmatic signifier" which might contribute to a great paradigmatic change; my proposition of reading the "sexual fingerprints" with the "enigmatic signifier" is another step in this direction. According to Laplanche, from parents unconscious or conscious efforts try to hide certain sexual things from a child emanate an impalpable "enigmatic signifier" which the child understands as having some erotic meaning, more precisely, as a seduction on the part of the caretaker (the parent in most cases, but that might not always be the case). While the full content of the message enters the mind of the child, it cannot be "metabolized" as such or assimilated by symbolisation, and so it forms the unconscious as a reservoir. The subject as a sexual being is constituted by the "enigmatic signifier" which in later life people still "emanate" as adults. We live in the world of hidden fantasies and speculations, mind-readings and often failed verbal and nonverbal communications which constitute the world of sexual paranoia, full of "enigmatic signifiers" in the air. But this might also be seen as the beginning of knowledge and epistemology seen as paranoid. I would say it constitutes hermeneutical sexuality—the one that Foucault tried to escape—and paranoid knowing. Certainly, as Bersani and Dutoit remark, this might also be seen as an "exciting" condition if one treats sexuality more as a game (Bersani and Dutoit 41; Bersani 107–108). Now, the problem is this: in order to grasp the "sexual fingerprint" we need to read the "enigmatic signifiers," or rather, in autobiographical writing, to read the subject's own reading of their "enigmatic signifiers" (as symptoms, i.e. without holding claims about the relation to some phantasmatic "true" personality) and readings of others. And this means the project of such readings will ever be "paranoid"—but it should include the repairing twist—and, to say the least, "capricious" (I prefer the word "idiosyncratic"), because the "enigmatic signifier," precisely because it is enigmatic, cannot be fully read—it might be, hopefully, traced, found in bits. And this is exactly what I aim to do right now in a series of close-ups on four "secret diaries."

Iwaszkiewicz: Sublimation and Shit

Sublimation was the preferred literary practice of Iwaszkiewicz when dealing with homosexual themes in his fictional works. But this writer also attempted to define it or justify this practice in his autobiographical writings belonging to the "official" category. Evoking of the concept of "sublimation" serves partially as a confession. In his *Book of My Memories* (1957), we read about his youth: "For the first time I understood the revelation for me at that time concerning relation between creativity and eroticism. The first book I have ever bought for my library was Plato's Symposium, the Lviv Altenberg edition. Through the lecture of this book and by the charming character of Maslieiev I discovered the perspectives of sublimating the instinct that I knew not what to do with" (Iwaszkiewicz Książka moich wspomnień [237]).[4] Iwaszkiewicz is not mystifying, then, but

---

[4] All the translations from "secret diaries" from Polish to English are mine since these works have not been published in any other languages yet.

neither is he speaking in full voice; nor is he denying that creativity is erotic in its source, it needs, however, sublime elaboration, elevation and purification. Thus the official fictional and autobiographical writings offered the readers "purified" traces of the originally "wild" instinct. The superego triumphed over the id. Yet the "secret diary," published in three volumes from 2007 to 2011, proves that the acts of sublimation do not just annihilate the lower or "dirtier" (instinctual) aspects. Richard Halpern in his book on sublimation drew on the alchemical theory of sublimation in a reading of a sonnet by Shakespeare. This theory, older than psychoanalytical understanding and traced back to a treatise by Nicolas Flamel (1624), proves that psychoanalytical theory was based on false assumptions: sublimation produces two substances, not one (the "high spirit"), as Iwaszkiewicz also wished for, and the real aim of the whole process is a reconciliation of the two:

> Alchemical sublimation thus produces two substances: a purified and spiritualized essence and, separated from this, a fecal discharge or remainder. In turning solid to gas, and gas back to solid, sublimation was seen as transforming body to spirit and spirit to body. The goal was not a separation of spirit from matter but a reconciliation of spirit with a purified matter (...). The fecal remainder, by contrast, was associated variously with earth, with menses, with putrefaction, and with death. Flamel writes of this discharge or remainder that it "stincks, and gives a smell like the odour of graves filled with rottenesse, and with bodies as yet charged with their natural moisture." (Halpern 15)

In these terms, all of Iwaszkiewicz's attempts at sublimation failed because they removed the waste, the reminder of the shadow, and therefore, perhaps, transformed body to spirit, but not spirit to body. It comes as no surprise, then, that in the "secret diary" we find an "anal attack" (as Klein would put it; and the rhetoric of the fragment clearly indicates the defense-attack strategy) as a means of defense of both (carnal) anal sex and gay love; in short, we are faced with this forgotten and repressed or projected "remainder" ("bad object"):

> And nobody understands this, this joy and happiness. Everybody thinks that this consists in fucking in the ass! And the very Socrates explained that to Alcibiades that this is not what makes two men happy and joyful when they share their presence. And for so many ages nobody has understood it correctly—and they always interpret it through shit. Why does a man always have to be dirty? (Iwaszkiewicz 193)

The aim expressed in this entry is still sublimation, but this time the language is not "purified." Melanie Klein describes the "anal frustration" as a process experienced by the child on the part of the mother who "castrates" the faeces, takes them away, when the child considers them as a "gift." The gift might then become an arm: the child wants to "throw mud," no, "mud" is a sublimated version, "throw shit" at the mother. In Iwaszkiewicz's case "the mother" is represented by Polish[5] culture which performs an "anal castration" (i.e. of homosexuality; note also the association of faeces with death in Flamel which implies that homosexuality as a nonreproductive sexuality brings death). "The good shit," transformed from the "bad object" into a "good" one via sublimation—as Iwaszkiewicz understands it and performs it—is a rejected gift by the culture which insists that it is always "bad." This causes an incidental attack on Iwaszkiewicz's part, the projection of "bad objects" from the inside to the outside, nevertheless still understood as the defense of the "good object." What Iwaszkiewicz fails to understand is that by his very understanding of "sublimation," i.e. of transforming the "bad object" ("carnal anal sex") into a "good one" so that the "bad one" is apparently invisible (in the "official" literary works), contributes to the very falseness of the culture which eventually turns back against him. The repressed returns.

Andrzejewski: Wife, Son, Lover—and Shoes

In 2003, a "secret diary" written by Jerzy Andrzejewski was published under the title *Paris Diary*. It is a collection of his letters to his wife sent from Paris between December 1959 and May 1960, when the writer was on a scholarship in France. The text was accepted for publication as a diary one year before the writer's death in 1983. *Paris Diary*, which disappointed many critics in Poland, offers a unique venture into queer family life during the communism. Andrzejewski's wife, Maria, was fully aware of her husband's homosexual desires, and he did not hesitate to confess to her his cruising stories and sugar daddy experiences with *gamins*. Yet there is another discourse in the diary, the rapture with the free goods market which leads soon to a commodity fetishism exemplified especially in buying shoes. The writer constantly plans to buy shoes for himself and his children, complains about his shoes, buys new pairs of shoes, etc. These two discourses—commodity fetishism and familial homoeroticism—meet and intersect in interesting ways in a few paragraphs I want to examine now. On April 12,

---

[5] Moreover, in Polish tradition "Poland" is generally understood as a woman, a mother.

1960, Andrzejewski writes: "for Marcin I bought sportive shoes, very sound, big, thickly-tailored, on huge rubber, top of sports I guess, or maybe a little too flamboyant, I don't know?, and another pair, navy-blue linen, light, summery, kind of tennis shoes" (92). The next day the writer has doubts about this first ("flamboyant") pair of shoes, about their looks and their size. It comes to his mind that his adult (51-year-old) foot must be the same size as that of his 17-year-old son: "I should try Marcin's shoes, but I am a bit ashamed to wear shoes so adolescent, I am worried now that maybe in Warsaw these shoes will be "too much," yet after wearing for some time they'll get darker, anyway, for autumn and winter they'll be perfect" (95). English phraseology helps us understand this wishful fantasy very well; "put yourself in my shoes," "try walking in my shoes" (="put yourself in my place"). Buying a pair of shoes which appeal to his taste and which he would like to wear, Andrzejewski fears that he is too old, so then he would like to "project them" on his son, yet fears that the pair might be "too queer" for both his son and for Poland. Finally, there is a third party in this triangle— Andrzejewski's 17-year-old lover(s). Perhaps Andrzejewski would have also liked him to wear these shoes. Possibly, he would have liked to be his son Marcin at that moment, and be coupled with another 17-year-old like Raphael. Andrzejewski has an identification problem with the split in his roles as a father ("gay father," to be precise), and a lover of boys of his son's age. As it seems, Andrzejewski was aware of the fact that Marcin was not gay (which proved to be true in later life), the reader of the diary might guess that while Maria, the wife, "knew," Agnieszka, the 14-year-old daughter "knew not," Marcin "might have been guessing." Yet I am not suggesting that Andrzejewski had a direct desire for his son (apart from the idea in psychoanalytic theories of fatherhood that any kind of fatherhood deals with homosexual love which might—or might not—be repressed). I think Andrzejewski was unable to decide whether to adopt the position of the "sugar daddy," a kind of "foster father" and "master" (spiritual and financial) to his *mauvais garçons* (as he calls them), the position of an adult living his "second youth," and to place his son in this game which outside of the familial context would be somewhat clearer or at least more culturally archetypical (not to say cliché). In an utterly striking confession to his wife, Andrzejewski compares Raphael, one of his boys, with his son:

> Our son is a bit too childlish. I have met a boy who is 17 and will graduate this year in this famous lycée Louis Grand, a son of a Spanish woman and Russian man, who are divorced, he is the admirer of my

"Ashes and Diamonds," the mother the translator of Dos Passos and the Spanish, he is going to film school, it's impossible to imagine what he saw and read, such receptivity, such intelligence, maturity. Raphael Sorin (certainly, simply Zorin). Actually he and Ania Jawicz are the only reasons I am staying in Paris. (72)

There is another "erotic thread" here: intellectual fascination as erotic. Perhaps what Raphael had—and Marcin had not—was an admiration for Andrzejewski's work and intellect that the writer was ever avid for. The question whether we admire people more when we desire them sexually, as Raphael presumably did (and Andrzejewski admiring Raphael's intellect for being capable of admiring the intellect of Andrzejewski, in a game of mirrors), or whether any "admiration" is sexual *per se*, only sublimated—will be left open.

Białoszewski: Loving and/as Writing against Proper Definitions

Miron Białoszewski's *Secret Diary* was meant for publication in 2010 as the writer's will stipulated, but it took another two years before it was published. The "erotic confessions" appear only in the last 100 pages (out of 850) in the part significantly entitled *Aggravation* that cover the last year of the writer's life (Sobolczyk, *Dokładka* 161–72).

Aggravation uses a pastiche of a Proustian trope to introduce the theme of sexuality: on May 19, 1982, Białoszewski relates how he was standing in a queue to buy ten (this was the limit) fruit drops without "paper blocks" (Poland was full of queues at that time and sweets were sold only in limited amounts with special "paper blocks"), although he did not like fruit drops anymore. He recalls his childhood when he liked fruit drops and instantly jumps into another thing he liked, i.e. sex adventures, which must have started before the age of fifteen (and with adults which he curiously compares to an alternative school of thought, wit, and criticism). But this marks the end of the Proustian strategy, although not the end of the memories: in the next move Białoszewski, who had the merited fame of a very original artist with his own recognizable style, supports the idea (recently issued also by queer theory) that the nonconformist style of writing derives from sexual nonconformity: "All the terms and invectives of such tastes did not bother me especially. This is how I trained my stubbornness and impermeability. In sex and in writing. Not caring about critiques. Or non-acknowledgement. It was a good and effective auto-training" (752). As a strategy this is the opposite of sublimation which is supposed to raise "unsocial" impulses into "socially acceptable" ones; however, Białoszewski's official literature did not produce any direct or all-out ejaculations. What he is suggesting, I believe, is this: my queerness (sexual, too, but an all-embracing category) is in my style, it is everywhere in my works, in every phrase. The mention of "terms" and "invectives," that is, words with their proper definitions or pragmatic oral meanings, is not accidental. If "sexual nonconformity" means being somehow deaf or indifferent to their proper use, there are two ways of dealing with this: first, by omitting it, behaving like it did not exist, and so does the sublimation in some cases, or second, if one wants to be "creative," by appropriating words and grammar not as demanded by definitions and rules—norms, in short—but by breaking them privately or individually. This is what most of Białoszewski's poetry does. Both the sucking fruit drops and literature here are oral activities, and they are connected to surveillance and also the mother. How? As a child, Białoszewski tricked the mother that he needed to pay a fee, and he bought himself fruit drops—but the mother found that he had lied. When he concealed his sexual adventures, on the other hand, she did not find out. Thus the pre-history of the neglect of invectives (as the establishment of the individual style) is also oral and based on concealing, conspiracy and lying, tricking or cheating (the mother). In Melanie Klein's terms this could be seen as an oral sadism directed toward the mother's breast by acts of biting, gnawing, and tearing. The reader of the diary who notices this "oral fixation" might add what is unsaid: the fruit drops represent a substitute of the "bad breast" of the mother which the poet tried to "repair" by sucking on the "good penises," for the fruit drops might easily symbolize both and thus may symbolize the very slippage or erotic transition from one object to another. "I threw my mother's cunning to devour fake signatures, fruit drops and flirting with fellows. Here mum suspected something. But I wasn't too terrified. What she did not discover were the affairs in the city with the adults" (752). Even the very expression "rzucić na pożarcie," "to throw somebody something to devour," that is, to offer them something small so that something of greater importance might be kept safe, evokes "oral sadism."[6] This is the projected sadism as cannibalism onto the mother

---

[6] Białoszewski prefers the pictorial verb "zwietrzyć" (something like "to smell the wind" = to find out) – "rozgryźć (coś)," like "to bite something out" (= to crack something, an enigma, a mystification). It probably comes from the image of biting nuts, but psychoanalytically and in Kleinian terms especially it would mean a sadistic impulse to "open" the mother to see what she has inside as a part of an epistemofilic impulse. There is also the verb "przygryzać" ("bite somebody bit by bit") which means "provoking" somebody with words, being mischievous. In English there is the oral (but less sadistic) expression

(probably the phallic mother) who would "devour" the child if she found out that he introjects the "bad penises" of various men; by projection the child wants to devour the mother, but since that cannot be done "really," the child attacks the mother by oral, that is, verbal tricks or lies. Therefore homosexuality has a double status here, first as the paranoid effort to keep one's subjectivity or coherence, but second, and probably even more so, it can be understood as a sadistic attack on what the mother represents and cherishes. It is coherent that what Białoszewski attributes to adult gay men he knew as an adolescent, is "wit" and "sharpness of thought and language," associated with cutting or biting, i.e. the very categories he used against his mother and later in life as a means of defense as well. The mother, then, is the first figure of surveillance and prohibition (in Foucauldian terms).[7] At the time of writing, 1982, the fruit drops in the shop that the writer does not like but buys anyway because they are available without "paper cards"[8] serve as a vehicle speaking of the state apparatuses of surveillance and repression. Here, the state is the mother. In the Polish language there is an expression, "przygryzać" (see the footnote on Polish idioms), which is more or less what Białoszewski does with his artistic creativity, especially through language games. In place of sadistic attacks on the mother's breast (biting), with his homosexuality and/as style of writing "podgryza," he now gets on the nerves of the state. Still this is the ambiguous and projected desire to destroy (devour) the state before it destroys (devours) the subject. This is how I see the perfectly planned logic of this apparently loose paragraph. Thus the sexual fingerprint is found in the idiosyncratic style and in an idiographic reading.

"to suck" but it originally had the penis as an object, not the breast. In Polish there is also the expression "wycyckać kogoś," like "to breast somebody" = to trick them.

[7] In Freud and in Lacan it would be le non du pere, a position reserved for the symbolical father. Certainly this is symbolical mother I am discussing here. After the World War II but still before becoming a famous writer Białoszewski's sexuality was revealed to the parents and in the future he had a positive relationship with her, a "reparative" one.

[8] In a way it also connotes a kind of an erotic fatigue (a doubtful term, but I will use it here) and the fatigue with the paranoid secretiveness which now seems less aggressive (generally, the state regulates sex—like it regulates the supply of sweets with "paper cards," which represent the prohibitive "scriptures"—but at times it can be avoided, yet now, in this age, it does not bring the subject the longed-for feeling of "liberation"). A connection with another Polish idiom might be detected, although I am not sure if it was in use in Białoszewski's times. "Ciurlać dropsa," meaning "to suck the fruit drop," is a slang expression for "to do a blowjob." On another level the fruit drops that in the young days were a "cover," are now disliked because Białoszewski does not want or need "covers" ("appearances") any more.

Gombrowicz: Intellect is not Sex(y)

The official *Diary* of Gombrowicz was, from the beginning, considered as a work of autobiographical autocreation. In *Kronos* Gombrowicz offers a counter-account of his sexual experiences with women and men in a wholly different rhetorical way. The attempt is to avoid creation and thus produce the narrative as "raw," which eventually, in the area of eroticism, leads to counting lovers (hundreds), and on another level to counting money, for these are the dominant themes in this diary. There is no intellectual brilliance. This very positioning says something about Gombrowicz's vision of sexuality—since it *must* be separated from intellectual activities in its "basic" form, and in the intellectual forms it might occur only when transformed (into a concept, wit, game, problem)—as it happens to be produced in his fictional works and in the "official diary"; the connection with money is not exactly a revealed secret in this "secret diary," and it creates a subtext of "love for sale," prostitution. If in *Kronos* Gombrowicz paraphrases and challenges the saying that "gentlemen don't talk about money (and sex alike)," the other side of the coin seems to be for him that "one cannot be a gentleman when he fucks." All in all this constitutes another variant of "sublimation," a defense of it. *Kronos* is boring—perhaps on purpose. In my opinion, Gombrowicz tries to prove that sexuality cannot be rendered interesting in a narrative without a special rhetorics. Yet the very quantity of his experiences shows that they were not too boring for him and that they required many repetitions. Therefore we have a "revelation" which at the same time reclaims the "inexpressibleness" of the subjective experience or attitude, the non-representativeness. What we get in this journal is actually very external. When the writer counts his male lovers, in most cases he says something about their profession which is always "proletarian." With this "sexual fingerprint," I think, our understanding of Gombrowicz's vision of the figure of the intellectual cannot be complete, although he himself denies that connection and tries to pigeonhole those categories apart. For when we read that he had *El carnicero de Avellaneda* (111),[9] that is, a butcher from a proletarian district, or *Carlos the sailor* (147) (sailors seem to be the most desired profession), or a shoe-cleaner, it shows that for Gombrowicz professions might have a sexual appeal; class is also a factor, but I think that this preference-code is a bit fetishistic in a different way as the professions need to be codified, deter-

---

[9] Originally written in Spanish, not in Polish, in just a one sentence note even without a verb.

mined, have a "proper definition"; probably also a visible "mark" on the body. The profession of the "intellectual," including "a writer," is vague, not codified, very individual, not always "readable" from the body, of "doubtful masculinity" if "masculinity" means concreteness and following rules or codes. The psychic life, which is the basis of the work of an intellectual, is not taken into account. Thus we know nothing about those men apart from their profession, their behaviour ("effeminate"), or their looks ("hairy"). The inside, Gombrowicz suggests, is not "sexual." There is, however, a huge difference regarding the perception of women as sexual objects. First of all, in the whole Argentinian period, as we learn, Gombrowicz had no sexual experiences with women. In his memories from the earlier life in Poland (he started writing his "secret diary" in 1952 or 1953) most of the girls he had sex with are called "whores," like in this expression: *A hysterical whore from Hala* (40).[10] Yet it seems not always to be their "profession," as is the case with sailors. Moreover, some of the "boys with profession" probably were actually "prostitutes" or had sex for money. This could be too easily discredited as mere misogyny. In my first reading (and writing) of *Kronos* I suggested that it was a projection of self-shame and self-aggression, for even though this is not said directly in the diary, it can be guessed, and Virgilio Piñera's account quoted by Reinaldo Arenas supports this view, that Gombrowicz probably prostituted himself in his first years in Argentina when he was very poor. I am not denying this reading now, on the contrary, I think my new understanding rather supports it. If Gombrowicz sought in men "properly constitued objects," defined, and understood them as sexually arousing, then women in his account are not "constituted objects." They do not have a profession, they have a condition or a quality—of being "whores." Using once again very simply Kleinian distinctions, Gombrowicz is able to situate men in the "depressive position" under certain circumstances, where the objects might be constituted as either internal or external (in this case—external), and he situates women in the "paranoid position" (note the use of the word "hysterical") which means that by refusing to see them as objects he tries to destroy them. The reparative impulse toward women appears later in life with Rita who eventually becomes the writer's wife. So in fact his own situation as an intellectual and that of women-whores are very similar in fuzziness and internal unreadability. Whether this was due to actually having sex for living, what might be latent in this equation, is unsolved; however it could explain also the boring money

---

[10] Hala is place in the Tatra mountains.

accounts in *Kronos* as reparative because they finally prove that one can make a living out of being an intellectual.

The research for this paper was subsidised by the Polish National Center for Sciences grant nr DEC-2012/04/S/HS2/00561.

Works Cited

Andrzejewski, Jerzy. *Dziennik paryski*. Warszawa: Open, 2003. Print.

Bersani, Leo. "'Sociality and Sexuality'. *Is the Rectum a Grave? And Other Essays*. Chicago: U of Chicago P, 2010. Print.

Bersani, Leo, and Ulysse Duto. *Caravaggio's Secrets*. Cambridge: October, 1998. Print.

Białoszewski, Miron. *Tajny dziennik*. Kraków: Znak, 2012. Print.

Edelman, Lee. *Homographesis. Essays in Gay Literary and Cultural Theory*. New York: Routledge, 1994. Print.

Gill, Jo. "Introduction." Gill, Jo, Ed. *Modern Confesionary Writing. New Critical Essays*. New York: Routledge, 2006. Print.

Gombrowicz, Witold. *Kronos*. Kraków: Wydawnictwo Literackie, 2013. Print.

Hall, Donald E. *Reading Sexualities. Hermeneutic Theory and the Future of Queer Studies*. London: Routledge, 2009. Print.

Halpern, Richard. *Shakespeare's Perfume. Sodomy and Sublimity in the Sonnets, Wilde, Freud, and Lacan*. Philadelphia: U of Pennsylvania P, 2002. Print.

Iwaszkiewicz, Jarosław. *Dzienniki 1956–1963*. Warszawa: Czytelnik, 2010. Print.

Iwaszkiewicz, Jarosław. *Książka moich wspomnień*. Kraków: Wydawnictwo Literackie, 1957. Print.

Kosofsky Sedgwick, Eve. *Epistemology of the Closet*. Berkeley—Los Angeles: TUof California P, 1990. Print.

Lionnet, Françoise. *Autobiographical Voices. Race, Gender, Self-Portraiture*. Ithaca: Cornell UP, 1989. Print.

Klein, Melanie. *Love, Guilt and Reparation, and Other Works 1921–1945*. New York: Free P, 1975. Print.

Laplanche, Jean. "Seduction, Persecution, Revelation." Transl. P. Slotkin. *Essays on Otherness*. London: Routledge, 1999. Print.

Radstone, Susannah. "Cultures of Confession / Cultures of Testimony." Gill, Jo, Ed. *Modern Confesionary Writing. New Critical Essays.* New York: Routledge, 2006. Print.

Sobolczyk, Piotr. "Dokładka—pogorszenie? Na(d)dawanie?." *Kwartalnik ARTystyczny* 2 (2012): 161–72. Print.

—. "Gombrowicz Bez Marynarki IZ Marynarzem." *Kwartalnik ARTystyczny* 3 (2013): 206–14. Print.

—. *Interpelated on Camp?.* Forthcoming (in print).

Steakley, James D. "*Per Scientiam ad Justitiam.* Magnus Hirschfeld and the Sexual Politics of Innate Homosexuality." Rosario, Vernon A, Ed. *Science and Homosexualities.* New York: Routledge, 1997. Print.

Sullivan, Nikki. *A Critical Introduction to Queer Theory.* Edinburgh: Edinburgh UP, 2006. Print.

"Glad Rags, Feather-Dusted Spiders and Horse-Drawn Harvesters": Gender, Truth, and Imagination in Three Approaches to Autobiography/Autoethnography at an Elder Care Home in Bristol

Seana Kozar

In the Irish folktale "The Wonders of the Three Donals,"[1] an inhospitable and unsociable farmer finds himself playing host to three travelling peddlars invited in by his kind-hearted wife. Each bears his Christian name, she reasons, and all are therefore equally deserving of charity. He agrees to hear a tale from each, promising that if it is the most wonderful he has ever heard, their labours will earn the best of them a good meal and a warm bed. Each decides to tell his life story.

The first man tells how he was sent out with two farm servants to cut peat, drank from a faery well and was transformed into a well-respected parish priest who, as his first act in his new vocation, marry the servants who have come with him. The pair have fallen madly in love—and switched genders—as a result of drinking from the same well. Some years later, he accompanies the young family on holiday and all drink from a clear, pure fountain found in the forest and fall asleep. Upon waking, the young Donal and the servants are restored to their former selves. Returning to Donal's father with their tale, they are cast out as bewitched. Six full years have passed in both worlds.

The second Donal, also a farmer's son, hides himself in the last stack of grain left in his father's haggard on All Hallows Eve. Despite a bountiful harvest, the stacks have been mysteriously disappearing one by one. While

---

[1] See MacManus (185–201) for the version of this story summarised in this paper.

dozing on watch, he is startled awake by the sight of 50,000 faery folk ranging all over the remaining stack. Each one takes a stalk of grain, mounts it like a horse, utters a spell and rides off on the wind. Donal tries the same incantation and is whisked away on a fine beast. He arrives at the palace of the Faery Queen. After a sumptuous banquet, he dances the evening away with the Queen, their skill much admired by the assembled guests. Fearing the late hour, he begs leave to go and rides home. When he reaches his father's stables he is very upset to find his wondrous horse suddenly gone from under him, the bridle replaced in his hand by a single piece of straw. He enters the house, now very grand, and is confronted by strangers who chase him away. He seeks shelter in a small cottage with an elderly couple. He asks after his father, only to be told he died decades ago. With a passing glance in a mirror, Donal is horrified to discover his aged self. His whole lifetime has passed in one night.

The third Donal, a fisherman's son, lives near the coast and is sent to fetch water from the well on the strand after coming in from fishing with his father. He takes a drink and looks up to behold a beautiful sailboat bobbing gently at the water's edge. He gets in and the boat takes him to an enchanted isle. He marries the Queen and stays away for 300 years. Eventually, he is seized with a great longing to see his homeland. The Queen cautions him not to set foot on shore, but upon seeing the strand and the well he moors the boat. Running to the well, he nearly trips over two carelessly discarded water buckets and turns to see the little boat casting off with the outgoing tide. Hearing his mother's voice, he fills the buckets and tries to tell his fantastic story to anyone who will listen. Centuries have passed in the enchanted realm, but only ten minutes have gone by in the real world.

Although folktales and autobiographies are clearly different genres, they share certain key features. Firstly, most stories, including "wonder tales" or märchen, are considered true on some level by their tellers and audiences. Even the most fantastic story, one that seems to challenge and overturn all the normal parameters of temporal and spatial possibility, may be in fact a narrative about coming of age, taking stock or confronting one's fear of death, to name but a few broad themes. Without exception, each of the Donals has to leave the life laid out before his youthful adventures, shoulder his pack and find his own way to the narrative moment at the farmer's hearth.

Secondly, the nature of narrated time across both genres is rich in what is known but unstated. In essence, this is because the storyteller knows how it ends and the autobiographer knows how it's gone so far. According to W.F.H. Nicolaisen:

> Once convincingly embedded in narrative time, any story's total recounted time is presented in narrated and non-narrated portions, of which the former ... are normally proportionally less extensive than the latter ... thus giving folktales in their very telling a paradoxical lopsidedness towards silence, towards the redundance of the unsaid. ("Past" 3)

In addition to being concerned with specially marked or signified time and featuring a central protagonist/self who is necessarily the centre of the story, folktales and autobiographies share a concern with a reflexive past and future that serve the narrator's present understanding. As Brockmeier states: "A life story starts in the here and now and reconstructs the past as if it were teleologically directed towards this specific present" (60). This knowledge in turn equips the individual with the ability to create the structures from experience of life *times*, that "give a meaningful diachronic order to a selected multitude of singular life events" (61). This structuring is likewise echoed in the folktale, where the protagonist receives detailed and often repeated admonishments and advice from various helpers, foreshadowing a way to avoid future calamity, if the warnings are heeded. As Nicolaisen observes: "By knowing in advance and by remembering that knowledge well at the right time, the future is harnessed and made serviceable" ("Concepts" 156).

In this chapter, I explore the oral and written autobiographical and autoethnographic styles of three residents of an extra care home site in Bristol, UK who are part of the Tangible Memories Project, an interdisciplinary study researching ways of creating community in elder care home settings by using digital technology to put residents' stories into personal objects with a view to self-curation and the creation of digital legacies. Looking at the interplay between creativity, memory, play and veridicality in the construction and performance of life stories, I will highlight three narrators' very different conceptions of time and voice. First however, I would like to clarify what is meant by *autobiography, autoethnography* and *autobiographical memory* in the context of this paper.

Because the creators of the texts presented here used spoken word as well as various genres of writing, including essays that were neither read aloud nor recorded and notes that were, autobiography in this instance cannot be restricted to a consideration of writing alone, but must take into account oral performance as well. Autobiography here might be better understood as a kind of *embodied communicative register*, since as Brockmeier points out:

> Autobiographical accounts, or fragments of it, are common and elementary practices of the self, neither bound to a particular age, education or social habitus, nor to the act or linguistic form of writing in the narrow sense. Rather, it is in many forms of discourse, oral and written, that we order our experiences, memories, intentions, hopes, desires, fears, and concerns in an autobiographical perspective. (53)

Defined as: "a self-narrative that critiques the situatedness of self with others in social contexts" (Spry 710), I would argue that while the narrators make use of autoethnographic techniques, they do so within certain culturally- and generationally-defined limits. The intentional, systematic, contextualised self-consciousness of the method, which practitioners cite as a distinctive feature and potential strength over more traditional autobiographical forms,[2] may be problematic for people brought up in an era when drawing too much attention to oneself was at least socially undesirable if not actively but informally proscribed. Each of the narrators defines and limits his or her transgression of perceived cultural norms in this regard either through play, which transforms the responsible voice of the self into one that doesn't have to answer for behaviour that might be interpreted as "showing off," or by situating their personal story within a larger, but still familiar, historical continuum of past generational experiences.

Furthermore, with respect to autobiographical memory, it may be useful to consider *life review* and *reminiscence* as well, since these terms all have to do with ways of talking about what are essentially personal experience narratives that centre on the past. According to Burnside and Haight, while both foreground the importance of memory: "Life review is a process of reviewing, organizing and evaluating the overall picture of one's life with the purpose of achieving integrity by seeing one's own life as a unique story" (56). Similarly, Bluck and Levine emphasize both the structured

---

[2] See Ngunjiri, Hernandez, and Chang (2010) for further discussion. Along these lines, although many of the residents in our project were happy to talk about their life stories to (younger) researchers, they had to develop a certain comfort level when faced with an audience of their peers. Their initial reticence around "not wanting to sound like I'm bragging" points less to Butler's notion that life review is almost a natural corollary of old age, than to Wallace's assertion that, like other forms of narrative, sharing life stories is a communicative performance that must be experienced within a constantly negotiated social context that includes the narrator's and audience's shared cultural expectations around reciprocity, even within a small, familiar group (1992, 124).

nature of life review and its relationship to conflict resolution, healing and personal integration, calling it a "particularly structured form of reminiscence" (188). Furthermore, they note that Butler's classic study on reminiscence among the aged put forward concepts—such as the reconstructed nature of personal memories—that come remarkably close to findings in experimental studies of autobiographical memory (186–187).

If life review can be seen as a structured form of reminiscence, it may be useful to see autobiographical memory as *the larger pool of recollected content from which life story narratives are derived.* Furthermore, if autobiographical memory can be generally viewed a superordinate concept—the set of all possible memories a person might have over the course of the lifespan whether those memories are recalled at any given time or not—and reminiscences are the essential components from which life stories are constructed, chaptered, edited, told and revised, then it follows that work in autobiographical memory could potentially benefit, as Harris, Rasmussen, and Berntsen suggest, from the adoption of a broader analytical framework that borrows from the reminiscence literature. By extension, more critical attention should be paid to how the autobiographical self is, to use Gullette's phrase, "aged by culture" (103)[3] and how the narratives we physically embody in the ageing process are reciprocally inscribed in and through our relationships on personal and cultural levels (2013).

Veridicality is a key concept in memory-based research, oral history and the study of narratives that draw directly on the remembered past. However, as Sarkar observes, one of the longstanding criticisms of oral history as a method, that it was too concerned with accounts from memory that may not be true, is now recognised as one of the methodology's potential strengths: "even so-called 'wrong' statements ... can be "psychologically true" and that this "truth"—as an index of what people might wish for or desire—is an important element of historical reality that is often glossed over in conventional historiography" (584).

Truth is of paramount importance to Barry, a conscientious, gentle man in his early nineties who took a keen interest in our project from the start and who since has taken on the role of "unofficial communications officer" between the mostly university-based members of the research team and other participating residents, printing out and distributing emails for

---

[3] And perhaps by extension how conventions of life storytelling are aged and transformed by cultural and social processes and their outcomes—increased lifespans, opportunities and information access, for example—acting on autobiographical memory across generations.

discussion and relaying the group's decisions through regular correspondence. If a parallel can be drawn with the folktale framing this discussion, Barry's narrative stance throughout his stories reflects that of the second teller. Decades have passed in what seems like a prematurely foreshortened time and the world has forever changed. Although he initially felt he was somewhat bereft of objects that still held much personal significance for him and slightly bemused that anyone else could be interested in the memories of someone who had lived such an ordinary life, Barry nevertheless strove to provide useful and factual accounts of rural life in the past. However, his memory wasn't what it was and he couldn't countenance the thought of even unintentionally misleading future generations. Initially therefore, he wrote his stories or worked from extensive written notes during oral interviews, spending much time in reflective preparation. While he asserted that he was no author, he felt the process of writing allowed him to create accounts that were more accurate and detailed. Describing early mechanical changes to harvesting, Barry wrote of early horse-drawn threshing machines:

> When it was set up ready for working the corn had to be lifted with pitch forks up to the two men on the top who fed it into the machine. The grain came out through spouts at the back into large sacks, which when filled and tied, weight about two hundred weight. Then they had to be carried away. Another back breaking job, and the man at the back who had to see to the sacks being filled, would be covered from head to foot in dust. The reed came through another machine, valuable for thatching if it was wheat reed, otherwise it would be used for bedding.
>
> The excitement came as the rick became smaller and the rats started running out. Hundreds of rats infested corn ricks, living with and eating grain that would eventually become meal or flour! A lot of people would be there with sticks and dogs, a few had guns to kill as many as possible. I remember seeing a large heap of dead rats after a rick was finished.
>
> I take my hat off to those men who drove that "train" through the narrow country lanes. The big steam engine pulled the threshing machine (nearly as big as a bus), another machine for typing up the straw and behind that a four-wheeled wooden caravan for the engine men to sleep in.

By contrast, Barry's second oral performance, which he allowed to be recorded—the first being "just for practice" to see if his memory was up to the task—does not include some of the same details as his written version, but it conveys a clear sense of a boy's wonder in seeing the progress of this steam-powered leviathan through his village, a mechanical marvel that pressed man and beast alike into its relentless service. His evaluative gaze however, is that of a young fellow already well acquainted with managing shire horses and driving hay carts, and what can go wrong if such journeys are not precisely orchestrated, never mind a linked chain of interrelated machinery or the complicating demands of steam:

> Barry: The threshing business was done in the winter. There was a farm near where I lived that had a complete threshing outfit, two steam traction engines and all the equipment. And that used to travel around the farms during the winter, threshing their corn. And that was all booked up of course.
>
> Well, it only stayed there two or three days to finish that lot and then move on. It was all booked up in advance you know. That was amazing really, because the farm lanes were very narrow, the roads. And when you consider that there was a traction engine, a steam traction engine, a threshing machine—which was a *big* machine, as big as a bus. In back of that another machine for tying up the straw into bundles, and all behind that again was often a caravan for the engine men to sleep in when they were away from home. Imagine that lot going on through those country lanes! Imagine trying—impossible to reverse it if something went wrong! They had to have it all worked out ahead of time for water. They constantly had to keep filling the tank with water. They had to know where all the streams were that they could drop the hose in to draw up water. I think those old chaps were marvelous that did that!

For Eileen, a highly creative and engaging woman in her eighties who moved into sheltered accommodation after an operation left her paralysed, play, movement and travel are some of the central themes in her writing. Perhaps most closely echoing the first of the storytelling Donals, Eileen's most vivid memories and liveliest stories come from the twice-yearly trips taken over a period of seven years with a group of female friends she met through an informal support group at the hospital where all of the women had spouses in palliative care. Like the first Donal's time as a parish priest, this was a period in Eileen's life marked by new independence, spontaneity and personal power. Even before the sudden onset of her paralysis and the death of the first of her friends that ultimately signaled the end of her travels, Eileen was no stranger to profound loss and abrupt change. Before the project, Eileen wrote the story of her travels and she keeps a large framed collection of snapshots on her wall that serve as a visual travelogue and daily reminder of trips taken and loved ones gone. In the following performance, which she recorded herself, Eileen reads a story written in response to a creative storytelling session using photographs that was done with the larger project group. Here, she recounts her version of an imaginary train journey to the seaside. The text is transcribed ethno-poetically[4] in order to give some idea of her pauses and emphases:

> Hello, the train went on. We had been traveling so far.
>
> I wonder what we'll see when we stop next?
>
> The train slowed down. I looked out of the window, I'd seen a small village. They said it was a hamlet.
>
> And on the table was a very large hamper with a lid. Everyone was getting off and going in until it came to a lady in a chair.
>
> "Oh, sorry Miss, you cant go in."
>
> "Why?"
>
> "We can't afford to rebuild it."
>
> Anybody would think that I was a nuisance in a wheelchair!
>
> "You just stay there, and I'll get you lovely cup of tea."
>
> On the way out, they had something out of the hamper.
>
> Oh, there goes a big man! He's fallen in the fishpond!
>
> I thought: "Oh, that was funny!"
>
> The man that had just put a cup of tea in my hand jumped up and down, crying out: "My poor fish! My poor fish" and went running towards the pond.
>
> When everyone was back on the train, the man who had got wet put his hand in his pocket and there was the fish!
>
> Nobody knew what had happened as it was our stop to get off and we let more people get on so they could enjoy the journey.
>
> Its been a lovely ride, all around all different places and people bringing back all sorts of things. And everyone enjoyed the jellied eels that went around!

---

[4] See Hymes (1994) for further explanation.

But there—but next time we'll go on another journey. But this time we may go on a coach and see where the coach takes us.

The reference to jellied eels was intended as a wry nod to another resident of the extra care home, a Londoner who saw this as a delicacy to be consumed at every opportunity. According to Eileen, *her* tale of the seaside trip was a thinly veiled attempt to convince her sceptical audience of the superiority of this comestible and was met with gales of laughter. In a later interview, aside from this neat homage to a decidedly acquired taste she did not actually share, Eileen was particularly pleased with the changes she made around the man who fell into the pond, based on a real-life hapless fellow observed on a trip to Paignton with her young children:

> Eileen: The story I wrote about the fat man, I was thinking about when my children were small. And we were walking around the ponds and my little girl was following her brother with his boat and she happened to fall in. But as we were having a picnic and there were lots of men walking around the pond, one did fall in and it was not the goldfish that came out on the grass, but it was all the swans that were flying away! But I thought that was a lovely thing to put into a story.
>
> When the man, when the fat man fell in the water I could imagine all the goldfish coming out. Because in places like that, in a little village or places you go to, you'll find there are always goldfish ponds, everywhere. At seaside places, or anywhere. And I thought that would be really amusing, to see the big man fall into the water and all the gold fish flying up into the air and landing on the grass. Especially when the keeper has seen what has happened, you can imagine him jumping up and down and shouting and running, saying: "Oh my goldfish! Oh my goldfish!" Perhaps it was his pride and joy, and he thought he lost the lot! And then I thought I'd add more to it by the man having one in his pocket. I thought that would be fun, to have him get back on the train and have him automatically put his hand in his pocket and guess what? There was a gold fish in there!

Similarly, the hamlet in the story refers the model village near Babbacombe, which Eileen visited with her family after her paralysis. She was prevented from seeing many of the miniature animatronic displays up close because of the inaccessibility of the site. Despite the rapturously horrified accounts of her grandchildren that accentuated her exclusion ("And of course, the little ones they came back and said: 'Nan, it was great! You see a lady in bed and the house was on fire!' They made it worse!"), Eileen made the best of it in her story, even transforming the site guard into a considerate host for, as she later admitted: "He's not like the man when we were on holiday, he never made me a cup of tea!"

Finally, the third narrator's work recalls the last storyteller in the folktale because it appears, initially at least, to be the most fictional and time-transcendent. On the one hand however, the third Donal is aware of staying away for centuries and for him one step, one second touching his past environment signifies the end of his otherworldly sojourn and the necessary beginning of his identity as a telling Other—a stranger with a story from some fantastic, timeless past who tells it in order to survive in an uncomprehending narrative present. On the other, Kathleen can draw on her past experience creating children's stories to travel freely between her past—elaborating on a tradition of tales she began years ago to entertain an adult sister in residential care and, by extension, the other sisters who were caring for her—and present using a skill that she has come to see as an important part of her future. Drawing a clear line of descent from "postscripts from Charlie" her pet budgerigar, written at the end of her letters, Kath has created Percy the spider and moved from communication that started out as "something between sisters" to a character with a definite public voice, composed orally in the style of children's "guessing" stories. Despite the familiar structure, Kathleen's lively and persistent voice and its underlying message, challenging stasis and loneliness and finding her strengths and using them to create a place for herself no matter the circumstances, comes through clearly:

> Kathleen: It's a story about children on their way to school and the lovely things they used to look at. And they used to say: "Oh, gosh let's see these lovely flowers! Look at the beautiful colours!"
>
> Now the house that they passed on their way to school there lived a family, Mrs. Boshier[5] and her cleaning lady, who we'll call Mrs. Mop. And in her house was Percy, a spider. He used to watch the children going to school in the mornings and he thought: "Oh, wouldn't it be lovely if I could be called beautiful and that. Whenever people see me, they just call me 'ugh.'"

---

[5] Kathleen pronounces this name "bo-she-yay," and said it is a name she invented to sound "foreign and posh." However, sometimes her pronunciation seems to deliberately soften the "sh," making the name more like "bossier," which she may have intended as a reference to the character's personality.

Anyway, he sat there in the dining room way out of anybody's reach this morning and the children had already gone to school and Mrs. [Boshier] came in with Mrs. Mop. And he kept a good eye out for this because he'd escaped her dusters the year before. And he noticed they were talking about they were going to start spring cleaning again, and he thought: "Uh-oh."

So the next morning, in came the lady of the house and with Mrs. Mop, and she'd got various cleaning articles. But Percy noticed that she's got a new— creature—he could only name it that, call it that.

And it had a long handled body and neck and its tail was all colours. And he thought: "I'll watch what she does with that." And so he kept a close eye on her and he noticed that she let it fly around her in circles. And he had to keep a wary eye to make sure that he didn't get caught with this. So gradually, Mrs. Mop came closer and closer. So Percy thought: "I'll have to keep an eye on this." And so as she swung this new thing around, she caught Percy and he went flying out of the window. He gripped on as tightly as he could on to some leaves as he was going down and he thought to himself: "Now, what can I do? So he decided to weave a web. And so he thought: "I can't go back into the house because Mrs. Mop's still there. I'd better use my web and stay out here," which he did for the night.

The next morning, the children came as usual on the path by the house and all of a sudden they were saying: "Oh, look at that lovely spider's web!" Percy had to look and said: "Are they talking about me? I've never been called lovely!" And he looked down, and his web, because it'd been frosty in the night, his web was all little strands of silver and a frosty look about them. And the dewdrops that had fallen were still hanging on and they hung like pearls. And he thought: "Doesn't it feel lovely to be called 'lovely'!" So he decided then he was going to stay for the spring term, he was going to stay outside. And he went back into—he didn't go back into the house—not until late summer.

And the one who was telling the storytelling said to the children: "Can you imagine what creature this was that Mrs. Mop used to swing around?" and they couldn't think of a creature that you know, would fly ... but it was a feather duster!

Kathleen recorded this story "on the first take" and there were very few pauses in her delivery. She paid particular attention to the description of the dew-covered spider's web and looked up and to the side during this description, as if she could see the entire scene in situ in her mind's eye. Unlike Barry who has few personal storied artefacts, or Eileen who has gotten rid of most of her souvenirs, choosing instead to keep and showcase her photographs, Kath has two nearly identical embossed copper plates which were made by her late husband in the 1940s, early in their marriage. Although well beyond the limits of this paper, in a recording of a group session in which Kath tells the story of these treasured objects, she stressed that he had to make his tools as well, fashioning two styli from bent nails of different gauges. As she showed the plates to the audience, gently tracing the contours and describing with no little wonder the process of bringing forth the pair of raised galleons that adorn them, Kathleen often remarked: "I'm not clever like this," ultimately suggesting that the artistic younger generations in the family got their genius from their father and grandfather. Not surprisingly perhaps, Kathleen sees her Percy stories as a way to communicate more than entertain. However, not unlike Anansi, the story-spinner worlds and cultures away, Percy gets bolder and his stories more elaborate with each instalment as his creator continues to challenge herself to learn new things and find new stories about and through her life.

Not to leave the fates of the three Donals hanging, at the end of each marvellous tale the enraptured farmer couldn't decide which of them spun the best yarn, so he fed and sheltered all three, promising ever after to have time and hospitality for anyone who came to his door with a story to tell. In this paper, I have explored three very different autobiographical perspectives and I hope I have been able to show that, in their own unique ways, each merits at least a similarly committed level of consideration and reflection—and hopefully a certain admiration for how each story, as a small excerpt of a life well-lived and told, has gone so far.

Works Cited

Bluck, Susan, and Linda J Levine. "Reminiscence as Autobiographical Memory: A Catalyst for Reminiscence Theory Development." *Ageing and Society* 18.2 (1998): 185–208. Print.

Brockmeier, Jens. "Autobiographical Time." *Narrative Inquiry* 10.1 (2000): 51–73. Print.

Burnside, Irene, and Barbara Haight. "Reminiscence and Life Review: Therapeutic Interventions for Older People." *The Nurse Practitioner* 19.4 (1994): 55–61. Print.

Butler, Robert N. "The Life Review: An Interpretation of Reminiscence in the Aged." *Psychiatry* 26 (1963): 65–76. Print.

Gullette, Margaret Morganroth. "From Life Storytelling to Age Autobiography." *Journal of Aging Studies* 17.1 (2003): 101–111. Print.

Harris, Celia B, Anne S Rasmussen, and Dorthe Berntsen. "The Functions of Autobiographical Memory: An Integrative Approach." *Memory (Hove, England)* November 2013 (2013): 37–41. Print.

Hymes, Dell. "Ethnopoetics, Oral-Formulaic Theory, and Editing Texts." *Oral Tradition* 9.2 (1994): 330–70. Print.

MacManus, Seumas. "The Wonders of the Three Donals." *Hibernian Nights*. New York: The MacMillan Company, 1963. 185–201. Print.

Ngunjiri, Faith Wambura, Kathy-Ann C Hernandez, and Heewon Chang. "Living Autoethnography: Connecting Life and Research." *Journal of Research Practice* 6 (2010): 1–15. Print.

Nicolaisen, W.F.H. "Concepts of Time and Space in Irish Folktales." *Celtic Folklore and Christianity Studies in Memory of William W Heist*. Santa Barbara: McNally and Loftin, 1983. 150–58. Print.

—. "The Past as Place: Names, Stories, and the Remembered Self." *Folklore* 102 (1992): 3–15. Print.

Phoenix, Cassandra, Andrew C. Sparkes, and Brett Smith. "Narrative Analysis in Aging Studies: A Typology for Consideration." *Journal of Aging Studies* 24 (2010): 1–11. Print.

Sarkar, Mahua. "Between Craft and Method: Meaning and Inter-Subjectivity in Oral History Analysis." *Journal of Historical Sociology* 25.4 (2012): 578–600. Print.

Spry, T. "Performing Autoethnography: An Embodied Methodological Praxis." *Qualitative Inquiry* 7.6 (2001): 706–732. Print.

Wallace, J B. "Reconsidering the Life Review: The Social Construction of Talk about the Past." *The Gerontologist* 32 (1992): 120–125. Print.

Rewriting Cure:
Autobiography as Therapy and Discursive Practice

Tanja Reiffenrath

"If I could not cure myself, perhaps I could begin to understand myself," writes American novelist and essayist Siri Hustvedt in her acclaimed 2010 memoir *The Shaking Woman or A History of My Nerves* (6). Her struggle for understanding, the uncertainty, tentativeness, but also the sense of possibility that her statement expresses, as well as the acceptance that cure might not conclude her illness experience and thus provide her narrative with a pre-configured triumphant ending, are characteristic of contemporary illness autobiographies.

These narratives have been on the rise since the second half of the twentieth century and their publication gained particular momentum in the wake of the Patient's Rights and Disability Rights Movement in the 1970s and the so-called 'memoir boom'[1] that has begun in the 1990s and continues unabatedly. While traditional autobiographers have treated illness as the mere interruption of the life originally intended to be the "proper concern" of the story (cf. Couser, *Recovering Bodies* 11f.), the writers of these texts take illness as their trajectory and focal point. Their works do not only represent the body with its ailments, anomalies and impairments, but lend a voice to the manifold experiences rendered silent and invisible in biomedical discourses. As they critically view their conditions, their bodies,

---

[1] In the 1990s, the memoir began to surge to unparalleled popularity and has now emerged as the dominant cultural mode of telling stories about one's own life, presenting arguments and floating ideas, and providing justification or (re)constructing reputations (cf. Yagoda 28f.). Especially the number of stories written beyond the limelight of politics, athletics, and entertainment has sky-rocketed and the sharp increase in the production and visibility of American memoirs has been excellently documented in Julie Rak's recent study *Boom! Manufacturing Memoir for the Popular Market* (Waterloo: Wilfrid Laurier UP, 2013).

and their selves against the backdrop of cultural and social norms, their private experiences enter the public arena, a dynamic that in itself subverts the traditional conception that patients are passive and silent (cf. Frank, "Reclaiming" 3).

First of all, such stories may well be seen as therapeutic, for they enable their writers to come to terms with the dramatic experiences diseases may entail. In this vein, Marylin Chandler describes autobiographical texts as a fundamental means of "restructuring, redescribing, reevaluating, and remythologizing the world" (*Healing* 5), since writing allows patients to craft a narrative that attributes (new) meanings to their experiences. For Chandler, this is analogous to healing, for both writing and healing are "purgative, reconstructive, integrative, [and] transformative" ("Healing" 6). In her choice of adjectives it becomes evident that healing cannot be grasped as a universal process, but rather in relation to the respective condition (cf. ibid.), where it may then be understood as catharsis, reinterpretation, reorientation, or the (re-)assembly of fragments into a coherent whole.

While all of these aspects are of great importance, autobiographical writing does not only serve the purpose of remediating individual health problems, as my reading of two exemplary texts, Audre Lorde's *The Cancer Journals* (1980) and Siri Hustvedt's *The Shaking Woman* (2010), aims to show. I argue that in recording their experiences and reflecting on their healing, contemporary autobiographers also reconsider established notions of cure and health. The recurring motifs of contingency and temporality serve to subvert the conventional script of the triumph narrative, a formulaic story recounting patients' cure and their return to health.[2] Secondly, temporality and contingency also function to challenge the authority of cultural and scientific discourses to account for the writers' ordeals.

In this vein, autobiographical texts like Lorde's and Hustvedt's respond to the technological progress and scientific discoveries that have profoundly changed medical care: While many diseases are nowadays treatable, they may not necessarily be fully cured (cf. Frank, *Will* 139), thus leaving individuals in an, at times uneasy, in-between existence. To elucidate these changes in the patient experience, sociologist Arthur Frank has devised the

---

[2] For a more thorough introduction to the triumph narrative and its cultural implications, please see Kathlyn Conway's *Illness and the Limits of Expression* (Ann Arbor: U of Michigan P, 2007) and Frank's analyses of so-called 'restitution narratives' (*Wounded* 77ff.).

concept of the 'remission society,' a theoretical framework originating in an autobiographical impulse[3] and affording a fresh perspective on the meaning of 'health.' This is because, in Frank's words, the 'remission society' is comprised of

> those who have had almost any cancer, those living in cardiac recovery programs, diabetics, those whose allergies and environmental sensitivities require dietary and other self-monitoring, those with prostheses and mechanical body regulators, the chronically ill, the disabled, those "recovering" from abuses and addictions, and for all these people, the families that share the worries and daily triumph of staying well. (*Wounded* 8)

Rather than employing the adjective "healthy" in his definition, Frank describes the members of the remission society as striving to "stay well," hence stressing that traditional notions of 'health' are no longer adequate, just like the idea of 'cure' ceases to be applicable.

Consequently, his framework opens up a discursive space for the plethora of autobiographers who may not fully recover from their ailments, but whose stories nevertheless limn healing and a sense of reconciliation. As their works constitute a significant breach of the tradition of storying illness, interpretations need to depart from dichotomous views on health and disease, as well as abandon the term 'pathography' that was initially used to refer to such life narratives[4] and turned the gaze on the writers' illnesses and their abnormalities. Linked to the traditional sense of health, defined as the absence of disease, the writers were found and found themselves lacking, an issue that has greatly impacted the motifs and tropes in their autobiographies as well as our responses to their stories. However, as writers examine the cultural construction of disease and health, new

---

[3] Frank first uses the term toward the end of his memoir *At the Will of the Body: Reflections on Illness* (1991), a book that is significantly influenced by his research as a sociologist and his preceding work with members of the medical profession. Throughout the narrative, he uses personal events, encounters with his doctors, friends, and strangers as trajectories for mediating larger questions on the nature of illness.

[4] Anne Hawkins has first used the term in *Reconstructing Illness: Studies in Pathography* (West Lafayette, Ind: Purdue UP, 1993) and Thomas Couser, too, uses it throughout *Recovering Bodies* and a number of essays to explain how "the medical becomes literary" and "the story of a patient's disease becomes the story of a person's life" (Couser, "Critical" 286f.), yet later critizes—and rightly so—its emphasis on the pathological, urging scholars to see such autobiographies as "antipathological," because "the impulse to write a first-person illness narrative is often the impulse to depathologize one's condition" (quoted in Smith and Watson 261).

motifs are created in the expanding genre of illness autobiographies and in the following I will turn to two in more detail and illustrate the role of temporality and contingency in Lorde's and Hustvedt's writing.

Both temporality and contincency are crucial when it comes to writing about cancer and Audre Lorde's *The Cancer Journals*, one of the earliest autobiographical works on breast cancer, is a particular case in point. It chronicles Lorde's experiences, thoughts, and feelings from an initial biopsy of her left breast which proved to be benign, the detection of a cancerous lump in her right breast in 1978, the ensuing mastectomy, and finally her coming to terms with her altered body. Recorded in the midst of the dramatic events, the journal entries, which make up a significant part of the book, do indeed have a therapeutic and cathartic function. Yet healing also has a further meaning for Lorde, which becomes evident when her journal entries and the polemical essays of the book are read side by side. Both text genres complement one another in the reconstruction of Lorde's body image, particularly in light of the fact that her body is never reconstructed, an issue that powerfully challenges the traditional narrative about breast cancer and the discursive frameworks that regulate the heteronormative views of the female, Black, queer and ill/disabled body.

Although the overall plot of Lorde's narrative is roughly chronological, her book does not follow a neat linear and progressive storyline and therefore subverts the 'triumph narrative' that conventionally depicts the experience of cancer as a story about individual triumph over the disease and the return to normality and health. In contrast to many narratives published around the "five-year mark," the time-span typically associated with survival (cf. Couser *Recovering*, 40), *The Cancer Journals* is far from celebrating recovery and a life after cancer. Instead, Lorde constructs her story as a call for a collective struggle and she is sternly aware of the new sense of temporality her life has gained through the disease: "Whatever I did," she concludes her decision to undergo mastectomy, "might or might not reverse that process, and I would not know with any certainty for a very long time" (*Cancer* 32).

This sense of uncertainty and contingency is underlined on the structural level by the great number of journal entries included in the introduction and the essays. With its immediacy, the journal appears as an adequate medium to record Lorde's experiences, for Kay Cook reminds that "one's cancer story is not easily written from a retrospective position, because one isn't sure when the 'retrospect' begins or if one will be around long enough to have the 'distant' take" (92). This is furthermore highlighted by the pervasiveness of dates in Lorde's narrative which stress the present dimension and the fleeting sense of time that informs her writing: not only is each journal entry dated, but aside from that, dates are also given at the end of the introduction, as well as at the end of each essay. Particularly at the end of the essays, the dates imply a sense of accomplishment and attest Lorde's survival, yet also convey the preliminary. In her introduction, she avers that her "work is part of a continuum of women's work, of reclaiming this earth and our power, and know[s] that this work will not begin with [her] birth nor will it end with [her] death" (*Cancer* 15). Lorde hopes that her experience will help other women in their struggle (cf. Keating 47) and secondly, she is confident that it will enable others to continue and expand her project.

A very significant part of her work concerns the discourse on the post-mastectomy body. Rejecting prosthesis is first of all Lorde's personal strategy of coping with the new asymmetry of her body and, secondly, rooted in her refusal to have her marked body normalized and rendered invisible. Instead, she needs her body to speak its own difference and remain visible to society as a constant reminder of things awry in "america."[5] Much of her outrage is therefore directed at the conceptualization of breast cancer as a mere cosmetic issue that may easily be effaced by means of prosthesis (cf. Barnes 770).

At great length, Lorde recounts an incident that takes place when she visits her doctor's office ten days after her mastectomy, having carefully tended to her post-surgical body. She lists numerous signifiers of bodily healing, such as her "shining" hair, and embraces the returning vitality of her body through a deliberate choice of bright and colorful clothing (*Cancer* 59). Particularly striking, though, is the "single floating bird dangling from [her] right ear in the name of grant asymmetry" (ibid), a beautifully conjured image that portrays Lorde as regal and dignified, celebrating the new shape of her body. While David Mitchell and Sharon Synder speak of leaving "the wound of disability undressed" (8), Lorde goes one step further by enunciating asymmetry through her choice of clothing.

This thoroughly positive image of pride, self-confidence and an emerging feeling of healing, however, is utterly disrupted when Lorde goes on to recount that the nurse at the doctor's office berates her for not wearing a prosthesis:

---

[5] Not only in *The Cancer Journals*, but throughout her oeuvre, she spells America in the lower-case, a choice in typeface that is without doubt to be understood as a derogative marker.

> [T]he nurse now looked at me urgently and disapprovingly as she told me that even if it didn't look exactly right it was "better than nothing," and that as soon as my stitches were out I would be fitted for a "real form." "You will feel so much better with it on," she said. "And besides, we really like you to wear something, at least when you come in. Otherwise it's bad for the morale at the office." (*Cancer* 60)

The nurse's assurance that prosthesis, however makeshift and temporary, will be "better than nothing," exposes a disparaging view of the body that Lorde has so carefully attended to and begun to make peace with. Her urge to cover the "nothing" in the right side of her chest suggests that the new body is seen as incomplete and in need to be restored to a "whole." Above all, prosthesis is made compulsory, which Lorde finds entirely illogical, given that she is in a room crowded with women who have shared or may potentially share her plight (cf. 61). Prosthesis not only ignores the need for individual healing; moreover, it will normalize women's bodies, thus making them invisible to one another and silencing any conversation about breast cancer, which is exactly what *The Cancer Journals* strives to avoid.

As Lorde chronicles her gradual healing despite the looming threat of a recurrence, writing and compiling journal entries is cathartic, since, throughout the story, the entries channel her pain and furious outcries, but also her gratefulness for "the love of women" (ibid. 27). Yet in her merging of the two text genres, journals and essays, a more complex form of healing surfaces, for autobiographical writing also serves the process of reconstruction beyond the biomedical quick fix of prosthesis. While Lorde assembles fragments of her breast cancer experience into a coherent political argument, she is indeed able to continue her work as an activist and advocate for social justice. For Lorde, wellbeing in the face of breast cancer becomes the ability "to live and to love and to do [her] work" (ibid. 32).

Another facet of Chandler's concept of healing may be detected in Siri Hustvedt's autobiographical narrative, an intricate book concerned with the integration of the eponymous "shaking woman." Although *The Shaking Woman* significantly differs from *The Cancer Journals* in both content and form, Hustvedt shares Lorde's engagement with the inadequacy of 'cure' and employs temporality and contingency to point to the inconstancy of medical and scientific knowledge and to subvert the diagnostic narrative many readers and critics[6] were sure would await them in the autobiography.

---

[6] On its publication, the book was met by many reviewers with utter surprise. Noting that despite the essays she has published and the lectures she holds, Hustvedt is

The book begins on the day Hustvedt returns to the college campus where her deceased father taught as a professor, in order to deliver a speech in his honor. As soon as she begins her talk, she starts to shake uncontrollably and can only stop when her speech comes to an end. Throughout the book, the narrating I returns to this day to explore the question of who the shaking woman, the "shuddering stranger," is and what role she takes up in her life (*Shaking* 7). Eventually, she integrates the shaking woman into her identity and abandons the inconclusive quest for a diagnosis and cure when she declares: "I am the shaking woman" (199). Her story hence undermines the firm divide between health and illness and promotes an alternative vision of healing in opposition to the biomedical cure.

Readers are first of all defamiliarized with the idea of diagnosis as Hustvedt takes them on a veritable "tour-de-force" through scientific concepts and discourses (cf. Mildorf 3f.), ranging from possession and hysteria to present-day discussions of neuroscientific data that all conceptualize one and the same form of shaking differently, depending on the respective historical and cultural context:

> Nature, God, and the devil could wrack your body, and medical experts struggled to distinguish among causes. How could you separate an act of nature from a divine intervention or a demonic possession? Saint Teresa of Avila's paroxysmal agonies and blackouts, her visions and transports were mystical flights towards God, but the girls in Salem who writhed and shook were the victims of witches. (*Shaking* 8f.)

Thus moving from "mythical flights towards God" and a "divine intervention" to "demonic possession," her narrative exposes the temporality and contextuality of medical knowledge that has been adapted arbitrarily in accordance with the respective social and cultural climate.

In passages such as this one it becomes clear that Hustvedt's book is not an objective scientific treatise but an exercise in critical writing as she—and here I fully agree with Christine Marks—confronts science with the eyes of a writer (194). It therefore comes of no surprise that it is not her meticulously documented research, but autobiographical writing itself that brings an epiphany and initiates Hustvedt's healing process. Automatic writing, triggered by the phrase "I remember," ultimately becomes a therapeutic

---

commonly perceived as a novelist, literary critics voiced their astonishment over the fact that *The Shaking Woman* appears to be rather a piece of academic work than a personal story (cf. Beyer 111). In an attempt to categorize her work, scholars have been tempted to create neologisms like "intellectual neuropsycho-autobiography" (Švrljuga 222).

strategy to blur the boundaries between her "narrating (...) conscious, telling self" and the "shaking (...) flashback self" (*Shaking* 52) and merge the mental and the corporeal aspects of her identity whose separation has posed problems thoughout the narrative. So Hustvedt becomes the shaking woman when she is writing, as Tougaw rightly observes, and "draws on what's unconscious to craft a sense of control—or agency—through writing (189). It is hence through automatic writing that she is able to not only develop an understanding for her condition, but also embrace it.

Whereas the integration of the shaking woman into her identity is still tentative in these scenes, it is made explicit when her story comes full circle at the end of the book, since Hustvedt rewrites the paragraph that has initiated her quest when she recounted the first incident of her tremors:

> I can't tell what it is or if it is anything at all. I chase it with words even though it won't be captured and, every once in a while, I imagine I have come close to it. In May of 2006, I stood outside under a cloudless blue sky and started to speak about my father, who had been dead for over two years. As soon as I opened my mouth, I began to shake violently. I shook that day and then I shook again on other days. I am the shaking woman. (*Shaking* 199)

In light of these final sentences, several reviewers have remarked that the ending is "slightly frustrating" or even "unoriginal," since Hustvedt does not reach a definitive diagnosis that explains the cause of her shaking (Albertyn 59; Magenau n.p.; my translation). Yet the question is of course for whom this presents a dissatisfying and unnerving ending. Similar to Lorde's *Cancer Journals*, *The Shaking Woman* departs from the script of the triumph narrative. While triumphant narratives re-inscribe the boundary between health and illness, the ending of Hustvedt's narrative refuses such a clear-cut distinction by withholding a diagnosis, and in fact, any need for further medical probing. By refraining from a diagnosis and accordingly suspending the structural and formal elements that would provide the narrative with closure, *The Shaking Woman* powerfully breaks with the conventions of the triumph narrative and overwrites this plot with a therapeutic story, albeit one that decidedly defies closure. This is in line with the argument devised throughout the book that diagnoses and medical knowledge may at best be contextual, dependent on a historical moment and a specific cultural context.

Both autobiographical narratives destabilize the dichotomy of health and illness as their writers may heal and attain well-being, even in the face of a persisting affliction. Yet while other members of the remission society are often known to pass as healthy when their conditions are rendered invisible, Lorde's and Hustvedt's memoirs do not permit such passing. Instead, their life narratives leave a distinctive mark, yet one which may work to effectively destigmatize disease and foster alternative visions of health.

Works Cited

Albertyn, Lynda. "The Shaking Woman or a History of My Nerves." *Journal of Child and Adolescent Mental Health* 23.1 (2011): 59–60. Print.

Barnes, Sharon L. "Marvelous Arithmetics: Prosthesis, Speech, and Death in the Late Work of Audre Lorde." *Women's Studies* 37 (2008): 769–89. Print.

Beyer, Susanne. "Die Doppelte Frau." *Spiegel* 2 (2010): 110–14. Print.

Chandler, Marilyn R. "A Healing Art: Therapeutic Dimensions of Autobiography." *a/b Auto/Biography Studies* 5.1 (1989): 4–14. Print.

—. *A Healing Art: Regeneration through Autobiography.* New York: Garland, 1990. Print.

Conway, Kathlyn. *Illness and the Limits of Expression.* Ann Arbor: U of Michigan P, 2007. Print.

Cook, Kay K. "Filling the Dark Spaces: Breast Cancer and Autobiography." *a/b Auto/Biography Studies* 16.1 (1991): 85–94. Print.

Couser, Thomas G. *Recovering Bodies: Illness, Disability, and Life Writing.* Madison: U of Wisconsin P, 1997. Print.

—. "Critical Conditions: Teaching Illness Narrative." Hawkins and Chandler. 282–88. Print.

Frank, Arthur W. "Reclaiming an Orphan Genre: The First-Person Narrative of Illness." *Literature and Medicine* 13.1 (1994): 1–21. Print.

—. *The Wounded Storyteller: Body, Illness, and Ethics.* Chicago: U of Chicago P, 1995. Print.

—. *At the Will of the Body: Reflections on Illness.* 1991. New York: Houghton Mifflin, 2002. Print.

Hawkins, Anne H. *Reconstructing Illness: Studies in Pathography.* West Lafayette: Purdue UP, 1993. Print.

Hawkins, Anne H., and Marilyn R. Chandler. Eds. *Teaching Literature and Medicine.* New York: Modern Language Association, 2000. Print.

Hustvedt, Siri. *The Shaking Woman or A History of My Nerves.* New York: Henry Holt, 2010. Print.

Keating, AnaLouise. *Women Reading Women Writing: Self-invention in Paula Gunn Allen, Gloria Anzaldúa, and Audre Lorde.* Philadelphia: Temple UP, 1996. Print.

Lorde, Audre. *The Cancer Journals (Special Edition).* 1980. San Francisco: Aunt Lute Books, 2006. Print.

Magenau, Jörg. "Kontrollverlust über den eigenen Körper." 15 Jan. 2010. 28 Aug. 2012. <http://www.dradio.de/dkultur/sendungen/kritik/1105494/>. Web.

Marks, Christine. *Identity Formation at the Beginning of the Twenty-First Century: Intersubjectivity, Art, and Medicine in Siri Hustvedt's Works.* Diss. Johannes Gutenberg-University, 2010.

Mitchell, David T., and Sharon L. Snyder. *Narrative Prosthesis: Disability and the Dependencies of Discourse.* Ann Arbor: U of Michigan P, 2000. Print.

Mildorf, Jarmila. "Narrative Refashioning and Illness: Doctor-Patient Encounters in Siri Hustvedt's *The Shaking Woman.*" forthcoming. 1–19.

Rak, Julie. *Boom! Manufacturing Memoir for the Popular Market.* Waterloo: Wilfrid Laurier UP, 2013. Print.

Smith, Sidonie, and Julia Watson. *Reading Autobiography: A Guide for Interpreting Life Narratives.* 2nd Ed. Minneapolis: U of Minnesota P, 2005. Print.

Švrljuga, Željka. *Hysteria and Melancholy as Literary Style in the Works of Charlotte Perkins Gilman, Kate Chopin, Zelda Fitzgerald, and Djuna Barnes.* Lewiston: Edwin Mellen P, 2011. Print.

Tougaw, Jason. "Brain Memoirs, Neuroscience, and the Self: A Review Article." *Literature and Medicine* 30.1 (2012): 171–92. Print.

Yagoda, Ben. *Memoir: A History.* New Haven: Riverhead, 2009. Print.

Notes on Contributors

ALICE GODFREY
Alice Godfrey is a PhD candidate in American literature at Bordeaux Montaigne University. She wrote her master thesis on Maya Angelou's identity building process in her autobiographical sequel. Her PhD extends this research by analysing identity building motifs in Afro-American and Caribbean women authors. She is also currently completing a Master degree in Peace and Conflict studies at the University of Oslo.

APARAJITA NANDA
Aparajita Nanda, Fulbright Faculty Scholarship awardee Visiting Associate Professor to the University of California, Berkeley, has taught at Jadavpur University, India, and now teaches both at UC Berkeley and Santa Clara University. Her most recent publications include *Black California*, *The Strangled Cry*, articles in *Ariel* and *Callaloo*; forthcoming publications include *Ethnic Literatures and Transnationalism* with (Routledge) and a chapter on California literature in a Cambridge University Press publication.

BELINDA HILTON
Belinda Hilton is a creative writer and academic from Queensland, Australia. Her creative writing PhD at Griffith University Gold Coast, set for completion in 2015, will produce her first novel a work of autobiographical fiction. She has a Bachelor of Arts with first class Honours in creative writing, and a Bachelor of Arts with majors in theatre and contemporary arts, both from Griffith University. Belinda teaches in the field of communications and her research interests include NSSI, mental health, social media and digital communication, life-writing and therapeutic writing.

BEN LEBDAI
Benaouda Lebdai is a specialist in Colonial and Postcolonial literatures written in English and French. He obtained a PhD in 1987 at the University of Essex (England), in comparative literature and has also a French doctorate on the Ghanaian novelist Ayi Kwei Armah. He has published

extensively on African writers and on trans-Atlantic slave trade narratives. He is currently Professor at the University of Maine, Le Mans (France). His latest publication is *Autobiography as a Writing Strategy in Postcolonial Literature* with Cambridge Scholars Publishing (2015).

CHRISTINE SAVINEL

Christine Savinel is Professor Emerita of American Literature at the University of Sorbonne Nouvelle-Paris 3. The author of two books on Emily Dickinson and numerous essays and articles on poetics and aesthetics in American literature and art. Her latest publication is an essay on "Gertrude Stein in 1913, A Policy of Disruption" (2013). She is currently completing a book on Gertrude Stein's *Untimely Autobiographies*.

CLAUDE DESMARAIS

Claude Desmarais is an assistant professor in German Studies in the Faculty of Creative and Critical Studies at UBC's Okanagan campus in Kelowna, BC, Canada. His work focuses on autobiography, disability studies, foreign language education, and popular German culture, and more particularly on the writers Elias and Veza Canetti. His translations include Edouard Jeauneau's *Rethinking the School of Chartres* (University of Toronto Press, 2009), and he is the editor of *A Different Germany: Pop and the Negotiation of German Culture* (Cambridge Scholars Publishing, 2014).

DAGMARA DREWNIAK

Dagmara Drewniak teaches American and Canadian literature at Adam Mickiewicz University, Poznań. Her research interests include: multiculturalism in English Canadian literature, images of Poland and Eastern Europe in Canada and Canadian literature, literature by immigrants from Poland and Eastern Europe, Jewishness in Canadian literature, life-writing, and postcolonial literature in English. She has published essays on Kulyk Keefer, Stachniak, Hoffman, Rushdie, Ondaatje, Appignanesi and other contemporary writers. She co-edited a second number of TransCanadiana *Canada and Its Utopia/Canada et ses utopies* (2009). In 2014 she published *Forgetful Recollections: Images of Central and Eastern Europe in Canadian Literature*.

DANIEL WARZECHA

Daniel Warzecha's field of research concerns Christian theology, apologetics, allegory, myth, autobiography and children's literature. He is particularly interested in the articulation between the religious discourse and fiction. He has published several articles about C.S. Lewis and George MacDonald and holds a PhD in Anglo-Saxon studies (2008). Daniel is a French specialist of C.S. Lewis and has published *L'imaginaire spirituel de C.S. Lewis* (2010). He teaches English in Charles-de-Gaulle Lille 3 University, France.

DANIELA CHANA

Daniela Chana, born in 1985, holds a doctoral degree in Comparative Literature from University of Vienna, Austria. She is an independent scholar, art mediator, and author of fiction. Her short stories and poems have been published in international literary journals and anthologies. Recent publications include essays on Italian and American literature, Italian independent cinema, confessional poetry, and female singer-songwriters (Tori Amos, Fiona Apple, Regina Spektor). In 2013 and 2014, she was a guest curator of art exhibitions at Essl Museum and the Mozarthaus Vienna.

DIPTI RANJAN PATTANAIK

Dipti Ranjan Pattanaik, Professor of English at the Faculty of Arts at the Banaras Hindu University, India, was a Fulbright Visiting Scholar at Ohio State University in 1996–97, Charles Wallace Fellow at Cambridge in 2000, Shastri Indo Canadian Scholar at Vancouver University in 2009 and Erikson Scholar in Residence at Erikson Institute at Stockbridge in 2011. His scholarly essays and short stories have appeared in among others, MELUS, Journal of Commonwealth Literature and Weber Studies. He has won the National Katha Award for creative writing among others.

EBERE NNENNA AGUGBUE NWEZE

Ebere Nnenna Agugbue Nweze holds a PhD in English and Literary studies, an MA degree in Literature and a BA (ED) degree in Education with emphasis on teaching English. The focus of her PhD thesis was cross-cultural gender studies with emphasis in women writing from Africa and her Diaspora (Caribbean and American). She was an Assistant Professor at the Abu Dhabi University, United Arab Emirates from 2008–2012 where she won the best teaching faculty awards for 2009–2010. At present, she works as a Senior English language and literature instructor in Stockholm.

ELISABETH BOUZONVILLER

Elisabeth Bouzonviller is Associate Professor at Jean Monnet University in St Etienne, France, where she has been teaching American literature since 1999. She is a member of the F. Scott Fitzgerald Society. She also works on Native American literature. In 2014, Bouzonviller published *Louise Erdrich: Métissage et Écriture, Histoires d'Amérique* (Université de St-Etienne).

EVA-SABINE ZEHELEIN

Eva-Sabine Zehelein is currently acting Chair of American Studies at the University of Regensburg. She specializes in North American literature of the 20th and 21st century in transnational contexts. Her publications include *Space as Symbol: John Updike's "country of ideas" in the Rabbit Novels* (2003), *Science: Dramatic – Science Plays in America and Great Britain 1990–2007* (2009) as well as articles on Johnny Cash, Starbucks, Joan Didion and Octavia Butler's neo-slave narratives.

FLORIANE REVIRON-PIÉGAY

Floriane Reviron-Piégay is a Senior Lecturer in 19th and 20th century English literature at the University of St Etienne, France. She has written a PhD dissertation about the "New Biography." Since then, she has written numerous articles about the Bloomsbury Group, about its relationships with the visual arts in particular, and about Virginia Woolf's most confidential works (her diaries, memoirs, and essays). She is working on the transition from the Victorian Age to Modernism and on the relationships between fiction and autobiography. She is also the Editor of *Englishness Revisited*, a series of essays on Englishness, published in 2009 by Cambridge Scholars Press.

GIULIA GRILLO MIKRUT

Giulia Grillo Mikrut completed her PhD in English literature at the University of Queensland (Australia) in 2014. She holds a BA and MA in English awarded by the University of Stockholm (Sweden). She also co-organized the international symposium on Toni Morrison (2013) and the international conference on Autobiography (2014) at Södertörn University (Sweden). She is the co-editor of *Living Language, Living Memory: Essays on the Works of Toni Morrison* (2014) in which she also authors one of the chapters.

JO WOODIWISS

Jo Woodiwiss is a Senior Lecturer in sociology and leads the critical narrative research group at the University of Huddersfield, UK. She has written and presented widely in the field of women's narratives of abuse, sexuality, self-identity, and recovered memories. Moreover, she is the author of *Contesting Stories of Childhood Sexual Abuse* (2009 Palgrave) and editor (along with Kate Smith and Kelly Lockwood) of the forthcoming edited collection *Feminist Narrative Research: Opportunities and Challenges* (Palgrave 2016).

JOHN C. HAWLEY

John C. Hawley is Professor and former Chair of the English department at Santa Clara University in California. He is the author or editor of 14 books, including *Postcolonial, Queer*; *The Postcolonial and the Global*; and *LGBTQ America Today*; and most recently, the essay "Trans Autobiographies as Performative Utterances." He is former president of the US chapter of the Association for Commonwealth Literature and Language Studies and has served on MLA executive committees on Postcolonial Studies, on Religion and Literature, and on Literature in English other than British and American.

KAREN FERREIRA-MEYERS

Karen Ferreira-Meyers is Senior Lecturer and Coordinator of the Institute of Distance Education (University of Swaziland) since October 2010. She obtained various qualifications: MA Romance Philology (French-Spanish), Honours Portuguese, Post-Graduate Diploma Translation (French-English-French), MA Linguistics, LLM Degree (Legal aspects of new technologies), PhD in French (feminine Francophone autofiction), Master in Instructional Design and Technology. She has published several articles (autofictional feminine writing, crime fiction, 20th and 21st Francophone, Anglophone and Lusophone African authors, distance and e-learning), participates regularly in international conferences and is a keen translator and interpreter.

KERSTIN W. SHANDS

Kerstin W. Shands is Professor of English at Södertörn University, Stockholm. Among her books are *Living Language, Living Memory: Essays on the Works of Toni Morrison* (co-editor), *Neither East Nor West: Postcolonial Essays on Literature, Culture and Religion* (editor), *Collusion and Resistance: Women Writing in English* (editor), *Embracing Space:*

Spatial Metaphors in Feminist Discourse, and *The Repair of the World: The Novels of Marge Piercy*.

KIRSI TUOHELA

Kirsi Tuohela is a postdoctoral research fellow at the University of Turku, a cultural historian interested in various kinds of autobiographical texts from letters and diaries to published autobiographies. She has written about cultural history of women's writing, cultural history of psychiatry, history of melancholia. Her monograph (PhD thesis) analyzed women's autobiographical texts on melancholia in the late nineteenth century Scandinavia. She is involved in two research projects, one on written madness–mental illness in Finnish autobiographies and novels and another on the 'inner child' in Finnish autobiographical literature.

LAMIA MOKRANE

Lamia Mokrane obtained a license in Didactics and the Sciences of the English Language at the University of Bejaia in 2011. Then, she started a master in Anglo-Saxon Civilization and Literature. The title of her thesis was "Women's Emancipation as a Form of Dissent in *The Bluest Eye* by Toni Morrison and *The Color Purple* by Alice Walker." Her PhD thesis is entitled: "Otherness and Belonging in Nella Larsen's Life and Works." She is interested in African-American literature, especially when concepts or identity are questioned.

LAURA CASTOR

Laura Castor is Professor in English literature and culture studies at the University of Tromsø, where she teaches American literature and culture, including a course on American Life Narratives. She wrote her PhD dissertation on the issue of historical memory, autobiography and art in the autobiographical narratives of Isadora Duncan, Hallie Flanagan, and Lillian Hellman (U of Minnesota, 1994). Castor has since published extensively on Native American literature. She is currently writing a series of interconnected articles exploring various ways in which the memory of historical and personal trauma is expressed and transformed in fiction by writers from a variety of backgrounds.

LAURE DE NERVAUX-GAVOTY

Laure de Nervaux-Gavoty is a former Fulbright scholar (2005). She is senior lecturer in English at the Université Paris-Est Créteil (France) and assistant editor of *Quaderna*, a multilingual and interdisciplinary online journal. She has written articles on women's poetry, autobiography, and the relationship between literature and the visual arts. She was co-organiser of a conference on experience in literature and the arts in 2011 and on transdisciplinarity in 2014.

MANUEL BRITO

Manuel Brito is Associate Professor of American Literature at the University of Laguna, Spain. He is the author of *Means Matter: Market Fructification of American Innovative Poetry in the Late Twentieth Century* (2010), and has recently edited *Reshaping Publishing in the Twentieth and Twenty-First Century* (2014). He is the editor of the small press *Zasterle* and the magazine *Nerter*.

MÉLANIE HEYDARI

A former student at the Ecole Normale Supérieure Lettres et Sciences Humaines, Lyon, France, Mélanie Heydari completed her PhD dissertation on Vikram Seth's protean opus in November 2012. She has published various articles on the works of Vikram Seth and Salman Rushdie. In 2013 she taught a literature course at New York University, USA; she is now a lecturer at Columbia University.

MELISSA SCHUH

Melissa Schuh completed her MSc in Modern Languages (University of Oxford) in 2013 and is currently a PhD candidate in English Literature at Queen Mary University of London. Her research interests are English and German contemporary autobiography/ life writing, specifically the works of Philip Roth, J.M. Coetzee, and Günter Grass.

MICHAEL ACKLAND

Michael Ackland is the inaugural Colin and Margaret Roderick Professor of English at James Cook University, Townsville. Author of numerous critical monographs, biographies and editions, his publications in Australian Studies extend from the colonial period through to contemporary writing. Most recently he has published the first book-length study of Murray Bail

(*The Experimental Fiction of Murray Bail* [Cambria Press, 2012]). He is currently researching Christina Stead's response to the socialist heritage.

MIKOŁAJ WIŚNIEWSKI

Mikołaj Wiśniewski teaches American literature at the Warsaw School of Social Sciences and Humanities. He defended his PhD thesis at Warsaw University in 2007. In 2004/2005 he was a Fulbright Scholar at the University of California, Berkeley. In 2013 he was awarded the Kosciuszko Foundation Fellowship to do research at the Mandeville Special Collections Library at the University of California, San Diego. Dr Wiśniewski also holds an MA degree in philosophy from Warsaw University. He is the editor and co-founder of the renowned Polish philosophical quarterly "Kronos."

PAMELA J. RADER

Pamela J. Rader holds a PhD in Comparative Literature from the University of Colorado at Boulder. She is chair and Professor of English at Georgian Court University, a liberal arts university in Lakewood, New Jersey, where she teaches world, women's, and multi-ethnic literatures. She has published internationally on Edwidge Danticat, Assia Djebar, Junot Diaz, Louise Erdrich, and Marjane Satrapi; her current project examines productive silences in literature.

PIOTR SOBOLCZYK

Piotr Sobolczyk finished his MA and PhD studies at Jagiellonian University with degrees in comparative literature and literary theory. He has been an Assistant professor at Institute of Literary Research, Polish Academy of Sciences and a Visiting Lecturer at Jagiellonian University and University of Oslo. His PhD thesis was awarded by the National Centre of Culture. He received an award from the Polish Ministry of Science, Polish Ministry of Culture, Foundation for Polish Science, National Centre of Science, Estreicher Foundation. Sobolczyk has published two scientific books *Tadeusza Micińskiego podróż do Hiszpanii* (2005) and *Dyskursywizowanie Białoszewskiego* (2013). He is currently working on a book on Polish queer literature and has published several articles.

SEANA KOZAR

As Seana Kozar is interested in the interplay between story, image, object and culture and how stories and the things to and through which we attach our most resonant narratives change and transform to reflect the dynamic creation and negotiation of personal truth and meaning over the lifecourse. A student of medieval studies with a particular passion for learning the techniques of manuscript illumination and a recent but avid sewer, Seana is currently writing a work of children's fantasy fiction.

TANJA REIFFENRATH

Tanja Reiffenrath is a doctoral candidate in American Studies at the University of Paderborn (Germany) where she also teaches undergraduate courses in American literature and culture. Her PhD project analyzes illness and disability memoirs in contact and in conflict with current scientific, philosophical, and cultural discourses on disease and health. In 2014 LIT Verlag published her book *From Ethnic to Transnational: Screening Indian American Families*.

English Studies

1. Kerstin W. Shands (ed.), *Collusion and Resistance: Women Writing in English*, 2002
2. Kerstin W. Shands et al. (eds.), *Notions of America: Swedish Perspectives*, 2004
3. Kerstin W. Shands (ed.), *Neither East Nor West: Postcolonial Essays on Literature, Culture and Religion*, 2008
4. Kerstin W. Shands, and Giulia Grillo Mikrut (eds), *Living Language, Living Memory: Essays on the Works of Toni Morrison*, 2014
5. Kerstin W. Shands et al. (eds.), *Writing the Self: Essays on Autobiography and Autofiction*, 2015

www.ingramcontent.com/pod-product-compliance
Lightning Source LLC
Chambersburg PA
CBHW031426160426
43195CB00010BB/628